EXPERT SYSTEMS FOR EXPERTS

EXPERT SYSTEMS FOR EXPERTS

Kamran Parsaye

IntelligenceWare, Inc.
Los Angeles, California

Mark Chignell

Department of Industrial and Systems Engineering
University of Southern California
Los Angeles, California

WILEY

John Wiley & Sons, Inc.

New York ■ Chichester ■ Brisbane ■ Toronto ■ Singapore

Intelligence/Compiler and Auto-Intelligence are trademarks of IntelligenceWare, Inc. dBASE is a trademark of Ashton-Tate, Inc. ORACLE is a trademark of Oracle Corporation. IBM is a trademark of International Business Machines Corporation. VAX is a trademark of Digital Equipment Corporation.

Library of Congress Cataloging-in-Publication Data

Parsaye, Kamran.
  Expert systems for experts / Kamran Parsaye, Mark Chignell.
    p.   cm.
  Bibliography: p.
  Includes index.
  ISBN 0-471-60175-6
  1. Expert systems (Computer science) I. Chignell, Mark.
II. Title.
QA76.76.E95P27   1988
006.3'3—dc19

87-32620
CIP

PREFACE

This book is both an introduction to a powerful set of tools for knowledge representation and inference, i.e., the *technology* of expert systems, and a practical guide on how to use these tools to build expert systems, i.e., the *methodology* of expert systems. Our view of expert systems is that they are an extension of earlier programming technologies and that seeing them in this light assists in designing, implementing, and using them.

The close relationship between knowledge and inference is a central theme in this book. We show how logic and frames can be combined into a powerful programming paradigm that can be used to write high-level programs as well as to implement expert systems. This paradigm provides a practical approach to knowledge, built around the tools of facts, rules, and frames.

We expect that a straightforward exposition of the unified approach to knowledge and inference will lead to broader-based and less expensive expert systems in the future. In this book we outline an approach to expert systems development that is grounded in theory yet practical and inexpensive.

The approach we describe is not a hypothetical wish list but is based on our practical experience with the Intelligence/Compiler™ system, which implements the unified approach to knowledge and inference discussed in this book.

Topics covered in this book include the relationship between predicate logic and the inference engines of expert systems, frames, hierarchies, multiple inheritance and attached procedures, knowledge acquisition, inference engines, and the connection between expert systems and conventional software. The evolution of expert systems as a computer programming paradigm is also covered, along with a comparison between the expert system lifecycle and the general software lifecycle.

This book can be used in a number of ways. People with expertise in business and industry can use this book not only to provide basic information about expert systems but also as a guide for building expert systems themselves in their own knowledge domains. A fundamental assumption that we made in writing this book is that experts can and should be more involved in the process of actually building expert systems. These readers should cover the entire book in the order that it is written, including those appendixes that deal with material that is new to them.

This book can also be used in college courses on expert systems and their use. Courses on expert system technology that emphasize knowledge representation and inference procedures from a computational standpoint should focus on the material presented in Chapters 3 through 7. One possible sequence for these courses is to begin with the introduction to expert systems in Chapter 1, move to a segment on logic and inference, and then cover knowledge representation, inexact inference, and the integration of relational databases and expert systems. The following sequence might be appropriate for such a course: Chapters 1, 3, 7, 4, 5, and 6. The section on inexact reasoning would be postponed until after Chapter 6 has been covered in this course. Knowledge acquisition could then be covered as an optional topic if time permits.

Courses that emphasize the application of expert systems, such as those frequently taught in business and engineering schools, may use the following sequence: Chapters 1, 2, 5, 6, 8, and 9. The material in these chapters should be reinforced with a knowledge engineering project that proceeds either in parallel with, or after, the presentation of the lecture material.

The final group of readers that we had in mind when writing this book were those who don't want to build expert systems but who need to know enough about them to be able to make intelligent decisions about whether projects should proceed, and to manage and evaluate knowledge engineering efforts. It is often critical to have the support of upper management in initiating a knowledge engineering effort and seeing it through to its completion. Managers must be able to distinguish between a good expert system project and a bad one and recognize problems when they occur. Reading and understanding this material (particularly Chapters 1, 2, 8, and 9) should allow managers to have a good grasp of what expert systems are to a point where they can talk to their technical people and make informed decisions about where and how to invest in the technology.

Throughout this book we have striven to simplify and unify related concepts without sacrificing the intellectual content of the material. Our notational conventions use only the letters of the English alphabet supplemented with underlining, single quotes, semicolons, and the like. We have also emphasized the practical nature of expert systems.

Our treatment of knowledge acquisition and validation in Chapter 9 emphasizes one of the major themes of this book, namely, the expanding role of the expert. As expert system technology progresses, an increasing number of expert systems will be developed by experts without the aid of intermediaries. We hope that this book will help to accelerate this trend.

We wish to thank a number of people who have assisted us both in general and in the preparation of this work: Jenny Ghielmetti, Sandra Chignell, David Thompson, Kenneth Combs, Kathrin Kjos, Thomas Higgins, Diana Lin, and Professor Clay Sprowls. We would also like to thank the students in courses we have taught with the early versions of the manuscript at the University of Southern California and the University of California, Los Angeles, who provided invaluable assistance.

KAMRAN PARSAYE
MARK CHIGNELL

Los Angeles, March 1988

CONTENTS

1.

BACKGROUND ON EXPERT SYSTEMS 1

2.

A FIRST GLANCE AT EXPERT SYSTEMS 29

3.

LOGIC 69

4.

KNOWLEDGE 119

5.

KNOWLEDGE REPRESENTATION WITH FRAMES 161

6.

UNCERTAINTY   211

7.

THE INFERENCE PROCESS   251

8.

BUILDING EXPERT SYSTEMS   287

9.

KNOWLEDGE ACQUISITION AND VALIDATION   327

10.
SUMMARY

APPENDIX A.
SEARCH

APPENDIX B.
GENERAL-PURPOSE REASONING

APPENDIX C.
PROPOSITIONAL LOGIC

APPENDIX D.

EXPERT SYSTEMS FOR EXPERTS

1

BACKGROUND ON EXPERT SYSTEMS

An expert system is a computer program that relies on *knowledge* and *reasoning* to perform a difficult task usually undertaken only by a human expert. Just as a human expert has knowledge of a specific field, say, chemistry, an expert system has a knowledge-base consisting of knowledge relating to a specific field. Human experts reason and arrive at conclusions based on their knowledge; expert systems reason and arrive at conclusions based on the knowledge they possess.

From a functional point of view, we may define an expert system as follows:

Definition 1: An expert system is a program that relies on a body of knowledge to perform a somewhat difficult task usually performed only by a human expert. The principal power of an expert system is derived from the knowledge the system embodies rather than from search algorithms and specific reasoning methods. An expert system successfully deals with problems for which clear algorithmic solutions do not exist.

Expert systems have been enthusiastically accepted by many in the business, industrial, and professional spheres as a way of making expertise routinely available wherever it is needed. Expert systems have been particularly welcome in fields where existing experts are expensive and in short supply.

The programming technologies used in developing expert systems may be viewed as the evolution of early computer languages to a new level of expres-

1

sion that permits us to represent and deal with knowledge. The early languages were close to the hardware that executed them and were very difficult to understand, except by computer experts. More recent computer languages are gradually becoming easier to use and closer to the patterns of expression of humans. Expert system programming technologies are another step in this direction.

To be used effectively, each new technology should be accompanied by a set of guidelines or methodologies for its use. This helps new users to avoid pitfalls and to maximize productivity. Thus, to use expert system technologies to deal with knowledge we need a new set of methodologies, based on experience gained in developing various applications.

As shown in Figure 1.1, the development of expert systems is based on two distinct, yet complementary, vectors:

   a. New programming *technologies* that allow us to deal with knowledge and inference with ease.
   b. New design and development *methodologies* that allow us to effectively use these technologies to deal with complex problems.

The successful development of expert systems relies on a well-balanced approach to these two vectors. In this book we view expert systems using both technological and methodological discussions. To discuss the technology, we provide a framework in which knowledge and inference may be viewed uniformly. Our basic technical tenet is that knowledge and reasoning should not be viewed as disjunct, separate, or disconnected entities within an expert system, but that expert systems are, in fact, the epitome of the union between knowledge and reasoning.

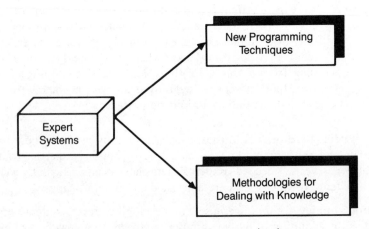

Figure 1.1 The vectors of expert system development.

The goal of this book is to provide the overall knowledge of expert system technologies and methodologies that experts need in order to play a larger role in the process of building expert systems. As the need for expert systems increases, an increasing number of experts are becoming interested in replicating their expertise. However, such experts often must deal with a large number of unfamiliar terms and concepts based on different views, approaches, and schools of thought.

The expert who perceives the need for an expert system in his knowledge domain may, of course, try to obtain the help of a knowledge engineer (i.e., a computer scientist skilled in expert systems) in building the expert system but may sometimes encounter a number of problems. For instance, much of the early interaction between the expert and the knowledge engineer may be spent in educating each other about their separate kinds of expertise. Since the knowledge engineer will generally be largely ignorant of the knowledge domain while the expert will have little knowledge about expert systems, a good deal of time will be spent (i.e., wasted) on these issues as the expert and knowledge engineer train each other to the point where a fruitful interaction can occur.

In some situations it may not even be possible for the expert to find a suitable knowledge engineer to work with since knowledge engineers are expensive and in short supply. This will engender a need for experts to be more knowledgeable about expert systems. As expert system tools become easier to use, it should eventually be possible for many experts to be as adept at using expert system tools as knowledge engineers are now. In any event, regardless of whether a knowledge engineer is involved in the project, it is likely that the process of building expert systems will be smoother and more efficient if the expert is knowledgeable about the technologies and methodologies of expert systems.

What knowledge do experts require? At a minimum, experts should be provided with a uniform view of what expert systems are, along with guidelines on how to build them. In this book we provide this uniform view by discussing and integrating many of the issues relating to knowledge representation, inference, and expert system development. This is, however, not a "hypothetical" approach, but one based on a fully implemented system that has been successfully used by many experts for the development of expert systems. The integrated inference and knowledge representation methods discussed in this book have been fully implemented in the Intelligence/Compiler™ system and utilized in a variety of commercial applications.

In our own experience, we have observed that (not surprisingly) experts are often very capable people and that, given the right introduction and sufficiently high level tools, they can understand the ideas of expert systems and use them without too much difficulty. For instance, we were surprised and impressed with the ease in which a group of geneticists could suddenly write

50-page programs in a rule-and-frame-based language. This brought us to the realization that rules and frames when combined in an expert system shell act as highly appropriate programming tools for experts. Thus expert systems shells may be viewed as high-level programming tools for experts who would not use a conventional programming language such as C or Pascal, but can implement their thoughts easily in these higher-level modes of expression.

Increasing the awareness of experts about expert systems and knowledge engineering should be extremely beneficial to the development of expert systems. In order to facilitate this awareness, we have attempted to distill the essential elements of knowledge representation, inference, and knowledge acquisition. Although expert systems raise many theoretical issues in computer science, cognitive science, and artificial intelligence, we will focus on practical applications and examples that can be readily assimilated by the reader. However, we will cover not only the basics of each idea, but more detailed issues as well.

In discussing expert system methodologies, we will provide a framework within which an expert's knowledge may be viewed, captured, and represented. Not surprisingly, such discussion often leads to questions involving the nature of expertise and issues relating to human psychology and lessons learned from the early days of artificial intelligence.

In addition to considering the basic mechanics of building and operating expert systems, we will also need to understand the social and organizational issues that determine when and how an expert system should be built. In our view, the power of expert system technology is best harnessed when an overall social and methodological vision of its purpose is used to govern the direction of its application.

The goal of this first chapter is to place expert systems within the broader context of artificial intelligence and emphasize one of the main lessons learned from the history of artificial intelligence: namely, that "general-purpose" problem-solving strategies often fail to achieve an acceptable level of performance and that success in building "intelligent" systems is most frequently obtained by focusing on narrow domains. This lesson should not be forgotten amid the plethora of technical terms and concepts involved in expert system technology.

We thus begin by reviewing the history of the search for machine intelligence and how expert systems evolved as a byproduct of this effort. We aim to teach history not for its own sake, but to motivate a better understanding of the guidelines and methodologies needed for the development and use of expert systems and to provide a perspective on where the technology came from, how it differs from previous technologies, and where future directions lie.

■ 1.2 THE QUEST FOR INTELLIGENT MACHINES

People have always been fascinated by lifelike machines. It is evident that a deep desire urges humans to create machines, playthings, or toys that mimic life. The court of Louis XVI, for instance, marveled at mechanical singing birds, while Napoleon himself was impressed by a chess playing machine secretly operated by a person hidden inside it.

Many lifelike machines have been envisaged as taking on approximately human form. Modern versions of the idea include Frankenstein's monster, Asimov's robots, and other science fiction characters. The earliest successes in mimicking human capability came in the domain of physical action.

By the seventeenth century, it was possible to gain precise mechanical control over machines such as clocks. These early developments in the realm of physical action, along with the creation of new power sources (e.g., steam engines) led first to the industrial revolution and ultimately, to the evolution of today's robots.

In spite of the successes achieved in the control of mechanical devices, most components of human capability were beyond the reach of mechanization until the twentieth century. Machines remained to all intents and purposes deaf, blind, and insensate, in spite of the ears, eyes, and fingers that were painted on them. The sensation and coding of physical stimuli in the environment was possible only after the invention of the microphone, the camera, pressure transducers, and similar devices. Although these peripheral senses were of interest, the fundamental goal of the search for machine intelligence was emulation of the human capabilities for thought and language by machines.

Early Greek philosophers had attempted to create formal tools for thought based on logic. Lacking computers, these philosophers had to use a pencil and paper (tablet) approach to implement the tools of logic. This "simulation by hand" was the precursor to the discipline now referred to as *automated reasoning*.

Some valiant attempts to build physical models that could perform mechanized reasoning were made centuries before the advent of computers. One celebrated example was that of the Spanish mystic Ramon Lull, who wanted to build a logic machine that could demonstrate the existence of God (Gardner, 1986). Lull used letters to symbolize words and arguments and then combined these symbols with each other using a system of rules. Lull demonstrated his system (which he called the "Ars Magna") with a mechanical device made up of a variety of geometric figures that rotated in relation to each other, producing new versions of logical arguments. Unfortunately for Lull, the three-dimensional geometry of his device was fixed and severely limited the number of operations that could be used. A more general computational method was needed that was not limited by physical shapes and structures.

This goal seemed impossible until the development of the modern computer and the intellectual revolution that it created. As technological capabilities advanced, the goal of mimicking (and perhaps surpassing) human capability became more realistic at the same time that the need for intelligent machines became more evident. The invention of the electronic computer provided an opportunity for machine intelligence to become a serious possibility.

1.2.1 The Computer: From Calculator to Reasoning Device

At first, the role of electronic computers as reasoning and thinking machines was overlooked. It seemed that the main virtue of computers was their ability to perform high-speed computations. Even after the invention of the first programming languages, thinking and reasoning appeared to be beyond the capability of computers that were seen as being efficient calculating devices. Thinking appeared to require something extra, the ability to reason with concepts other than numbers.

As computers began to spread through engineering and accounting applications, people interested in lifelike machines began to use them as symbol processing systems. In addition to mathematical computation, device control, and so on, they realized that one could program computers to do things that required *thinking* by humans (e.g., play chess or checkers, solve problems, and prove theorems). Within select research establishments people began to develop "smart" programs. Most of this activity, however, was for the sake of intellectual interest rather than commercial gain. Everyone was talking about *interesting* programs; hardly anyone said anything about making programs that did *useful* things. Consequently, interesting demonstrations were constructed, but no applications were developed.

The realization that computers could reason came with the understanding that computers were symbol processors, and that these symbols could be numbers, text, or even concepts. This led to the *physical symbol hypothesis.* A physical symbol system (Simon, 1981) is essentially a machine that can manipulate symbols, such as a computer. The basic tenet of the physical symbol hypothesis, as depicted in Figure 1.2, is that:

  a. Thoughts correspond to language.
  b. Language can be captured in symbols.
  c. By manipulating symbols on a computer, one can simulate the thinking process.

Armed with the physical symbol hypothesis and with the willingness to build lifelike machines, many early artificial intelligence researchers attempted to solve problems by representing them in symbolic computer languages. In spite of this early enthusiasm, however, the inherent difficulties of machine reasoning were greater than early researchers realized. An apparently serious problem, initially, seemed to be that the computer hardware was limited in terms of memory size and processing power. Early researchers hoped that with more powerful computers, the machine reasoning problem would soon be solved.

This, however, did not suddenly happen with faster hardware or with improved symbolic processing languages. As it eventually was realized, the major

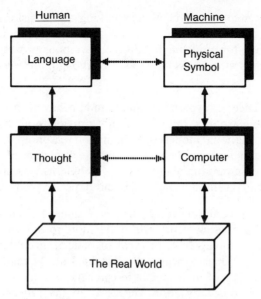

Figure 1.2 The physical symbol hypothesis.

stumbling block in machine reasoning was not merely the hardware or the software (although they were certainly important considerations), but rather the approach to representing and using large amounts of relevant knowledge.

▪ 1.3 THE HISTORY OF ARTIFICIAL INTELLIGENCE

The antecedents of artificial intelligence include an intellectual tradition dating back to the Ancient Greeks (Gardner, 1986), but the ideas that sparked the formation of the discipline stem from the research into human intelligence and formal reasoning that was conducted by various groups in the United States and Europe in the years prior to and following World War II. This research included pioneering work on cybernetics, behavior, and theories of computation.

The central idea of cybernetics was that intelligent behavior could be based on the principle of "negative feedback" (Wiener, 1948). The basis of negative feedback is to have opposing mechanisms that achieve a range of stability within a system. In the case of human body regulation, for instance, shivering and sweating act to keep the body temperature stable.

The basic idea of negative feedback control worked well with physical quantities, but it was not clear how it could be generalized to form the basis of intelligent thought. Others argued for a view of human behavior (initially from the standpoint of economics) based on rational decision making. According to those investigators, this rationality was often impossible to express as formulations of quantitative analytic techniques such as those of operations research. They pointed out that human thinking and decision making do not depend greatly on numbers. Since the existing tools of numerical reasoning were inappropriate for modeling intelligence, symbolic processing was investigated as the means through which models of thought and reasoning could be built.

The evolving sciences of cybernetics and human behavior inspired those interested in machine reasoning, but they did not provide tools that could be used in building computational models of thought and reasoning. Computation was to become the driving force behind the infant discipline of artificial intelligence. Without computational procedures, people had to illustrate the concepts of machine reasoning using pencil and paper or physical models.

As the potential for computer reasoning began to be realized, it was necessary to incorporate the research efforts within the more formal structure of a discipline. For artificial intelligence, the year of official inception was 1956, and the event was a Summer Research Project held at Dartmouth College that consolidated the ideas of many active researchers. The term "artificial intelligence" (AI) was coined by John McCarthy in the process of naming the meeting.

The new ideas about cybernetic systems and human intelligence, along with the availability of the modern computer at the end of World War II, led a number of scientists to the conclusion that the problem of building intelligent machines was now solvable. The 1956 Dartmouth meeting acted as a catalyst for researchers who had been thinking about the problem of how to build intelligent machines. This meeting had a deep impact on AI research for the next 20 years.

The Dartmouth meeting marked the unveiling of the "Logic Theorist" (Newell, Shaw, and Simon, 1963), a computer program that was capable of proving theorems in mathematical logic taken directly from *Principia Mathematica,* the well-known book on logic by Whitehead and Russell. The success of this theorem proving program had a strong influence on the direction of AI research in the next two decades.

Russell's work was extremely highly regarded for validating the foundations of mathematics and for contributing to the theory of computing systems. The ability to prove theorems taken directly from Russell's work seemed to be a "true" sign of intelligence. From one perspective, the Logic Theorist had a positive impact on AI in that it helped to encourage a great deal of research activity after the Dartmouth meeting. On the other hand, much of the research it inspired had exactly the same flavor as it did and focused on viewing AI as a method of automating mathematical logic. Thus machine reasoning at the time appeared to be simply a natural evolution of the theory of computation that began with Aristotle, Euclid, and other early philosophers and mathematicians. Today, this trend has long been forgotten.

In any case, after 1956, AI became a discipline and a more or less systematic search for machine intelligence began. Although computational techniques dominated AI research, with time the ideas and findings of psychologists, linguists, and neuroscientists were also incorporated into the endeavor.

1.3.1   AI as a Field of Study

In some sense, one goal of AI was (and still is) replication of the *functionality* of the human mind. Often, this approach has even gone further in attempts at replicating the *internal structure* of the brain, just as many of the earliest attempts at aviation tried to replicate the moving wing structure of birds.

Some modern proponents of the replicate-the-brain approach aim to arrive at the structure of the brain by simulating its evolution in computer models of neural networks (Ackley, Hinton, and Sejnowski, 1985). Such attempts use automata models as a starting point and try to achieve the formation of mind through accelerated simulation of learning processes. Other attempts use networks of interconnected processors that resemble the connectivity of neural networks within the brain (Hopfield, 1982). When this type of connectionist approach was first attempted (McCulloch and Pitts, 1943; Rosenblatt, 1962), however, the massively parallel computing devices needed to mimic the circuitry of the human brain were not available. The early work on connection machines was effectively halted by the work of Minsky and Papert (1969), who showed basic flaws in the existing approach. Recently, however, there has been a great deal of renewed interest in parallel computing architectures and their utilization in thinking (Hinton and Anderson, 1981; Feldman and Ballard, 1982; Hopfield, 1982; Rumelhart, McClelland, and the PDP Research Group, 1986).

Over the years, AI subsumed a range of topics that include planning, machine vision, and robotics, among many others. Although the exact definition of AI remains controversial even today, the class of activities considered to be AI are considerably broader than the problem of machine reasoning for expert systems that we address in this book.

On the basis of the desire to mimic the functionality of the human mind, distinct subfields of AI emerged that aimed at mimicking different human faculties. These subfields included the following:

- *Machine vision,* which aims at recognizing patterns in much the same way as the human visual system does.
- *Robotics,* which focuses on producing mechanical devices capable of controlled motion.
- *Speech processing,* which aims at recognizing and synthesizing spoken human speech.
- *Natural language processing,* which attempts to understand and produce written natural language.

- *Theorem proving,* which attempts to automatically prove theorems in mathematics and logic.
- *General problem solving,* which aims at solving general classes of problems expressed in a formal language.
- *Pattern recognition,* which focuses on the recognition and classification of patterns.
- *Game playing,* which builds competitive game playing programs.
- *Machine learning,* which aims at producing machines that accumulate knowledge by observing examples.

Interestingly, many of these subfields such as pattern recognition and speech processing have now left AI research. It would not surprise us if, after a few years, rule-based expert systems will no longer be associated with AI research, once their structure and properties are sufficiently well understood.

Expert systems benefit from research that has been carried out in a number of fields within AI. Figure 1.3 shows the relationship of expert systems to the rest of AI. At present, expert systems are most directly associated with knowledge representation and reasoning. Expert systems have, in fact, led to the development of the new field of knowledge acquisition that is a specialized form of learning where knowledge is acquired directly from an expert. Other AI issues that expert systems touch on include explanation, intelligent tutoring, planning, machine learning, distributed problem solving, and other research issues currently addressed in AI.

1.3.2 The Age of Small-Scale Experiments
Rather than being a monolithic discipline of groups organized to achieve the goal of machine intelligence, prior to its commercialization in the 1980s, AI research consisted of a number of small groups of researchers, each pursuing particular aspects of the overall AI problem. Consequently, the early work on AI was a patchwork quilt of largely independent demonstrations of particular principles and techniques. Progress was often measured in terms of quantum jumps from one Ph.D. dissertation to the next, resulting in the construction of small-scale systems that demonstrated concepts rather than having an actual application.

Games such as checkers, backgammon, and chess became popular test cases for the new ideas because people (including the researchers) liked to play them, the formal representation of the problem was fairly obvious, and one could judge the success of the program according to the playing strength of the human players that it managed to beat.

Research on game playing programs was built largely on the precepts of game theory that had been laid out by von Neumann and Morgenstern (1944). One essential principle of the game theory approach to game playing was to minimize the maximum amount of damage that the opponent could do. This prin-

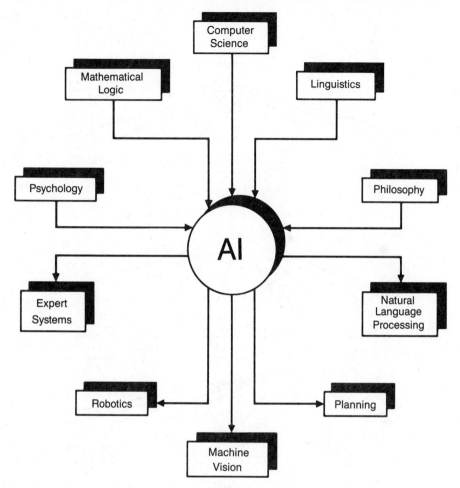

Figure 1.3 An input-output model for artificial intelligence.

ciple was called the *minimax* strategy. Using this approach in planning a move, a player "searches" for the worst thing that the opponent can possibly do and chooses the move that leads to the least damaging result (assuming the best possible play by the opponent). The concept of searching for a solution was an integral but not immediately obvious part of these game playing programs.

The gameplaying approach to AI research led to a concentration on what became known as "search and optimization" techniques. These techniques construct scenarios of possible situations (or states) and search among them for solutions. For instance, in the case of a tic-tac-toe game, we can construct a scenario of all possible moves in terms of a tree (see Figure 1.4). Such trees of possibilities came to be called "search trees." By searching through a search tree and considering all the possible moves an opponent could make, one could

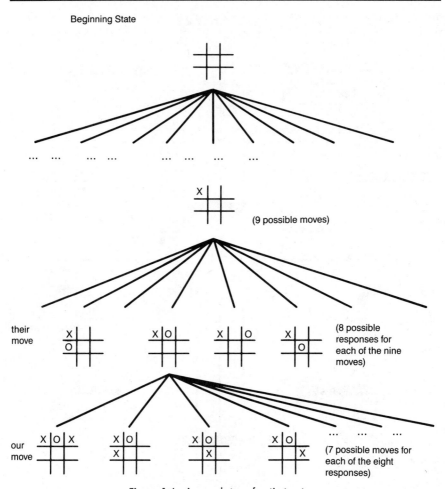

Figure 1.4 A search tree for tic-tac-toe.

actually play a reasonable game of tic-tac-toe. A discussion of game playing and search is given in Appendix A.

Soon, search became a popular approach to AI since it seemed that apart from games, many other problems could be formulated in terms of search among a number of possible states. However, a major problem still remained: although one can construct a search tree for tic-tac-toe with about 100,000 nodes, the search tree for chess is totally unmanagable, since it has close to 10^{70} nodes. These astronomic numbers of possible scenarios begin to approach the number of particles in the known universe.

Thus, search-based models of games that humans play with relative ease can blow up into monstrous structures. This combinatorial explosion in the number of pathways that can occur precludes the use of exhaustive look-ahead in game playing. In other words, you can't play a game of chess by going through all the possible lines of play and then choosing the move that leads to the best outcome given a strategy such as the minimax principle.

Initial success with small problems where search was manageable led to optimistic projections of how AI could solve larger problems. These projects were mistaken in many cases because they ignored the fact that the size of the search tree would increase extremely rapidly making generalization from toy systems to real systems impossible. For instance, a program that plays a game on a 4 × 4 board can seldom be easily generalized to a similar game on an 8 × 8 board, since the size of the search tree increases dramatically. The spirit of this lesson should be remembered as a methodologic guideline in dealing with expert systems today: i.e., the knowledge representation and inference methods used in a small-scale prototype may not easily lend themselves to more complex cases.

1.3.3 Heuristic Search and General Problem Solving
In answer to the problem of combinatorial explosion in search trees, a number of algorithms were developed to make search more efficient. These algorithms attempted to either:

    a. Construct a smaller search tree, i.e., construct fewer scenarios to begin with.

    b. Search only part of a search tree, i.e., consider fewer of the constructed scenarios.

These algorithms were based on *heuristics*. A heuristic is a rule of thumb most often used to make problem solving or searching easier. A heuristic will not lead to correct performance all the time and is not guaranteed to find the best solution, but it is sometimes a plausible way of reducing the search effort. Heuristics can be used to limit the amount of branching in a large tree. This idea has produced a number of smart heuristics for limiting the amount of search necessary for solving some problems.

Heuristic search became the basis of a well-known approach to *general-purpose* problem solving, called "GPS" (the General Problem Solver) developed by Newell and his coworkers (Ernst and Newell, 1969; Newell and Simon, 1972). GPS is described in more detail in Appendix B.

The rationale for GPS was to have a single problem solving framework for many applications. We review GPS and heuristic search here since the reasons for the failure of GPS were the same as those for the success of many expert systems; in other words, focusing on a narrow task and using domain specific knowledge is more important than general problem solving strategies in reasoning about specific domains.

In GPS a problem may be described as a collection of goals (*ends*) along with methods for operating on states of the world (*means*). This approach to problem solving is often referred to as *means–ends* analysis.

In GPS the world was viewed as a set of *states* that were transformed with a set of *operators*. For instance, a given arrangement of pieces on a chess board was a state, while the legal chess moves acted as operators transforming one state to another. The key factors in implementing GPS are to construct a measure of the distance between different states and a set of rules outlining which operators are applicable at different times and what the results of applying an operator will be.

A major difficulty with GPS is that the method requires a complete specification of the problem where the various states, operators, differences, and so on are described exactly. Although it is designed to be a general-purpose reasoning system, GPS depends on the ability of the programmer to produce a suitable representation for the given problem. Of necessity, this representation normally includes a considerable amount of detailed information about the specific domain, intricately related to the way the operators are constructed and the differences calculated. Although GPS did use the general-purpose reasoning strategy of means–ends analysis, getting the method to work in practice required a considerable amount of problem specific information to be built into the representation.

An example of GPS use is in making a robot arm move a number of blocks in a toy world (Figure 1.5). Each state corresponds to a given position and the cost of a solution corresponds to the number of pieces that are moved. It turns out that even a relatively few blocks can create a difficult task for a program such as GPS. Consider a world of eight blocks that are to be placed into two towers, each consisting of four of the blocks in a particular order. There are, in fact, 576 unique combinations of two towers that can be built, but there are many more combinations of one, two, or three blocks that can be constructed on the way to achieving the goal.

A system such as GPS works by effectively pruning the search tree. In the case of GPS, this is done by using a measure of closeness to determine whether a move or sequence of moves will lead to a more promising situation. GPS must be careful to tear down a promising solution that, although "close" to the solution, incorporates some flaw that prevents it from being on the path to an efficient solution. Consider a situation where the goal is to have four blocks in the order A–B–C–D (where D is on the bottom of the tower or pile) and the current order is A–B–C–E. This situation *appears* to be close to the solution but is, in fact, a long way off since the law of gravity does not allow us to simply remove the E block and replace it with D. Although GPS used the closeness of the current situation to the goal to prune the search tree and avoid combinatorial explosion of possibilities, closeness is itself a domain-specific concept that incorporates a considerable amount of domain knowledge. Thus

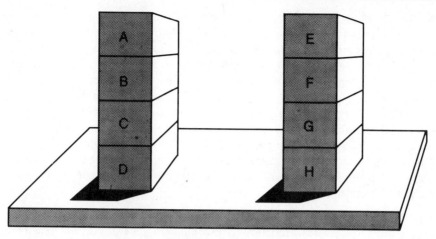

Figure 1.5   A toy world.

even a method that supposedly implements general-purpose reasoning actually requires a certain amount of domain specific knowledge to work, or else continue to face the problem of exponential search.

The General Problem Solver was not the only program of its kind to face the exponential search problem and the need for domain-specific knowledge. A number of other programs such as STRIPS (Fikes and Nilsson, 1971), AB-STRIPS (Sacerdoti, 1977), and MPS (Korf, 1985) had to deal with similar problems. These programs utilized the means–ends analysis approach of GPS but added methods for measuring closeness (sometimes referred to as "difference information") that was critical for pruning the otherwise massive search trees.

1.3.4   The Origins of Expert Systems
In the years following GPS and similar programs, AI matured, not only through the invention of new techniques, but also by the modification of the scope of its goals to focus on specific problems rather than trying to solve all of humanity's problems at once through general-purpose reasoning.

Experience with many early AI systems showed that general-purpose reasoning could, *in principle,* be done in problem solving, as long as the problem was *very small.* Otherwise one would soon bypass the limits of space and time on most computers by many orders of magnitude. A major resurgence and commercialization of AI began in the late 1970s on the basis of the success of a few programs that performed specific tasks almost as well as human experts and thus came to be called *expert systems.*

The expert systems breakthrough was not part of a large-scale organized effort aimed at inventing it (breakthroughs are usually hard to schedule). In the 1960s

NASA was planning to send a vehicle to Mars and asked researchers at Stanford University to build a program that would go on board the craft to perform chemical analysis of the soil on Mars. In order to perform the chemical analysis, the expertise of an expert chemist had to be encoded into a computer program. The aim of the program was to identify the chemical structure of a substance (such as the type of substance shown in Figure 1.6) from its mass-spectogram. Eventually, the program (and the computer it ran on) were too large to fit aboard the craft, but the idea of capturing knowledge from a human expert seemed to be a good one. The resulting program, called DENDRAL, continued to prosper, sometimes outperforming human experts in doing mass-spectogram analysis of chemical structures and discovering errors in published literature.

DENDRAL (Lindsay, Buchanan, Feigenbaum, and Lederberg, 1980) was created when most AI researchers were working on general-purpose reasoning and machine translation. What distinguished the approach used in DENDRAL from previous attempts at constructing intelligent programs was that a number of highly specific rules were captured from a human expert in order to perform a task in a very narrow area of expertise.

DENDRAL was soon followed by a number of other expert systems that used a similar approach to "clone" human experts. One of the most prominent such systems was MYCIN, also developed at Stanford University. Many of the lessons that were learned in building DENDRAL influenced the design of MYCIN. Most importantly, perhaps, the rule-based representation was used in MYCIN. MYCIN acts as a consultant for physicians, diagnosing bacterial infections and prescribing treatments for them. Many features of MYCIN have, for better or for worse, had a particularly strong impact on later expert systems work.

From a general functional point of view, an expert system was defined as a program that relied on a body of knowledge to perform a somewhat difficult task usually only performed by a human expert. From an architectural point of view, most of the early programs that managed to fit the description of an expert system had the following three characteristics:

    a. They have generally dealt with a focused task with a rather narrow range of applicability.

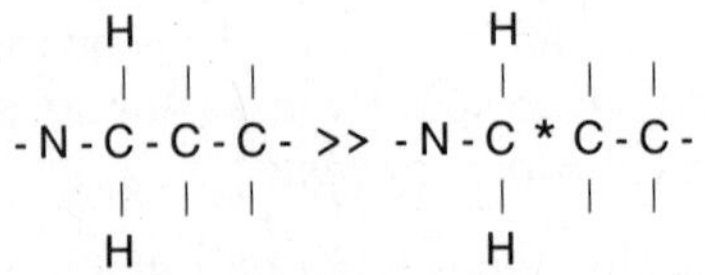

```
        H              H
        |  |           |  |
  - N - C - C - C -  >>  - N - C * C - C -
        |  |           |  |
        H              H
```

Figure 1.6 A type of structure identified by DENDRAL.

b. They have explicitly separated the knowledge from the reasoning method used to draw conclusions based on that knowledge.

c. They have been able to explain their own actions and lines of reasoning.

The separation between knowledge and inference should not be overemphasized. As we show in Chapter 5, expert systems are the epitome of the union between knowledge and inference.

Following DENDRAL and MYCIN, over the next few years expert systems captured the imaginations of many in the scientific and commercial worlds. By 1980 several expert system projects had accomplished significant results.

For instance, INTERNIST contained nearly 100,000 judgments about relationships among diseases and symptoms in internal medicine, representing a breadth of knowledge and problem solving performance that began to approach that of most human specialists in internal medicine (Pople, Myers, and Miller, 1975).

Another system, known originally as R1 (subsequently renamed XCON), used about 1000 if-then rules to configure orders for VAX computers. This eliminated the need for Digital Equipment Corporation (DEC) to hire and train many new people to perform a task that had proved difficult and that had resisted solution by conventional computer techniques (McDermott, 1979, 1982). Today, a host of expert systems are in use within business and industry. The domains of application range from telephone switching systems (Goyal, et al. 1985) to cancer therapy (Shortliffe, et al. 1984) to oil field drilling fluids (Kahn and McDermott, 1984).

The development of expert systems required a new kind of person who could capture the expert knowledge and express it in the form of facts and rules. Since many experts were not used to programming computers (and even if experts can program, they may not be able to access all the relevant knowledge that they have without external assistance) the expert knowledge was usually captured and encoded by an intermediary known as a *knowledge engineer.* Methodologies for capturing knowledge became known as *knowledge engineering* techniques.

Two major lessons were learned by the time expert systems burst on the scene, contributing much to the success of those systems. First, the limitations of general purpose reasoning were discovered and the criticality of explicit knowledge in problem solving and reasoning was realized. Since the use of highly specific domain knowledge led to successful reasoning, we learned that it was beneficial to deal with problems that have a narrow focus. Second, once a number of sharply constrained real-world problems were solved with success, it became clear that fairly simple knowledge representation tools, coupled with straightforward reasoning techniques, could be used to solve, or assist in the solution of, commercially important problems.

The trend toward knowledge-based reasoning, i.e., the use of highly specific knowledge in reasoning, has had a major influence on AI, but the greatest benefit of the knowledge-based reasoning approach has been the development of expert systems.

Although one component of the fascination with expert systems stems back to the old dream of intelligent machines, discussed earlier in this chapter, expert systems have become the center of attention for AI applications for very practical reasons. They can provide power and utility for reasoning that matches and surpasses that of human experts in limited domains.

Human expertise is well regarded and even vital in many situations. While human expertise is remarkable, there are convincing reasons for backing it up, or even replacing it with artificial expertise in the form of an expert system. It takes a human expert years to learn the necessary skill, whereas an expert system can be copied on magnetic media in seconds or minutes. Human experts become sick, retire, and die, whereas expert systems continue to work consistently and predictably. Finally, human expertise is expensive, whereas once the costs associated with building the expert system have been absorbed, the expert system may be used again and again with minimal charge.

■ 1.4 A BRIDGE TO HUMAN COGNITION

Heuristic search found little use in practical applications in spite of the large amount of research devoted to it. Heuristics were hard to come by and did not appear to conform to the methods used by human experts. Although we must be cautious in blindly aiming to replicate the structure of the human brain, a good deal of insight can often be gained by considering some relevant aspects of human cognition.

Analysis of human problem solving has shown that while general GPS-like methods such as means–ends analysis are sometimes used by people, in many situations where expertise is demonstrated, the human problem solver attempts to capitalize on as much of the *problem specific* knowledge as is available. In general, human experts appear to do little search. In fact, human experts are often admired not for doing lots of search, but for formulating the problem in a way that makes its solution apparent. This is well illustrated by the difference between an expert who on the basis of personal knowledge can quickly diagnose a malfunctioning piece of equipment and a novice who must search through a vast number of possibilities.

The development of "smart heuristics" that search massive trees of possibilities is generally not as effective as the structuring of knowledge and the development of much smaller sets of possibilities, i.e., using "smart trees." It is this emphasis on knowledge structuring rather than on search heuristics that distinguishes the expert systems approach from early AI approaches to problem solving (Feigenbaum, 1977).

Analysis of human behavior has also suggested that a large component of reasoning can be captured in the form of production systems that use a set of if–then rules (Anderson, 1983; Newell and Simon, 1972). In such cases, people simply follow a set of rules of the form "If X happens, then I will do Y." Such systems provided a convenient format for combining general-purpose reasoning with specific knowledge.

A further fact to consider is that considerable amount of research supports the hypothesis that human memory is organized into at least two separate storage mechanisms: long-term and short-term memory. Long-term memory persistently stores many facts and structures over a period of time, while short-term memory is relatively transient and information within it is soon forgotten if it is not transferred to long-term storage. An example of short-term memory operation is encountered by many people when they are dialing an unfamiliar telephone number. After looking up the number, we remember it long enough to make the call, but unless we make a special effort to remember it, the number is soon forgotten once we have made the call.

Many experimental studies have investigated the capacity of short-term memory (i.e., how many items it can hold). Generally, about seven distinct items or concepts appears to be the limit for most people (e.g., Miller, 1956), although memory-aiding (mnemonic) techniques (Yates, 1966) and grouping of related items can lead to higher apparent limits. One of the most compelling examples of the phenomenon was de Groot's (1965) demonstration of the important role that memory for specific board positions plays in skilled chess performance.

Chess masters spend many years in studying and playing chess. Many people who are normally regarded as highly intelligent do not make good chess players, while many chess masters are not regarded as being particularly intelligent when it comes to other tasks. De Groot (1965, 1966) wanted to know what separated the expert chess player from the novice. He found that, if anything, chess masters considered fewer moves than did novices. Thus it was not extensive search that gave the human experts an edge in performance.

In one task, however, he found a critical difference between the masters and the novices. He presented players of both types with legal chess positions that were removed after five seconds of inspection. The chess masters could reconstruct the positions of more than 20 pieces after only the five seconds of study, whereas the novices, under the same conditions, could remember the positions of only four or five of the pieces. However, when the players were presented with random (nonlegal) chess positions, the masters remembered no more than did the novices. It appeared that the master chess players' knowledge of common board positions allowed them to group chunks of pieces together as one memory item. The chess master's detailed knowledge consists of a vocabulary of chess positions, along, perhaps with rules guiding the search for good moves; this knowledge makes the chess player an expert.

Study of human long-term memory also suggests the use of knowledge structures that aid in the storage and retrieval of knowledge. One of the clearest demonstrations of this occurs when people recall words. It has been found (e.g., Bousfield, 1953) that people tend to recall information by categories. Thus, if the words:

chair
nose
table
dog
eyes
hair
cat
cupboard

are presented to a person, they will tend to recall them later ordered by category (e.g., furniture first, followed by animals and then human features):

chair
table
cupboard
. . .
dog
cat
. . .
eyes
nose
hair

In such experiments it is often observed that once the person recalls a category such as furniture, the items within that category are remembered fairly quickly, and then there is a pause until the next category is recalled.

This type of behavior indicates, along with a considerable amount of related evidence collected by cognitive psychologists, that people structure their knowledge into categories. The category of furniture for instance, consists of tables, chairs, and other objects. Other evidence (e.g., Rosch, 1975, 1978) has shown that people have strong notions about what features *typical* members of a category should have. A typical table, for instance, has four legs and a flat top. A particular table, however, may be supported by just one large leg.

Machine knowledge may also be organized and structured in terms of objects and their features. Human knowledge provides a good model of how machine knowledge may be organized. In return, the computational techniques that are used in expert systems suggest interesting hypotheses about how reasoning is carried out within the human brain. There is thus a bridge between human and machine cognition. Nevertheless, it is probably neither possible nor desirable to build expert systems as exact replicas of human reasoning. For one thing, humans tend to forget from time to time and there is no point in building forgetful expert systems just so that they mimic human behavior.

One challenge for machine reasoning and expert systems is to exploit the bridge to cognition so that human expertise can be utilized and emulated by machines. This requires that the knowledge structures that people have can be expressed in a computational form. Later, in Chapters 4 and 5 we will see how a particular type of knowledge structure, i.e. frames, can be used for this purpose.

Human experts are of particular interest to those building expert systems. Two of the characteristics associated with experts are as follows:

- They are usually expert only with respect to a narrow area of expertise.
- They rely on shortcuts that they have distilled from their previous experiences.

Experts are typically not very adept at dealing with problems that are outside their area of expertise, and they may not be skillful in dealing with novel situations where reasoning from first principles, rather than experience, is important.

The critical importance of domain-specific knowledge in intelligent behavior is a lesson that took years to learn, but it can be observed in the behavior of human experts. The analysis of chess skill and other types of skilled reasoning in human experts has shown that:

- Human experts do relatively little search.
- Highly specific domain knowledge is invaluable.
- The use of specific rules relating situations to actions is a powerful and plausible model of skilled performance.
- Many people have preconstructed structures for dealing with situations.
- The way in which a problem is formulated, and the way that knowledge about the problem is represented can make it much easier (or harder) to find a solution.

A number of demonstrations of this last point exist, of which the mutilated checkerboard (Figure 1.7) is merely one example. The problem is to decide how many dominoes are required to cover all 62 squares on the mutilated checkerboard. Each domino can be used to cover two adjacent squares in a

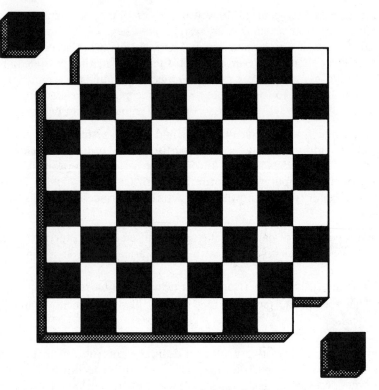

Figure 1.7 A mutilated checkerboard.

row or column (but not a diagonal). An intact checkerboard with all 64 squares will require 32 of the dominoes. Is it possible to cover the mutilated checkerboard with just 31 dominoes, or will 32 dominoes still be needed? The solution to this problem is very simple (see the end of this chapter) once an appropriate representation is chosen.

■ 1.5 AN EVOLUTIONARY VIEW OF EXPERT SYSTEMS TECHNOLOGY

In spite of the many different problems that have been addressed by AI research, lying underneath all the specific details of robotics, planning, machine vision, game playing, etc. is a general thread of evolving machine reasoning capability that represents a new technology for symbolic reasoning.

Programming languages are the tools for machine-based reasoning, computation, and data manipulation. Like all tools, the primary goal of programming languages is to "get things done." Success in building and using tools is often related to the invention of new technologies. At first, the technologies that appeared to be most important in computing concerned hardware. The development of logic circuits, memory registers, vacuum tubes, and transistors resulted in new computing tools. In AI, however, aside from the development of specialized AI workstations for symbolic processing, the emphasis has always been on the development of software tools.

Artificial intelligence languages grew out of techniques developed for managing non-numerical information. Early applications of computers in data processing soon led to the use of computers to manipulate and process textual data, and thus the era of word processing began. At this stage there was a significant difference between how the computer performed data processing and manipulated textual information. In performing operations on data, such as when multiplying numbers, the computer had separated the components of the information on which it was operating and had explicit instructions for dealing with each component. For instance, in dealing with (2 + 3), the computer was aware of the significance of '+' with respect to its position between 2 and 3. In manipulating text, however, the computer had no internal representation for the meaning of the text, e.g., in dealing with "inflation *is* high," it did not realize the significance of *is* with respect to its position between "inflation" and "high." New languages were needed that could use the technique of symbolic processing to manipulate and understand ideas as well as numbers.

Expert systems and symbolic computation usher in a new era in information processing in which computers can separate and classify the components of symbolic information and manipulate them on the basis of explicit instructions. In this era, computers manipulate textual information which represents knowledge, reason with this knowledge, and draw conclusions from it. We should not be distracted by the different motivations that people have in dealing with expert systems. Depending on one's perspective, expert systems are tools for simulating human behavior, tools for solving problems, and a new software technology. Each of these perspectives has a certain amount of validity.

1.5.1 New Programming Paradigms

In this section we discuss expert systems as a new step in the evolution of programming paradigms. This discussion is aimed at readers who are familiar with programming paradigms and may be skipped by other readers.

Artificial intelligence has often provided important new ideas that have enriched traditional computing. Symbolic compilers, multiwindow high-resolution displays, object oriented software architectures and the like were once available only within AI laboratories; today they are becoming widespread within mainstream computing environments.

These ideas were in fact invented within the AI world due to the need for dealing with higher levels of complexity. However, the flow of ideas has not yet ended. Today, we are witnessing the emergence of new *programming paradigms* based on AI techniques. From a software designer's point of view, these paradigms may represent a new step in the evolution of programming techniques.

The interesting point is that these paradigms are often obtained by removing some of the fundamental assumptions on which traditional programming stands. For instance, the following statements generally apply to traditional (e.g., FORTRAN or COBOL) programs:

a. The *flow of execution* in nonbranching program segments always moves forward; i.e., each line of the program is executed after the previous one. This direction cannot be reversed, e.g., in executing

$$A: = 4$$
$$B: = 5$$

we always move from A to B.

b. Programs usually have some *input* and some *output* variables, e.g.,

$$Y : = Factorial(X)$$

always takes X as input and returns a value to Y as output.

c. Data elements (arrays, files, etc.) are *passive,* and are acted on, i.e., *read* or *modified* by other control elements that are *active.,* e.g.,

$$read(X)$$

simply reads a value for X and performs no computation.

As we shall show in the next chapters, each of these statements becomes invalid as we introduce new paradigms for computing. For instance,

a. Backtracking can be used to execute the same program backward (Chapter 7).

b. In logic programming the distinction between input and output becomes irrelevant (Chapter 3).

c. Active values in frames may be used to represent active data elements that cause side effects whenever they are accessed (Chapter 5).

Thus, from a software designer's point of view, expert systems involve a form of program architecture that characterizes a new generation of software technology. This generation is significantly more advanced than the previous four generations of software.

Each programming paradigm consists of two aspects:

- Methods for organizing and structuring data
- Methods for controlling the flow of computation

These methods are characterized by the equation

Programs = data structures + control.

These two components of programming paradigms correspond to knowledge representation, and inference, respectively. The difference between a data structure and a knowledge structure is largely a matter of the complexity and organization of the information being stored. Bits, bytes, alphanumeric symbols, words, sentences, and frames (see Chapter 5) are all methods for organizing and structuring data.

Thus the two main features of a programming paradigm are (1) the way that knowledge (data) is represented and (2) the way that reasoning (computational control) is carried out. We can trace the lineage of data and knowledge structures through traditional languages as shown in Figure 1.8. The general classes of control paradigm can be summarized as follows:

Goto/Jump. This was the very first control paradigm, used in assembly language programming, and it still exists in a number of languages.

For-Loop/Do-While. This was the next step away from Gotos and was used in FORTRAN and other Algol-like languages. This paradigm provided more structure for the programmer and grouped the information to enable the programmer to think in terms of loops rather than individual program statements.

Recursion. This method of repeating a program segment was used in ALGOL, C, Lisp, etc. A recursive definition may actually call itself. In many situations recursive definition of program control is convenient for the programmer.

Backtrack/Fail. This style was first used in Prolog (Clocksin and Mellish, 1987). It relies on going back and repeating a statement again with a new variable value, once computation fails to progress successfully (see Chapter 7).

Do Whenever. This style of computing was advanced by forward chaining rule-based languages such as OPS5 (Forgy 1981). In this paradigm, there is no explicit flow of control and the program consists of a number of if–then rules that are executed according to a conflict resolution strategy (see Chapter 7).

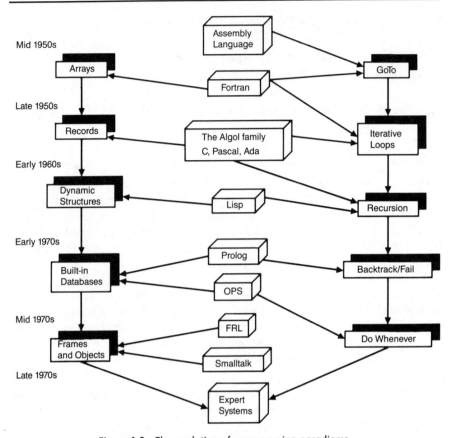

Figure 1.8 The evolution of programming paradigms.

Similarly, we can trace the evolution of data structuring techniques as follows:

Arrays. These are commonly used in assembly language, FORTRAN, and similar languages. Arrays are a natural way of storing tabular data.

Records/fields. These are used in PASCAL, C, Ada, etc. Records are used to group information together, and each record contains fields with specific information such as part numbers and retail prices.

Dynamic data structures. Such structures are used in symbolic languages such as Lisp and Prolog, which provide a convenient way of dealing with an undetermined number of items of different types.

Built-in databases. Prolog's built-in database and OPS5's working memory are examples of such structures. They provide the ability to store information in an abstract form, as though it had been placed in a relational database.

Frames. Frames (and objects) were first implemented in FRL (Roberts and

Goldstein, 1977), Smalltalk (Goldberg and Robson 1983) and a number of other recent languages. Frames extend record structures by providing means of inheriting information between records and allow active data elements.

We may, in fact, view each programming language or system as a collection selected from a pool of general programming features (Goguen and Parsaye, 1981). Thus expert system technology has enriched this pool of features by providing important new paradigms.

■ 1.6 SUMMARY

In this chapter we reviewed the evolution of expert systems and introduced some of the key trends in artificial intelligence and showed how early programs designed to show interesting behavior led to practical programs that were found to be useful.

The key to practical success in machine reasoning was the realization that general-purpose methods which attempt to use a single approach to deal with a variety of problems fail because of their dependence on searching large numbers of possibilities.

Programs that focused on narrow tasks and included large amounts of domain-specific knowledge fared much better and began to approach and exceed the performance of human experts.

We also discussed how expert system technology may be viewed as an evolution from existing programming paradigms to more advanced programming techniques for knowledge representation and inference.

■ 1.7 SOLUTION TO THE MUTILATED CHECKERBOARD PROBLEM

The checkerboard cannot be covered with just 31 dominoes. Each domino must cover one black and one white square. Thus, with 31 dominoes we can cover 31 black squares and 31 white squares. But the mutilation removed 2 white squares, so that there are still 32 black squares to be covered, and therefore 32 dominoes are still needed.

2

A FIRST
GLANCE AT
EXPERT SYSTEMS

■ 2.1 INTRODUCTION

In Chapter 1 we introduced expert systems and placed them in the context of the evolution of artificial intelligence. The success of expert systems provides one of the major lessons that has been learned in AI, namely, that general-purpose reasoning, by itself, is not powerful enough to produce acceptable levels of performance in many tasks. To achieve success in performing difficult tasks, we need to focus on narrow domains and use knowledge relevant to these domains.

The technique of focusing on narrow problems that expert systems use is helpful for two reasons: (1) it reduces the overall complexity of the situation, and (2) it allows the use of domain-specific knowledge. This restricted type of domain-specific knowledge can also be observed in the behavior of human experts. Experts typically know "a lot about a little," having a great deal of knowledge about a narrowly defined problem domain. Human experts do not appear to perform a great deal of search among possible alternatives. Chess masters, for instance, appear to use their knowledge to restrict the number of possible moves to only a few promising ones and then perform an extensive analysis on a relatively few continuations of these move possibilities. Similarly, most expert systems use knowledge to reduce the amount of search they have to do.

The basic concepts necessary to understand and use expert systems are (1) the components of knowledge, (2) methods of inference, and (3) methodological guidelines. Once they are explained in the right way, these concepts can be understood and utilized by experts.

29

In this chapter we outline the essential elements of expert systems. We first describe expert systems and outline their structure. We then focus on the knowledge structures used in expert systems and discuss how facts, rules, and frames are combined. The discussion then turns to reasoning methods for expert systems and their use.

■ 2.2 EXPERT SYSTEMS

In Chapter One we defined an expert system as a computer program that relies on knowledge and reasoning to perform a difficult task usually performed only by a human expert. Just as a human expert reasons and arrives at conclusions based on personal knowledge, an expert system reasons and arrives at conclusions based on the knowledge it possesses.

Expert systems generally deal with a focused task with a rather narrow range of applicability and use highly specific knowledge for reasoning. In doing so, they are also able to explain their actions and lines of reasoning.

Expert systems have become commercially important because they provide a way of archiving expertise and making it available when it is needed. There are good reasons for backing human expertise up with artificial expertise in the form of an expert system. It takes a human expert years to learn the necessary skill, whereas an expert system can be copied on magnetic media in seconds or minutes. In addition, human expertise is often expensive to use, while an expert system may be used again and again with minimal charge. Finally, expert systems can be far more available and accessible than human experts.

2.2.1 People Involved in Expert System Development

The development of expert systems calls for cooperation between a team of skilled people, as shown in Figure 2.1. The *domain expert* typically provides the knowledge that will be used in the expert system. For instance, a physician, a chemist, or any other specialist is a domain expert. *Domain knowledge* is knowledge relating to the expert's domain, e.g., knowledge of chemistry or medicine.

Rather than being disinterested members of the team, domain experts typically have a great deal of interest in the expert system because:

> Management wants them to assist in building the expert system.
> Talking about their knowledge is interesting and may lead them to new insights.
> The expert system may eventually assist them with their work.

The knowledge used by the expert system is captured and encoded by the *expert system developer*. In the early days of expert systems, the developer was usually a computer scientist referred to as a *knowledge engineer* who inter-

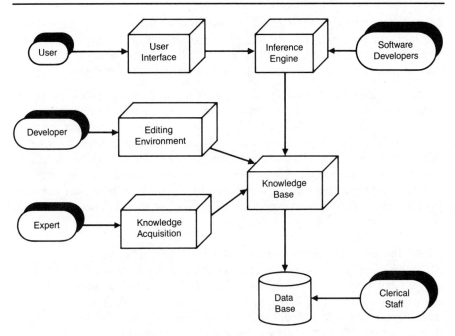

Figure 2.1 The expert system development team.

viewed the expert, extracted the knowledge, and built the expert system. This was due mostly to the fact that experts were not familiar with Lisp (the main language for early expert systems). In this scenario, the expert acted as an assistant for the knowledge engineer, and the methodologies used for dealing with experts in this manner became known as *knowledge engineering* techniques.

Gradually, as expert system building tools have become higher level and easier to use, the role played by the domain expert in building the expert system has expanded. In many cases, experts can learn enough about the tools and techniques to build expert systems themselves, although, in complex applications, knowledge engineers may still be needed.

Users should also be involved in developing expert systems to ensure that the expert system works in a way that the user understands. The user brings a number of concerns to the development process, such as:

Will the expert system work on the task that I need to have done?
Will the expert system be reliable?
How will I know when the expert system makes a mistake?
Will the expert system be easy to use?
Can I get help if I find an error in the expert system?

Other people may also be involved in data entry, data collection, and software development and maintenance for the expert system or for interfacing it to, or embedding it in, other applications. They will be concerned about the presence of adequate programming aids such as editors and debuggers.

Since there are a number of people involved in building and using expert systems, and since these people may have widely differing backgrounds and interests, the coordination of their activities is a significant issue. As with any project of this type, there should be a leader who can act as the "glue" keeping this collection of individuals focused on the task. One of the principal functions of this leader is to ensure that the concerns of the various players are communicated to other members of the team. The needs and capabilities of the user, for instance, should be apparent to the developer so that the user can interact with the expert system most effectively.

2.2.2   The Structure of an Expert System
A human expert uses knowledge and reasoning to arrive at conclusions. Similarly an expert system relies on knowledge and performs reasoning. The reasoning carried out in an expert system attempts to mimic human experts in combining pieces of knowledge. Thus the structure or architecture of an expert system partially resembles how a human expert performs. Thus, there is an analogy between an expert and an expert system, as shown in Figure 2.2.

The first part of human expertise is a long-term memory of facts, structures, and rules that represents expert knowledge about the domains of expertise. The analogous structure in an expert system is called the *knowledge-base*. The second part of human expertise is a method of reasoning that can use experts' knowledge to solve problems. The part of an expert system that carries out the reasoning function is called the *inference engine*.

In this analogy the process of inference mimics thinking while knowledge is contained in the knowledge-base. The knowledge that an expert system has

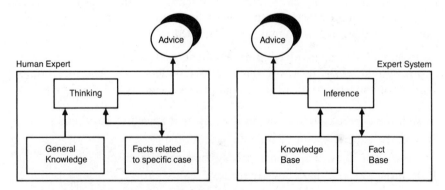

Figure 2.2   An analogy between human experts and expert systems.

will include general problem solving knowledge as well as specific domain knowledge.

The difference between the knowledge base and the inference engine parallels somewhat the distinction between general-purpose reasoning and domain-specific knowledge that we made in Chapter 1. In general, the domain knowledge is contained in the knowledge base. The general problem solving knowledge is mostly built into the way the inference engine operates. Thus the same inference engine can be used to reason with different knowledge-bases.

In addition to the knowledge-base and the inference engine, the expert system environment will include a number of tools for helping the various people who build or use the expert system. When building the expert system, the developer uses expert system building tools to acquire, encode, and debug knowledge within the knowledge base. Tools for the developer include tools for acquiring knowledge, knowledge base editors, debuggers, compilers, and validation tools, as discussed in Chapter 9.

Once the expert system has been developed, users utilize a variety of tools and interfaces to interact with the expert system. The expert system may be connected to real time data and external databases, or be embedded in larger applications.

Human experts need a way of communicating with sources of information and with their clients. This allows them to explore the particular details of a problem and to share their conclusions with clients. Similarly, to interact with users an expert system has a *user interface* that allows users to query the system, supply information, receive advice, etc.

The user interface aims to provide the same form of communication facilities provided by the expert but often has much less capability for understanding natural language and general world knowledge. However, sometimes graphic user interfaces can provide a form of human–machine communication that has no direct analog in human–human communication.

The user interface is an essential part of an expert system. It is the task of the interface to handle all the communication between the user and the expert system. The user's impression of the expert system usually depends a great deal on the nature of the interface. The way that information is presented to the user should conform to the user's model of the task and expectations. This issue is generally referred to as *cognitive compatibility*. The basic idea of compatibility is that what users see conforms with concepts that are familiar to them and that the information is presented in a nonconfusing and understandable way.

Just as human experts explain their recommendations or decisions, expert systems need to justify and explain their actions. The part of an expert system that provides explanations is called an *explanation facility*. The explanation facility not only satisfies a social need by helping an end-user feel more assured about the actions of the expert system but also serves a technical purpose by helping the developer follow through the operation of the expert system.

Figure 2.3 shows the basic structure of an expert system, which includes the user interface, a knowledge base, an inference engine, and methods for building and updating the knowledge base.

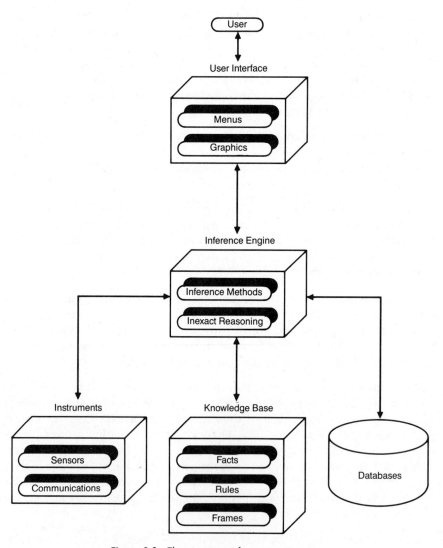

Figure 2.3 The structure of an expert system.

■ 2.3 STRUCTURING AND REPRESENTING KNOWLEDGE

Expert systems derive their power from knowledge. The heart of any expert system is the knowledge it contains, and it is the effective use of knowledge that makes its reasoning successful.

It is extremely difficult to define knowledge in the abstract, and we shall avoid entering an argument that has been waged in philosophy for millennia. Since we are ultimately concerned with expert system applications, we consider knowledge from the perspective of its use in reasoning. Thus we restrict ourselves to a pragmatic definition of what knowledge is based on what it does:

Definition : Knowledge is information about the world that allows an expert to make decisions.

In order to represent knowledge in a machine, it must be possible to define objective versions of knowledge for each domain of interest. Thus expert systems must deal with knowledge that has been structured and codified.

Expert systems employ knowledge to perform tasks that usually require a high level of reasoning ability in humans. To mimic the behavior of a human expert, an expert system typically uses the same sort of knowledge as the expert.

The knowledge used by an expert system needs to be represented and employed in a form that can be used for reasoning. This is in contrast to most computer programs that work with data. Thus, *knowledge structures* are used to store knowledge and reason with it, just as data structures are used to store and deal with data.

The first type of knowledge structure that we consider is a *fact*. The following are facts that make general statements:

> House prices <u>are</u> high
>
> Radiator coolant <u>contains</u> Ethylene-Glycol
>
> Fine cutlery <u>contains</u> Silver

The first fact is more transient than the others. We may use facts to refer to either permanent or temporary knowledge.

Another basic knowledge structure often used by experts is a *rule*. The following are some simple rules:

> If
>> The inflation rate <u>is</u> high
>
> Then
>> House prices <u>are</u> high;

    If

        Ethylene-Glycol comes in contact with Silver

    Then

        A fire hazard is present;

    If

        A hazard is present

    Then

        Injury or death may occur;

When combined with the facts, rules can be used to arrive at *conclusions,*
which are new facts. For instance, you can probably see that the conclusion:

    House prices are high

is true, if the fact:

    The inflation rate is high

is true. Figure 2.4 shows the information used in drawing this conclusion. All
that is needed in this case is one fact and one rule. Figure 2.5 shows how the
fact and the rule are combined to give the conclusion.

Experts often relate their concepts in knowledge structures. For instance, a
safety expert's knowledge of hazards may relate hazards as follows:

    A fire hazard is a hazard

    An electrical hazard is a hazard

    A shock hazard is an electrical hazard

These and similar statements can be used to organize knowledge about hazards
in a hierarchy, as shown in Figure 2.6.

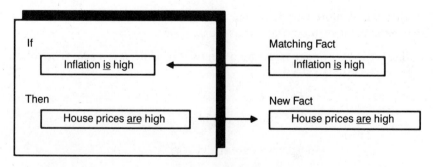

Figure 2.4   A simple knowledge system consisting of one fact and one rule.

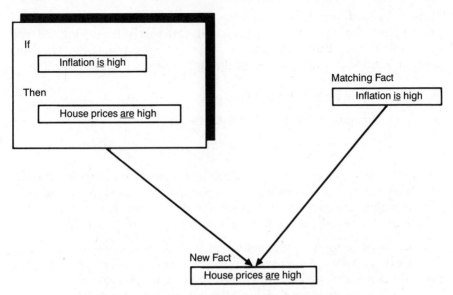

Figure 2.5 Deducing a conclusion based on the knowledge in Figure 2.4.

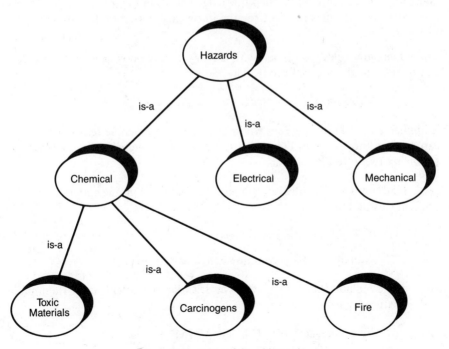

Figure 2.6 A hierarchy of hazards.

Facts, rules, and knowledge hierarchies correspond fairly closely to the way that we think about the world. Facts and rules are part of the rules of the road that each licensed driver must learn, while structure hierarchies are often deeply ingrained into our knowledge through organizing concepts such as

> A municipal bond is a type of bond
>
> Cirrhosis of the liver is a liver disease
>
> A Ford is a type of automobile.

Hierarchies are often used in representing and organizing knowledge in terms of related concepts. Each concept in the hierarchy is related to a higher-level concept, called its *parent*. Thus the parent of the concept shock hazard is electrical hazard; similarly, shock hazard is a *child* of electrical hazard.

The advantage of using hierarchies is that they allow us to organize concepts and to express knowledge in a more compact manner. Anything valid for a higher-level concept is generally assumed valid for lower-level versions of that concept; e.g., statements applying to all bonds also apply to municipal bonds. This avoids the need for repetition in storing information that is actually shared among a related class of concepts.

Facts, rules, and knowledge hierarchies may be used to deal with both simple and complex tasks. Consider the knowledge shown in Figure 2.7, which shows a set of facts and rules relevant for the knowledge structure hierarchy shown in Figure 2.6.

These facts and rules, combined with the organizing knowledge in Figure 2.6, can be used to draw conclusions. The fact

> A fire hazard <u>is</u> present

is implied by the knowledge shown in Figure 2.7. A machine reasoning system can use the knowledge in Figure 2.7 to prove this conclusion by applying the following two inference steps:

1. Find out what chemical substances are contained in fine cutlery and coolant using the facts

    > Fine cutlery <u>contains</u> Silver
    >
    > Radiator coolant <u>contains</u> Ethylene-Glycol

    and conclude that Fine Cutlery and Radiator coolant are a flammable mixture by using the fact

    > Silver <u>interacts with</u> Ethylene-Glycol

    along with Rule 1.

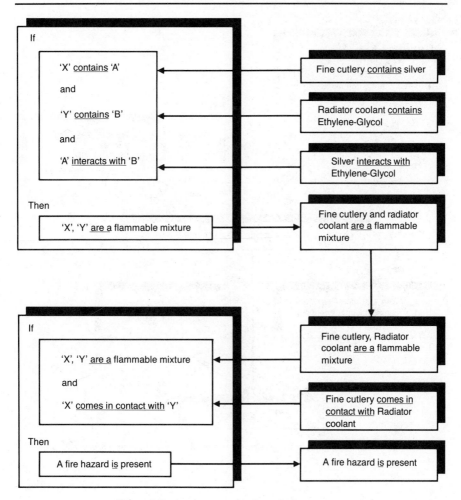

Figure 2.7   A more complex knowledge system.

2. By using this conclusion and the fact

Fine cutlery <u>comes in contact with</u> Radiator coolant

along with Rule 2, conclude that

A fire hazard <u>is</u> present.

Figure 2.8 illustrates the reasoning process. The same *method* of drawing conclusions can be used to carry out commercially important hazard analysis in large organizations. We can build systems of facts and rules of considerable complexity to represent knowledge about industrial hazards.

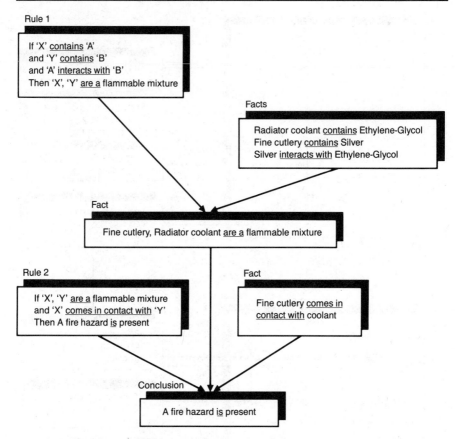

Figure 2.8 Deducing a conclusion based on the knowledge in Figure 2.7.

For instance, the knowledge structures shown in Figure 2.9 describe the components of three types of system that may be produced by a large company. Each of these components may have certain types of hazard associated with it. In a laser system, for instance, there may be chemical hazards associated with the optical coatings used on the lenses. Facts and rules can be combined with this information to draw conclusions about the presence or absence of various hazards in different industrial systems.

The only obstacle to effectively representing knowledge of different systems with facts, rules, and frames is our ability to keep knowledge modular and manageable. In describing one concept, we must ensure that we don't overlap or interfere with the descriptions of other concepts. This can be achieved by using partitioned knowledge bases and hierarchies.

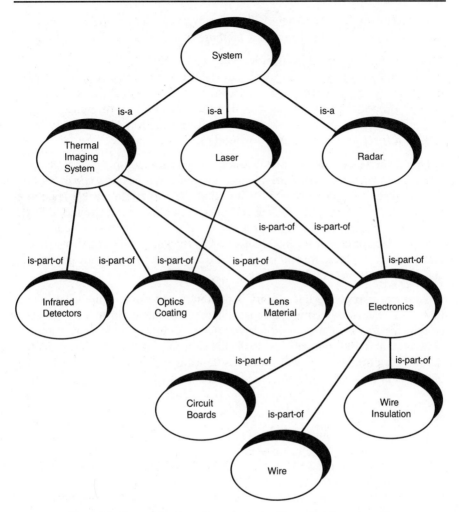

Figure 2.9 Representation of a system as a hierarchy of components.

2.3.1 Facts

Facts are pieces of information that can be used by expert systems. We saw earlier (e.g., Figures 2.7 and 2.8) how facts may be combined with rules to draw conclusions. Facts often refer to specific cases and individuals, e.g.,

> The patient <u>is</u> 24 years old
>
> The patient <u>has a</u> previous history of allergy

Facts are statements about the world, and as such they are mostly transient and subject to change. John Smith's age can change from year to year, and the status of the current patient will change with each new appointment. In an expert system, facts are stored in a *factbase,* which is a database of facts.

Although one can not always know how experts think, in many cases the observed behavior of experts suggests that they combine knowledge and current facts to arrive at conclusions. Expert systems seek to mimic the results of the thought processes of human experts by using reasoning or inference to reach conclusions. Rules in the knowledge base of an expert system express knowledge in a form that can be used for inference.

Human experts can often make decisions based on incomplete, imprecise, or uncertain information. Similarly, facts may sometimes be *uncertain* or *inexact.* For instance, we may be only 70% sure that the real estate market is good at a particular point in time. This uncertainty may result from the fact that the situation is inherently uncertain or because we are missing some of the knowledge we need for certainty. Regardless of why the knowledge came to be uncertain in the first place, we will often need a way of expressing our uncertainty about different pieces of knowledge.

One way of expressing uncertainty is to state it in terms of one's confidence that a fact or rule is true. To represent our confidence in a fact, we use a *confidence factor* or a *certainty factor* (CF). A certainty factor is a number between 0 and 100 that reflects our belief in a fact. A CF of 100 means that the fact is definitely true, while a CF of 0 means that a fact is definitely false. Numbers in between 0 and 100 are inexact; e.g., a CF of 80 means pretty sure.

For instance,

> the real estate market is good   CF = 70
> Helen is old   CF = 90
> the investor will accept high risk investments   CF = 30

are examples of inexact facts. We shall return to the problem of uncertainty in Chapter 6, where we show the different methods of defining uncertainty. We will show how uncertainty can be incorporated into inference in Chapter 7.

The final feature of facts that we want to discuss here is how they may change over time. An expert system needs a way of getting access to new information as it becomes available. New facts may be provided to an expert system in a number of ways:

They may be entered in the factbase before execution.

The user may provide them during the operation of the expert system.

They may be read from external devices (e.g., real-time data input such as satellite telemetry).

They may be read from external databases.

Facts can be considered as the elementary components of knowledge. In some sense, the facts that are known guide the reasoning of an expert system since they determine which rules are currently applicable. The quality of the reasoning process will be greatly affected by whether all the relevant facts are available to the system.

2.3.2 Rules

In spite of their importance, facts by themselves cannot be used for reasoning. We need to relate facts together with rules to reason and to derive new facts. Rules are a general way of representing information.

A rule can be expressed in the general form

> If *premise*
>
> Then *conclusion;*

The premise is, in turn, made of one or more conditions. A rule suggests that the conclusion follows the premise in a logical or action-oriented way. We can also write rules using the format

> *conclusion*
>
> If *premise;*

where the order of the premise and conclusion is reversed. We shall use both of these formats to represent rules. Consider the following rule:

> If
> > the unemployment rate < 7.6%
> and
> > the GNP growth rate > 4%
> Then
> > the economic outlook <u>is</u> good;

In this rule the premise consists of two conditions. The first condition expresses unemployment rates covered by the rule, while the second condition expresses the GNP growth rate covered by the rule.

A rule is *proved* when the premise ("If" part) of the rule matches known facts. The effect of proving a rule is to confirm its conclusion ("Then" part). In the case of the rule shown above, proving the rule leads to the conclusion of projecting a good economic outlook. In other situations the conclusion of a rule can be used to get something done in the real world as in

> If
> > the economic outlook <u>is</u> good
> Then
> > more sales people <u>should be</u> hired;

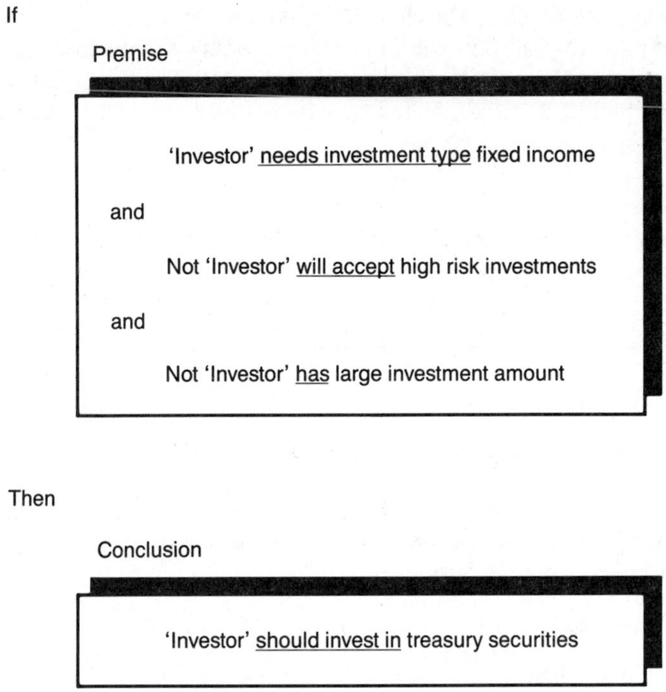

If

Premise

'Investor' <u>needs investment type</u> fixed income

and

Not 'Investor' <u>will accept</u> high risk investments

and

Not 'Investor' <u>has</u> large investment amount

Then

Conclusion

'Investor' <u>should invest in</u> treasury securities

Figure 2.10   An investment rule.

For instance, the structure of an investment rule is shown in Figure 2.10. This figure emphasizes the way in which rules provide a structure for facts. We can use facts, rules, and knowledge structure hierarchies to describe the knowledge of a financial adviser, a safety engineer, or experts in a wide variety of other knowledge domains.

Rules have a number of desirable features. First, they are straightforward and seem to correspond to the way in which experts discuss their own knowledge (e.g., Newell and Simon, 1972). Second, in many cases, rules can describe how the system should react to incoming data, often without worrying in advance about the order in which actions should be taken by the reasoning system. However, situations may arise where more than one rule is appropriate and the order in which rules are matched against facts affects the reasoning process.

Some rules may also be true some, but not all, of the time; i.e., they may be *uncertain* or *inexact*. We can express our uncertainty about a rule by adding a *certainty factor* to the rule. The rule certainty indicates the degree to which the rule is held to be true.

The following rule is from the domain of investment advice. It contains three conditions in its premise and a statement about its own certainty (or CF):

CF = 50

If

      'Investor' <u>needs</u> investment type real estate

and

      'Investor' <u>needs</u> tax shelter

and

      'Investor' <u>needs</u> inflation protection

      real estate market <u>is</u> good;

Even if all three facts in the premise of this rule turn out to be true, we are still only 50% sure that the conclusion is true. By using inexact rules like this, we can capture the knowledge of experts even when the knowledge is inexact.

2.3.2.1   Specific and General Rules   Another feature of rules is that they can be expressed at varying levels of generality (Figure 2.11). The more generally a rule is expressed, the more situations it may cover. Consider the following rules:

If

      an electric drill <u>has a</u> damaged electrical cord

Then

      the electric drill <u>constitutes</u> a shock hazard;

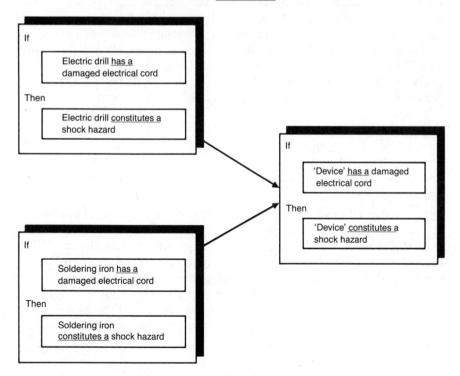

Figure 2.11   Specific and general rules.

and

> If
>
> a soldering iron <u>has a</u> damaged electrical cord
> Then
>
> the soldering iron <u>constitutes a</u> shock hazard;

Both of these specific rules can be accounted for in a single more general rule:

> If
>
> 'Device' <u>has a</u> damaged electrical cord
> Then
>
> 'Device' <u>constitutes a</u> shock hazard;

The advantage of expressing the rule in this more general form is that this single rule can now apply to all devices that have electrical cords. We don't have to make a separate version of the rule for each new device that is considered.

Once we have the general rule, we can make similar deductions for all devices that people have access to and which have damaged electrical cords. Note here that we have created a rule of knowledge that can apply to a large number of objects. When we say 'Device' in the rule, we really mean "any device," so the knowledge will apply to any device that may have a damaged electrical cord. By using more general forms, we can derive many conclusions from relatively few rules. Naturally, the same will hold true for any rule that refers to a class of objects or a general knowledge structure. Thus we could have:

> If
>
> 'Substance' <u>is</u> flammable
> Then
>
> 'Substance' <u>is a</u> potential fire hazard;

indicating that all substances that are flammable can be classified as potential fire hazards. In the preceding case, the rule applies broadly. However, we must be careful in using such rules, since the more general the rule, the more likely there are to be exceptions. Note that we are using a term such as 'Substance' to refer to all possible substances. 'Substance' is thus acting as a *variable* that can be matched with a variety of actual substances. It is the use of the variable inside the rule that allows the rule to be general. Instead of having a different version of the rule for each possible substance, we can have a single general rule that covers all the substances.

Consider a rule such as:

If

'Substance' is a Class IA liquid

and

'Substance' is stored in a glass container

Then

the capacity of that container must not exceed one pint;

This rule may be part of a fire protection code. However, there may be an exception where an alternative type of container is not available, i.e.,

If

'Substance' is a Class IA liquid

and

'Substance' is stored in a glass container

and

'Substance' causes excessive corrosion of a metal container

Then

the capacity of that container must not exceed one gallon;

The original rule is inappropriate in the case of a highly corrosive substance. The general rule, which did not distinguish between corrosive and noncorrosive substances, created ambiguity within the knowledge domain that was removed by using a more specialized version of the rule that did recognize the distinction.

Rules allow the generation of new knowledge in the form of facts that are not originally available but can be *deduced* from other pieces of knowledge. These facts are generated as the conclusions of rules that have been applied. The process of deduction using facts and rules works as follows:

1. Knowledge exists in the form of facts and rules.
2. New facts are added.
3. Combining the new facts with the existing facts and rules leads to the deduction of further facts.

This type of deduction forms the basis of symbolic reasoning that uses knowledge structures such as those shown above much as other programs use data to perform numeric reasoning.

Of course, using symbolic reasoning in an expert system does not immediately guarantee that the expert system will generate correct results or show desired behavior. Incorrect knowledge will lead to faulty conclusions. Thus the quality of the knowledge that they employ is a critical determinant of how well expert systems perform.

2.3.2.2 *Metarules* Although rules represent a fairly simple knowledge structure, they can be used in a number of different ways. For instance, some rules can be designed to control the behavior of other rules. Imagine the case of a small company that begins to expand. Initially all the employees are directly involved in basic activities such as production, development, and marketing. Later, as the company becomes more complex and more employees are hired, some of the employees begin to manage the activity of other employees.

The same sort of thing can happen in an expert system. When there are only a few rules in the knowledge base, each rule represents part of the knowledge domain. As an increasing number of rules are added, an overhead develops for organizing the activities of the rules. Rules, known as *metarules,* are developed that manage the activities of other rules. An example of a metarule in a financial advisor might be:

> If
>> the age of the client is greater than 65
>
> and
>> there are rules that mention blue chip risk in their premise
>
> and
>> there are rules that mention speculative risk in their premise
>
> Then
>> use the former set of rules before using any of the latter;

Building this type of *metaknowledge* into the knowledge base can be difficult. One problem with metarules is that there will always be exceptions. In the preceding example, for instance, there may be a class of senior citizens who already have a secure income and who would be interested in speculative risks.

2.3.3 Frames: Packaged Structures

Facts and rules are important knowledge structures, but we also need a way of packaging knowledge that makes it easily accessible. Packages provide modularity, hierarchical organization, and compactness of expression.

Hierarchical organization enhances modularity by allowing us to describe or refer to a class of concepts using a single high-level representative of that class. Hierarchies also assist the system in knowing where to look for information. For instance, finding information about automobiles begins by looking in the automobile section of the hierarchy. Compact expression is achieved by having to define something only once. It can then be shared by lower-level instances of the same concept.

Packaged structures can assist the expert in reasoning in a variety of ways. They make it easier to organize and retrieve knowledge. In analyzing hazards, for instance, the expert knows what information, such as voltage, is important and what sorts of situations may lead to an electrical hazard. Packaged structures can also guide the expert in carrying out the task by specifying the important information that should be known about an object. All hazards, for instance, will have causes, effects, and possible strategies for controlling or removing them, and for each hazard, this type of information should be packaged with other information about that hazard.

Structures seem to be a natural way of organizing knowledge. There is a considerable amount of evidence that human memory contains knowledge structures that aid in recall of information. An early study of human long-term memory (Bartlett, 1932) demonstrated the existence of patterns derived from previous experience that are used in interpreting new experiences. Bartlett used the term "schema" to refer to these patterns. Packaged knowledge structures in machines perform similar functions in organizing and interpreting knowledge.

Consider the concept of an automobile. Most people already know a great deal about what an automobile should be like and have concepts such as:

> Automobiles are a type of vehicle
>
> Automobiles carry passengers
>
> An automobile requires a driver
>
> An automobile uses gas for energy

These statements represent reasonable expectations about what properties an automobile should have. However, listing general statements about automobiles in this fashion does not show how they are related to each other. Instead, we need to package this information into a more usable form. Thus we might create a standardized form of representation that captures the critical elements of the automobile structure in a way that allows the structure to be related to other structures. We might, for instance, standardize our general notions about automobiles in the form shown in Figure 2.12.

In representing knowledge about a domain, a knowledge base needs to store knowledge in a form that can be used for efficient storage, retrieval, and reasoning. One knowledge structure that fulfills these purposes and which is frequently used in expert systems is the *frame*. Frames are a way of packaging knowledge within a well defined structure.

The basic idea of a frame was outlined by Minsky (1975), who in introducing the notion of frames, wrote:

> . . . the ingredients of most theories both in Artificial Intelligence and in Psychology have been on the whole too minute, local, and unstructured to account . . . for the effectiveness of common-sense thought. The "chunks" of

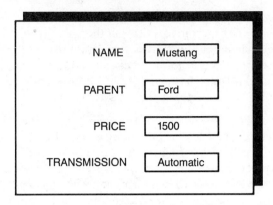

Figure 2.12 A "packaged" version of basic knowledge about an automobile.

reasoning, language, memory, and perception ought to be larger and more structured; their factual and procedural contents must be more intimately connected in order to explain the apparent power and speed of mental activities.

Frames were seen as a way round this problem. A frame is a specialized structure that represents a stereotypical situation. Additional power is added to the frame concept by allowing information to be attached to each frame. These attachments can include instructions about how to use the frame, what should happen next, and what to do if the expectations are not confirmed.

Each frame has a higher-level frame (parent frame) to which it belongs. For instance, the parent frame for Ford may be Automobile. The characteristics of each frame are captured in its *slots* or *attributes*. A frame may contain a number of *slots* that can be filled with specific instances or data.

Consider automobiles and their role in transport. The following information describes some relevant knowledge about automobiles:

An automobile is a land vehicle

A Ford is an automobile

A land vehicle is a vehicle

A vehicle is a form of transport

An automobile is powered by an engine

An automobile can usually carry from 2 to 6 passengers

Information about automobiles, and about vehicles in general, can be linked into a hierarchy, as is shown in Figure 2.13. The description of our knowledge about automobiles should also organize the knowledge in a way that includes the information in each statement listed above.

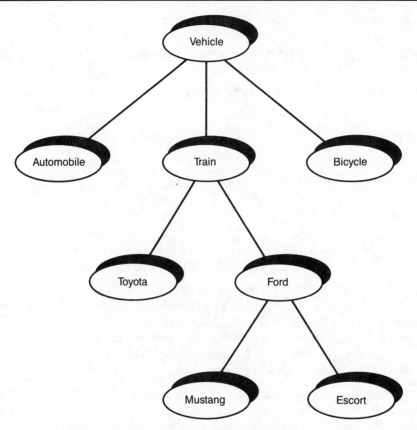

Figure 2.13 A hierarchy representing knowledge about automobiles.

The knowledge structures shown in Figure 2.13 suggest that vehicles share the function of transportation and that land vehicles share the function of transportation over land. The frames become more specific as we move down the hierarchy. Vehicles are manufactured in all shapes and sizes, however, when we get down to the more specific level of automobiles we have a fairly strong set of expectations about an automobile's structure and function.

Automobiles also have general attributes such as the engine size, the capacities of the passenger and luggage compartments, the mileage on the speedometer, the size of the tires, and so on. These shared attributes can be expressed as slots in the general automobile frame. Specific automobiles will have additional attributes that are not shared with other automobiles. While most automobiles have four wheels, relatively few are convertible, have sun roofs or heavily tinted windows.

Much of the power of frames as knowledge representation tools is derived from their ability to handle default reasoning. In the absence of external information, a slot in a frame can be filled with a default value that will be assumed until new information is obtained. Thus we might assume that a power plant burns coal, or that a teacher has a college degree until told otherwise, or that all automobiles have four wheels.

If we establish the syntactic structure for frames:

> Frame Name
> Parent Frame
> slot1 filler1
> slot2 filler2
>
> . . .
>
> slotN fillerN

then we can develop an equivalent pictorial representation. The frame representations of vehicles and automobiles is illustrated in Figure 2.14.

An important aspect of this frame hierarchy is that general attributes described by slots in higher-level frames are shared by all automobiles and specific attributes are stored locally in slots in lower level frames (with each particular instance of an automobile). The relationship between Figures 2.13 and 2.14 is very close. Each parent slot in a frame in Figure 2.14 is equivalent to the link between corresponding nodes in Figure 2.13.

Using the frame hierarchy in Figure 2.14, we can draw conclusions about a particular Ford Escort based on the fact that it is a Ford and that it is an automobile. Knowing that it is an automobile, we can conclude that the 1983 hatchback model has four wheels and an engine unless told otherwise.

We can build a hierarchy of frames where the topmost nodes represent general concepts and the lower nodes represent more specific instances of those concepts. This is done by connecting frames in a series of *parent–child* relationships. Thus the parent frame for Ford is Automobile.

Each frame thus represents a concept as a collection of attributes that are referred to as *slots*. Slots can be filled with *values;* the value of the Engine slot for the Ford Escort frame is 4-Cylinder.

If we want to collect information from a frame, and we don't find that information in the frame itself, we can try and obtain the information from its parent and so on using the process of *inheritance*. For instance, suppose that we tried to find out how many wheels a Ford Escort has using the frame hierarchy shown in Figure 2.15. Since this information is not stored in the Ford Escort frame, we try its parent, but the information is not present in the Ford frame, either. We then move to Automobile, the parent of Ford, and it is here that we get the answer, i.e., that there are four wheels. We can paraphrase the kind of reasoning involved in this example of inheritance as follows:

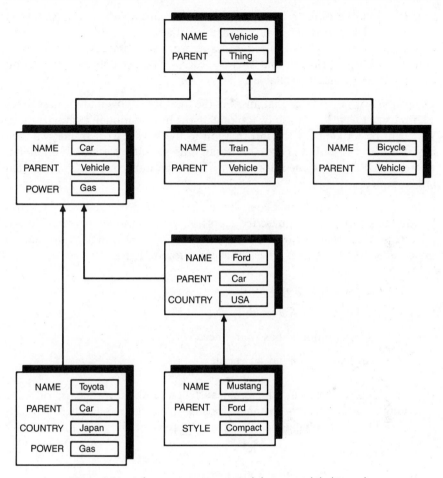

Figure 2.14   A frame representation of the automobile hierarchy.

Since I know that a Ford Escort is a Ford

and I know that a Ford is an automobile

and I know that an automobile has 4 wheels

I can assume that a Ford Escort has 4 wheels

Inheritance saves us the trouble of explicitly going through this type of reasoning process each time we want to retrieve information from a frame hierarchy. Inheritance is a natural consequence of using knowledge structures organized in hierarchies. One uses a hierarchy by placing information at the highest level where it can reasonably be expressed. It can then be shared by all the concepts that are children or descendants of the concept that contains the information.

Inheritance is the process of making the information stored in a high-level concept available to lower-level instances of that concept. Inheritance works well when knowledge is organized into a network or hierarchy. Inheritance is both a structuring principle and a set of processes that search for information that is not immediately available.

The process of inheritance that answers the question "how many wheels does a Ford Escort have?" does so by looking up the information in a set of frames. We begin by looking for the information in the Ford Escort frame; we then look for it in the parent (Ford) and finally the parent's parent (automobile), where, in fact, we find the information. This inheritance process is illustrated in Figure 2.15.

Inheritance should not immediately be confused with organized facts. The following facts, for instance, describe a portion of a hierarchy, but they do not provide a mechanism for inheriting the number of wheels that a Ford has on the basis of the number of wheels that an automobile has:

> A Ford Escort is a Ford
>
> A Ford is an Automobile
>
> An Automobile has four wheels
>
> An automobile has an engine

If we use facts to represent a hierarchical structure we must then use rules for inheriting information. For instance, we could find out the number of wheels that a Ford has by applying the following rules for inheriting that information:

> If
> > 'Object' is a Ford Escort
> Then
> > 'Object' is a Ford;
>
> If
> > 'Object' is a Ford
> Then
> > 'Object' is an automobile;
>
> If
> > 'Object' is an automobile
> Then
> > 'Object' has four wheels;

However, it is more convenient to use frames, since we would have to create a similar rule for each step in the inheritance path, and we wouldn't have the packaging of information that frames provide.

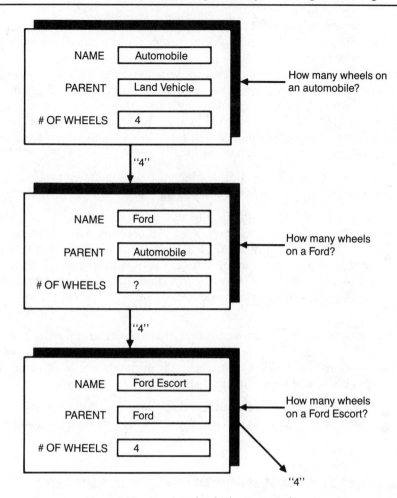

Figure 2.15 An example of inheritance in frames.

Rules and frames should not be seen as competing ways of representing knowledge. Frames are a good way of packaging knowledge and handling the storage and retrieval of that knowledge. Rules, on the other hand, work best at making deductions. The functionality of frames can certainly be implemented in rules, but this creates a whole new set of extra rules, and the resulting rule system will be harder to work with. Further, implementing frames in rules results in computational performance degradation and slow response time.

We have now introduced three important features that frames provide:

Hierarchical representation.
Attribute packaging.
Inheritance.

There is one more feature still to be introduced. What happens if the system needs some information but that information is not available, even after inheritance has been tried? One solution is to allow the system to somehow determine the information, by asking someone, proving a rule, etc. Thus we might have a rule called "Go ask for it" that is invoked when the original search for the information in the frame hierarchy fails. In a frame hierarchy, this type of behavior is achieved by attaching the "Go ask for it" rule to the appropriate slot in the frame. A rule such as "Go ask for it" is generally referred to as an *attached* procedure, or an *attached predicate*.

Consider the frame for an automobile which has been modified to include an attached predicate on the fuel consumption slot, as shown in Figure 2.16.

In this case we are trying to obtain information from the frame, so the attached procedure is referred to as an *if-needed* procedure. Now, if the system needs to find the fuel consumption of a Ford Escort, it looks in the Ford Escort frame, draws a blank, and then works its way up the hierarchy using inheritance. When it gets to the fuel consumption slot in the automobile frame, it finds the if-needed rule and then uses "Go ask for it" to get the information it needs.

If-needed procedures are used when information is needed from a slot but the slot is empty. Several other types of attached procedure have been suggested for frame systems. An *if-added* procedure, for instance, is invoked when the system attempts to add something to a slot.

It should be clear from this introduction that frames provide a versatile way of organizing knowledge. In practice, the majority of expert system tasks can

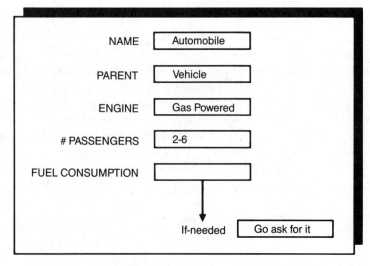

Figure 2.16 A frame containing an attached procedure.

be efficiently implemented using rules or frames. However, since frames are a good way to manage knowledge and rules are well suited to reasoning, it seems natural to combine rules and frames when building expert systems.

■ **2.4 REASONING WITH KNOWLEDGE**

Expert systems work with knowledge structures and rules of knowledge, but how? An expert system typically includes:

Facts, which are elementary pieces of knowledge.

Frames, used to organize knowledge.

Rules, which relate facts and frames.

We collectively refer to these facts, rules, and frames as the knowledge the expert system possesses. To arrive at conclusions, the expert systems needs to relate pieces of knowledge by performing *inference* or deduction. The part of an expert system that performs inference is called an *inference engine.*

The task of the inference engine is to take the knowledge in the knowledge base and carry out a set of actions that will utilize the knowledge in finding a solution to the problem. The same knowledge may be used for performing different types of task.

Human experts are able to use similar pieces of knowledge in more than one way. For instance, knowledge of medicine can be used for diagnosing a patient, prescribing treatments, or suggesting preventive regimens.

Consider how inference works for a safety expert who is dealing with garage fires and related hazards. The expert has a core of knowledge to be used for a number of different purposes. The expert may use this knowledge to diagnose why a fire took place, to predict the existence of a hazard, or to recommend how hazards may be eliminated.

Imagine that a garage fire has just occurred. In searching for a cause of the fire, the expert discovers that a set of fine cutlery had been left in the garage prior to the fire and now suspects a cause for the fire. The expert knows that:

Silver is a precious metal

Fine cutlery contains silver

Radiator coolant contains Ethylene-Glycol

Asbestos particles are potent carcinogens

Radiator coolant is used in servicing automobiles

Automobiles are housed in garages

etc.

By themselves, these pieces of information don't seem very compelling. After all, the expert's knowledge consists of numerous facts that may or may not be relevant to the case. The expert needs some way of tying these facts in with the fact that a fire occurred and needs to find the *right* rule or fact among all the known rules and facts. In this case the right fact might be expressed in the form:

Ethylene-Glycol interacts with Silver

Once the relevant facts and rules are identified, the pieces fall into place and a reasonable scenario is constructed. It is possible that radiator coolant was stored in the garage. The coolant (which contained Ethylene-Glycol) somehow spilled onto the cutlery, which was made of silver. The reaction between the Ethylene-Glycol and the silver then resulted in the fire.

In this example, the expert uses a straightforward, but effective, reasoning process: collecting a set of facts and then examining which rules are relevant to these facts. In this case the joint presence of Ethylene-Glycol and Silver activates a particular rule in the expert's memory, and it is this rule that suggests a probable cause for the fire.

Note that this scenario is a plausible, but by no means certain, explanation of the cause of the fire. Fine cutlery is often, but not always made of silver. Without carrying out a detailed forensic analysis, the expert might only be 75% certain that the cutlery contained silver, for instance. Then there is additional uncertainty regarding whether the Ethylene-Glycol was actually spilled on the cutlery.

This type of uncertainty creates an additional complexity for expert systems to deal with. We might quantify our uncertainty about whether fine cutlery contains silver in the following fashion:

Fine cutlery contains Silver   CF = 75

In this example the knowledge that the mixture of Ethylene-Glycol and Silver can cause fires is used to *diagnose* the course of a fire. Related information could be used to *predict* the existence of a hazard providing that we have knowledge expressed in rules such as the following:

If

      'Substance1' contains 'A'

and

      'Substance2' contains 'B'

and

      'A' interacts with 'B'

Then

      'Substance1', 'Substance2' are a flammable mixture;

If

'Storage site' <u>contains</u> 'Substance1', 'Substance2'

and

'Substance1', 'Substance2' <u>are a</u> flammable mixture

Then

'Storage site' <u>has</u> a fire hazard;

A third application could use the same essential knowledge, but this time to *recommend a strategy* for eliminating fire hazards. For this, we need to reformulate the expression of the knowledge:

If

'Storage site' <u>contains</u> 'Substance1', 'Substance2'

and

'Substance1', 'Substance2' <u>are a</u> flammable mixture

Then

<u>separately store</u> 'Substance1', 'Substance2';

In this case, we changed the conclusion of the second rule. The intent of the rule shown above can be represented as:

If

a flammable mixture causes a fire hazard

Then

that fire hazard may be eliminated by storing the components of the mixture in separate locations;

However, we had to make sure that the way that we expressed this rule would enable it to be *linked* to other facts and rules. For machine reasoning to process the knowledge, it should be expressed in a formal and consistent fashion. The way in which we name things so as to maintain consistency in rules and facts is discussed in Chapters 3 and 5.

Another point illustrated by this example is that the expert used two separate kinds of knowledge: temporary knowledge about the specific garage the expert dealt with and permanent knowledge about fire hazards in general. Figure 2.17 shows the distinction between his temporary and permanent knowledge. The rule defining a flammable mixture is an example of permanent knowledge. In addition to this permanent knowledge, there will be temporary knowledge (consisting of facts) that is situation-dependent. These facts will change as each new case is considered.

Rules are generally permanent, while facts may be temporary or permanent. For instance, the molecular structure of particular substances does not change at an abstract level, e.g.,

Ethylene-Glycol <u>is an</u> organic compound

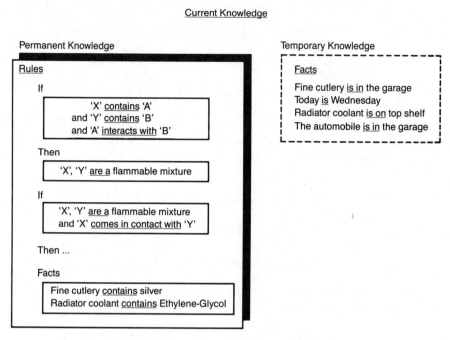

Figure 2.17 Permanent and temporary knowledge.

is an example of a permanent fact. Although temporary facts are not directly retained, human experts often *learn* from patterns they have observed in previous cases; e.g., a safety expert may learn to associate certain flammable substances such as paint thinners with garage fires.

■ 2.5 METHODS OF INFERENCE

An inference engine combines facts and rules to arrive at conclusions. But what happens if a large number of facts and rules may be matched? How can the system choose the right facts or rules? The wrong choice may set the system on a wild goose chase where most of the reasoning is of little assistance in performing the task. Thus the system needs methods of inference that can select which rule should be applied at each step in the reasoning process.

In performing inference, the inference engine tries to establish the truth or falsity of a statement called a *goal*. A goal is a fact whose truth value is to be determined. For instance,

The patient has an allergy

may be a goal, or a hypothesis provided to a medical expert system.

A series of rules can be joined together to form a line of reasoning. All the possible lines of reasoning that can be used by an expert system form a network, as in Figure 2.18.

The task of the expert system is to start from an initial position of the network and find the best path through the network in order to reach the goal represented by the correct conclusion. We can further illustrate this problem with an intuitive analogy, discussed in the next section.

2.5.1 An Intuitive Analogy for Inference

Networks are formed in many problems, not just in inference. One example of a network is a *flight path network* which connects various cities in the world. Flights between cities may be routed through *connections*. Thus a flight from Los Angeles to New York may be direct or may be routed through Chicago or St. Louis. There are a number of similarities between this network and the network of rules that the expert system works with. A rule of the form

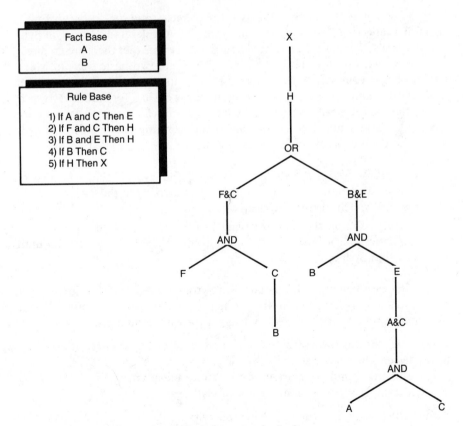

Figure 2.18 A network of rules.

If

      A

Then

      B;

can be viewed as if it were a flight that leaves city A and arrives at city B. Thus a flight from Los Angeles to New York will resemble the rule

If

      Los Angeles

Then

      New York;

When we consider rules in this way, the problem of deciding where to go next in an inference tree begins to resemble the problem of finding connecting flights between cities in our network of scheduled flights. In this analogy, chains of rules resemble chains of connecting flights.

Suppose that you are a travel agent in Los Angeles and are trying to find a chain of connecting flights originating from Los Angeles and arriving at Sydney, Australia. To make the example nontrivial, assume that there are no direct flights between Los Angeles and Sydney. There are two basic ways in which you can begin your search for this chain of flights. You can either start with Los Angeles and look for connecting flights working forward (westward) across the Pacific until you get to Sydney, or you can assume that you are already in Sydney and find connecting flights working backward (eastward) across the Pacific. Thus the two methods are

> *Backward.* Look up the flights arriving in Sydney and find which cities they arrive from. Then look up the flights arriving in those cities and so on until you find Los Angeles.
>
> *Forward.* Look up the flights leaving Los Angeles and find their destination cities. Then look up the flights leaving those cities and so on until you find Sydney.

In the first case you are working backward from Sydney and thus are using a backward chaining strategy. In the second case you are working forward from the initial condition toward Sydney using a forward chaining strategy.

Now, which strategy works better, going forward or backward? As you may have guessed, the answer actually depends on the pattern of flight connections, your destination, and your origin. To illustrate this point, we will consider a simpler example focused on a portion of California.

Figure 2.19 shows a section of California with some flight connections. The figure shows connections between eight locations: San Francisco, Los Angeles,

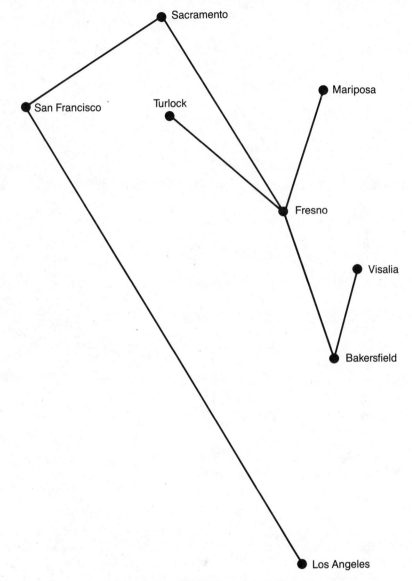

Figure 2.19 A flight network in California.

Sacramento, Fresno, Bakersfield, Visalia, Mariposa, and Turlock. These connections are, however, given for illustrative purposes only and may not represent currently available flight connections in the area.

Imagine that we are in Visalia and want to fly to Fresno. Which would be a more efficient strategy for planning our trip, working forward from Visalia or working backward from Fresno? Figure 2.20 shows the two trees generated

Backward

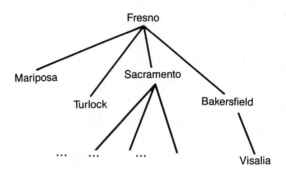

Forward

Figure 2.20 Forward and backward search paths from Visalia to Fresno.

for the alternative strategies. It can be seen that there is only one path working forward from Visalia, whereas by starting to work backward, we could immediately become sidetracked by heading off to Turlock, Sacramento, or Mariposa. Thus in this case at least, forward chaining works better. The reason is that there are more paths originating out of Fresno than there are originating out of Visalia. In this example it makes more sense to work forward from Visalia in finding the route since there is no point in working backward from Fresno to cities like Turlock or Sacramento and then finding that there is no connection to Visalia in sight.

In other situations, working backward can be more efficient. Consider the problem of going forward from Sacramento to Turlock. The backward and forward search trees for this problem are shown in Figure 2.21. Working for-

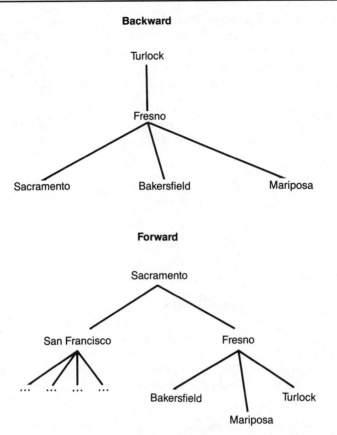

Figure 2.21 Forward and backward search paths from Sacramento to Turlock.

ward from Sacramento, we may immediately take a long detour to San Francisco or Los Angeles and from there, might become further sidetracked to any number of places. Working backward from Turlock, in comparison, has fewer distracting possibilities. We can still get sidetracked when we reach Fresno, but we do not encounter the same degree of problem that we have with a major flight connection such as Sacramento. The trick here is to constrain the problem to a small region of the network rather then allowing it to blow up so that we eventually circumnavigate the globe during our planning activity.

We can combine the two types of strategy and inspect the intersection of flights leaving Sacramento, say, with the flights arriving at Turlock. This is called *mixed-mode* chaining. However, this can often lead to far too much search (see Appendix A for a discussion of search techniques), since it is possible for the two flight chains (one working forward, the other backward) to pass each other without intersecting.

2.5.2 Forward and Backward Chaining

The preceding airline example illustrates the problem of how to ensure that reasoning is efficient and that rules are invoked in an appropriate order. It also shows how one can reason forward or backward and that the direction of inference makes a difference in the efficiency of reasoning.

So far we have expressed such rules as forward rules, but any rule can be expressed in two different ways. For instance, the rule "If the piston rings are worn, then overhaul the engine" can be expressed in the following ways:

Forward rule:

> If
>
> the piston rings <u>are</u> worn
>
> Then
>
> <u>overhaul</u> the engine;

Backward rule:

> <u>Overhaul</u> the engine
>
> If
>
> the piston rings <u>are</u> worn;

It is not enough simply to reverse the rule, however. Completely different inference processes are required for reasoning forward versus reasoning backward.

There are two broad strategies for controlling a reasoning process. The first strategy is to reason forward from the available facts and hope that the deduction of new facts will eventually lead to the deduction of the goal. This type of reasoning uses what is known as a *forward chaining* strategy.

The alternative to forward chaining inference is *backward chaining,* where the inference process works backward from the goal. Backward chaining inference takes the goal as a hypothesis and then tries to prove a series of subgoals working backward from the goal. Each subgoal, in turn, becomes a hypothesis during the reasoning process.

In forward chaining production systems the inference engine cycles through the rules until one is found whose premise matches a fact. This rule is then *proved* or *fired,* and the conclusion is added to the factbase. Forward chaining inference works well in situations where the system has to interpret a set of incoming facts. Without modification, however, forward chaining does not provide a mechanism for focused reasoning.

In backward chaining inference, the system accepts a goal or hypothesis and tries to determine which other goals need to be proven in order to prove the initial goal. If these goals are not immediately available, they serve as new hypotheses that require further inference, and so on. This type of reasoning is referred to as "backward chaining" because one is reasoning backward from the hypotheses to the data. In forward chaining inference, the system moves in the reverse direction.

■ 2.6 SUMMARY

Expert systems embody knowledge and inference procedures that can use that knowledge. The knowledge represented in facts, rules, and frames is used by an inference process to reach conclusions. Reasoning can be performed by controlling inference so that a series of rules is invoked with one conclusion leading to another.

The task of an inference engine is to invoke rules in an orderly sequence that will eventually produce the conclusions required by the task. The two major methods of controlling inference are referred to as *forward* and *backward chaining*.

While the knowledge base and inference engine are the basis for the expert system's reasoning, the user interface may also influence whether the expert system's advice will be accepted and put to use.

3

LOGIC

■ 3.1 INTRODUCTION

In chapter two we discussed how expert systems work and described the operation of the knowledge-base and the inference engine. The process of using the knowledge-base and inference engine to make inferences is a logical reasoning process.

Understanding the principles of logic is important for understanding expert systems. Further, logic may be viewed not only as a system for inferencing but also as a high-level programming method. This chapter focuses on a discussion of logic and logic programming.

There are many systems of logic, including predicate and propositional logic. Propositional logic is a simple and well-known system that includes basic concepts such as truth values and logical connectives. An introduction to propositional logic is provided in Appendix C. Predicate logic is a more powerful form of logic that includes the notions of variables, quantifiers, and predicates. Predicate logic provides a precise and natural way of representing knowledge.

In logical knowledge representations we represent facts, knowledge, and rules in terms of predicates and logical sentences. Rules become readable and easy to understand when a suitable syntax for defining predicates is chosen, as we will show in this chapter. Logic can be used to both describe knowledge and carry out inference. The way in which inference is carried out is modified by changing the goals that are to be proved.

The ability of logic to both describe and infer makes it a unifying formalism. However, the role played by logic in this relationship between knowledge and inference is often considered as controversial. While logic has some desirable features, it is not a good way of structuring and organizing knowledge. One approach to remedy this is to integrate frames and logic within a hybrid system that allows a unified approach to knowledge and inference, as discussed in Chapter 5.

In this chapter, after a brief review of the history of logic, we discuss the basic concepts of formal logic and inference. A formal syntax for describing facts and rules is introduced and concepts involving variables and pattern matching discussed. The focus then turns to predicate logic and its application in logic programming, illustrating how logic may be used as a general programming language. The issue of style in logic programming is also discussed. We extend "pure logic" with the addition of extra logical constructs and illustrate how logic programming and conventional languages may be combined.

■ 3.2 A BRIEF HISTORY OF LOGIC

Aristotle is generally considered to be the founder of logic. The ancient Greeks valued oratory highly. Oratory called for the ability to put forward or refute extended arguments as part of the process of public debate. In response to the need to construct persuasive arguments for oneself and refute the arguments of others, Aristotle devised systematic methods for analyzing and evaluating arguments. He developed *syllogistic logic* and cataloged a number of fallacies often used in arguments.

A century after Aristotle, another Greek named Chryssipus developed *propositional logic* in which the fundamental elements were whole propositions (i.e., sentences that were either true or false). He developed procedures for determining the truth or falsity of compound propositions based on the truth of falsity of their components.

Over a thousand years passed before further major progress occurred in logic. In the early twelfth century, Abelard distinguished arguments that were valid because of their form (intensional meaning) from those that were valid because of their content (extensional meaning). The work of the medieval logicians culminated in that of William of Occam, who developed modal logic in the fourteenth century. Modal logic includes concepts such as possibility, necessity, belief, and doubt.

Another 300 years passed before further developments occurred. In the seventeenth century Leibniz outlined an ambitious scheme for machine reasoning. Leibniz envisioned (but never implemented) a "Characteristica Universalis," a calculus that would cover all thought and replace controversy by calculation. Leibniz's calculus was to cover all knowledge; it therefore presupposed as a basis an encyclopedia that would contain all that was known so far. The calculus also needed the knowledge to be stated in a systematic form. Leibniz believed that the logical dependence of one proposition on another had to be shown by reducing complex concepts to the simple concepts that are their constituents (c.f., the atomic theory of matter). The aim of Leibniz was to represent knowledge in a form that could be used for mechanized reasoning. Unfortunately, Leibniz did not have the tools needed to implement his ideas. It is only with the capabilities of the modern computer that it becomes conceivable to even remotely approximate the knowledge representation and reasoning systems that Leibniz envisaged.

Leibniz, in pursuit of his Characteristica Universalis, attempted to develop a symbolic language that could be used to settle all forms of disputes. Progress in symbolic logic continued with the work of nineteenth-century philosophers and mathematicians such as Bolzano, DeMorgan, Boole, Venn, and Frege.

In 1854 Boole published *An Investigation of the Laws of Thought on Which are Founded the Mathematical Theories of Logic and Probabilities.* The major achievement of the book was the demonstration that the tools of algebra could be modified and applied to logical deduction. Boole took the arithmetic operators of addition, multiplication, and subtraction and created their logical equivalents—union, intersection, and the connective "not." Boole also invented the truth table (discussed in Appendix C) in order to test the truth of the compound propositions he constructed out of the new logical connectives. Today, *Boolean Logic* still forms a convenient form of modeling large numbers of hardware components used in computers.

It was Frege who invented the first complete theory of first-order logic. Whitehead and Russell (1910) then codified symbolic logic in its present form as a system for reducing mathematics to logic. The foundation of modern formal logic is often attributed to them.

Formal logic has been developed in spite of innate tendencies of humans toward irrational and emotional behavior often founded on anything but logic. Even eminent logicians have not always applied logic to the conduct of their own lives. Some of the most important work in formal logic was carried out in an environment charged with emotions. Whitehead, whose son was killed in World War I, could not see eye to eye with Russell, who was a pacifist. Thus although their work was started together, the bulk of it was completed by Russell.

Part of the attraction of formal logic is that it acts as a counterweight to human irrationality. This vision of logic as a prosthetic for the irrational human mind can be seen in such diverse forms as the Characteristic Universalis sought by Leibniz and the various rational machines and beings envisioned by science fiction writers.

■ 3.3 FORMAL LOGIC

The essential idea behind formal logic is rather simple and is as follows:

a. We have a number of statements that are assumed true (these are called *axioms* or *facts*).
b. We have a set of general methods for combining some axioms to derive new conclusions. These are called *inference methods*.
c. The methods of inference are used to combine the axioms and obtain new facts.

The axioms describe the domain of interest in terms of logical structures that correspond to facts and rules. The rules of inference determine what can be inferred if certain axioms are assumed to be true. Thus logic consists of two basic steps, namely, *representation* and *inference*, which are analogous to the knowledge-base and inference engine of an expert system. Logic representations are operated on using the rules of logic to make inferences about the state of the world implied by the logical assertions. As an example, we may know the following facts:

>All men are mortal.

>Aristotle is a man.

Using logical inference, we can then deduce that Aristotle is mortal. Logic can be used to generate important, and not always immediately obvious, conclusions. Thus the same type of reasoning that allows us to make somewhat hypothetical and academic statements about Aristotle can also be used in more modern and practical settings. For instance, on the basis of the information:

>Every metal is dissolved by Sulphuric acid

>Copper is a metal

we might deduce

>Copper is dissolved by Sulphuric acid.

Formal logic allows us to say things precisely since it is based on formal definitions and methods of inference. The *axioms* here (which correspond to knowledge) are:

>Copper is a metal

>If 'X' is a metal
>Then 'X' is dissolved by Sulphuric acid;

The rule of inference used here is that by knowing (A) and (If A Then B), we then know (B). This rule of inference is usually referred to as a *syllogism.*

Formal logic may be expressed in a large variety of notations. Despite the abundance of notation, logic is much more palatable to most people if it is expressed in a way that conforms to the expectations that they have built up after years of using natural language. In this chapter we define a notation for logic that is designed to reflect these expectations. In addition, we introduce predicate logic and show how the notions of variables, quantifiers, and predicates can be combined to create a formalism for reasoning. We have included information about propositional logic, truth tables, and other topics in formal logic in Appendix C.

■ 3.4 THE COMPONENTS OF LOGIC SENTENCES

The basic units of logic are the terms that logical statements are composed of. We adopt a systematic way of expressing facts and rules in logic, beginning by considering terms, the basic elements of a logical representation. The three basic types of *term* are:

- A *constant,* e.g., a, Pipe–1
- A *variable,* e.g., 'X' or 'pipe'
- An *expression,* e.g., 'X' + 3 or 2 * 9

We will also use a fourth type of term that is used to make information in frames accessible to logic representations:

- A *frame term,* e.g., (age of John).

We will discuss frame terms and their use in Chapter 5.

A *constant* is any string of nonreserved characters (e.g., John, Ohio, X, Y, 1, 12). Constants may be numbers or alphanumeric strings. The exact definition of how constants and variables are developed can vary. Different implementations of logic systems will typically have sets of reserved characters that are set aside for special use.

In our notation, a *variable* is obtained by enclosing a constant within single quotes; e.g., 'X', 'y12', 'John', 'Mary Jones' are variables. Terms that are not enclosed in single quotes are assumed to be constants.

An *expression* is either:

- A single expression, e.g., 'X', 3, or 'Y'
- An arithmetic expression, e.g., 'X' + 3
- A function expression, e.g., sin('X') or cos('X')

A *single expression* is either a single variable or a single constant, e.g., 'X', 'Y3', John, 4.

An *arithmetic expression* is obtained by applying an arithmetic operation to single statements, function statements, or other arithmetic expressions. The *arithmetic operators* are:

+ (plus)
− (minus)
* (times)
/ (divide)

For instance, 'X' + sqr(256) and ('X' + 'Y' + 4.3) * 36 are arithmetic expressions.

The components of logic sentences are represented visually in Figure 3.1.

3.4.1 Predicates and Clauses

In mathematics, a variable is a number that can take on different values, depending on the situation. We can talk about the average of a set of numbers without knowing what that average actually is. In similar fashion, variables allow us to describe classes of object in predicate logic. Consider the two statements:

> Container One contains a Class IA liquid

> Container Two contains a Class II liquid

Propositional logic takes propositions such as the first of the two propositions shown above and creates a propositional variable (say, P) that stands for the sense of the expression. The proposition is taken as a whole and no attempt is made to analyze it into its components. Thus the expression:

> Container Two contains a Class II liquid

might be assigned the propositional variable Q. In terms of flammability and fire safety, there is a significant difference between a Class IA liquid and a Class II liquid but there is also some similarity between the statements since they both refer to containers containing liquids. Propositional logic has no way of capturing these similarities. Instead, it labels the statements completely differently. One could then have a third statement:

> A municipal bond is a type of bond

and this might be assigned the propositional variable R. The fact that the first two statements are closely related while the third is the odd one out cannot be captured by using propositional variables.

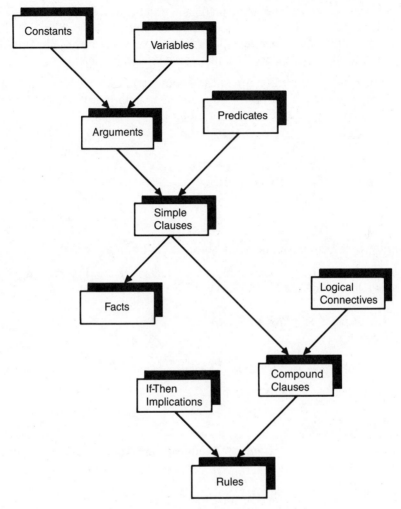

Figure 3.1 The components of logic sentences.

In contrast, predicate logic provides a way of capturing both the similarities and the differences between statements. Instead of the unanalyzable proposition P, we can use the form x P y to represent the assertions, where P is referred to as a *predicate* and x and y are *arguments*. In this case, we could represent the fact that Container One contains a Class IA liquid as:

Container One <u>contains a</u> Class IA liquid

Similarly, we would describe the second fact using the following predicate form:

Container Two <u>contains a</u> Class II liquid

In these examples *contains a* is the predicate, and the objects on either side of the predicate correspond to the variables x and y in the general form x P y. In the second statement shown above, Container Two is the first argument to the contains a predicate and Class II liquid is the second argument.

Underlining is used to signify a predicate. Some systems of logic use the notation P(x,y), referred to as *prefix* notation. Our notation with underlines is called *infix*. In general, the prefix notation of a predicate:

P(x,y)

has the corresponding infix notation:

x P y

We will generally use infix notation since we find it more readable.

The combination of a predicate and its arguments is referred to as a *clause*. A clause is a logical statement that has a truth value. For instance,

Road–1 is joined to Road–2

5 > 3

John meets with David, Mary

'X' is between 'Y', 'Z'

are all clauses. A clause thus consists of a *predicate* (sometimes referred to as a *verb*) and a number of *arguments*. Arguments are separated from each other by commas, as in

Valve–1 is a junction for Pipe–2, Pipe–3

The construction of clauses from predicates and arguments is shown in Figure 3.2.

The mapping between predicate logic and natural language is often fairly straightforward. Predicates typically map onto verbs with the arguments of the predicate being the subject and object of the verb. Other common types of predicate map onto the notion of possession and instance in language. In general, the following basic rules will work reasonably well:

Definition 3.1: Constants should be used to represent proper names such as John or Sydney.

Definition 3.2: Transitive verbs such as "activate" correspond to predicates with two arguments (e.g., X activates Y).

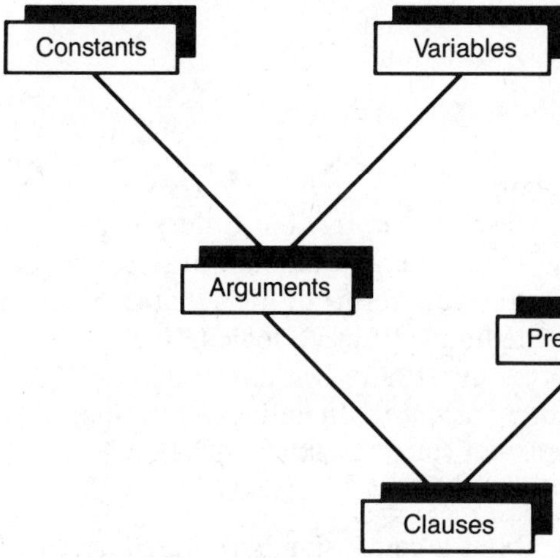

Figure 3.2 The construction of clauses from predicates and arguments.

In general, it will be convenient to map verbs into predicates, but it is also possible to use the following rule in some cases:

Definition 3.3:   Predicates with one argument express nouns such as "book" or "machine" (e.g., book X), adjectives such as "heavy" (e.g., heavy X), or intransitive verbs such as "swims" (e.g., swims X).

Although rules such as these are helpful, there is no hard-and-fast transformation between language and logic at this superficial level.

Predicates are not just a convenient shorthand for describing assertions; we can also map their arguments into truth values, so that they can be used in inference. The number of arguments of a predicate is often referred to as the *arity*. In theory, predicates may have any number of arguments, although in most situations, the arity of predicates should be fairly low (five to seven or less) to keep sentences readable.

3.4.2 Compound Clauses

A clause with only one predicate is referred to as a *simple clause*. When a clause consists of a number of simple clauses linked by *logical connectives* (and, or, not), it is referred to as a *compound clause*. The following are compound clauses:

> 'X' > 4 and 'X' < 12

> 'Investor' needs tax shelter and
> 'Investor' needs inflation protection and
> NOT real estate market is good

risk of inflation is high or
expected rate of inflation is high

'X' > 4 and not 'X' > 12

3.4.3 Truth and Uncertainty

Predicate logic has many useful features, but it does not explicitly represent uncertainty in reasoning. A considerable amount of research has been done in extending predicate logic to create forms of logic that explicitly handle uncertainty. One well-known method is "fuzzy" logic (Zadeh, 1965, 1978a). *Fuzzy logic* allows one to express uncertainty within a rule. We refer to reasoning with uncertainty as *inexact reasoning*. In an inexact reasoning system such as fuzzy logic a conclusion is not stated as either TRUE or FALSE, but as being probably, or possibly true to a certain degree.

The degree of certainty about a conclusion is captured as a *truth value*. We shall assign truth values on a scale from 0 to 100. Often, in dealing with uncertainty, we are not completely sure of a fact, but we have reason to believe that it is "probably" true. Rather than taking such uncertain information and arbitrarily categorizing it as either certainly true (truth value = 100) or certainly false (truth value = 0), we need a way of dealing with uncertain information in its own right. Our convention for assigning truth values is as follows:

FALSE: Truth Value = 0
TRUE: Truth Value = 100
UNCERTAIN: 0 < Truth Value < 100

In this chapter we will deal with certain information, i.e., facts, rules, and conclusions that have truth values of either 0 or 100. We shall postpone our discussion of logical analysis of uncertain information until Chapter 6.

■ 3.5 FACTS AND RULES IN PREDICATE LOGIC

A fact is a clause that has been asserted as true. Facts are stored in a factbase. Facts are thus clauses that are true regardless of what other information is available. Thus

Pipe–1 is joined to Pipe–2

Dean Johnson has social security number 559–87–3494

are examples of facts. The fact that Pipe–1 is joined to Pipe–2 does not depend on other information.

Since many machine reasoning systems will work cooperatively with humans in some way, it is also important to allow humans to input facts that for some reason are not available to the system. The system can prompt the user for assistance if an unknown fact is *askable*. Thus, if we don't have a patient's blood pressure in a database, we might render that information askable so that when it is required to prove a goal, the system asks:

> What is the blood pressure of the patient?

The response of the human is then treated as a fact and can be used in later reasoning.

Facts may be added and deleted at execution time. The predicate <u>assert</u> adds facts to the factbase. This predicate has the form

> <u>assert</u> clause

where *clause* will be added to the factbase. For instance,

> <u>assert</u> The patient <u>looks</u> pale

adds the fact *The patient looks pale* to the factbase and succeeds.

The predicate <u>retract</u> deletes facts from the factbase. It has the form

> <u>retract</u> clause

where *clause* will be removed from the database. The predicate <u>retract</u> succeeds if the clause matches the factbase and may be removed. If the clause does not match the factbase, <u>retract</u> will fail. Thus executing the two goals:

> <u>assert</u> clause and <u>retract</u> clause

will leave the factbase unchanged, since as soon as the clause is added, it will be removed. The <u>retract</u> predicate also accepts clauses with unbound variables as an argument; e.g., we may write

> <u>retract</u> 'X' <u>looks</u> pale

to delete the first fact in the factbase that matches *'X' looks pale*. Thus if we have a factbase containing:

> John <u>looks</u> pale
> Mary <u>looks</u> pale
> David <u>looks</u> pale

the attempt to prove the goal *retract 'X' looks pale* will succeed and will remove *John looks pale*. However, the goal *retract* 'X' *looks healthy* will fail, since it will not match a clause in the factbase. To distinguish between temporary facts asserted during program execution and permanent knowledge in a factbase, we may use a predicate such as retract-all-new, which removes only new and temporary assertions.

3.5.1 Rules

A predicate can be used to express a fact, but it can also be part of a rule. Rules can be formed by joining clauses together by *logical implication* (see Appendix C for a discussion of logical implication). Thus, from the perspective of predicate logic, the abstract structure of a rule is:

If

Clause$_2$ (is true)

and

Clause$_3$ (is true)

and

. . .

and

Clause$_n$ (is true)

Then

Clause$_1$ (is true);

Note that the rule above was written in the form "If P, Then Q". We can also write this rule in the form Q If P as in:

Clause$_1$ (is true)

If

Clause$_2$ (is true)

and

Clause$_3$ (is true)

and

. . .

and

Clause$_n$ (is true);

These two forms of expressing the implication are equivalent. For instance, the statement: "If you trust someone you also like them" may be expressed in the following ways:

Forward rule:

If

'X' trusts 'Y'

Then

'X' likes 'Y';

Backward rule:

> 'X' <u>likes</u> 'Y'
>
> If
>
> 'X' <u>trusts</u> 'Y';

A forward chaining rule (or *forward rule*) has the form:

> If
>
> premise
>
> Then
>
> conclusion;

which means that if the premise is true, the conclusion is true. Using our syntactic conventions, a forward rule should begin with the keyword *If* and should include one *Then*.

A *backward rule* has the form:

> conclusion
>
> If
>
> premise;

which means that the conclusion is true if the premise is true. A backward rule should begin with the conclusion clause followed by the word *If* and the premise.

The basis ideas behind forward and backward reasoning were outlined in Section 2.5. For forward reasoning, the clauses in premises are matched against current facts and the conclusions are used to generate new facts until the goal is reached. For backward reasoning, the conclusions are matched against the current goal (or hypothesis) and the clauses in the premises then represent new hypotheses to be proven. This process continues until no further hypotheses remain (usually when one runs up against the initial facts).

We can also express a rule in a third way that includes an assessment of how certain we are about the knowledge expressed in the rule. The inexact rule is as follows:

> $CF = 75$
>
> 'X' <u>likes</u> 'Y'
>
> If
>
> 'X' <u>trusts</u> 'Y';

Inexact rules are discussed further in Chapter 6.

Rules often define relationships between different objects or concepts. We can draw an analogy between rules and human relationships that gives a good intuitive understanding of how a system of rules work.

Consider the predicate *is grandfather of*. We will show how this relationship (i.e., rule) can be expressed in terms of more basic relationships such as *is father of*. We might, for instance, have the following statements in our fact-base:

> Philip is father of Charles
>
> Charles is father of William.

One of the defining rules for the related predicate is grandfather of may be:

> 'X' is grandfather of 'Z'
>
> If
>
> 'X' is father of 'Y'
>
> and
>
> 'Y' is father of 'Z';

The relationship between facts, rules, and clauses is shown in Figure 3.3. Note that this rule captures an aspect of the meaning of what a grandfather is, but

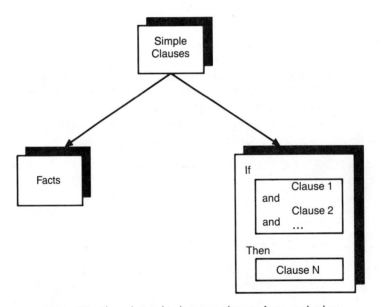

Figure 3.3 The relationship between clauses, facts, and rules.

it would be a mistake to assume that the structure of the clause uniquely identifies and defines the concept. We could also have said:

Philip is bigger than Charles

Charles is bigger than William

with the corresponding rule

If   'X' is bigger than 'Z'

          'X' is bigger than 'Y'

and   'Y' is bigger than 'Z';

There is obviously a natural human inclination to read more into a well-named predicate than is really there. We should remember, as stressed in Chapter 2, that the meaning of a proposition or clause is given by the conditions under which it will be true.

3.5.2 Variables

In defining the grandfather rule in the previous section we used *variables* to denote the fact that anyone who is "the father of a father" is a grandfather. In general, clauses can include variables as arguments to provide greater generality.

Clauses expressing facts can include variables as in:

Container Two contains 'Substance'

In this example the variable is enclosed in single quotes and the clause refers to an unspecified substance that is contained in Container Two. In such cases, when a variable is specified without knowledge of its actual value, we refer to it as a *free* or *unbound* variable. After we assign a value to the variable, it is referred to as *bound*. The value given to a variable is sometimes called its *binding*.

Along with the extra benefits of allowing variables in predicate logic come additional responsibilities. In assessing the truth of a statement that contains variables we will need to assess the truth of that statement under each possible binding of the variable (or variables) within it.

We might, for instance, try to express the idea that employees at Company-A finish their workday at 5 P.M. as:

          'Employee' finishes work at 5 P.M.

If

          'Employee' works at Company-A;

This rule might work adequately for most employees, but it will fail for those who work outside of standard office hours. In this case the scope of the variable 'Employee' is too wide for this rule and the inference mechanism will attempt to apply the rule indiscriminately to all the Company-A employees. The scope of the variable can be limited by applying additional conditions to the rule as in

If

'Employee' finishes work at 5 P.M.

'Employee' works at Company-A

and

'Employee' works during standard hours;

3.5.3 Quantification

Variables are very useful, but we need to know whether a free variable refers to just one instance or, potentially, to every object that can act as an argument for the current clause. We saw in Section 3.5.2 how the scope of a variable within a rule could be limited by adding extra clauses to the rule.

Quantifiers are the traditional way of defining the scope of a variable in predicate logic. Consider a situation where we are trying to determine whether the contents of a container are flammable. Part of our knowledge might be expressed in a general statement such as

"All metal containers contain flammable liquids."

Another general statement might be

"A metal container contains flammable liquids."

In comparing these two statements, we see that while both of them refer to metal containers as a variable, the first statement refers to *all* containers while the second statement refers to *at least one* container that contains flammable liquids.

These two statements illustrate the difference between the two types of quantifier used in predicate logic. *Universal quantifiers* assert that a statement is true *for all possible* values of the variable (as in the first statement above). *Existential quantifiers* are used to represent the information that there is *at least one* value for which a statement is true (the second statement above).

The phrases that denote the two types of quantifier are as follows:

Universal Quantifier	Existential Quantifier
For every	There exists

If you wanted to express the information that there is a metal container that contains flammable liquids, you might say:

> there exists 'X' where 'X' <u>is a</u> safety container

and

> 'X' <u>contains</u> flammable liquids

The use of the variable 'X' allows us to be deliberately vague about which particular metal container we are referring to, and the use of the existential operator ensures that we don't have to be concerned as to whether there is a second metal container that also contains flammable liquids.

The universal quantifier, on the other hand, allows us to make generalizations such as "all safety containers contain flammable liquids," which can be represented as:

> For every 'X'

If

> 'X' <u>is a</u> metal container

Then

> 'X' <u>contains</u> flammable liquids;

In this rule the variable 'X' remains *free* (or unbound) until we assign a particular value to it, at which point it becomes *bound*. Since 'X' refers to metal containers in general, there are many potential values for 'X'. The bindings or assignments that are made during reasoning will depend on which metal containers are actually described in the factbase.

Let's consider the example of a metal container of a type that is known to sometimes contain flammable liquids but whose current contents are unknown. Although the identity of the liquid is unknown, it may be possible to test some of its properties such as its flash point and vapor pressure. Our earlier version of the rule can be modified to reflect the availability of this additional information:

> For every 'X'

If

> 'X' <u>contains</u> 'Liquid'

and

> 'Liquid' <u>has flash point</u> low

and

> 'Liquid' <u>has vapor pressure</u> moderate

Then

> 'X' <u>contains</u> flammable liquids;

To determine whether a particular metal container contains a flammable liquid, we bind 'X' with the particular container under consideration and check the preceding rule against the available facts, i.e., the flash point and vapor pressure of the liquid in the container.

3.5.4 The Scope of Variables

The concept of *variable scope* is central to the operation of an inferencing system since it is used to distinguish between the different uses of the same variable symbol. In purely logic-based systems, variable names are completely *local* to the rule in which they appear. This means that the variable 'X' used in one rule has absolutely nothing to do with variable 'X' used in another rule; i.e., the scope of each variable is only one rule.

For instance, the use of the variable 'X' in the rule:

$$\text{If} \quad \begin{array}{l} \text{'X' is mortal} \\[6pt] \text{'X' is a man;} \end{array}$$

has no relation to the use of 'X' in the rule:

$$\text{If} \quad \begin{array}{l} \text{'X' is healthy} \\[6pt] \text{'X' is an athlete;} \end{array}$$

In fact, the preceding rule is logically equivalent to the rule:

$$\text{If} \quad \begin{array}{l} \text{'Y' is healthy} \\[6pt] \text{'Y' is an athlete;} \end{array}$$

This means that the variable names on their own have no significance; all that matters is how the variables relate compound clauses together, i.e., within a compound clause such as:

$$\text{and} \quad \begin{array}{l} \text{'X' contains Class II liquid} \\[6pt] \text{'X' is a safety container} \end{array}$$

the value of 'X' remains the same for both of the single clauses.

This concept of scope implies that there are no *global variables* in pure logic. In practice, however, global variables are often added to implementations of logic-based systems as a matter of practical convenience.

During evaluation of a rule, a variable may be bound to a value. This means that during evaluation of that rule, whenever the variable is used, the variable assumes the value to which it is bound. After the execution of a rule, the variables appearing in the rule lose their values, i.e., are no longer active components of the execution environment.

The predicates and variables appearing within rules may be viewed as logical predicates and axioms. The quantification of variables is an important part of predicate logic. In general, however, we can write facts and rules that include the concept of quantification, without explicitly having to associate "there exists" and "for every" with each reference to a variable.

This is possible because the necessary quantification is usually implicit in the way that the rules are written. We may view all variables as *quantified variables*. When a variable is used in the conclusion of a rule, that variable is assumed to be true for all constants to which the rule applies. We therefore say that variables appearing in the conclusion of rules are *universally quantified*, e.g., in either the backward rule:

$$
\begin{aligned}
&\text{'X' is \underline{trustworthy}}\\
\text{If}\quad\quad\\
&\text{'X' is \underline{honest}}\\
\text{and}\quad\quad\\
&\text{'X' is \underline{reliable};}
\end{aligned}
$$

or the forward rule:

$$
\begin{aligned}
\text{If}\quad\quad\\
&\text{'X' is \underline{honest}}\\
\text{and}\quad\quad\\
&\text{'X' is \underline{reliable}}\\
\text{Then}\quad\quad\\
&\text{'X' is \underline{trustworthy};}
\end{aligned}
$$

the variable 'X' is *universally quantified*, since the rule is true for any 'X'.

Variables that appear only in the premise of a rule, but not in the conclusion of that rule, are *existentially* quantified. For instance, either in the backward rule:

$$
\begin{aligned}
&\text{'X' is \underline{athletic}}\\
\text{If}\quad\quad\\
&\text{'Y' \underline{is a} sport}\\
\text{and}\quad\quad\\
&\text{'X' \underline{plays} 'Y';}
\end{aligned}
$$

or the forward rule:

If
     'Y' is a sport

and
     'X' plays 'Y'

Then
     'X' is athletic;

the variable 'Y' is *existentially quantified,* while 'X' is universally quantified. For *every* given value for 'X', the rule is true, if *some* value may be found for 'Y'. In some sense, as long as we find a 'Y', it does not matter which 'Y' we have found.

The reason for using this convention follows from an analysis of how rules work. Consider a more general version of the grandfather rule:

     'X' is grandfather of 'Z'

If
     'X' is father of 'Y'

and
     'Y' is parent of 'Z';

     'Parent' is parent of 'Child'

If
     'Parent' is mother of 'Child'

or
     'Parent' is father of 'Child';

Variables in the conclusion part of these two rules (i.e., the first lines of each rule) are universally quantified. This makes sense because we want to be able to apply the rule for all grandfather–grandchild relationships. When it comes to the premise part of the grandfather rule, though, we only need to prove that there exists "someone" who is the parent of the grandchild and the child of the grandparent in order to prove the grandfather goal. It is unnecessary to prove the rule twice, once for the grandchild's mother and once for the father.

3.5.5 Pattern Matching

Just as variable names are local to a rule, so are their bindings. Variables are bound to values through the process of *pattern matching.* An exact definition of pattern matching will be given in Section 3.5.6, but first we describe the concept in an intuitive manner.

Suppose that we have a rule:

     'X' is mortal

If
     'X' is a man;

and only the fact "John is a man." When we attempt to find the truth value of the clause "John is mortal," we will first look in the factbase to see whether the fact is present.

Since this fact cannot be found in the factbase, we will now try to find a rule which may be used to prove this fact. The preceding rule states that *for every* 'X', if *'X' is a man* is true, then *'X' is mortal* is true. This must also be true if 'X' is John.

The inference mechanism therefore gives 'X' the value John, i.e., it *binds* 'X' to John in the rule. The rule now becomes:

John is mortal

If

John is a man;

When a variable is bound to a value, all its occurrences within the rule are bound to that value. We now try to prove "John is a man" and succeed by finding it in the factbase.

We can also match compound clauses through variable bindings, e.g.,

John likes 'X' and 'X' knows Mary

matches

John likes Julie and Julie knows Mary

because 'X' matches Julie successfully. To match compound clauses, we match them piece by piece, matching each of the simple clauses on their own.

The definition of clauses and facts is only one part of using logic. Inference involves ascertaining the conditions under which certain facts are true. Thus we might want to know whether Philip is grandfather of William. To answer questions such as this, we have to apply relevant clauses to the available facts.

The definition of is grandfather of given earlier applies to any person because it is expressed in terms of variables rather than specific people. The notion of a variable is extremely useful in both mathematical and logical reasoning because it allows us to express general concepts and later substitute particular values (bindings) at the appropriate time.

Variables are also extremely useful in inferential reasoning. In the definitions of is grandfather of given above, it is much easier to define two rules relating the concept of grandfather to known concepts of father and mother than it is to enumerate all the possible grandfather–grandchild relationships.

In order to use variables in inference, however, we need to have some way of binding the variables with particular values at some point in the reasoning

process. <u>Pattern matching</u> is the process of comparing two clauses to determine whether they are identical or can become identical by substitution for
variables. We can see how basic pattern matching works by referring back to
the grandfather example.

Given the facts and rule shown in Figure 3.4, we ask the question, i.e., pose
the hypothesis:

Philip <u>is father of</u> Charles

(i.e., "is Philip the father of Charles?").

This is obviously true since there is an identical clause in the factbase. If we
pose the hypothesis "who is the father of Charles?", i.e.,

'X' <u>is father of</u> Charles

we are looking for a known fact that matches the structure. Since 'X' is a free
variable, the statement:

Philip <u>is father of</u> Charles

Facts

Rule

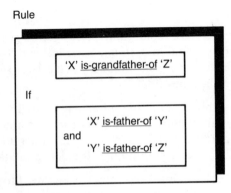

Figure 3.4 A miniature knowledge base.

is a match and 'X' can be bound to Philip. It turns out that pattern matching is a powerful inferencing technique, which is used by many machine reasoning systems.

The form of pattern matching discussed here is often referred to as *unification*. In general, two clauses may be *unified* either if they are identical or if we can make them identical by substituting suitable values for some of their variables, i.e., binding their variables with values. For instance, we may unify the two clauses:

> Philip <u>is father of</u> Charles
>
> 'X' <u>is father of</u> Charles

by binding 'X' to Philip.

When matching two clauses, one must first check that the clauses have:

- The same predicate (verb) name.
- The same number of arguments.

If not, the clauses cannot match. Now suppose that two clauses have the same predicate name, say, predicate, and the same number of arguments, say, n. Then to match the general clauses

> predicate $a_1, a_2, \ldots, a_n$
>
> predicate $b_1, b_2, \ldots, b_n$

we try to match their corresponding arguments, i.e., match a_1 to b_1, a_2 to b_2, $\ldots$, a_n to b_n, etc. Arguments are matched as follows:

a. *Constant Matches.* Two constants match only if they are identical, i.e., if they consist of exactly equal lists of characters (e.g., *John Smith* matches *John Smith*), but does not match *JohnSmith*.

b. *Constant/Variable Matches.* A variable may match a constant as follows:

    b1. *Unbound Variable.* If a variable does not currently have a value, i.e., is not bound, it will match any constant, and will be bound to that constant.

    b2. *Bound Variable.* If the variable has a value, i.e., is bound, the constant value will be matched according to **a** above.

c. *Variable/Variable Matches.* Two variables may match each other as follows:

    c1. *Two Unbound Variables.* Two unbound variables always match each other. If one of them is later bound to a constant, the other will also be bound to that constant.

   c2. *Bound and Unbound Variables.* If one variable is unbound and the variable has a value, they will be matched according to **b** above as though the bound variable had a constant value.

   c3. *Two Bound Variables.* If both variables have values, they will be matched according to **a** above as though they both had constant values.

In forward rules, pattern matching always begins with the premise. Any bindings made in this pattern matching process will be reflected in the conclusion, i.e.,

Definition 3.4:   Bindings in the premise of a forward rule are effective in the conclusion.

For instance, given the rule:

> If
>> 'X' <u>likes</u> 'Y'
>
> and
>> 'Y' <u>likes</u> 'Z'
>
> Then
>> 'X' <u>likes</u> 'Z';

if 'X' is bound to John and 'Y' is bound to Mary in the rule premise, these bindings will be the same in the conclusion. Thus the rule becomes:

> If
>> John <u>likes</u> Mary
>
> and
>> Mary <u>likes</u> 'Z'
>
> Then
>> John <u>likes</u> 'Z';

In backward rules, pattern matching always begins with the conclusion. Any bindings made in this pattern matching process will be reflected in the premise, i.e.,

Definition 3.5:   Bindings in the conclusion of a backward rule are effective in the premise.

For instance, given the rule:

>> 'X' <u>likes</u> 'Z'
>
> If
>> 'X' <u>likes</u> 'Y'

and

> 'Y' <u>likes</u> 'Z';

if 'X' is bound to John and 'Z' is bound to Julie in the rule conclusion, these bindings will be the same in the premise. Thus the rule becomes:

> John <u>likes</u> Julie
>
> If
>
> John <u>likes</u> 'Y'
>
> and
>
> 'Y' <u>likes</u> Julie ;

3.5.5.1 *Examples of Pattern Matching*   To illustrate the concept of pattern matching and variable bindings, we now provide a few examples of how pattern matching works in practice.

Let us consider the following clauses and the reasons why they may or may not match each other:

1.

> Dean Johnson <u>will accept</u> high-risk investments

matches

> Dean Johnson <u>will accept</u> high-risk investments

because they are identical clauses.

2.

> Dean Johnson <u>will accept</u> high-risk investments

does not match

> Dean Johnson <u>will accept</u> a low rate of return

because high-risk investments and a low rate of return do not match.

3.

> Dean Johnson <u>will accept</u> high-risk investments

does not match

> Dean Johnson <u>should invest in</u> commercial real estate

because the predicate names are different.

4.

Dean Johnson <u>will accept</u> high-risk investments

matches

Dean Johnson <u>will accept</u> 'X'

binding 'X' to high-risk investments, since 'X' is unbound.

5.

Dean Johnson <u>will accept</u> high-risk investments

matches

'X' <u>will accept</u> 'Y'

binding 'X' to Dean Johnson and 'Y' to high-risk investments, because both 'X' and 'Y' are unbound.

6.

Dean Johnson <u>will accept</u> high-risk investments

does not match

'X' <u>will accept</u> 'X'

because once 'X' is bound to Dean Johnson it can no longer match high-risk investments.

7.

'X' <u>will accept</u> 'Y'

matches

'A' <u>will accept</u> 'B'

binding 'X' with 'A' and 'Y' with 'B'.

8.

'X' <u>will accept</u> 'Y'

does not match

'A' <u>will accept</u> 'B', 'C'

because now one of the predicates has three arguments.

■ **3.6 GOALS AND INFERENCE**

Often many conclusions can be drawn from a given set of facts and rules. The reasoning process should thus be *focused* by being given a purpose or a *goal*. The operation of focused reasoning can be seen in the way that an expert chess player selects moves. In most chess positions, an expert will quickly focus on a small set of promising moves and continuations.

The concept of goal is quite simple:

> A goal is a clause whose truth-value should be determined.

Computation within a machine reasoning system relies on trying to prove goals, i.e., find the truth value for goals. Let us return to the knowledge-base of Figure 3.4 and consider how we can prove that Philip is the grandfather of William. We begin by posing this goal as a hypothesis, i.e.,

> Philip is-grandfather-of William.

Using the paternal is-grandfather-of rule, we transform this into two separate clauses, each of which must be true if the original clause is true:

> Philip is-father-of 'X'
>
> 'X' is-father-of William

In attempting to solve the first of these clauses, we use unification to bind 'X' to Charles using the statement

> Philip is-father-of Charles

which is present in the knowledge-base. Since 'X' is now bound to Charles, the second clause becomes

> Charles is-father-of William

which matches directly with the corresponding fact in the factbase. Since both clauses are proved to be true, the original clause is also proven to be true and we can assert that Philip is, indeed, the grandfather of William. The proof process that we went through is summarized in Figure 3.5.

Although our previous example used backward chaining inference, goal-oriented reasoning does not necessarily have to work backward. For instance, consider the following rules:

Forward rule:

> If
>
> Inventory manager needs Part-A
>
> Then
>
> Inventory manager buys Part-A;

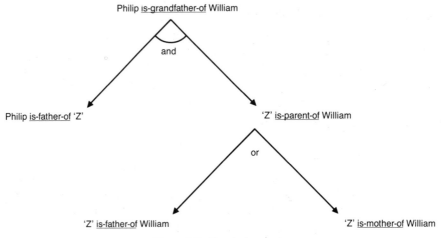

Figure 3.5 Proof of a goal.

Backward rule:

If

　　　　Inventory manager <u>buys</u> Part-A

　　　　Inventory manager <u>needs</u> Part-A;

The forward inference engine will begin with the goal *Inventory manager needs Part-A* and if successful in proving it will add the clause *Inventory manager buys Part-A* to the factbase. Thus:

　　　Forward rules try to prove the goals in their premise.

The backward rule will begin the goal *Inventory manager buys Part-A* and tries to prove it by turning the clause *Inventory manager needs Part-A* into another goal to be proved. *Inventory manager needs Part-A* may itself be proved by another rule. Thus:

　　　Backward rules try to prove the goals in their conclusion.

Computation in general, and reasoning in particular, is closely related to the *proof of goals,* or the *execution of goals.* This means that whenever we need to perform a computation, we try to *prove,* or *execute,* a goal. We often use the terms *prove* and *execute* interchangeably.

The concept of goal also applies to inexact reasoning. Consider the inexact rule:

CF = 75

If

               Inventory manager <u>buys</u> Part-A

               Inventory manager <u>needs</u> Part-A;

The inexact inference process will begin with the goal *Inventory manager <u>buys</u> Part-A* and tries to determine a truth value for it, by turning the clause *Inventory manager <u>needs</u> Part-A* into another goal. *Inventory manager <u>needs</u> Part-A* may itself be proved by another rule or may be found in the factbase to have a truth value of 100. In this case the truth value for *Inventory manager <u>buys</u> Part-A* will be 75. Thus:

> Inexact rules try to find truth values for the goals in their conclusion.

Forward and backward chaining rules include clauses that return exact truth values in two-valued logic, while inexact rules use clauses with certainty factors in the range 0–100, i.e.,

> A clause in a forward or backward rule will return either 0 or 100.

> A clause in an inexact rule will return a CF in the range 0–100.

Thus the idea behind the proof of goals is very simple:

> Given a goal, the reasoning system will try to find a truth-value for the goal.

In the process of proving goals, variables may be bound, output to the screen may be produced, subroutines in other languages may be invoked, and so on. Thus, in trying to prove a goal we may also get interesting side effects that simulate the output of a more procedural computational process. These side effects allow us to link the reasoning of a logic-based system with surrounding software and hardware environments.

∎ 3.7 LOGIC PROGRAMMING

The purpose of using logic is to reason about the state of the world. Backward and forward chaining are methods of inference through which logic-based reasoning can be applied. The general discipline of applying logic to the problem of reasoning is referred to as *logic programming*.

The goal of logic programming is to provide a framework for writing descriptions of situations or systems by using logic. These descriptions can then be executed as sets of rules that predict and control occurrences within the environment. Used in this fashion, logic programming may be used as a tool for information retrieval, simulation, diagnosis, planning, and reasoning in general. For instance, after building a logical representation of an electric circuit, we can describe the connectivity and functionality of the circuit and simulate its behavior under different conditions.

In building an appropriate description for a logic programming application we can consider the world as being composed of objects, relations, and operations. As an example, two objects that may exist in a portion of the world are a hammer and a nail. There may be a number of relations between them, including the fact that the hammer is larger, the fact that they are lying side by side, and so on. A relevant operation will be that of hammering, which could operate on the nail (with the hammer) to drive it into a wall or some other object.

Corresponding to the objects, relations, and operations in the world, we can define symbols, predicates, and operations expressed as rules within a logic representation. We can then use an interpretation to create a mapping between the objects, relations, and operations in the world and the object symbols, predicates, and rules in the logic representation (see Section 1.2.1 on the physical symbol hypothesis). This interpretation allows us to simulate operations and events in the world by proving appropriate goals in the logic representation. In essence, logic programming renders the logic representation programmable, so that the symbolic simulation can take place.

The appealing aspect of logic programming is that once you have described a system adequately, you immediately have an executable model that can be used to simulate the behavior of the system, retrieve information about the system, troubleshoot failures in the system, and so on.

In practice, however, "pure logic programming" can be difficult for a number of reasons. One problem is the lack of explicit packaging and modularity constructs of the type discussed in Section 2.3.3, in logic itself. Another problem is that "pure logic" does not tell you which inferences to draw at a particular stage in reasoning, but instead tells you which inferences can be made. (The choice is yours.) Thus, the more you know, the more inferences you can draw and the greater your search problem. Unless you have a good way of choosing which inference to make next, extra knowledge may actually make it more difficult to find a solution.

People do not seem to work in this way. In general, the more knowledge that people have about a problem domain, the more likely they are to solve the problem. There are two explanations for how people handle extra knowledge so that it does not confuse their reasoning. The first explanation says that people use heuristics to guide their inference making. The second explanation states that people structure their knowledge better so as to narrow down the potential proof trees. We favor the second explanation. The implication of this for writing descriptions for reasoning systems is that knowledge should be rendered specific in order to avoid excessive inference.

More specific and structured knowledge should also lead to shorter proofs, thus simplifying the reasoning process. This appears to be the best explanation for why people can be adept at reasoning despite being generally poor at multi-step logical inference. Short proofs are also desirable because they restrict the growth of uncertainty during reasoning.

However, "pure logic" may be supplemented and combined with other techniques so as to make it more managable and practical as a tool for building programs and expert systems. For instance, in Chapter 5 we discuss how logic and frames can form a fruitful partnership, and in Chapter 7 we show how logic programming and inexact reasoning may be effectively combined. Later in this chapter, we show how logic can be extended with extralogical features.

3.7.1 Programs in Logic

We may use logic not merely as a method of making inferences, but as a *programming method*. To do so, we view the proof of a goal as a *computational procedure* and construct logic programs out of proof procedures. Thus:

> A program is a collection of proof procedures.

A procedure is a collection of rules and facts that define a single predicate. Thus the procedure for the grandfather predicate can be written as:

> 'X' is-grandfather-of 'Z'
> If
> 'X' is-father-of 'Y'
> and
> 'Y' is-father-of 'Z';

When we view logic as a programming method, we also have to have a method of *debugging* logic, just as we debug a program in any language. Typically, rules are modified (debugged) over time as bugs are found that lead to faulty inference. In the case of the is-grandfather-of predicate, for instance, we might find that the system is ignoring maternal grandfathers until we debug it by adding another rule:

> 'X' is-grandfather-of 'Z'
> If
> 'X' is-father-of 'Y'
> and
> 'Y' is mother-of 'Z';

> 'X' is-grandfather-of 'Z'
> If
> 'X' is-father-of 'Y'

and
>   'Y' is-mother-of 'Z';

In this example the grandfather predicate consists of two rules. In order to find someone's grandfather, we would start to determine whether the goal was a known fact; if not, we would use the two rules in the procedure.

The representation of family relationships and similar concepts in logic can also be made by using relational tables. The mapping between clauses and tables is direct, with predicates corresponding to the names of tables and arguments corresponding to field names within the table. Figure 3.6 shows the

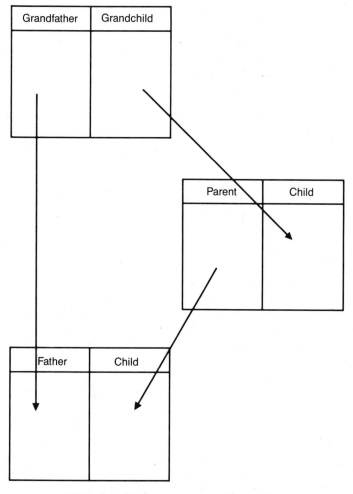

Figure 3.6 Predicates represented as tables.

operation of the is-grandfather-of procedure in terms of tables. In Chapter 5 we will further discuss the relationship between logic and relational databases.

Each predicate in a logic program is defined as a *procedure,* and each procedure can, in turn, utilize other predicates that are themselves defined as procedures. In the case of the grandfather predicate, for instance, we can express the procedure in only one rule provided we have a predicate is-parent-of that indicates whether someone is the mother *or* father of someone else, i.e.,

> 'X' is-grandfather-of 'Z'

If

> 'X' is-father-of 'Y'

and

> 'Y' is-parent-of 'Z';

The is-parent-of procedure could then be defined with two rules:

> 'X' is-parent-of 'Y'

If

> 'X' is-father-of 'Y';

> 'X' is-parent-of 'Y'

If

> 'X' is-mother-of 'Y';

What we have done here is sometimes known as procedural abstraction, i.e., we are constructing new predicates (procedures) out of combinations of old procedures. Procedural abstraction is part and parcel of logic programming. Ideally, each high-level procedure should be expressed as simply as possible, without loss of functionality. In the case of the grandfather procedure, for instance, we simplified things by saying that the grandfather was the father of the parent, instead of the father of the father or the father of the mother. This was possible because we expressed the new version of grandfather in terms of is-parent-of, which was a higher-level abstraction of the two predicates is-mother-of and is-father-of.

What would happen now if we wanted to define a grandmother procedure? As things stand, we would be best to copy and edit the grandfather procedure to produce:

> 'X' is-grandmother-of 'Z'

If

> 'X' is-mother-of 'Y'

and

> 'Y' is-parent-of 'Z';

However, we could instead use the principle of simplifying higher-level predicates and create an is-grandparent-of predicate. This would build on the is-parent-of predicate as follows:

> 'X' is-grandparent-of 'Z'
>
> If
>
> 'X' is-parent-of 'Y'
>
> and
>
> 'Y' is-parent-of 'Z';

We can now define both grandmothers and grandfathers in a simple and uniform manner, i.e.,

> 'X' is-grandfather-of 'Z'
>
> If
>
> 'X' is-grandparent-of 'Z'
>
> and
>
> 'X' is male;

> 'X' is-grandmother-of 'Z'
>
> If
>
> 'X' is-grandparent-of 'Z'
>
> and
>
> 'X' is female;

It is important to note that often in logic programming the concept of "input" variable and "output" variable disappears. In a conventional language we may write a function,

> F(X): returns Y

which accepts a value for X and returns a value for Y. For instance, we may have two functions,

> Father(X): returns Y
>
> Child(Y): returns X

which are used to relate fathers and children. However, as the procedures (i.e., predicates) exemplified above illustrate, in logic programming the same procedure is used for both input and output. For instance,

> 'X' is-father-of William
>
> Charles is-father-of 'Y'

correspond to two queries for finding a father and a child. However, both queries use exactly the same procedure.

3.7.2 Logic Programming Style

Logic programming is a recently developed programming method that has received a good deal of attention. Style in logic programming is important to the extent that it facilitates writing, understanding, and debugging logic programs. We now discuss some basic issues in logic programming style.

Some stylistic issues revolve around the use of the logical connectives. For instance, an expression such as:

> 'Investor' <u>needs</u> inflation protection
>
> If
>
> risk of inflation <u>is</u> high
>
> or
>
> expected rate of inflation <u>is</u> high;

can alternatively be represented as:

> 'Investor' <u>needs</u> inflation protection
>
> If
>
> risk of inflation <u>is</u> high;
>
> 'Investor' <u>needs</u> inflation protection
>
> If
>
> expected rate of inflation <u>is</u> high;

where the failure to confirm the first version of the rule results in an attempt to confirm the second version of the rule.

However, the two most important elements of logic programming style are probably the development of simple procedures that can be reused by other procedures and the naming of predicates and arguments to reflect their *logical meaning*. We gave an example of simplifying and generalizing predicates in the example of the <u>is-grandfather-of</u> procedure. We now turn to the problem of naming.

It is helpful to express facts and rules in a logic representation so that their meaning is apparent in the choice of names for the predicates and arguments. However, since there is no homunculus (little man) inside a machine reasoning system to interpret the meaning of a clause such as:

> low cash flow <u>attracts</u> hostile takeovers of companies

as it stands, the clause could just as easily read:

> low cash flow <u>repels</u> hostile takeovers of companies

The meaning of the clause in a logic system is derived from the way that it is used, not from the particular wording. This can be quite a problem in debugging a logic representation, since we can hardly help ourselves from reading meaning into the facts and rules based on the way that they are worded. Thus there may be a case for using less meaningful naming conventions when building and debugging logic programs and using much more meaningful names when the program is in operation.

There is an interesting demonstration of the fact that people tend to automatically grasp the meaning of words when they see them at the expense of the physical structure that is actually present. In one version of what is known as the Stroop effect (e.g., Anderson, 1985), people are asked to read the physical colors of words that are actually the names of different colors. Thus the word "red" might be written in green ink, and so on. People find this task surprisingly difficult and can hardly resist the temptation to read out the meaning of the word rather than the actual color in which it is written.

You can demonstrate the Stroop effect yourself by writing out a list of color words in varying colors. If you or your friends seem to be mastering the task, try going faster, and you should experience the kind of difficulty that arises from this conflict between meaning and form. We have generally observed a similar effect in reading logic representations. Labeling the intended meaning of a rule by choosing appropriate names for the predicates and arguments helps in informing people of what the rule should be doing, but if there is a logical flaw in the structure of the rule, this normally helpful labeling may block the perception of the logical meaning of the rule.

Ideally, a well-written logic program functions as both a declarative and a procedural description of knowledge. The grandfather procedure, for instance, can be read in both ways. We actually developed three declarative definitions of what a grandfather is:

1. A grandfather of a person is the father of that person's father or the father of that person's mother.
2. A grandfather of a person is the father of that person's parent.
3. A grandfather of a person is a male grandparent of that person.

The corresponding procedural interpretations are as follows:

1. To find the grandfather of a person find the father of that person's father or the father of that person's mother.
2. To find the grandfather of a person, find the father of that person's parent.
3. To find the grandfather of a person, find a male grandparent of that person.

Note here the small change in our use of language that is used to indicate the transition from a declarative to a procedural definition. Instead of saying:

'X' is . . .

the procedural definition says:

to find 'X' . . .

The inference engine in a logic programming system is what allows us to take a definition in the form of 'X' is . . . and use it as if it were written in the form "to find 'X'. . . . "

Sometimes one needs to think procedurally even when using logic programming. This may occur because one is dealing with a problem that is best dealt with procedurally, or because the interaction between the inference engine and the logic program is producing bugs that are procedural rather than logical in nature.

We shall illustrate the problem of dealing with procedural issues in logic programming with one small example. Consider the problem of defining a procedure for the is-sister-of predicate. Our first attempt might be

                'X' is-sister-of 'Y'

If

                'X' is female

and

                'Z' is-parent-of 'X'

and

                'Z' is-parent-of 'Y';

If we try to run this procedure, we find an error, i.e., the system says that someone can be her own sister (Jane is-sister-of Jane). The problem is that we wouldn't think of calling someone her own sister, it wouldn't be "common sense." But since logic doesn't contain common sense, we have to incorporate the idea that the two arguments of the sister predicate have to represent different people.

We can now use another predicate, namely, is different from. Since the clauses in the condition of the rule are all connected by logical ands, it won't make any difference where we insert the new clause in the rule from a logical or declarative perspective. But it will make a difference from the procedural perspective since the behavior of the inference engine will depend on the order in which the variable bindings are made.

Consider the following version of the procedure:

If
    'X' is-sister-of 'Y'

and
    'X' is different from 'Y'

and
    'X' is female

and
    'Z' is-parent-of 'X'

    'Z' is-parent-of 'Y';

Say that we are trying to find all the sisters in the knowledge-base and that we enter the goal:

    'X' is-sister-of 'Y'

In order to find a pair of sisters. The problem is that the first subgoal that will be executed is:

    'X' is different from 'Y'

and the arguments 'X' and 'Y' will be unbound variables. Since two unbound variables can always be matched, the clause fails. Since the system has no way of supplying bound variables to the is different from clause, it will always fail. Depending on the inference engine, the whole is-sister-of procedure will respond that there are no sisters, or else the system will loop indefinitely.

The solution to this problem is to delay calling the is different from clause until after both the arguments are bound. This is done by placing it as the final clause in the condition of the rule:

If
    'X' is-sister-of 'Y'

and
    'X' is female

and
    'Z' is-parent-of 'X'

and
    'Z' is-parent-of 'Y'

    'X' is different from 'Y';

This example shows how procedural issues can arise in logic programming. The use of the no-backtrack predicate is a particularly important procedural issue, which we will discuss in Chapter 7.

The procedural issues in logic programming can be tolerated, however, if the applications are sufficiently important, as in the construction of a rapid prototype. A logic programming application may often begin by building a logic representation of the system of interest. The performance of this logic representation may then be assessed and the logic program refined so as to produce appropriate procedural behavior. If the logic program has been defined in sufficiently abstract fashion, some important predicates may then be rewritten in a conventional language for greater efficiency. These conventional language functions can then be linked with the rest of the logic program, as discussed in Section 3.8,' and treated as if they were the original predicates.

■ **3.8 EXTRALOGICAL CONCEPTS**

In a practical logical inferencing system, two forms of predicates are needed:

- *Built-in* predicates
- *User-defined* predicates.

The *built-in* predicates provide some of the basic features of a programming language that are otherwise absent from "pure logic." Examples of built-in predicates include input and output predicates (for saving files, communicating with the user, etc.) and predicates that assert or remove information to or from a database. The additions that are made to make logic "programmable" are a mixed blessing, with a necessary tradeoff between the clarity of the logic representation and its functionality as a programming system. Logic as a programming language only works in practice if we add some extralogical concepts. In the following we discuss some logical and extralogical features.

Equality clauses are used to test for equality of terms and to achieve variable bindings. An equality clause has the form:

$$term_1 = term_2$$

where $term_1$ and $term_2$ may be any terms. The equality clause fails (i.e., returns a truth value of FALSE) if the terms have different values. The equality clause succeeds (i.e., returns TRUE) if the two terms have equal values. Further, even if one of them has no value, the equality clause will succeed, and in doing so, the term with no value is bound to the value of the term with a value (if any).

The notion of equality is used in two ways. First, one can *test* whether two expressions are equal as in:

$$1 + 1 = 2 + 2$$

One can also assign values with an equality as in:

$$'X' = 3$$

The equality predicate is useful as a pattern matching predicate because it can be used to calculate values for use in other clauses. We can indicate a matching process using the equality predicate as in

$$\text{expression}_1 = \text{expression}_2$$

The equality predicate matches expression$_1$ with expression$_2$ in accordance with the unification process discussed above.

Although the implementations of techniques for pattern matching can be fairly complicated, the basic idea behind it is not. During the reasoning process we want to know whether a particular fact or rule is relevant. We establish relevance by attempting to show that the current situation fits the requirements of the rule or the details of the fact.

The equality clause evaluates both sides of = and then compares the values. For instance, if the variable 'X' has value 3, the test:

$$'X' = 3$$

will return TRUE, but the test:

$$'X' = 'X' + 1$$

will fail and return FALSE. If the variable 'X' has no value, the test:

$$'X' = 3$$

will succeed and give 'X' the value 3. Further, if 'X' has a value, then:

$$'X' + 3 = 1 + 'X' + 2$$

is syntactically valid and will succeed since both sides evaluate to 6.

However, if either 'X' or 'Y' have no value, then:

$$'X' + 3 = 'Y' + 3$$

cannot be evaluated, since assessment of the equality requires that the variables be bound and there is no basis for assigning the bindings for 'X' and 'Y'.

Another built-in predicate that is in some respects similar to, but in general very different from, equality is the *assignment* predicate. The assignment predicate is used to *set values* to variables, as in conventional programming. Thus

Definition 3.6: Assignment can *change* the value of a bound variable, but equality cannot.

An assignment has the form:

variable : = Expression

For instance,

'A' : = brown

'X' : = 'X' + 1

'X' : = sin('Y' + 30)

'X' : = ('X' + 12) * 'Z'

are all assignments. An assignment changes the value of the variable to the value of the expression on the right-hand side.

Assignment to variables differs from the equality clause since if the expression can be evaluated, the assignment always succeeds and changes the value of the variable on the left-hand side of the assignment, even if the variable has a value. On the other hand, if the variable has a value, the equality test will fail if both sides of = do not have the same value.

If 'A' has no value or has the value brown, the effect of:

'A' = brown

is the same as the effect of:

'A' : = brown

However, if 'A' has value red, the preceding assignment will change its value to brown and succeed, while the equality test will simply fail.

Relational clauses are used for numeric comparisons. A relational clause has the form:

Exp1 operator Exp2.

An operator is one of:

> (greater than),

< (less than),

> = (greater or equal),

< = (less than or equal) or

< > (not equal).

Relational operators may involve any form of arithmetic expression; e.g., we may have:

'Y' + sin('X') < > cos('X') * 'Z'.

The addition of features such as built-in predicates can have an important effect on the practical use of logical procedures.

3.8.1 Programming Language Features

We may define a large number of built-in predicates that may be used for general-purpose programming. Any of these predicates return either TRUE or FALSE and thus naturally fit in the formalism of logic programming. In this way, we can even write "every-day" programs in logic.

The built-in predicate <u>write</u> always succeeds and writes a value to a screen, etc. For instance,

<u>write</u> Hello

will write "Hello". Similarly, the predicate <u>read</u> reads a value; e.g.,

<u>read</u> 'X'

reads a value and assigns it to the unbound variable 'X'. We may combine these basic predicates in a simple *logic program:*

	<u>say</u> hello
If	
	<u>write</u> What is your name?
and	
	<u>read</u> 'X'
and	
	<u>write</u> "Hello ", 'X';

This example shows how we may use the logical inference process to perform procedural and sequential types of programming normally carried out in conventional languages. We may perform many other programming tasks such as cursor control with goals. For instance,

<u>move-cursor-to</u> 'A', 'B'

<u>cursor-is-at</u> 'A', 'B'

allow you to move the cursor on the computer screen, or find its location. As another example, consider a logic program that deals with files on the IBM PC™. To read from a file, we *open* the file for reading with the goal:

> Open-Read File

where File is the name of an IBM PC™ file. This goal is simply treated as just another goal provided to the inference engine. If we succeed in opening the file, the goal will succeed and return TRUE; otherwise, it will fail. We may then read from File with the goal:

> File-Read File, 'X'

which reads from File. Here 'X' is an unbound variable and will be bound to the value read from File. The goal:

> File-end File

succeeds if we are at the end of File. You may close a file with the goal:

> Close-File File.

In the next section we use these predicates in programs that deal with files.

3.8.2 Higher-Level Control Predicates

The use of logic programming does not obviate the need to use procedural constructions such as iterations and loops. We can define a number of predicates that give us this kind of procedural control over the execution of a logic program.

The "do until" programming construct is useful in directing an end to computation when a fact becomes true. The clause:

> do Clause$_1$
> until Clause$_2$

performs Clause$_1$ until Clause$_2$ becomes true. This predicate may be used for defining iterative loops as in conventional languages. For instance, we may use it to write the contents of a file to the screen with the built-in predicates discussed in the previous section. The procedure show file 'File' is defined as follows:

> show file 'File'
>
> If
>
> Open-Read 'File'

and

> do show one line 'File'
> until File-end 'File'

and

> Close-file 'File';

and uses the procedure show one line 'File', defined by:

> show one line 'File'

If

> File-Read 'File', 'X'

and

> write 'X' ;

This show file procedure thus reads each line in the file and writes it to the screen until the end of the file is reached. As another example, consider the predicate show squares 'X', defined as:

> show squares 'X'

If

> 'N' := 0

and

> do write square 'N'
> until 'N' = 'X' ;

which uses the predicate write square 'N' defined by:

> write square 'N'

If

> 'N' := 'N' + 1

and

> 'M' := 'N' * 'N'

and

> write 'M' ;

The quantified goal show squares 15 executes the predicate write square 15 times. We see here the incorporation of a procedural programming construct within the definition of this rule. The first clause of the goal sets the initial value of the counter, N, which is then accumulated in the write square procedure. The value of 'N' is incremented to ensure the termination of the loop.

While the "do until" predicate checks for termination, the predicate:

> for every Clause$_1$
> do Clause$_2$

finds all possible pattern matches or proofs for Clause₁ and for each such match or proof will perform Clause₂. The goal:

> for-every 'X' is-a suitable investment
> do write "consider ",'X'," as an investment.";

will prove the clause 'X' *is a suitable investment* repeatedly to obtain new bindings and executes the write statement for each binding. For instance, if the factbase contains the three facts:

> Real Estate is a suitable investment
> Stocks is a suitable investment
> Bonds is a suitable investment

then the three statements:

> Consider Real Estate as an investment.
> Consider Stocks as an investment.
> Consider Bonds as an investment.

will be written to the screen. Similarly, the goal:

> for-every 'X' is-grandfather-of 'Y'
> do write 'X'," is a grandfather";

will prove the clause *'X' is grandfather 'Y'* repeatedly to obtain new bindings for 'X' and will execute the write statement for each binding.

The "for-every do" quantifier can be used to cycle through all the possible ways of satisfying an expression. However, we may not be interested in this exhaustive information, but only in carrying out the rule until a certain condition is reached. In such cases we may use the "do until" quantifier.

There is yet another extra logical quantifier that may be used to test clauses. The predicate:

> for-all Clause₁
> is-true Clause₂

will succeed if whenever Clause₁ is true, then Clause₂ will also be true. Thus it means that:

> Clause₁ *implies* Clause₂

For instance,

> for-all 'X' is a major city
> is-true 'X' is near a river

will succeed if for every value of 'X':

> If *'X' is a major city* is true, then *'X' is near a river* is true.

This will succeed if we have a factbase such as:

> London is a major city
> New York is a major city
> London is near a river
> New York is near a river

However, if the factbase contains:

> London is a major city
> New York is a major city
> London is near a river

then the for-all clause will fail, since when 'X' is bound to New York, the is-true part of the clause will no longer succeed.

The for-all clause allows us to perform metalogical reasoning, since by using it we can test whether *rules imply each other,* e.g., suppose that we had two rules:

Rule #1:

>   Conclusion$_1$
> If
>   Premise$_1$;

Rule #2:

> Conclusion$_2$
> If
> Premise$_2$;

the clause

> for-all Conclusion$_1$
> is-true Conclusion$_2$

will be true if:

> whenever Rule #1 succeeds, Rule #2 also succeeds.

We may thus use this predicate to test the relative truth of rules during execution. This can be very useful for debugging and for testing rules to discover obscure errors. For instance, to test whether our definition of grandparent matches our definition of grandfather, we could prove the goal:

<u>for-every</u> 'X' <u>is-grandfather-of</u> 'Y'
<u>is-true</u> 'X' <u>is-grandparent-of</u> 'Y'

The uses of the additional quantifiers in the preceding examples shows how logic can be used as a general programming language. Thus a system that combines knowledge representation and a versatile inference engine can be used as a very high-level programming luaguage as well as for building expert systems.

It should be clear from the preceding discussion that when used to solve problems that require reasoning, the basic goals and techniques of logic programs and expert systems are very similar. The major difference is one of emphasis. Logic programming tends to focus on the use of logic as a high-level programming language, whereas expert systems focus on getting machines to reason like human experts. It is possible, however, to do high-level programming in a powerful expert system shell, and it is possible to build expert systems using logic programming. This is not surprising since expert systems and logic programming are largely based on the same set of tools and technologies.

From the discussion in Section 1.5, where we viewed expert system technologies as the evolution of programming paradigms, both expert systems and logic programming techniques may be viewed as augmenting the set of features available to programming paradigms.

3.8.3 Combining Logic with Conventional Languages

Although the use of logic programming can often accelerate the development process in high-level applications, in some applications it cannot replace or even approach the efficiency and the procedural functionality of conventional languages such as C or Pascal. Thus, to be used in practical applications, logic should be combined with existing programming technologies.

It is, however, conceptually rather straightforward to link logic programs with conventional programming languages. To do so, we may use an *interface clause* that provides access to functions and procedures in other languages.

For instance, to provide interfaces with C functions, we use the built-in predicate <u>C</u>. A C *interface clause* has the form:

<u>C</u> function-name, Arg_1, Arg_2, . . . , Arg_n

where function-name is the name of an *interface function* written in C and Arg_1, Arg_2, . . . , Arg_n are its arguments. The arguments Arg_1, Arg_2, . . . ,

Arg$_n$ may be constants or variables used within rules, frames, etc. User-defined C functions may thus alter the value of variables used within the logic system.

Since each C interface clause is just another clause, it should return a truth value as an integer between 0 and 100. When the C interface clause is proved the arguments Arg$_1$, Arg$_2$, . . . , Arg$_n$ are passed from the logic system to the C function. The C function may then call any other user-defined functions or library procedures to compute values, print, or assign values to the arguments Arg$_1$, Arg$_2$, . . . , Arg$_n$.

For instance, suppose that you have a C function called *compute* that computes a specific function for the arguments 'X', 'Y' and returns a value 'Z'. To use it from within rules, you could define:

> . . . .
>
> and
>
> C do__compute, 'X', 'Y', 'Z'
>
> and
>
> write 'Y'
>
> and
>
> . . . .

where the function *do__compute* calls compute to get a value for 'Z'. One may thus interface rules to graphic functions, for instance, by proving goals such as:

> C draw__circle, 'X', 'Y', 'Radius'

from within rules. By connecting logic and conventional languages, we have a powerful programming style that provides both efficiency and ease of expression. Further, in Chapter 5 we show how logic, frames and relational databases may be combined.

■ **3.9 SUMMARY**

Propositional and predicate logic both utilize the logical connectives along with the notions of truth, validity, and proof. However, predicate logic is more powerful because it introduces predicates that can contain variables, and these variables may be either existentially or universally quantified. In propositional logic, the fundamental reasoning tool is the syllogism. In predicate logic we need to deal with the more complicated form of inference necessitated by the introduction of variables.

Logical inference requires a predicate logic representation of knowledge along with mechanisms for pattern matching. *Pattern matching* is a process of assigning values to unbound variables consistent with the constraints imposed by the relevant facts and rules.

Logic representations are utilized in reasoning through the technique of *logic programming*. One weakness of logic as a knowledge representation formalism, however, is that it does not address the issues of how knowledge can be organized and interconnected. In Chapter 5 we develop a powerful methodology for organizing and structuring frame-based knowledge that can be connected to a logic representation in a straightforward way.

4

Knowledge

■ **4.1 INTRODUCTION**

Expert systems derive their power from knowledge. The heart of any expert system is the knowledge it contains, and it is the effective use of this knowledge that makes its reasoning successful.

As discussed in Chapter 2, it is difficult to define knowledge in the abstract, and we shall avoid entering the philosophical arguments relating to the "nature" of knowledge that have been waged for millennia. We consider knowledge from the perspective of its practical use for reasoning within expert systems. In this context, knowledge can be defined in terms of what it does:

Definition 4.1: Knowledge is information about the world which allows an expert to make decisions.

The knowledge used by an expert system needs to be *represented* and employed in a form that can be used for reasoning. *Knowledge structures* are used to store knowledge and reason with it, just as data structures are used to store and deal with data.

According to our discussion in Section 1.5, where we viewed expert system technology as an evolution of conventional programming paradigms, knowledge structures represent an evolution of data representation methods. Most people realize that there is no "best" data structure for all computing purposes; one needs a set of different data structures for use in different applications. Similarly, we need different knowledge structures and knowledge representation methods for different applications.

In discussing knowledge, we should consider questions such as:

What are the components of knowledge?

How can knowledge be represented?

How can we evaluate a knowledge representation method?

How do different forms of knowledge representation compare with each other?

In this chapter we address these questions. We begin with a general discussion of knowledge and its relation to language and intelligence and discuss levels at which knowledge may be expressed. We then present a basic model for viewing knowledge in terms of a set of entities or objects and discuss how knowledge may be organized in terms of this model. Next we discuss the basic components of knowledge that any knowledge representation method should deal with. We then outline various approaches to knowledge representation and discuss a set of evaluative guidelines that may be applied to any knowledge representation method. Finally, we provide examples of knowledge representation in the system of logic discussed in Chapter 3. Later, in Chapter 5, we will present a detailed account of knowledge representation with frames.

■ 4.2 KNOWLEDGE

To use knowledge on machines, we must bring that knowledge out in the open and represent it formally. The process of representing knowledge formally is referred to as *knowledge representation.*

The type of knowledge representation that is appropriate in a given situation depends on what sort of knowledge is being represented and how it is to be applied. Various methods of knowledge representation have been proposed, each attempting to determine how knowledge should be represented by identifying the essential components of knowledge that allow us to reason about interesting and practical problems.

In building expert systems, we may treat knowledge as a commodity that can be transferred between people and systems rather than an inherent property such as intelligence. Although intelligent behavior relies on knowledge, it would be a mistake to equate knowledge with intelligence. If not provided with appropriate knowledge, an intelligent person may act foolishly and a great deal of knowledge will not result in intelligent behavior if it is irrelevant in the current situation.

We can illustrate this point with the example of a genius who becomes lost in the jungles of Borneo. This person's outstanding intelligence and powers of deduction may be inadequate in the face of the rigors and demands of the unfamiliar environment. Thus this genius will fare worse than someone with far fewer deductive powers but who is familiar with the environment. Assuming that the genius survives the first few hours and days of this ordeal, this person's intelligence may make it easier to adapt to the strange environment. Initially, however, this high level of intelligence will not completely compensate for an extremely small amount of knowledge about the new environment.

We avoid a definition of the term "intelligent." In our view, the answer to the question "But are expert systems *really* intelligent?" is: "We do not care. We are interested in what we can *do* with them." We believe that extended discussions of this question will simply distract us from the important issues involved in practical applications of expert systems.

From a goal-oriented perspective of solving problems, specific knowledge about the domain of interest is far more important to an expert system than is general intelligence. An expert system for configuring computers, for instance, knows nothing about geography or tax planning. Certain people are very adept at one thing (such as mental arithmetic or playing music) and completely ignorant about almost everything else. These people are called *idiot savants*. Expert systems function in much the same way, each system having expertise in only a narrow domain of knowledge (Figure 4.1).

The knowledge that an expert system needs to have is a reflection of the type of behavior it should exhibit. Some expert systems deal with fairly static environments where knowledge is always applied in the same way whereas other systems must adapt in some ways to a more variable environment. In general, adapting to a variable environment requires a deeper level of knowledge that takes into account the causal structure of the knowledge domain.

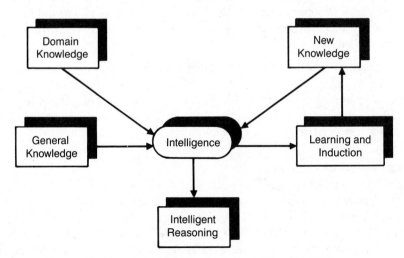

Figure 4.1 The relationship between knowledge and intelligence.

4.2.1 Knowledge and Language

Of course, most people have some knowledge. So why don't we simply ask them what their knowledge is and type their responses directly into a computer? Doing so involves a number of transforming operations, each of which is quite difficult in its own right. First, we have to understand the surface level and grammatical structure of sentences, using a process known as *parsing*. For instance, we have to identify and distinguish verbs, pronouns, etc. This in itself requires access to a considerable vocabulary (including technical terms) and considerable linguistic knowledge (Winograd, 1983).

Next, we must explicitly recognize, analyze, and relate the concepts expressed by the speaker. The real problem here is that most people have a set of deeply ingrained concepts that are "buried" within their natural-language responses. Taking sentences at face value quickly leads to misleading results, illustrated by the example session with the ELIZA program discussed in the next section.

A typical conversation in natural language almost always includes a complex knowledge representation scheme, where the listener and the speaker must make numerous transformations between the deep structure of ideas and the surface structure of words used to express those ideas. Humans tend to take these complex transformations for granted. We are seldom even aware of them as we carry out everyday conversation. However, linguists have long been perplexed by the nature of these transformations. Observing the acquisition of linguistic constructs in children demonstrates the nontrivial nature of these transformations.

A totally natural language-based knowledge representation system must take into account a great deal of "everyday" or common-sense world knowledge. Creating a knowledge representation and inferencing systems that copes with the full range of knowledge about the world as expressed in natural language by humans leads to deep trouble, or as some would say, to a fruitful and intriguing research area.

However, after an expert system has been developed by using a formal knowledge representation method, we may choose to allow users to interact with it using a natural language interface. In such a scenario, the natural language system is part of the user interface, and not a component of the knowledge representation system, as shown in Figure 4.2.

4.2.2 Levels of Knowledge

Knowledge can be represented at different *levels,* depending on the degree to which fundamental principles and causal relationships are taken into account. *Shallow knowledge* handles only surface level information that can be used to deal with specific situations. *Deep knowledge,* on the other hand, represents the internal and causal structure of a system and considers the interactions between its underlying components.

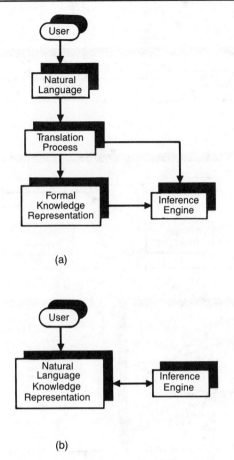

Figure 4.2 Natural language and the interface.

Shallow knowledge is concerned only with the type of information that is needed to solve a particular kind of problem, while deep knowledge can be applied to different tasks and different situations. One way of viewing the distinction between shallow and deep knowledge is shown in Figure 4.3. Although the system of interest represents a complex set of causal interactions, all that is represented in the shallow version of the knowledge is the overall input–output behavior of the system. For shallow knowledge, the internal structure of the system is hidden within a black box that cannot be opened and examined. However, deep knowledge takes the internal structure into account and tries to solve problems by relying on the interactions between the fundamental components of a system.

The distinction between shallow and deep knowledge can be seen in the use of language. As we discussed in the previous section, people are used to handling

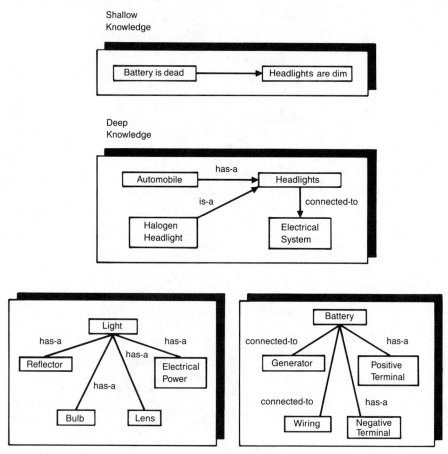

Figure 4.3 A schematic representation of the difference between shallow and deep knowledge.

knowledge in terms of the surface structure of words and sentences, and they carry out complex transformation of the surface structure into deep-structure meaning without much awareness of the processes they use. The deep-structure form of understanding concepts is very different from the surface structure of the speech and text that people say or write.

The fact that we cannot rely on the facile presentation of knowledge in terms of surface structure was well illustrated with an early program called ELIZA (Weizenbaum, 1966). ELIZA was designed to simulate aspects of the dialog of Rogerian psychotherapists, who reflect patient responses in the hope that the patients can then analyze their own feelings and gain insight into their emotional difficulties.

ELIZA worked by echoing the patient's responses using keyword recognition. When the patient used words such as "love" or "hate," this would trigger a special response related to that keyword. ELIZA's knowledge about English and psychology were contained in a set of rules that were indexed by keywords. An ELIZA-like rule might be:

> If the patient says "I like 'X'" then
> respond with "Why do you like 'X'?"

If no rules matched a particular input, default responses would be made by the program such as:

> Uh-huh

or

> Tell me more about yourself.

In this way, ELIZA could initially carry out seemingly interesting conversations with a patient. A typical dialog with ELIZA is shown in Figure 4.4.

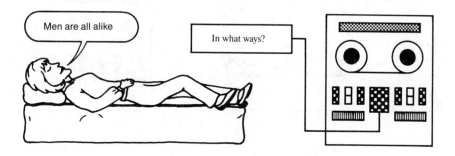

...They are always bugging us about something or other.

...Can you think of a specific example?

...Well, my boyfriend made me come here.

...Your boyfriend made you come here?

...He says I'm depressed much of the time.

...I am sorry to hear that you are depressed.

...Its true, I am unhappy.

...Do you think coming here will help you not to be unhappy?

...I need some help, that much seems certain.

...What would it mean to you if you got some help?

...Perhaps I could learn to get along with my mother.

...Tell me more about your family.

Figure 4.4 A sample of output from the ELIZA program.

In the sample ELIZA session shown in Figure 4.4, for instance, we see a number of methods that ELIZA uses to keep the conversation going. When the patient types in "my boyfriend made me come here," ELIZA transforms it into the question "your boyfriend made you come here?". Similarly, in the final statement shown in Figure 4.4, ELIZA takes a reference to the patient's mother and uses it as a cue to ask about her family in general.

ELIZA understood almost nothing about human relationships and emotions and contained very little knowledge, yet it was able to manipulate surface representations of knowledge in a reasonably convincing fashion some of the time.

However, the total reliance on surface-level knowledge that ELIZA used meant that the program would make gross blunders with certain types of input. For instance, the two sample dialogs shown in Figure 4.5 illustrate how the program can go astray because it simply matches surface-level keywords without understanding what they mean.

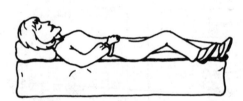 

Conversation 1

...Things are bothering me.	...What is bothering you?
...My boyfriend.	...Where is your boyfriend?
...My boyfriend is away.	...How long has your boyfriend been away?

Conversation 2

...Things are bothering me.	...What is bothering you?
...My head.	...Where is your head?
...My head is on my shoulders.	...How long has your head been on your shoulders?

Figure 4.5 A misleading session with ELIZA.

The use of appropriate words does not imply more than a fairly shallow level of understanding, yet the small amount of success that ELIZA had in dealing with people suggests that it is fairly easy to develop a conversational mode of interaction between people and machines. The danger, of course, is that creating clever surface-level methods of directing conversation leads the user to believe that the system is smarter than it really is. This is an effect that should be avoided in expert systems since it may eventually lead to disappointment and rejection of the system in the same way that most users of ELIZA quickly found the system to be an inadequate therapist.

Once we move beyond the surface-level structure to represent knowledge, the question arises as to how deeply we should express the knowledge. Depth of knowledge is not a dichotomy, but a continuum. Referring back to Figure 4.3, we can move from the shallowest level to a deeper level of knowledge by opening up the black box into its components. Some of these components will again be treated as black boxes. We can then move to a still deeper knowledge level by opening up these smaller black boxes, and so on.

However, we eventually need to stop somewhere; otherwise, we must deal with microscopic pieces of knowledge, e.g., the behavior of subatomic particles in diagnosing a car. Thus the level of knowledge description should be determined by the needs of the expert system and its application domain.

Consider the electrical system of a car. In troubleshooting the electrical system, a simple rule of thumb is that dim headlights indicate a faulty battery. Thus we have the following shallow rule showing the relationship between dim headlights and a faulty battery:

> If
>
> the headlights are dim
>
> Then
>
> the battery is faulty;

Shallow rules such as this do not tell us how the electrical system actually works. A deeper representation, on the other hand, may represent the underlying components (battery, battery cables, wiring, lights, the ignition system, etc.) and their interactions. The deep knowledge about the system includes the following:

Definition 4.2: The battery is connected to the battery cables, which, in turn, connect to the wiring of the electrical system. One part of the wiring provides charge to the ignition system while another part supplies charge to the lights. In order to permit the ignition system to work, the battery must be sufficiently charged, and the cables and wiring must transmit the charge from the battery to the ignition system. When the battery does not contain sufficient charge, the lights are dim. The transmission of electrical charge by cables and wires is normally all or none.

On the basis of this knowledge we could then build deep facts, rules, and frames reflecting not only the connectivity of the system and the propagation of charge through these connections but also the causal relationship between the status of the battery and the wiring and the resulting behavior of systems such as the headlights.

This knowledge could be generalized further by adding deeper knowledge that explains aspects of the behavior of all electrical circuits, not just those that appear in cars. Examples of such knowledge would be rules expressing Ohm's law (the voltage is equal to the product of the current and the resistance), Kirchhoff's current law (the sum of the currents flowing into a component or node must be zero), and the fact that an ideal battery supplies a constant voltage.

One approach to representing deep knowledge is to capture the underlying principles in the knowledge domain by modeling the functions carried out by each object in the domain. We could, for instance represent each of the components of an automobile in terms of what it does and how it affects other components under different conditions. This functional model could then be used for "what if" simulation by adding different facts as inputs and then seeing how each component is affected. Another example of this is the representation of the behavior of piping structures and scenarios for the failure of a feedwater system, discussed in Section 4.6.

There are sometimes a number of advantages in building expert systems based on deeper representations of knowledge. These include:

An ability to explain reasoning using deeper principles, thereby enhancing the credibility of the system

An ability to invoke deeper knowledge structures that can be used in solving difficult problems within the knowledge domain

However, shallow knowledge is usually easier to capture and to use and is appropriate in many situations. The need for deep knowledge arises when an expert system has to deal with diverse situations. If we have a fairly simple mechanical troubleshooting system where we are only interested in knowing whether the battery is supplying adequate charge, we might only need a single rule expressing much more shallow knowledge.

The depth of knowledge should not be confused with the type of knowledge representation, as demonstrated by the diverse approaches to representing deep knowledge (Chandrasekaran and Mittal, 1982; Davis and Shrobe, 1983; Michie, 1982). The same deep knowledge can be represented using a number of different knowledge structures. Rules and frames, for instance, can represent both shallow and deep knowledge. The adequacy of a knowledge representation is determined not by how "deep" it is but by whether it captures the essential components of knowledge in a form that supports the operation of the expert system.

■ 4.3 THE COMPONENTS OF KNOWLEDGE

Any method of representing knowledge must include a way of discussing knowledge at multiple levels and be able to describe, relate, and organize a set of elementary concepts or entities. We shall refer to the generic concepts or entities used in a knowledge representation system as *objects.*

Determining the right level at which to describe objects has a major impact on knowledge representation. In some knowledge domains, the right level at which to define objects is often fairly obvious and can be recognized by the conceptual objects used by experts in performing reasoning. In other knowledge domains, however, many different sets of objects may be used. In modeling transportation within a city, for instance, the objects may be particular vehicles such as buses, cars, and trucks, along with intersections, times of day, and related concepts. Viewing the same city from the perspective of crime prevention or health maintenance might lead to a very different set of objects being defined.

Once we have settled on a set of objects to use for knowledge representation, it is necessary to define them and their interactions. These definitions are based on the elementary components of knowledge (as shown in Figure 4.6):

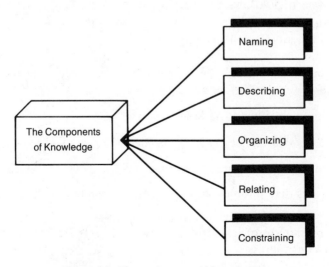

Figure 4.6 The components of knowledge.

Naming
Describing
Organizing
Relating
Constraining

These components of knowledge are generally present within many knowledge representation systems. However, each knowledge representation method deals with these components in its own way.

These components have intuitive analogs in the parts of speech used in natural language. The function of *naming* is usually performed by *proper nouns,* which can be signified by capitalizing the first letter or the name. For instance, we may name a chemical compound such as "acetone" or a component in a computer such as the "hard disk."

The function of *describing* is performed by *adjectives,* such as happy, blue, and tall. Adjectives generally modify nouns, which makes sense since they are describing objects. For instance, we may say that a patient is old, or that a chemical substance is hazardous. In formal notation, we may use *values,* as well as adjectives for describing an object. For instance, we may say that the age of the patient is 67 or that a chemical substance is a Class IA liquid. Such values reflect attributes or properties of an object.

The function of *relating* is performed by *transitive verbs* and special *nouns* that describe relationships. From a knowledge representation perspective we can distinguish between different relationships expressed by verbs, e.g.,

Action—electricity flows through the wire
Structural description—the pipe is connected to the valve
Relation—John is-father-of Mary

The function of *organizing* objects is handled in a variety of ways including *categorization* and *possession,* e.g.,

municipal bond is-a bond

which indicates that one object is an instance of a general class of objects or:

automobile has-an engine type

which indicates that an object possesses some attribute type.

Constraints are generally handled by *conditions* that define what descriptions of objects or patterns of relationships between objects are admissible. An example of a constraint is:

Any person whose age is less than 18 should not consume liquor.

We may describe this constraint as a rule:

> If
>
>   (age of 'X') < 18
>
> Then
>
>   'X' should not consume liquor;

We will now consider these basic components of knowledge in more detail.

4.3.1 Naming

To represent knowledge, we should be able to denote objects by name. For instance, "General Motors" may be the name of a company, "acetone" the name of a substance, and so on. The names that we assign should be unique so that we do not become confused as to whom or what we are talking about. If more than one person is called John Smith, then we need further identification to single out a particular John Smith. Methods for picking out a person or object uniquely include:

Adding more detail to the name (e.g., John Q. Smith)

Assigning a special code (e.g., Social Security number)

Attaching properties to the name (e.g., the John Smith living at 209 Wisdom Place)

The name of an object is really a symbol that can stand in place of the actual object. We tend to think of naming as a rather simple operation and perhaps even take it for granted. Yet there is evidence that learning the name of something may be one of the last steps in the development of core concepts (Nelson, 1974). For instance, when children are given sets of objects, they are able to classify them into groups of related objects even if they do not have labels to describe each group. The results of classification experiments with children (e.g., Nelson, 1973) suggest that functional concepts dominate the thinking of infants. For these children the world appears to be dominated with information such as "balls roll" or "a hole is to dig." There may well be an important lesson here for building knowledge structures: Understand the concept and its functionality at a higher level before you try to name it at a lower level.

4.3.2 Describing

We should be able to describe the important properties that an object has in representing the knowledge about the object. Obviously, there are a huge number of properties that potentially describe most objects. A complex object such as a person will have a wide range of properties such as physical features, experience, age, occupation, and skills. In describing people, we could focus on aspects of their personality, their appearance, their past experience, as in:

The age of John is 25

The height of John is six feet

John has had a history of allergy

John has a fever

John has held many different jobs

and so on. The properties that should be described depend on the application we are dealing with. A medical diagnostic system will focus on the physical properties, whereas a personnel selection system might focus on qualifications and employment history.

Some properties will be shared by different types of object, whereas other properties are fairly unique. The length of *antenna,* for instance, is a property that may be useful in classifying insects, whereas the *term until maturation* of an investment will be a more pertinent property for a financial advising system. Similarly, a person's weight may be of interest to a physician, but not to a tax adviser. Part of the skill in describing an object for an expert system will be in deciding what the system has to know about the object in order to be able to carry out its reasoning task.

Although the basic process of description is very straightforward, it can lead to different forms of expression in different knowledge representation methods. In logic, for instance, description is handled by predicates and arguments. Thus we could describe someone's age in logic as:

John has-age 24

In frames, however, the same description would be made by placing the value of the age in the corresponding slot of the frame that described John:

(age of John) : = 24

These notational differences should not obscure the fact that all knowledge representation methods must be able to describe the relevant objects.

4.3.3 Organizing

In addition to methods for describing objects and their relations, there should be methods for organizing objects into conceptual categories. One way of organizing objects is to describe some objects as instances of more general objects. Thus an automobile is a type of vehicle.

The analogy of the parent and the child is often used to capture the essential features of the relationship between a general concept and a specific instance of that concept. Thus "vehicle" is a parent concept of automobile that is, in turn, a parent concept of "1987 Ford."

The organization of objects creates categories which will generally contain objects with similar properties. Categories appear to be useful in organizing information in memory (Bousfield, 1953). Some experimental findings (e.g., Smith, Shoben, and Rips, 1974) suggest a view of long-term memory as a collection of categories nested within a large hierarchy (see Figure 4.7 for an example of what a portion of this hierarchy might look like), but the complexity of knowledge and the different perspectives that can be adopted have led some researchers to relax the assumption of nesting and to look at a network organization of knowledge (e.g., Anderson, 1983).

The same types of category that help people to recall information can also assist in the retrieval of information in a machine reasoning system. The most important feature of organizing objects into categories is that it then becomes possible to "know where to look" for information.

It is almost axiomatic that a knowledge representation method should include efficient methods of organizing knowledge. The type of practical, complex knowledge that can be used in expert systems must be organized in some fashion in order to be usable. One can compare disorganized knowledge to a messy desktop where the papers are stacked into piles randomly. The only way to

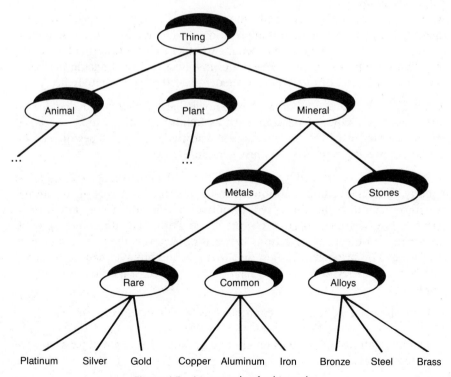

Figure 4.7 An example of a hierarchy.

find a particular paper is to search through the stacks exhaustively until the right paper is found. In contrast, a filing system (Figure 4.8) provides an organizational scheme that allows the searcher to search within a much smaller region of papers for the particular paper that is the target of the search. In a well-ordered filing system, the search might proceed as follows:

1. Select the appropriate filing cabinet.
2. Select the appropriate drawer within that cabinet.
3. Select the appropriate file within that drawer.
4. Select the appropriate paper within that file.

This type of hierarchical organization of knowledge is the one that we shall generally use, where possible. In some cases, however, the same paper may really belong in more than one category. Thus one topic discussed in a particular meeting might be filed under the topic itself or under the meeting at which it was raised. This problem of how to organize knowledge is not new, of course; it has traditionally been faced by librarians and led to the development of cataloging systems such as the Library of Congress Subject Headings and the Dewey Decimal System.

4.3.4 Relating

After we have named, described, and organized objects, we need to *relate* them. Part of the skill in describing relationships between objects is in choosing the right level of analysis and deciding whether to include particular entities in a relationship. The number of entities involved in a relationship may thus depend on the level of analysis and the depth of the knowledge used.

Relations represent a gray area where knowledge representation shades into inference. Some types of relation, such as family relations, can be expressed naturally in terms of the organization of knowledge. Other types of relation are best expressed as procedures involving inference.

At some point one has to aggregate entities and approximate the situation underlying a relationship. An object can be described in terms of its internal structure, including the conceptual primitives of which it is composed, or in terms of how it relates to other objects in the world. The difference between properties of objects and relations between objects is sometimes a source of confusion. For instance, the fact that Mary is an employer can be regarded as either a property of Mary or a relationship between Mary and each of her employees.

Relationships act as links that connect objects. For instance,

> Family relationships such as parent and grandparent relate objects that are individuals.

A) The Messy Desk

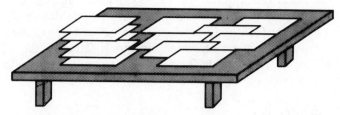

Method: Search the Stack Exhaustively.

B) The Filing Method

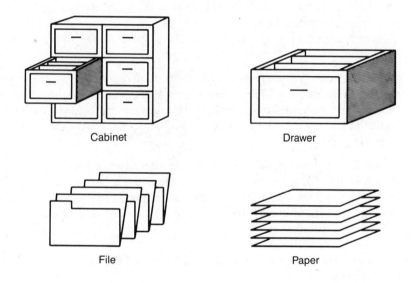

Cabinet   Drawer

File   Paper

Method: Choose Cabinet
          Choose Drawer
          Choose File
          Choose Paper

Figure 4.8 Searching desktops and filing cabinets.

A hazardous relationship produced by the combination of a dangerous substance with an inappropriate container relates the attribute of one type of object (chemical substance) with another type of object (container).

The relationships between the inflation rate, the interest rates, and house prices involve at least three conceptual objects, and potentially many more.

Different knowledge representation systems express relationships in different ways. In logic, relationships are expressed with clauses and rules, while in frames, relationships are expressed in terms of either slot values or inheritance. When combining logic and frames, the issue arises as to which method is most appropriate, e.g., do we represent someone's father as the value of a slot "father," or as a fact in the factbase? The answer is most often determined by the application.

4.3.5 Constraining

Constraints govern the properties of objects. They are used to limit ranges of values, relationships, and organizational structures. For instance, a constraint can be used to express the fact that the property of an object can take on only a certain range of values, as in the case in the age or height of a person, where the range does not exceed a certain value. Constraints can also be used to determine one property based on other properties. Thus an employee's telephone number may be constrained by the place of work, while the city of an address may be constrained by its zip code.

Constraints can be used to check the validity of knowledge, infer information that is not directly available, and regulate access to information. The rules of the road are examples of constraints that govern the behavior of motorists, while the laws of the land are examples of constraints that govern behavior in general.

Constraints can be designed to protect the integrity of a knowledge-base. Consider a system for managing patients in a medical practice. Relevant portions of the patients' records might include their names, age, weight, medical information, etc. There are a variety of constraints that one can impose on the patient records, such as:

> *Check for duplication.* No two patients may have identical names and addresses.
> *Check age.* No patient may have a birthdate indicating that the patient is older than 125 or that the age is negative.
> *Check gender.* A patient whose gender is male cannot be pregnant.

Constraints on knowledge may focus the reasoning process that uses knowledge by restricting the objects that may be considered in a given situation.

■ 4.4 APPROACHES TO KNOWLEDGE REPRESENTATION

Some of the inspiration for developing knowledge representation methods has come from observing how humans in general cope with the problem of representing and organizing knowledge. The human mind, like other reasoning systems, faces the problem of storing knowledge in some type of memory, retrieving knowledge from that memory when it is needed, and acting on knowledge.

The earliest explicit attempts at knowledge representation in artificial intelligence (AI) reflected psychological models of human memory and drew on the analogy between knowledge and natural language to build structures that represented the meaning of words. This approach resulted in the definition of *semantic networks* (Quillian, 1968; Anderson and Bower, 1973; Norman and Rumelhart, 1975; Fikes and Hendrix, 1977).

Although semantic networks were an early approach to knowledge representation, they introduced a number of important concepts, such as inheritance of properties, which are still in use in modern knowledge representation systems. The term "semantic network" has, however, been used by many different people to mean many different things. For instance, Brachman (1979) asks the question: "Will the real semantic network please stand up?".

Despite these differences, all approaches to semantic networks rely on two fundamental units:

    Nodes—which represent objects, concepts, or events

    Links—which represent relations between nodes

Graphically, nodes are drawn as boxes, ovals, or circles. Links (also called *arcs*) are drawn as arrows connecting the nodes, as in Figure 4.9. Nodes within a semantic network can be instances of other nodes using a special link

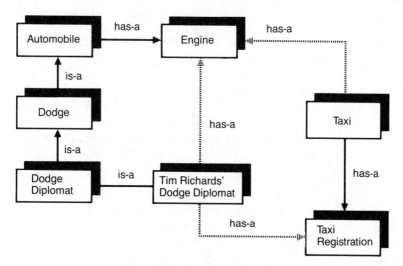

Figure 4.9 A semantic network.

called the *is-a* link. The is-a links provide the concept of inheritance, earlier mentioned in Section 2.3.3 and discussed further below.

Although semantic networks were popular in the 1970s, today semantic networks on their own are used in relatively few systems. In our view, this is due partly to the fact that semantic networks can soon become unmanageable as the size of a knowledge-base increases and that it is easier to interface other methods of knowledge representation to an inference engine. However, ideas based on semantics networks still exist in some recent knowledge representation environments (Brachman and Levesque, 1986).

Another early approach to knowledge representation was based on *production rules* (Newell and Simon, 1972). In this approach knowledge was represented as a series of If–Then rules based on propositional logic, discussed in Appendix C. Newell and Simon demonstrated that a surprising amount of human problem solving could be explained using such production rules.

Because rules were a straightforward method of representing expertise, they were used by Shortliffe in building MYCIN, one of the best known early expert systems (Shortliffe, 1976). The attention that MYCIN generated helped to establish rules as a prominent method of knowledge representation.

Another approach to knowledge representation relies on the use of *logic.* The use of logic in dealing with knowledge goes back to the ancient Greeks, who attempted to capture knowledge in terms of propositions. Their goal was to develop methods for determining whether an argument was correct. They recognized that words could sometimes obscure the essential features of an argument. In Chapter 3 we illustrated some of the problems that arose in using propositional logic and discussed how predicate logic provides a much more powerful method for reasoning. Predicate logic can be also used as a knowledge representation method, as we show in Section 4.6 in this chapter.

4.4.1 Frames and Scripts
However, a number of other knowledge representation methods were developed independently. These included both the work of Minsky (1975) on *frames* and the work of Schank and Abelson (1977) on *scripts.* The basic idea here was that human behavior can often be characterized in terms of standard ways of dealing with familiar situations.

Frames and scripts represented one line of research on how to combine declarations and procedures within a knowledge representation environment. The fundamental organizing principle underlying frame systems is the packaging of knowledge. Scripts permit reasoning based on expectations about what should happen next in stereotyped situations. A script is an outline of an episode of a certain type. This outline serves two purposes. First it organizes a set of actions. Second, it predicts the presence of activities that are not specifically referred to. Going to a restaurant is a well-known example of a script. A typical restaurant script is shown in Figure 4.10. This script can also be represented in terms of rules, as shown in Figure 4.11.

Scripts are composed of a number of parts:

- The constrained context in which the script is appropriate.
- The role to be played by each participant in the script.
- The conditions under which the script is activated.
- The results of completing the script.
- The scenes which occur as the script is executed.

Research has shown that structures such as frames and scripts can be an important organizing principle in human long-term memory (e.g., Smith, Giffin, Rockwell, and Thomas, 1986; Bower, Black, and Turner, 1979).

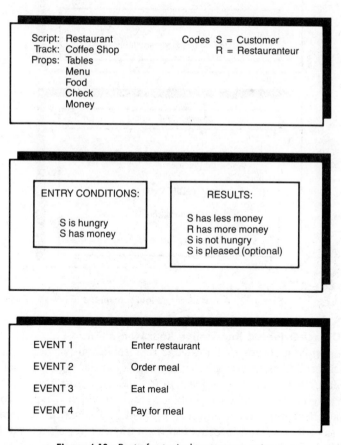

Figure 4.10   Part of a typical restaurant script.

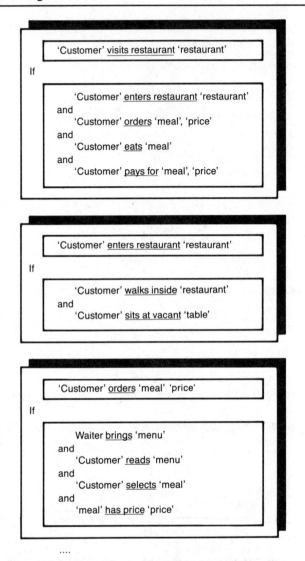

Figure 4.11 A restaurant script represented in rules.

4.4.2 Object-Oriented Knowledge Representation

Object-oriented methods of knowledge representation provide an alternative but closely related methodology for representing knowledge that shares a number of features with frames and semantic networks. In this approach knowledge is viewed in terms of a set of objects, each of which is capable of exhibiting certain behaviors. Each object is situated in a network or hierarchy and can access properties and information from higher-level objects (Bobrow and Stefik, 1983; Goldberg, Robson, and Ingalis, 1983; Stefik and Bobrow, 1986).

One feature of objects is that the properties of the object judged to be relevant depend on the situation. Thus the properties of a refrigerator that you consider when you are moving it are very different from the properties that relate to its use in storing perishable foods. In one case you see it as a heavy piece of furniture; in the other case it is a kitchen appliance.

Much of the arguments made in favor of objects as knowledge structures relate to the style of description being used rather than to fundamental properties of objects. Part of the object description style is that description is a process of comparison, so that a new object is described by saying in what ways it is similar to, and different from, the objects that are already known. This comparative method of description allows people to *copy and edit,* where they take a description for a related object and then modify it in accord with the special characteristics of the new object. In describing a sports car, for instance, one might take a generic description of a car and modify it (specialize it) to include features of streamlined design, powerful engine, low center of gravity, etc.

In the object-oriented paradigm, objects communicate with each other by sending and receiving *messages.* An object that has received a message checks its database and decides what action to take. Actions can be taken by invoking a *method.* Any action that it does decide to take is again passed on in the form of a message (Figure 4.12).

To represent knowledge about restaurants in an object-oriented form, we might include objects representing tables, waiters, customers, cashiers, and so on. Each object then interacts with the others by sending messages; e.g., a customer object may send a message to a waiter object.

Objects are very similar to frames. Description by comparison (using copy and edit) looks very much like specialization of specific instances used in frames. Objects use attributes, while frames have slots. Both objects and frames can be organized in hierarchies in which lower-level elements share the properties of higher-level elements (i.e., inheritance). Objects have methods, while frames have attached procedures. Objects send messages, while frames can use rules to perform computations.

Today, object-oriented and frame-based systems are rapidly converging toward an integrated form in which it is difficult to distinguish between them. In Chapter 5, we show how object-oriented behavior can be easily achieved in terms of frames and rules.

4.4.3 Inheritance

However we choose to represent knowledge structures, the problem of connecting and organizing the components of knowledge must be dealt with. Networks and hierarchies can be used for this purpose, but the issue of how to retrieve information that is shared among different members of a category or class of objects within a hierarchy still remains.

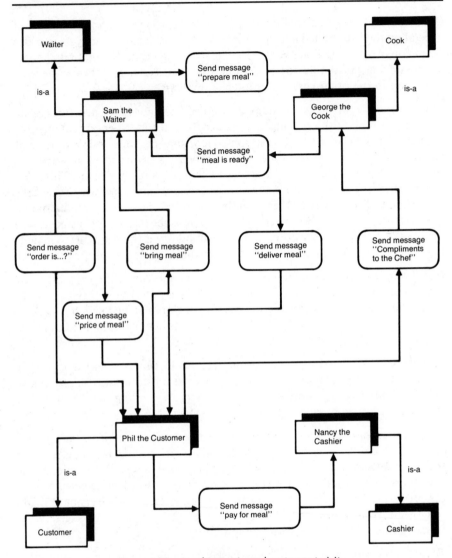

Figure 4.12 An object-oriented restaurant visit.

For instance, we may know that most automobiles have four wheels, but we don't want to explicitly store that information for each separate instance of an automobile that we have in our knowledge-base. Instead, we can express this information as a property of automobiles in general. Thus we store the fact that automobiles have four wheels as a property connected to the automobile category node. If we need the number of wheels for a particular instance of an automobile, we retrieve it by using *inheritance* from the parent category of automobiles.

Inheritance is based on the concept that objects or concepts tend to form groups and that members within a group tend to share common properties. By using inheritance we can organize our knowledge in a way that allows the inference of information that is not directly available.

For instance, a shock hazard is a type of electrical hazard, which is, in turn, a type of hazard. Thus we expect a shock hazard to retain all the basic properties of electrical hazards and hazards in general, but with further restrictions. Similarly, if we know that a machine is an assembly of parts and that a drill is a machine, we can deduce that a drill is an assembly of parts. We can represent this information efficiently by storing drill as a special instance of the machine concept and then inheriting information that also applies to machines in general as it is needed.

Inheritance is a good way to find information that is not stored in the place where we first look. It leads to what is known as *cognitive economy,* where information is only stored in one place, but can still be retrieved from different parts of the network or hierarchy.

The process of inheritance normally proceeds as follows. First, we examine the appropriate object, concept, or frame directly. If the information is not stored there, we go to the parent (superordinate) object, concept or frame and check whether the information is stored there. Then, if the information is still not found, we repeat the same process with the parent of this current object, concept or frame; until either the information is found, or we reach the top of the hierarchy. Inheritance is a powerful way of retrieving information. It allows us to get the same information from a variety of sources, even though it has been stored in only one location.

Hierarchies are easy to search for information in, but most real-world knowledge is not strictly nested and a hierarchy can only approximate the true structure of a knowledge domain. Thus we often need to allow each object to have more than one parent. The inheritance of properties from multiple parents is called *multiple inheritance.* Figure 4.13 shows an example of multiple inheritance.

4.4.4 Representing Knowledge in Blackboards

An interesting approach to knowledge representation suitable for implementation on a multiprocessing or distributed computer system is the *blackboard* model. The blackboard model was developed for the HEARSAY-II speech understanding system (Erman, Hayes-Roth, Lesser, and Reddy, 1980) and is reminiscent of the earlier work of Selfridge (1959), who proposed an early model of speech recognition.

The idea behind the blackboard model may be intuitively explained as follows:

We have a group of human experts, each of whom is highly qualified in a specific field. We are trying to coordinate the knowledge of these experts to solve a diffi-

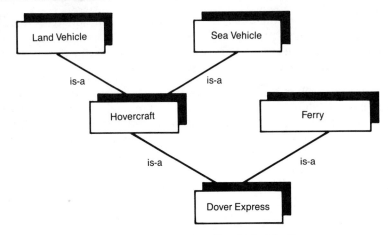

Figure 4.13 Representation of multiple inheritance.

cult problem. As it turns out, the experts will not speak to each other directly, but in order to help solve the problem will agree to interact with a *coordinator* or *scheduler* and to read from and write on a *blackboard.*

We thus gather the experts in a room with a large blackboard and write the initial statement of the problem on the blackboard. The experts read the problem statement and will begin to think. As each expert comes up with an interesting hypothesis or an important idea, he writes it on the blackboard for everyone to see. This will help the other experts in their thinking, and provides them with important clues based on knowledge outside their own domain. Eventually, one of the experts will solve the problem and will write the final solution on the blackboard.

When this model is used in an expert system context, we call each participating expert a *knowledge source.* A knowledge source need not be a human expert, but may be a knowledge-base devoted to performing a specific task. The blackboard then becomes a way of sharing hypotheses and information among the knowledge sources.

This model of problem solving was used in HEARSAY-II, an early speaker-dependent speech understanding system that attempted to generate a coherent interpretation of spoken sentences drawn from a 1000-word vocabulary. The system had 12 knowledge sources. Each knowledge source carried out a different task. This allowed the use of diverse types of knowledge, such as phonetic knowledge and grammatical knowledge. For instance, PREDICT hypothesized all words that might syntactically precede or follow a given phrase, and so on. Each knowledge source functioned as a rule-based system. More recent blackboard environments include HEARSAY-III (Erman, London, and Fickas, 1981), AGE (Nii, 1980), and BB1 (Hayes-Roth, 1984, 1985).

From a general perspective, the blackboard model aims to address three distinct problems that appear as the size of a knowledge-base grows:

1. The system becomes harder to understand, since there are many rules, facts, etc.
2. Different types of knowledge and different knowledge representation and inference methods need to be integrated.
3. Response time begins to deteriorate as the amount of required computation increases.

The blackboard model deals with these issues by separating knowledge into modular knowledge sources that use different knowledge representation and inference methods and that may reside on separate computers. A blackboard architecture is thus made up of three basic components:

A global database (the *blackboard*).

Independent *knowledge sources* that have access to the blackboard.

A *scheduler* to control knowledge source activity.

The knowledge sources are independent and influence each other by responding to and modifying information on the blackboard. Blackboards are distinguished more as an architecture for distributed problem solving than as a distinct method of knowledge representation. In fact, a number of different knowledge representation methods can be used for each knowledge source without disturbing the overall blackboard structure, providing that any information on the blackboard can be read and used by the knowledge sources that need it.

Thus the blackboard model provides three distinct advantages:

a. It can be used to organize knowledge in a modular way.
b. It can easily integrate different knowledge representation methods.
c. It may be executed in a distributed computing environment for greater efficiency.

Although a blackboard system may be implemented on a single computer, the blackboard model is ideally suited for distributed problem solving. Each knowledge source can be implemented as a knowledge-base on a separate processor to work independently on a component of a problem. Of course, one must ensure that only one knowledge source at a time writes on the blackboard. But this is not a major issue compared to the problem of "coordinated thinking," which appears if we do not have a truly distributed (or multiple processor) implementation of a blackboard.

On a single computer, advantage **c** above disappears and the activities of the knowledge sources need to be carefully coordinated since they are all sharing the same processor. Depending on which knowledge source receives more computation time, different intermediate hypotheses may be posted on the blackboard. In the intuitive analogy shown above, the scheduler now assumes the role of "thought police officer" who has to grant "thinking time" to each expert. Thus, in a single processor system the method of construction of the scheduler is critical, and often becomes reminiscent of attempts to devise heuristic search algorithms, as discussed in Chapter 1.

We can simulate the blackboard architecture, using the logical constructs of Chapter 3:

> If
>   begin blackboard
>   do execute knowledge sources
>   until goal;

> If
>   execute knowledge sources
>   for-every 'K' is a suitable knowledge source
>   do operate 'K' ;

> If
>   operate 'K'
>   read blackboard 'K' and
>   form results 'K' and
>   update blackboard 'K' ;

Each knowledge source 'K' can then be implemented individually with a separate predicate, which reads the blackboard, forms some results with form results, and writes the results on the blackboard. The predicate form results can be implemented as a disjunction of a set of diverse predicates so that it takes a dramatically different set of actions depending on which knowledge source it is dealing with, e.g.,

> If
>   form results 'K'
>   'K' = Phonetics and
>   perform phonetic analysis
>
> or
>   'K' = Grammar and
>   perform grammatical analysis
>
> or
>   . . .

To write results on the blackboard, each knowledge source may simply assert them in a common factbase. The predicate goal can then be implemented to check whether a particular result has been achieved; if so the blackboard activation cycle is terminated.

Note that the goal *'K' is a suitable knowledge source* may be implemented either to try all knowledge sources, or to select a specific set of knowledge sources for activation at each time, depending on the contents of the blackboard, and thus achieves the effect of a scheduler.

4.4.5 Message Passing with Frames

Some object oriented systems, such as Smalltalk (Goldberg and Robson 1983), rely on *messages* for communication between objects. In this paradigm, objects may send messages to each other and take actions upon the receipt of messages. This means that:

a. An object may have a *method* of computation associated with a slot.

b. Upon the receipt of a message from other objects, the object invokes the *method* to perform computation.

c. An object may inherit methods from its parents.

This method of computation may be easily achieved by using our integrated rule and frame system. To do so:

i. For each method, we define a slot with that method name.

ii. We attach the computation to be performed by the method to the slot with an if-added or if-needed predicate.

iii. To send and respond to messages, we either read or assign values to the method slots.

For instance, we may define a frame as follows:

> Frame: F1
> Parent: Thing
> Slot: Method–1 Value: V1
>   If-added: perform computation New-Value, Method–1

We then define a message predicate with:

> send message 'Frame', 'Method-name', 'Content'
> If
> ('Method-name' of 'Frame') : = 'Content';

Thus the goal *send message F1, Method-1, Content-1* will invoke the method predicate *perform computation Content-1, Method-1* within the frame F1. Of course, methods may be inherited, e.g., if we have:

> Frame: F2
> Parent: F1
> > Slot: Method-1 Value: V2

The goal *send message F2, Method-1, Content-2* will invoke the method predicate *perform computation Content-2, Method-1,* by inheritance of the attached predicate. If a child of F1 has no explicit slot called Method-1, the value will be obtained from F1, e.g., if we have:

> Frame: F3
> Parent: F1

The goal *send message F3, Content-3* will invoke the method predicate *perform computation Content-3, V1* by inheritance of both the attached predicate and the value of the slot Method-1.

■ 4.5 WHAT TO LOOK FOR IN A KNOWLEDGE REPRESENTATION METHOD

We have outlined several approaches to knowledge representation. But what are the features that a good knowledge representation method should have? Representation of knowledge requires that relevant objects in the knowledge domain be named, described, and organized, and that relationships between objects be expressed including constraining relationships that govern the storage and retrieval of object properties. The goal of a knowledge representation method is to carry out these functions in an efficient and effective manner.

The selection of an appropriate knowledge representation method requires that we have evaluation criteria for determining whether a particular method is appropriate. The following general questions can be used in evaluating a knowledge representation method for use with an application or class of applications:

A. *The Quality of Basic Knowledge Structures*
   1. What is the basic vocabulary of the knowledge representation system? Does this vocabulary permit adequate expression of the important concepts within the knowledge domain?
   2. How modular is the representation? Does changing one piece of knowledge force one to make a complicated sequence of changes in related objects?
   3. Can knowledge be simultaneously represented at multiple levels of detail? (For instance, is it possible to describe a car, the electrical system

of a car, or the behavior of the battery, and so on, depending on the level of detail required by the problem?)

4. Is the basic form of the knowledge structure easily understood by some-one reading through the coded knowledge? Can someone pick up the source code of the knowledge-base and understand its content by read-ing it?

Some of the issues that determine the effectiveness of a knowledge repre-sentation system concern the basic knowledge structures that are used. These structures should be easily understood. One important test of this is the amount of time it takes most people to learn how to read and under-stand the source code in which knowledge is expressed. Knowledge struc-tures should be modular so that minor changes can be made on one or two of the knowledge structures without requiring an update of the whole knowledge-base.

The basic vocabulary used in the system is an important factor. The basic knowledge structures should be as general as possible; otherwise, we are constrained by concepts that refer to other knowledge domains that may not be relevant for the current application. We could, for instance, have a knowledge representation system that included a basic vocabulary of how objects can be moved, or what types of container there are, but such vo-cabularies would only be useful in restricted knowledge domains.

Knowledge representation systems that incorporate a minimal basic vocab-ulary are generally preferable. One advantage of such system is that it can be used to describe the objects and concepts in a knowledge domain at many different levels of detail with the same vocabulary.

B. *The Quality of Storage Mechanisms*

1. How is new knowledge added? Can new knowledge be linked to the old knowledge in a way that is consistent with the overall structure of the knowledge?

2. What mechanisms are available for organizing knowledge? Can the var-ious relationships between objects be expressed adequately?

3. Can the structures that are used to organize the knowledge be updated reasonably easily? Can new objects be expressed as generalizations or specializations of old objects?

4. Is it possible to distinguish between permanent and temporary knowl-edge?

A knowledge-base, and the inference based on it, is only as good as the knowledge that it contains. Storage mechanisms have to deal with the problem of organizing and updating knowledge, in addition to expressing the basic concepts. Two important features are the ability to express new knowledge as revised versions of old knowledge and the ability to distinguish between permanent and temporary knowledge that should be stored only for the duration of a consultation or for a certain time period.

C. *The Quality of Retrieval Mechanisms*

1. What kind of retrieval is possible? Is it easy to retrieve knowledge from the knowledge-base after you have put it in?
2. Can the knowledge structures be browsed over or reviewed during the updating or debugging of the knowledge-base?
3. Can the inference system easily access the internal structure of objects?

In many ways the retrieval mechanisms are the most visible feature of a knowledge-base. Ideally, the retrieval system should be able to return the value of information if it is known directly and to infer the value of that information on the basis of other facts that it does know about otherwise. Thus an ideal system will allow inference mechanisms to be inserted into the knowledge structures to enhance retrieval.

D. *The Quality of the Knowledge Representation Environment*

1. Can the knowledge representation method handle the size of knowledge-base that the application demands? Will storage and retrieval times degrade gracefully as the knowledge-base grows?
2. Can the knowledge representation method itself be modified or extended? Can new knowledge structures be developed if they are found necessary?
3. How efficient is the representation? Does the same piece of knowledge have to be stored in more than one place?
4. How easily can the knowledge be linked to the rules of an inference process? That is, how easy is it to use the knowledge in reasoning?

A knowledge representation system will in practice be part of a programming environment determined by the hardware and software architectures utilized for developing the expert system.

In viewing knowledge representation in abstract and theoretical forms, one can develop a variety of complex methods. But these methods are of no use to a practitioner if they do not run on available computer equipment with reasonable efficiency. Storage and speed are important factors, as is the extent to which one can customize the knowledge representation system using subroutines written in other languages. Finally, since our focus is on the development of expert systems, from our viewpoint it is most critical that the knowledge representation system be well integrated with an appropriate inference engine.

The evaluative questions outlined above express what we should know about a knowledge representation method when evaluating it for possible use in an application. However, sometimes one doesn't have the luxury of choosing all features and one must make difficult tradeoffs between two or more evaluation criteria. One such tradeoff occurs when a complex representation may improve flexibility at the expense of the overall efficiency of the system in terms of speed and memory utilization.

Particular applications may lead to more specific criteria that will also need to be considered in the evaluation process. The clarity of the knowledge representation, for instance, will depend on who is building and maintaining the knowledge-base. A computer scientist may be much more tolerant of abstruse source code and skimpy browsing facilities than experts and other types of user.

▪ 4.6 LOGICAL KNOWLEDGE REPRESENTATION

Like all knowledge representation methods, logic must deal with the fundamental issues of naming, describing, organizing, relating, and constraining that constitute the components of knowledge. The constructs available for knowledge representation in logic are predicates, clauses and rules.

The problem of naming is straightforward in logic. Objects are named as the arguments of predicates in clauses. Thus the clause:

> Dean Richards is 24
> Container-1 contains acetone

names the person called Dean Richards, a container called Container-1 and the substance "acetone."

Descriptions can be handled in logic by creating predicates that relate objects to their properties. Thus the description of a person's height might be:

> Dean Richards is tall

The is predicate can then be used to describe properties of objects in general. We can also define a has predicate with a similar function:

> Tim Richards has blue eyes

The problem of organizing knowledge in logic is also handled by the creation of predicates. The fact that Tim Richards is a student can be represented as:

> Tim Richards is a student

where the is a predicate is used to denote that its first argument (Tim Richards) is an instance of the parent concept (student) in the second argument.

The relationship between objects is handled by clauses, or rules. Examples of clauses that express relationships are:

Paul <u>is brother of</u> Ian
Pipe–1 <u>is connected to</u> Valve–3

Rules can be used to constrain relationships to a particular form. The fact that each person in the knowledge-base may have at most one father maybe checked with the rule:

If
<u>duplicate exists</u> 'Y'

and
'X' <u>is-father-of</u> 'Y'

and
'Z' <u>is-father-of</u> 'Y'

not 'X' = 'Z';

In the next two sections, we provide two examples of how knowledge may be represented in logic.

4.6.1 Representing Rule-Based Knowledge

In this section we illustrate the use of logic for representing rule-based knowledge with an example that deals with investment selection. In this example we use a set of "exact" rules that relate to investments. Later, in Chapter 6 we present inexact versions of rules.

The first set of investment rules define the predicate <u>should invest in</u>. The meaning of this predicate should be self-evident. Consider the following rule for this predicate:

If
'Investor' <u>should invest in</u> real estate syndicate

and
'Investor' <u>needs investment type</u> real estate

and
'Investor' <u>needs</u> high addition to investment

not 'Investor' <u>needs</u> long term investment;

The effect of this rule is to recommend an investment strategy based on the needs of the client. Further examples of <u>should invest in</u> rules are shown in Figure 4.14.

We immediately notice a number of components of knowledge that are reflected in this rule. First, the objects or concepts, such as an investor, or real estate, are defined as arguments in each clause, while relationships such as <u>needs</u> are written as predicates.

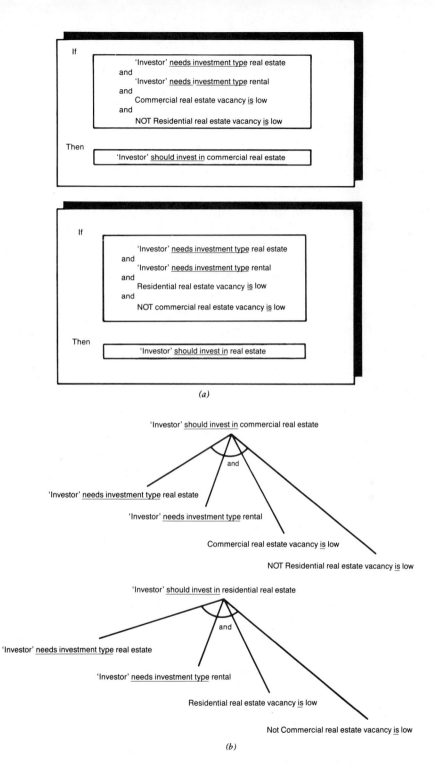

Figure 4.14 (a) Rules for advising the client on what to invest in. (b) Rules expressed as and/or goal trees.

The first rule in Figure 4.14 contains the clause:

> commercial real estate vacancy is low

which shows how an object or concept can be *described* using a special predicate is where one of the arguments is the object and the other argument is the description that is assigned to the object.

The second set of rules, shown in Figure 4.15, define the predicate needs tax shelter which reflects a motivation for investment. Finally, the third set of rules, shown in Figure 4.16, define the meaning of the predicate needs investment type that maps the type of investment considered into the characteristics of the investor. This third set of rules implies an organization of the knowledge about investments.

The remaining information referred to in these rules can be available as facts that can either be asked of the investor or that are already available in the factbase for the current case.

We can use special predicates such as is a and are that capture the organization of knowledge explicitly, as in:

> Savings Bond is a government obligation

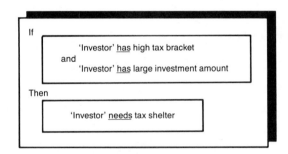

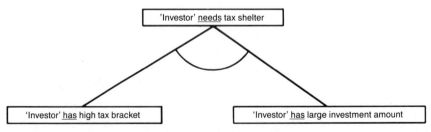

Figure 4.15 A rule for tax shelters.

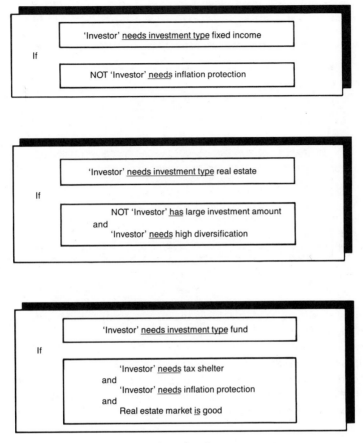

Figure 4.16 Some rules related to investment types.

We can then define a network or hierarchy through a combination of separate is a facts, as in:

Municipal Bond is a bond

Government Obligation is a bond

Corporate Bond is a bond

Savings Bond is a Government Obligation

Treasury is a Government Obligation

Treasury Bond is a Treasury

Treasury Bill is a Treasury

Treasury Bond is a Treasury

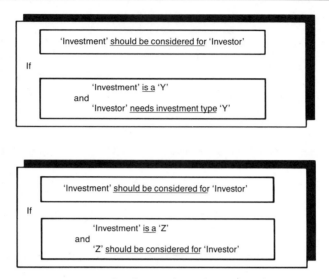

Figure 4.17 Rules that simulate inheritance in logic.

These concepts can be used to achieve the effects of inheritance with rules such as those shown in Figure 4.17.

4.6.2 Representing Structural Knowledge in Logic

As a second example of logical knowledge representation, we consider the representation of the structure of the emergency feedwater system for a nuclear power plant. This example illustrates the use of logic for representing "deep" knowledge.

An emergency feedwater system is used when the main feedwater system for a nuclear power plant is not available. The emergency feedwater system provides the capability to remove heat from the reactor coolant system during emergency conditions, including small loss of coolant accident (LOCA) cases. The emergency feedwater system operates over a time period sufficient to cool down the reactor coolant system to temperature and pressure levels at which the residual heat removal system can operate. The emergency feedwater system plays a very important role during the occurrence of a LOCA.

The emergency feedwater system consists of piping structures that take water from condensate storage tanks to steam generators. The piping structure consists of *pipes* to carry the water, *valves, pumps,* and *vessels* which are interconnected by the pipes (Parsaye and Lin, 1987). The structure of an emergency feedwater system can be viewed in terms of two basic constructs:

Pipes, which carry water
Valves or nodes, which occur at pipe connections

Emergency feedwater systems can be very complex, but we will convey the basic concepts with a simple example. As in Figure 4.18, suppose that A, B, and C are nodes and that water has to reach A either from B or C. To carry the water, we need pipes such as P1, P2, and P3. In this example, water can flow from either B or C to A, provided water reaches B or C from other parts of the emergency feedwater system and if B and C are operative.

We can use logic to represent the interconnectivity of the components. We represent the fact that a pipe is joined to a valve in terms of logical predicates. The predicate is joined to indicates the fact that two components are joined to each other. This predicate performs the task of *relating* the objects that are *named* in its arguments. The structure shown in Figure 4.18 can be captured with the logical assertions involving the predicate is joined to. These facts are then placed in a factbase representing the connectivity of the emergency feedwater system.

Once the facts about interconnectivity are available, we can capture the *topology* of the system in logic using a basic set of rules that will work with piping

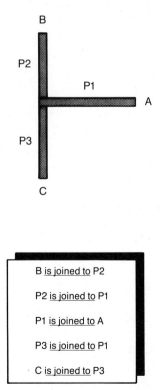

Figure 4.18 A simple piping diagram.

structures in general. Rules can be defined for representing flow and the basic concepts of pipe interconnectivity. For instance, the rule:

> 'Pipe' has multiple joins
>
> If
>
> 'X' is joined to 'Pipe'
>
> and
>
> 'Y' is joined to 'Pipe'
>
> and
>
> not 'X' = 'Y';

may be used to prove that pipe P1 in Figure 4.18 has multiple joins; i.e., it is joined to both P2 and P3.

Rules such as these are quite generic and apply to almost any piping structure. The generic nature of these rules stems from the fact that they do not specify particular pipes or nodes but refer instead to variables representing pipes or nodes. Thus the rule above can be paraphrased in the following way:

Definition 4.3:   A pipe has multiple joins if two distinct additional pipes are joined to it.

We may use the rules:

> 'Pipe' leads to 'Node'
>
> If
>
> 'Pipe' is joined to 'Node' ;

> 'Pipe' leads to 'Node'
>
> If
>
> 'Pipe' is joined to 'X'
>
> and
>
> 'X' leads to 'Node' ;

to prove that pipe P2 leads to node A. To prove *P2 leads to A,* we use the first rule twice, i.e.,

> P1 leads to A
>
> If
>
> P1 is joined to A ;

> P2 leads to P1
>
> If
>
> P2 is joined to P1 ;

We then use the second rule, using these facts:

If
> P2 leads to A

and
> P2 leads to P1

> P1 leads to A ;

To represent water flow, we may use the extralogical quantifiers defined in Section 3.8.1 to define the relationship dominates between nodes. The predicate dominates indicates that one node is the only source of water for another node, i.e., that it is the only node leading to the another node. We define this predicate by

If
> 'Node-1' dominates 'Node-2'

> for-all 'Other Node' leads to 'Node-2'
> is-true 'Other Node' leads to 'Node-1' ;

This tells us that in case water fails to reach 'Node-1' or if 'Node-1' somehow fails, water will fail to reach 'Node-2', as in Figure 4.19.

By using this predicate we may predict failure modes within an emergency feedwater system. We may consider different scenarios and pose hypothetical questions to the emergency feedwater system, e.g., "Suppose that node V–125

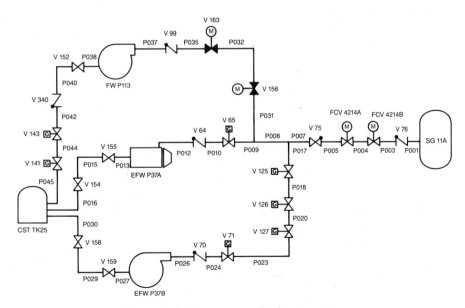

Figure 4.19 An emergency feedwater system.

fails. What are the consequences?'' With a sufficient number of rules such as these it is possible to dynamically simulate the behavior of piping structures and emergency feedwater systems.

■ 4.7 SUMMARY

This chapter has provided a general discussion of knowledge. We discussed levels of knowledge representation and differentiated between shallow and deep knowledge. We pointed out that the level at which knowledge is represented should depend on the type of application.

We introduced the basic components that any knowledge representation method should deal with in terms of naming, describing, organizing, relating, and constraining. We discussed several approaches to knowledge representation, including semantic networks, rules, frames, scripts, objects, and blackboards. We pointed out the commonalities, such as the concept of inheritance, that exist between these methods and illustrated how each method must deal with the five basic components of knowledge.

We then provided a set of evaluative guidelines for knowledge representation. These guidelines relate to four fundamental aspects of knowledge representation: basic knowledge structures, storage methods, retrieval methods, and the representation environment. Finally, we focused on logic and provided two distinct examples of how the system of logic discussed in chapter three can be applied to knowledge representation.

In Chapter 5 we show how frames fit into the general scheme of knowledge representation methods and describe the use of frames and their integration with facts and rules.

5

KNOWLEDGE REPRESENTATION WITH FRAMES

Chapter 4 discussed knowledge from a general point of view. We presented an overall view of knowledge and knowledge representation and outlined the underlying concepts of a number of knowledge representation paradigms.

In discussing knowledge, we noted how a number of knowledge representation methods are gradually converging toward a common point. We saw the concept of *basic entity* viewed in terms of nodes, frames, objects, etc. and the concept of *property* expressed in terms of attributes, slots, etc. Further, the underlying concept of inheritance was shared amongst these methods.

To develop a method of knowledge representation, we begin with frames as a starting point since they capture the essential characteristics needed for use in commercial expert systems. Our treatment of frames, however, extends traditional concepts and incorporates features from other approaches, such as the object-oriented paradigm.

Further, this treatment is enhanced with a logical flavor, allowing the integration of frames and inference. In Chapter 4 we showed how logic on its own can also be used for knowledge representation, but noted that it lacked some facilities, such as packaging, built-in inheritance, and the form of procedural attachment discussed later (Section 5.5). However, this does not mean that we intend to abandon logic. Predicate logic provides a powerful system for reasoning and once combined with frames, allows for a flexible method of knowledge representation and inference.

In this chapter we provide a formal introduction to frames and show how they can be combined with logic to provide an integrated knowledge representation

161

and inferencing system. We begin by discussing how frames fit into the overall components of knowledge discussed in Section 4.3. Then a formal syntax for representing knowledge in frames is given, along with a description of basic storage and retrieval methods, including attached predicates. Methods of building inheritance hierarchies are also discussed. We then show how frames can be linked to rules, and we evaluate the resulting hybrid rule–frame system of knowledge representation using the guidelines developed in Chapter 4. The chapter concludes with a description of two applications of frame-based knowledge representation.

■ 5.2 FRAME-BASED KNOWLEDGE REPRESENTATION

Frames provide a method of combining declarations and procedures within a single knowledge representation environment. The fundamental organizing principle underlying frame systems is the packaging of both data and procedures into knowledge structures.

Frames are a way of organizing, as well as packaging, knowledge. Frames are organized into hierarchies or networks that can be used to inherit information, i.e., to retrieve properties that a lower level concept shares with a whole class of concepts. In addition to organizing knowledge in inheritance hierarchies, frames can also be linked to rules, allowing predicates to be activated when knowledge is stored and retrieved.

Frames, as discussed in this chapter, can be used to implement much of the functionality of objects (discussed in Section 4.4.2.). Thus we use the terms "frame," "object frame," and "object" interchangeably.

The essential feature of a frame is that it contains *slots* that can be filled with values. Frames are essentially composed of their slots, just as record structures in traditional programs are composed of fields. Slots are the building blocks of the body of frames.

Like any knowledge representation method, frames must deal with the five components of knowledge introduced in Chapter 4. The basic components of knowledge are incorporated in frames as follows:

Naming. A unique *name* is assigned to each frame. A frame name may be any constant.

Describing. The body of a frame is composed of a number of *slots* or *attributes* that have values. We often use the terms "slot" and "attribute" interchangeably. These slots or attributes can be used to describe the properties of the frame or to link different frames together.

Organizing. Each frame (except the top level frame in a hierarchy) has one or more *parents,* providing an *inheritance* mechanism.

Relating. The values of frame slots may be other frames. Frames may thus be related by having one frame as the *value* of a slot in another frame. Frames may also be related by *rules*.

Constraining. Each slot in a frame may have attached *predicates,* which are invoked whenever the slot is read or modified. Attached predicates include an *if-needed* predicate that is activated when information is retrieved and an *if-added* predicate that is activated when information is stored.

The basic components of frames thus correspond closely to the basic components of knowledge (discussed in Section 4.3). The frame name provides a label, the slots provide a mechanism for describing properties and relations, and organization of frames can be achieved by defining parent–child relations. Relations may also be defined with slots or with rules. The resulting knowledge base can then be constrained by using attached predicates to control the processes of storing and retrieving information.

5.2.1 The Structure of Frames
The basic structure of a frame consists of:

The name of the frame.
The parents of the frame.
The slots (if any) of the frame and their values.
The attached predicates (if any) for each slot.

The components of a frame slot are:

Slot Name. Each slot should have a *unique* name within the frame. However, slot names are local to frames. Hence two distinct frames may have the same slot name.

Naming slots within frames uniquely achieves data abstraction by avoiding naming conflicts between frames. For instance, the slot "age" may be used both for people and cars with no conflict. We can draw an analogy here with the scope of rule variables (as discussed in Section 3.5.4), where variable names are local to the rule in which they are used.

Slot Value. Each slot should have a *value* field, as well as a name. The value field in a slot may be empty when the slot is first defined and may be later assigned and read.

In the frame "John Smith" for instance, we might have the slot "age" with the value 24. The situation where a slot has been defined, but no value for it is yet available, is like knowing that something must have a property, because of the type of frame that it is, without knowing what the value of the property is. Thus we know, for instance, that someone must have an age, even if we do not know what the value of that age is. In such cases, the default value NO-VALUE may be used.

If-Needed Predicate. Each slot may have an *if-needed* predicate. If a slot has an if-needed predicate, before the value of the slot can be read and obtained, the if-needed predicate must be successfully proven. The use of an if-needed predicate is optional with each slot.

If-needed predicates are frequently used to enhance the flexibility of retrieval. For instance, when the value of a slot is not available directly, we might be able to consult a table of expected values on the basis of other information that we know about the frame. Thus, if we do not know the age of a person, but the birthdate is known, an if-needed predicate can calculate the desired information by subtracting the current date from the birthdate.

If-Added Predicate. Each slot may have an *if-added* predicate. If a slot has an if-added predicate, before the value of the slot is assigned a value, or the value is changed, the if-added predicate must be successfully proved. The use of an if-added predicate is also optional with each slot.

If-added predicates can be used to screen erroneous values before they are added to slots. For instance, an if-added predicate might accept a number as the age of a person only if it is less than 125 and greater than 0.

Figure 5.1 shows the general template for a frame, including slots and their values. Figure 5.2 gives a representation for individual slots within a frame, including procedures that may be added to the slots. Figure 5.3 provides a pictorial representation of a frame showing how if-needed and if-added predicates function as filters in storage and retrieval.

■ 5.3 STORING AND RETRIEVING KNOWLEDGE IN FRAMES

Frame representations of knowledge need mechanisms that permit the storage and retrieval of information. Storage and retrieval are processes for manipulating descriptions. Information that we may need to store in a knowledge representation system includes:

the value of a particular property
the category to which the frame belongs.

To store and retrieve such information, we extend the definition of terms given in chapter three by defining frame terms. A *frame term* has the form:

(slot-name of frame-reference)

A) Written Form:

Frame: Frame Name

Parent: Frame Parent-1

...

Parent: Frame Parent-N

Slot: Slot-1　Value: Value-1 (or empty)

Slot: Slot-2　Value: Value-2 (or empty)

...

Slot: Slot-N　Value: Value-N (or empty)

B) Pictorial Form:

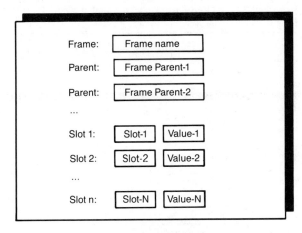

Figure 5.1　The general template for a frame.

where *slot-name* is the name of a slot and *frame-reference* is either the name of a frame or another frame term. The keyword "*of*" is used to separate the slot-name from the frame-reference. A frame term should always be enclosed within parentheses. We may, for instance, write:

(brother of John)

(teacher of John)

A) Written Form:

Slot: Slot name   Value: val (or NO-VALUE)

If-added: Arg A_1,... predicate-1..., Arg A_n

If-needed: Arg B_1,... predicate-2..., Arg B_n

B) Pictorial Form:

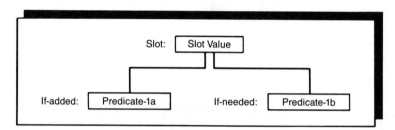

Figure 5.2 The general template for a slot.

Frame:	Name	
Parent:	Frame Parent-1	
Parent:	Frame Parent-2	
...		
Slot:	Slot-1 Value-1	
If-added	Predicate-1a	If-needed: Predicate-1b
Slot:	Slot-2 Value-2	
If-added:	Predicate-2a	If-needed: Predicate-2b

Figure 5.3 A pictorial representation of a frame.

('X' of 'John')

(age of 'X')

('X' of 'Y').

This notation provides a readable format for slot references. For instance, we often request information about a person's telephone number with a statement such as:

Please give me the telephone number of Dean Johnson.

The general form *('X' of 'Y')* is frequently used in natural language to describe the attribute of a frame (consider the five words preceding the left parenthesis of this comment).

The frame term *(Slot of Frame)* is assigned the value of the slot *Slot* in the frame *Frame*. For instance, consider the frames:

Frame: Peter Johnson
Parent: Student
Slot: Teacher   Value: Simon Richards
Slot: Telephone   Value: 123 7654

Frame: Simon Richards
Parent: Staff
Slot: Position   Value: Teacher
Slot: Department   Value: Mathematics
Slot: Office   Value: 321E
Slot: Telephone   Value: 627 3758

The frame term (Teacher of Peter Johnson) will have the value Simon Richards, while the frame term (Telephone of Peter Johnson) will have the value 123 7654.

Frame terms can be used to implement the functions of description and organization in knowledge representation. The term:

(Telephone of Peter Johnson)

describes one of the attributes of Peter Johnson, namely, his telephone number. We can also use frame terms to refer to other frame terms as in:

(Telephone of (Teacher of Peter Johnson))
(Department of (Teacher of Peter Johnson)).

We can use frame terms of this sort to retrieve information during reasoning. Retrieval is only one aspect of the problem in working with frames. We also need methods for storing the information that is later retrieved. How do we express the storage of information in natural language? One way of specifying information is as follows:

> The telephone number is 555 1212

The use of the word "is" generally indicates storage or communication of information, but we could instead have the following use:

> Is the telephone number 555 1212?

In this case the word "is" asks a question that compares the stored value of the telephone number to another number.

In using frames, there is a clear distinction between the processes of *assignment* (storage) and *comparison* (testing). As discussed in Section 3.8, the two predicates:

> $=$ (equality)
> $:=$ (assignment)

are distinct and have different meanings. Thus the clause:

> (Telephone of Peter Johnson) $=$ 123 7654

will succeed, since it is equivalent to the evaluation of:

> 123 7654 $=$ 123 7654

However,

> (Telephone of Peter Johnson) $=$ 888 7654

will fail, since it is equivalent to:

> 123 7654 $=$ 888 7654

However, if we use the assignment predicate, the clause:

> (Telephone of Peter Johnson) $:=$ 888 7654

succeeds and *changes* the telephone number of Peter Johnson. The frame now becomes:

Frame: Peter Johnson
Parent: Student
Slot: Teacher   Value: Simon Richards
Slot: Telephone   Value: 888 7654

Assignment is thus the process of adding or modifying a description within a frame, while comparison is the process of comparing the value of a slot in a frame's description with a particular value.

A great deal of flexibility can be achieved by allowing frame terms and variables to appear in logical statements as part of rules. We may also write:

(Telephone of (Teacher of Peter Johnson)) := 'Z'

'X' := (Telephone of (Teacher of Peter Johnson))

In the first statements we store a value of the variable in a frame slot; in the second statement we retrieve information from a frame slot and assign it to a variable. This example shows that by using a frame term on the *right-hand side* of an assignment, we can retrieve its value; while by using a frame term on the *left-hand side* of an assignment statement we can change its value. Thus there are two ways in which frame terms may appear in assignment statements:

For obtaining the value of a slot.
For assigning a value to a slot.

To obtain the value of a slot, we may use an assignment statement of the form:

'Variable' := Frame-term

In this case, the value of *Frame-term* is found and is assigned to *'Variable'*. To assign a value to a slot, we may use an assignment statement of the form:

Frame-term := Expression.

In this case, the *value of Expression* is found and is assigned to *Frame-term*. We may even use frame terms as both parts of an assignment statement, e.g.,

(age of John) := (age of Mary)

(Telephone of (Teacher of Peter Johnson) := (Telephone of (Teacher of Mary Smith))

We can also use information retrieved from frames to test whether it conforms to a certain value or range of values. Thus we could use an expression such as:

(capacity of Container–1) < 21

The use of assignment and equality statements will, of course, depend on whether the terms are bound. For example, if (Teacher of Peter Johnson) has value Simon Richards and 'X' is unbound, then:

$$(\text{Teacher of Peter Johnson}) = \text{'X'}$$

will bind 'X' to Simon Richards, but:

$$(\text{Teacher of 'Y'}) = \text{Simon Richards}$$

is meaningless if 'Y' is unbound. However, a variable appearing within a frame term may be bound when used within a rule; i.e., we may use clauses of the form:

$$\text{'X'} := (\text{'Y' of 'Z'})$$
$$(\text{'Y' of 'Z'}) := \text{Value}$$

provided 'Y' and 'Z' are bound before evaluation of the clause begins. For instance, we may write a rule involving slots 'S$_1$' and 'S$_2$' of a frame 'Frame' as follows:

> If
>
> <u>swap values 'S$_1$', 'S$_2$', 'Frame'</u>
>
> 'Temp' := ('S$_1$' of 'Frame')
>
> and
>
> ('S$_1$' of 'Frame') := ('S$_2$' of 'Frame')
>
> and
>
> ('S$_2$' of 'Frame') := 'Temp';

This rule will swap the values of slots 'S$_1$' and 'S$_2$' in the frame 'Frame', regardless of the frame, as in Figure 5.4. Note that we need the extra variable 'Temp' to keep track of the value of the frame-term ('S$_1$' of 'Frame') as the swap is being made.

■ 5.4 ORGANIZING KNOWLEDGE IN FRAMES

The general rationale for the use of frames for knowledge organization is to group together related pieces of knowledge within one structure. Many programming languages include record structures which may seem similar to frames. However, frames are much more powerful than records since they allow for inheritance and enable the use of attached predicates, as discussed in Section 5.5.

We can apply frames to a variety of types of knowledge such as general information about people. The information may be about people's age, sex, tele-

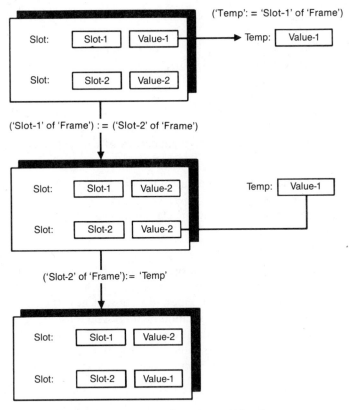

Figure 5.4 Swapping slot values within a frame.

phone, address, etc. Frames can be used to create a general template describing information about a person and to store the description of each person in a separate frame. For example, we may construct a frame:

Frame: Person
Parent: Thing
Slot: Social Security Number   Value:
Slot: Age   Value:
Slot: Sex   Value:
Slot: Address   Value:
Slot: Telephone   Value:

We may then define each specific person as a child of the frame above, e.g.,

Frame: Dean Johnson
Parent: Person

Slot: Social Security Number	Value: 123 45 678
Slot: Age	Value: 25
Slot: Sex	Value: Male
Slot: Address	Value: 11 Second Street
Slot: Telephone	Value: 321 7654

Organization of frames into structures such as hierarchies is useful for two main reasons: (1) information can be inherited in a network or hierarchy and (2) relationships between classes and subclasses of concepts can be made explicit.

The concept "person" refers to a vast number of instances of actual people. Similarly, the concept "hazard" refers to a number of types of hazard. We can organize concepts into taxonomic classes by using frames in a number of applications.

For instance, consider the the emergency feedwater system discussed in Section 4.6.2. This system includes piping structures that transfer water from condensate storage tanks to steam generators and *nodes* which may be *valves, pumps,* and *vessels* interconnected by the pipes. We showed how the connectivity of structures such as pipes and valves could be represented using facts and rules. We can now use frames to describe these pipes and valves. In Section 4.6.2 we used the generic term *"Node"* to refer to devices that are connected by pipes, but now we make further distinctions between these entities using frames.

We represent a *generic gate* with the frame *Gate* and define specific kinds of gates as children of Gate. For instance, a *gate valve* will allow water to flow in both directions, whereas a *check valve* will allow water to flow in only one direction. This distinction is captured in the frame representation shown in Figure 5.5.

Figure 5.5 defines the overall structure of some valves within the emergency feedwater system. We can build frame representations for the nodes shown in Figure 4.19. Part of this representation is shown in Figure 5.6. We can continue to add rules and frames until we have a representation of the emergency feedwater system for trouble shooting, fault diagnosis, and simulation.

5.4.1 Inheritance
As discussed in Section 4.4.3, inheritance in knowledge representation allows for the sharing of information among a set of elements with uniform structure. Frames are organized into a hierarchy or network, with each element at a lower level *inheriting* the properties of the elements at a higher level.

Since frames realize the concept of inheritance, each frame must have at least one *parent*. A frame *inherits* the properties of its parents. A frame may have more than one parent. In this way, we have an *inheritance* network. We say that a frame is a *child* of its parent and is a *descendant* of all frames from which its parent inherits in the inheritance network.

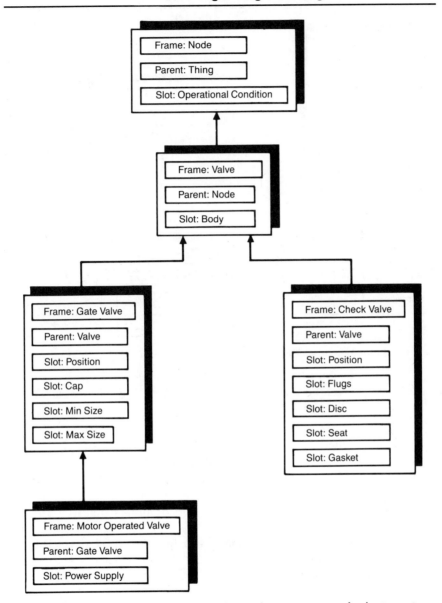

Figure 5.5 Partial frame representation for valves within an emergency feedwater system.

The parent represents a higher-level concept. For instance, Dean Johnson is an instance of the more general concept of person. We can make assumptions about some of the characteristics that Dean Johnson has on the basis of our knowledge about people in general.

At some point, there must be a highest frame in the inheritance network, from which all frames are descended; i.e., any inheritance network needs a highest

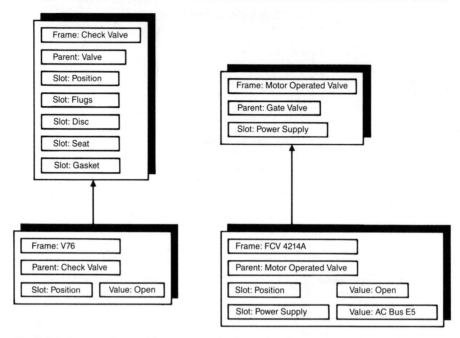

Figure 5.6 Instance frames for two types of valve within the emergency feedwater system.

or root node. We refer to this highest frame as *Thing*. Thing is the only frame with no parent. It also has no slots.

Each frame within the hierarchy, except the top-level frame Thing, may have a number of explicit slots which are defined within the frame itself. Inheritance allows us to define a slot once in some frame and have that slot shared by all the descendants of that frame. This means that:

Definition 1: Each frame includes all the slots of all its parents.

This, in turn, means that each frame will in fact inherit all slots of all its ancestors, since its parents will inherit the slots of their parents, etc. For instance, consider the following frames:

Frame: Person
Parent: Thing
Slot: Age   Value:
Slot: Sex   Value:

Frame: Man
Parent: Person
Slot: Sex   Value: Male

Frame: Woman
Parent: Person
Slot: Sex   Value: Female

Frame: John Smith
Parent: Man
Slot: Age   Value: 25

In this example, the frame Person includes the explicit slots Age and Sex. The frames Man, Woman, and John Smith inherit the slots Age and Sex from their ancestor Person.

Each frame also inherits the values, if any, of inherited slots. This means that the assignment:

'X' := (Sex of John Smith)

will assign the value Male to 'X'; i.e., the frame John Smith inherits the value Male from its parent Man. Thus although the slot Sex is not explicitly defined within the frame John Smith, this slot is implicitly present within the frame by inheritance from Man. The frame Man also implicitly includes a slot Age. The frame John Smith inherits the slot Age from its ancestor Person but inherits no value for Age. If either Sex or Age had any attached predicates, these predicates would have also been inherited by John Smith.

As another example, consider the following frames:

Frame: Car
Parent: Land Vehicle
Slot: Engine Type   Value: Gas-powered

Frame: Ford
Parent: Car
Slot: Wheels   Value: 4

Frame: New Mobile
Parent: Car
Slot: Wheels   Value: 3

In this example, the frame Ford has an explicit slot Wheels. However, the frame Ford also implicitly includes the slot Engine Type with value Gas-powered, since it is a child of the frame Car, and Car includes the slot Engine Type with value Gas-powered. Similarly, the frame New Mobile implicitly includes a slot Engine Type with value Gas-powered.

Thus the assignments:

'X' := (Engine Type of Ford)
'Y' := (Engine Type of New Mobile)

will assign Gas-powered to both 'X' and 'Y'. The assignment:

'A' := (Wheels of New Mobile)

will assign 3 to 'A', since this value is explicitly present within the Frame New Mobile. Figure 5.7 shows how Ford and New Mobile fit into the hierarchy of cars.

5.4.2 Multiple Inheritance

Each frame may have more than one parent. This means that a frame may inherit slots, values, and attached predicates from multiple parents. This is referred to as *multiple inheritance.*

Multiple parents are defined in the same way as single parents, e.g.,

Frame: Hovercraft
Parent: Sea Vehicle
Parent: Land Vehicle
Slot: Maximum Speed   Value:

In this case, the frame Hovercraft will inherit all slots, values, and attached predicates of Sea Vehicle and also all slots, values, and attached predicates of Land Vehicle. In general, given:

Frame: Frame-Name
Parent: Parent1
Parent: Parent2
. . .
Parent: ParentN
Slot: Slot-name   Value:

Frame-Name will inherit from all of Parent1, Parent2, . . . , ParentN. But what happens if two parents include the same slot name? Which do we inherit from first? The issue of which parent should be inherited from first is dealt with differently in different implementations. Some systems forbid multiple inheritance if two parents share a slot name, others select the first slot found, etc.

Multiple inheritance is a powerful feature, but it raises fundamental questions about the circumstances under which a concept may inherit information from more general concepts. Consider the example of the substance mercury. Its function will depend on the application being considered. It can be used in the

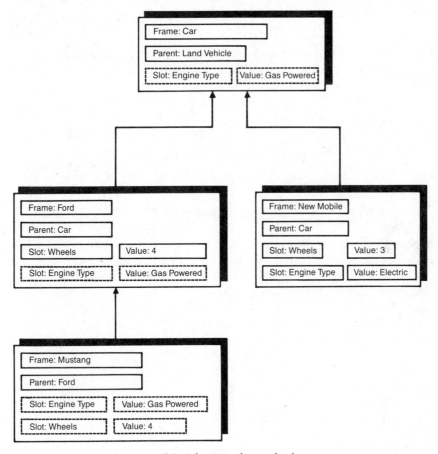

Figure 5.7 Inheriting slots and values.

process of gold refining, in the construction of thermometers, etc. The ability to carry out multiple inheritance places more responsibility on the designer of a frame system to ensure that the information retrieved will be consistent with the current application or context of the system.

5.4.3 Exceptions and Defaults

In many everyday activities, we often assume that events have regular or default behavior, e.g., that all automobiles run on gasoline. However, regular events usually include exceptions. Defaults and exceptions are thus very useful in knowledge representation.

Although frames are useful whenever there are regularly structured circumstances, sometimes there are exceptions to general structures. It is therefore necessary to deal with these as *exceptions*. For instance, conceptually we think that all birds fly; but, in fact, there are a number of species of birds that do not fly.

Frames provide exception handling by allowing the redefinition of the value of an inherited slot. For instance, consider the following frames:

<u>Frame</u>: Bird
<u>Parent</u>: Living Creature
<u>Slot</u>: Has Wings?   <u>Value</u>: yes
<u>Slot</u>: Flies?   <u>Value</u>: yes

<u>Frame</u>: Penguin
<u>Parent</u>: Bird
<u>Slot</u>: Flies?   <u>Value</u>: no

In general, any frame of type Bird should have the value yes for the slot Flies?. However, the frame Penguin has an exception value assigned to its Flies? slot. Thus the value yes is the default value for all Birds, and Penguin is an *exception*. Now consider the following frame:

<u>Frame</u>: Penguin-1
<u>Parent</u>: Penguin
<u>Slot</u>: Age   <u>Value</u>: 3

The assignment

'X' : = (Has Wings? of Penguin-1)

will assign the value yes to 'X', by searching upward to the ancestor frame Bird. However, the assignment

'Y' : = (Flies of Penguin-1)

will assign the value "no" to 'Y', since it will find the value "no" in the immediate Parent of Penguin-1. In this case, once the value "no" is found within the frame Penguin, the search will no longer continue and the frame Bird is not even examined. However, any attached predicates for Bird will still affect Penguin-1.

5.4.4 Modifying Inherited Slots

When the value of a slot in a frame is to be found, we look for that slot name in the frame. If the frame does not include that slot name, we look for the slot name in the parents of that frame. If a parent does not include the slot name, we look at its parent, etc. until either the slot name is found or Thing is reached.

This means that to find the value of a slot, we continue working our way upward in the inheritance tree and look for the slot name. When the slot name is found, we return the appropriate value. But what about modifying the values for inherited slots? Can we use a similar approach to change values of inherited slots? In this case we must be careful to assign the new value not to the ancestor of the frame that appears in an assignment, but to the frame itself.

For instance, consider the following frames:

Frame: Car
Parent: Land Vehicle
Slot: Engine Type   Value: Gas-powered

Frame: Ford
Parent: Car
Slot: Wheels   Value: 4

Frame: Mustang
Parent: Ford
Slot: Price   Value: 15000

If we try to evaluate the clause:

'X' := (Wheels of Mustang)

The following actions should occur in our system:

The frame Mustang is searched for the slot Wheels.
Since Mustang has no slot called Wheels, its parent frame, i.e. Ford, is searched for the slot Wheels.
Ford has a slot called Wheels, and the value 4 is returned.
The value 4 is assigned to 'X'.

Now what if all Mustangs suddenly became electric cars and we had to change the value of the slot Engine Type for all Mustangs, but not for all Fords or for all Cars? What if we needed to perform the assignment:

(Engine Type of Mustang) := Electric

to change the Engine Type of all Mustangs? In this case, the system would act as follows:

1. The frame Mustang is searched for the slot Engine Type.
2. Since Mustang has no slot called Engine Type, its parent frame, i.e., Ford, is searched for the slot Engine Type.

3. Since Ford has no slot called Engine Type, its parent frame, i.e., Car, is searched for in the slot Engine Type.
4. Car has a slot called Engine Type, so the slot assignment is valid.
5. The slot Engine Type is explicitly added to the frame Mustang.
6. The value Electric is given to slot Engine Type of frame Mustang.

Note that the value Electric was not assigned to Car, but to Mustang. Step 5 above is the key step. Here we are actually adding an explicit slot to a frame so that we can modify its value. Steps 2, 3, and 4 above are necessary to determine that:

The slot Engine Type is a valid slot name.

If an attached if-added predicate for Engine Type had existed in the frame Car, it would have been invoked before the assignment of the slot value Electric to Mustang could take place.

The frame Mustang now has the form:

> Frame: Mustang
> Parent: Ford
> Slot: Price   Value: 15000
> Slot: Engine Type   Value: Electric

In this example, the frame Mustang has become an *exception* to all other Fords as far as Engine Type is concerned.

■ 5.5 ATTACHED PREDICATES

Attached predicates monitor the storage and retrieval of information in a frame system. Rules may be attached to the slots of frames using attached predicates. Thus attached predicates allow us to invoke rules from within frames without difficulty.

Attached predicates extend conventional data structuring paradigms by providing *active structures* (cf. our discussion in Section 1.5.1). In this frame-based structuring paradigm, data is no longer passive. In accessing data, or knowledge, rules may be automatically fired, output may be sent to the screen or other devices, etc.

The frame *Address,* for instance, may have an attached predicate that suggests that if the value of the slot *State* is California, the zip code must begin with the number 9. This type of rule can be used to maintain the integrity of the knowledge, so that names of states are always consistent with the zip codes. Because each particular address, e.g., John Smith's address, is an instance of the general structure Address, we would need to assert this rule only once and inherit it for any particular address.

Attached predicates can also assist in making inferences about knowledge that we do not have exact information on. If we have a sphere of known radius, we can use an attached predicate to calculate the volume rather than having to store the information explicitly. Similarly, if we don't know a person's weight, we can use an attached predicate to make an informed guess on the basis of their sex, height, and build. A system that cannot infer information in this way is ineffective in practical applications. Why store the volume of every possible sphere when it can be easily calculated from the radius when needed? The use of one rule obviates the need to store explicitly the radius of every sphere.

Attached predicates provide the concept of trigger, i.e., an action that automatically takes place under certain circumstances. Attached predicates modify the basic structure of frames. Thus, in addition to slots and their values, there may be separate information referring to attached predicates. We show the effect of attached predicates in frames in Figure 5.8.

Attached if-needed predicates are invoked when the value of a slot is retrieved. Attached if-added predicates are invoked when values are assigned to slots. Thus, if-needed predicates monitor *retrieval,* while if-added predicates monitor *storage.*

Whenever the value of a slot is to be retrieved in a statement of the form:

$$'X' := (\text{slot-name of frame-reference})$$

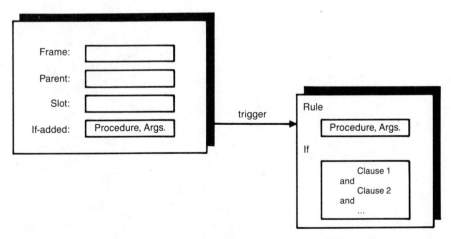

Figure 5.8 A frame with an attached procedure.

the if-needed predicate attached to *slot-name* is invoked and must be proved successfully before the assignment takes place. Similarly, when a value is to be stored in a slot with a statement of the form:

(slot-name of frame-reference) := 'Y'

the if-added predicate attached to *slot-name* is invoked and must be proved successfully before the assignment takes place. When the name of a slot is used as an argument to an attached if-added or if-needed predicate, it represents the value of the slot.

Attached predicates can provide a powerful style of programming. For instance, an attached if-needed predicate may be used for monitoring the behavior of an expert system and may be used as a debugging tool. Whenever the value of a slot is read, the predicate may write a message to the screen. This type of trace, which describes the use of knowledge, might supplement traditional methods that focus on the rules that are being invoked during reasoning.

The use of attached predicates along with inheritance provides a new programming paradigm with a number of benefits. In the next two sections we outline only two of these many applications.

5.5.1 Integrity Maintenance with Attached Predicates
One way to use attached predicates is as guardians for information retrieval and storage. In this mode the predicates restrict the information that may be retrieved from a slot or stored in a slot.

As an example of this type of application of an if-needed predicate, one may restrict access to parts of the data in a frame by defining a password predicate. Consider the following frames:

Frame: Employee
Parent: Person
Slot: Employee Number   Value:
Slot: Salary   Value:
          If-Needed: check password hidden3

Frame: John Smith
Parent: Employee
Slot: Employee Number   Value: 1925364
Slot: Salary   Value: 50000

Here the if-needed predicate check password is attached to the slot Salary in the frame Employee and will be inherited by the frame John Smith. When the value of John Smith's Salary is to be read or obtained through an assignment operation of the form:

'X' : = (Salary of John Smith)

the attached if-needed predicate will be proved as a goal. The following backward rule may then be called by this predicate:

<u>check password</u> 'X'

If

<u>write</u> Please Enter Password and
<u>read</u> 'Y' and
'X' = 'Y' and
<u>write</u> Thank you ;

When invoked, the attached predicate matches 'X' to hidden3 and tries to prove the premise of the rule. The user is prompted for a password value, and the result is compared with *hidden3*. If this test succeeds, the attached predicate succeeds and the salary of John Smith will be retrieved. However, if the test fails, the retrieval operation will also fail.

We can also use *check password* as an if-added predicate to protect the slot Salary from changing without a password of higher level authority. For instance:

<u>Frame:</u> Employee
<u>Parent:</u> Person
<u>Slot:</u> Employee Number   <u>Value:</u>
<u>Slot:</u> Salary   Value:
            If-Needed: <u>check password</u> hidden3
            If-Added: <u>check password</u> mystery4

<u>Frame:</u> John Smith
<u>Parent:</u> Employee
<u>Slot:</u> Employee Number   Value: 1925364
<u>Slot:</u> Salary   Value: 50000

In this case, if the value of John Smith's Salary is to be changed through an assignment operation of the form:

(Salary of John Smith) : = 60000

the attached if-added predicate will be proved as a goal. Thus to obtain the salary, we need to know the password hidden3; however, to change the salary, we need to use the password mystery4.

If-added predicates may also be used to safeguard information storage. For instance, consider the following frame:

> Frame: Employee
> Parent: Person
> Slot: Employee Number   Value:
> Slot: Year of Birth   Value:
>   If-added: check year Year of Birth

The predicate check year checks the validity of an age. Note that in this example, when used as an argument within the attached predicate, the term "Year of Birth" refers to the value of the slot Year of Birth. The attached predicate is defined by:

>   check year 'Year'
> If
>   current year 'Date'
> and
>   'Year' < 'Date'
> and
>   'Year' > 'Date' - 150 ;

Here the predicate current year retrieves the current year from a factbase. The attached predicate then ensures that no employee has negative age and that no employee is more than 150 years old. Thus, if the current year is 1987, an attempt to set an employee's Year of Birth to 1500 or 3000 will fail.

5.5.2 Dynamic Data Management with Attached Predicates

Another mode for using attached predicates is for dynamic information retrieval and storage. In this mode, one may either directly calculate the value of a slot on the basis of other information or dynamically determine the possible range of values for a slot.

For instance, an if-needed predicate may calculate a person's age by retrieving the current date and the birthdate of the person and subtracting the birthdate from the current data to obtain the age. Consider the following frames:

> Frame: Employee
> Parent: Person
> Slot: Employee Number   Value:
> Slot: Year of Birth   Value:
> Slot: Age   Value:
>   If-Needed: calculate age Age, Year of Birth

Frame: John Smith
Parent: Employee
Slot: Employee Number   Value: 1925364
Slot: Year of Birth   Value: 1959
Slot: Age   Value:

The attached predicate calculate age may be defined as a backward rule. For instance:

> If   calculate age 'Age', 'Year'
>
> and   current year 'Date'
>
>   'Age' := 'Date' − 'Year' ;

Here current year is again a predicate that retrieves the current year from the factbase. In this way the value of the slot Age is always dynamically determined. There is no need to update this slot as time changes. This facility may be used in a myriad of applications, such as simulations and strategic analysis.

If-needed predicates may also be used to dynamically determine a range of admissible values for a frame slot during inference. When a user is interacting with an expert system, situations often arise where data needs to be supplied by the user. However, all data values supplied by the user may not be valid, or the user may be unaware of the range of possible answers. The user thus needs to be informed of the acceptable set of possibilities for the value of a slot during inference.

Of course, in some situations, these values may be *predetermined* and displayed to the user when the need arises. However, in many cases, the admissible values are dependent on a number of factors and need to be determined *during* inference. In such cases, attached predicates are very useful since they can invoke rules that *dynamically* determine a set of acceptable values from which the user may select.

For instance, consider a financial expert system that makes investment recommendations to a user. After obtaining some basic data such as age, amount of desired investment, and current tax bracket, the system begins to interact with the user. During the interaction, the user may need to make some decisions or suggestions; e.g., the user may have to suggest a certain type of investment. Not all investments may be applicable to the user, however, and there is little point in showing the user a long and potentially distracting list of investments, many of which are not relevant.

What is needed here is a facility for dynamically determining the suitable investments for an investor and then asking for a choice. For instance, consider-

Frame: Investor
Parent: Person
Slot: Tax Bracket   Value:
Slot: Amount   Value:
Slot: Risk   Value:
Slot: Length   Value:
Slot: Main Investment Type   Value:
If-Needed: get choice Investor, Main Investment Type

Frame: Dean Johnson
Parent: Investor
Slot: Tax Bracket   Value: 30
Slot: Amount   Value: 50000
Slot: Risk   Value: high
Slot: Length   Value: short
Slot: Main Investment Type   Value:

In this example, after Dean Johnson has supplied his current tax bracket, amount of investment, etc., we need to show him a set of possible "Investment Types" (Stocks, Bonds, etc.) to choose from. His choice will then be placed in the slot Main Investment Type.

However, the choices to be displayed will depend on the answers Dean Johnson has provided to the earlier questions, as well as other facts such as the current inflation rate and the current prime interest rate. For instance, there is no point in displaying the choice Real Estate to someone interested in a very short term investment and who wishes to invest a small amount of capital.

To calculate the value of the slot, we simply perform an assignment involving the slot Main Investment Type. The predicate get choice will then calculate the possible values based on its other arguments. The assignment:

'X' := (Main Investment Type of Dean Johnson)

will thus invoke the predicate:

get choice Dean Johnson, Main Investment Type

which will may select a number of options. This predicate may be defined by:

get choice 'Investor', 'Investment'
If

for-every 'Investor' should invest in 'X'
do display investment 'X'
and

get user selection 'Investment' ;

Here, the clause *'Investor' should invest in 'X'* may itself be defined with a set of investment rules, such as those defined in Chapters 3 and 4. The clause *display investment 'X'* displays the suitable investments on the screen in a pop-up menu, etc., and the clause *get user selection 'Investment'* will select one of the displayed choices.

The key point of this example is that the investment choices displayed in the *pop-up* menu are *dynamically determined during a consultation based on a set of rules* and are different for each investor. Attached predicates thus allow us to have dynamic menus whose contents are not fixed before the execution of the program begins, but are dynamically adjusted with a set of rules.

5.5.3 Slot Names in Attached Predicates

Attached predicates often need to either use or refer to the values of some of the slots within a frame. In order to use attached predicates, we need conventions for referring to existing slot values within a frame and to new values that may be assigned to the slot.

For instance, consider the following frames:

Frame: Document
Parent: Thing
Slot: Classification   Value:
Slot: Location   Value:
        If-Needed: check class Classification

Frame: Business Plan
Parent: Document
Slot: Classification   Value: classified
Slot: Location   Value: File 321

First, note that the if-needed predicate check class is inherited by the frame Business Plan, since Business Plan is a type of Document. We may define the if-needed predicate check class with a backward rule such as:

            check class 'X'
    If
            not 'X' = classified
    or
            check password hiddenpass;

This rule checks whether the value of the slot Classification is equal to classified. If not, the rule succeeds, or else the predicate check password is invoked to ask for a password.

Within the frame definition, the attached predicate should be able to include the value of the slot *Classification*. To represent this value, we simply use the slot name Classification. For instance, the term Classification listed above is used as an argument to the predicate check class. In this case, Classification represents the value of the slot Classification within the frame, i.e., *classified*.

We must be careful in assigning values to slots to avoid the danger of confusing the current value of the slot and the new value that is being assigned to the slot. Suppose that we tried to enforce the condition that the salary of an employee can never decrease, i.e., that whenever the value of the slot Salary for an employee is changed, the new value must be greater than the current value. We must then distinguish between the old value for the slot Salary and its new value.

We may use the term *New-Value* as an argument to an if-added predicate to refer to the new value being assigned to a slot. The current value of the slot is referred to with the slot name. For instance, consider the frames:

> Frame: Employee
> Parent: Person
> Slot: Salary   Value:
>   If-added: check salary New-Value, Salary

> Frame: John Smith
> Parent: Employee
> Slot: Salary   Value: 50000

The predicate check salary may be defined by:

>   check salary 'New', 'Old'
>   If
>   'New' > 'Old'
>   or
>   issue failure message;

where issue failure message can fail after writing a message, e.g.,

>   issue failure message
>   If
>   write "Sorry. Salaries can only increase."
>   and
>   fail;

Note again that the if-added predicate check salary is inherited from Employee by John Smith. Now if we try to change the salary of John Smith with an assignment of the form:

> (Salary of John Smith) : = 60000

the if-added predicate check salary is invoked. When the if-added predicate is invoked, the value of Salary is 50000. However, the value of New-Value is now 60000. Thus in this case, we try to prove the goal:

$$60000 > 50000$$

and succeed. The value of the slot Salary in the frame John Smith will then be changed to 60000. However, if we had tried the assignment:

$$(\text{Salary of John Smith}) := 40000$$

we would have had to prove the inequality:

$$40000 > 50000$$

which would fail after writing an error message. The assignment statement would then fail and the value of the slot Salary in the frame John Smith would remain unchanged at 50000.

When the term New-Value is used in an if-added predicate, it refers only to the slot to which the appropriate predicate is attached. Thus we may use the term New-Value several times within a frame as arguments to if-added predicates for different slots without conflict.

▪ 5.6   A COMPUTATIONAL VIEW OF FRAMES

Although the concept of frames is straightforward and intuitive, we should also have a formal definition of how a frame system behaves from an algorithmic point of view. We now outline a formal definition of how a frame system deals with storage and retrieval. Because of the existence of inheritance and attached predicates, the efficient implementation of such algorithms is often nontrivial. Readers not interested in the algorithmic details of a frame system may skip this section.

The assignment predicate provides access to values of slots in frames. We obtain the value of a slot by an assignment of the form:

$$\textit{'Variable'} := \textit{(Slot-name of Frame-reference)}$$

where *Frame-reference* is either a frame name, e.g., *John Smith,* or a frame term, e.g., (teacher of John Smith). To perform the assignment, we follow these steps:

a. *Find Slot*

   a1. If *Frame-reference* is a simple frame term, i.e., simply a frame name, we search for the slot *Slot-name* within this frame, and if found, we proceed with step **c** below. If the slot is not found, we move to step **b** below.

a2. If *Frame-reference* is a compound frame reference of the form (*Slot2 of Reference2*), we obtain the frame (Slot2 of Reference2) recursively according to this algorithm and proceed with step **c** below.

b. *Check Inheritance*

We look for the slot *Slot-name* in the parents of the frame, and if not found there, we continue searching in their parents (and ancestors) by moving further up the inheritance network. We perform this operation for all parents of the frame until the slot is found. If *Thing* is reached and the slot may not be found, the search fails. If the slot is found in some parent or ancestor, we move to step **c**.

c. *If-needed*

c1. If the slot *Slot-name* has an attached if-needed predicate we try to prove the if-needed predicate as a goal. If the predicate succeeds we return the value of the slot, if any. The value of the slot may in fact be determined by the if-needed predicate.

c2. If the slot *Slot-name* has no attached if-needed predicate, we try to find an if-needed predicate for its parent, then its parent's parent, and so on. If an if-needed predicate is found in any ancestor, it is treated according to step **c1** above. If no if-needed predicate exists, we continue with the retrieval operation.

Values of slots are assigned by statements of the form:

Frame-reference := *Expression*.

or

Frame-reference := *Frame-reference1*.

The steps taken for performing this operation are as follows:

a. *Evaluate Expression*

First, *Expression or Frame reference1* is evaluated to obtain a value, say, *Value*. *Frame reference1* is evaluated according to the retrieval algorithm described above. If the right-hand side of the assignment has no value, the assignment fails.

b. *Find Slot*

b1. If *Frame-reference* is a simple frame term, i.e., simply a frame name, we search for the slot *Slot-name* within this frame, and if this slot found locally, we continue to step **d** below. If the slot is not found, we move to step **c** below.

b2. If *Frame-reference* is a compound reference of the form (*Slot2 of Reference2*), we find the frame (*Slot2 of Reference2*) recursively according to the retrieval algorithm and proceed with step **d**.

c. *Check Inheritance*

We look for the slot in the parents of the frame, and if the information is not found there, we look in the corresponding slot of their parents and ancestors, until the slot value is found. If *Thing* is reached and the slot may not be found the search fails. Otherwise, we move to step **(d)**. If the slot is found in an ancestor of the frame, we shall explicitly "add" the slot to the frame itself.

d. *If-added*

d1. If the slot has an attached if-added predicate we try to prove the if-added predicate as a goal, treating the term "New-Value" as the value "Value" found in step **a** above. If the predicate succeeds, we continue to step **e** below; otherwise, the assignment fails as a whole.

d2. If the slot has no attached if-added predicate, we try to find an if-added predicate among its parents, then their parents and ancestors, etc. When found, the if-added predicate is treated according to step **d1** above.

e. *Assign Value*

If the attached predicate has succeeded, we assign Value to the slot. If the frame does not explicitly include a slot for the assignment, but had inherited the slot, we now explicitly "add" the slot to the frame locally, before the assignment takes place.

These algorithms define the basic storage and retrieval operations on frames. They may be implemented in a variety ways to integrate frames with rules or conventional languages.

■ 5.7 LOGICAL OPERATIONS ON FRAMES

The previous sections showed how information can be stored and retrieved within frames by using frame-terms, assignment statements, and attached predicates. The mechanism used for storing and retrieving information in slots involves *assignment clauses* that may be directly used in rules and attached predicates. Thus in discussing frames, we have already entered the realm of logic.

However, a full range of other logical operations may be performed on frames to provide further flexibility. This means that we can define a set of *built-in* logical predicates that operate on frames. Such predicates facilitate the complete integration of frames and logic.

One such class of predicates allows for the dynamic management of frames during inference. A knowledge base may, of course, include a number of pre-defined frames and slots that are determined before inference begins. However, in many applications we need the creation or modification of the frames *during inference.*

New frames can be created dynamically by using the clause:

> new-frame Frame-Name, Parent

which creates a new frame named Frame-Name that has a parent named Parent, while frames may be deleted with:

> delete-frame Frame-Name

For instance,

> new-frame Electrical Hazard, Hazard

specifies the creation of a new frame of the form

> Frame: Electrical Hazard
> Parent: Hazard

Electrical Hazard will, of course, inherit all the properties of Hazard, but local slots can also be dynamically added as they are needed with:

> add-slot Frame-Name, Slot-Name.

For instance, the clause:

> add-slot Electrical Hazard, Voltage

will succeed and will result in the frame:

> Frame: Electrical Hazard
> Parent: Hazard
> Slot: Voltage   Value:

Such predicates provide frames with a very dynamic flavor that is useful in applications such as simulation. Further, to distinguish between temporary and permanent knowledge, we use logical predicates such as delete-new-frames, which delete all new frames created during execution but do not delete permanent frames.

However, we may also wish to deal with the properties of frames during inference. The predicates *is-a* and *has-a* provide such facilities. These predicates correspond to the way that we organize knowledge as it is often expressed in natural language. Consider statements such as:

> A bond has a maturity date.
>
> A person has a Social Security number.
>
> Ralph is a lawyer.
>
> A Mustang is a Ford.

The first two statements refer to the possession of properties or attributes, while the last two are examples of belonging to a type. We represent these general concepts by using the following corresponding clauses:

> Bond has-a Maturity date
>
> Person has-a Social Security number
>
> Ralph is-a lawyer
>
> Mustang is-a Ford.

Thus the predicate has-a reflects the relationship between a frame and its slots, while the predicate is-a reflects the relationship between a frame and its ancestors. The clause:

> Frame has-a Slot

thus determines whether the frame Frame has a slot Slot. To ask the question "What kind of properties does a bond have?" we can prove the goal

> Bond has-a 'X'

which will bind 'X' to Maturity date. Similarly, to ask the question "What kind of thing is a Mustang?" we can prove the goal:

> Mustang is-a 'Y'

which will bind 'Y' to Ford. In general, the clause:

> 'Frame' is-a 'Ancestor'

succeeds if 'Frame' is an ancestor of 'Ancestor'. The predicate is-a may thus be used for general searches in the inheritance network and will find an ancestor–descendant relationship across any number of levels in the network. In some cases, however, we may want to test only whether one frame is the *immediate* parent of another. This type of search can be carried out by using the predicate has-parent which, like is-a, is sufficiently important to be built into the basic frame system. The clause:

'Frame' has-parent 'Parent'

succeeds only if 'Parent' is an *immediate* parent of 'Frame'. For instance, consider the following frames:

Frame: Employee
Parent: Person
Slot: Employee Number   Value:
Slot: Salary   Value:

Frame: Manager
Parent: Employee
Slot: Department   Value:

Frame: Dean Richards
Parent: Manager
Slot: Employee Number   Value:

The following clause will have the indicated truth values:

Manager is-a Employee   succeeds
Dean Richards is-a Employee   succeeds
Employee is-a Manager   fails

Employee has-a Employee Number succeeds
Dean Richards has-a Salary   succeeds
Employee has-a Department   fails

Logical predicates may even allow the bypassing of some underlying frame operations. For instance, suppose that we have a Frame that has an attached if-needed predicate:

Frame: Frame-Name
Parent: Parent-Name
Slot: Slot-Name   Value:
      If-Needed: predicate-name Slot-Name.

In this case, the slot Slot-Name may or may not have a value. But how can we determine whether the slot has a value? Of course, one way is to use the clause:

(Slot-Name of Frame-Name) = NO-VALUE.

But as we evaluate the frame-term *(Slot-Name of Frame-Name),* we will trigger the attached predicate predicate-name, which may calculate a value for the slot. This defeats our purpose of checking whether the slot originally had a value. The logical predicate:

has-value Frame-Name, Slot-Name

may be used to test whether Slot-Name has a value, without triggering the attached if-needed predicate. The predicate succeeds if the value is different from NO-VALUE but does not trigger the attached procedure.

■ 5.8 CONNECTING RULES AND FRAMES

To have a totally integrated system for knowledge representation and inference, we need to connect frames with rules and rules with frames. The connection should work in both directions, i.e., from frames to rules and from rules to frames. Although integration of frames and rules is possible, some skill is required in deciding which knowledge to incorporate within frames and which knowledge to include within rules.

Working in the first direction (from frames to rules), frames can have rules (known as attached predicates) that control the storage and retrieval of information. This allows us to maintain the integrity of knowledge and provides for dynamic information management, as discussed in Sections 5.5.1 and 5.5.2. In a hybrid system, though, it will be natural to go in the second direction (from rules to frames) during inference and to use logic predicates to control reasoning and to use frames as an intelligent database that maintains the knowledge required for reasoning.

The storage and retrieval properties of frames make them a good way of implementing an intelligent database. Many expert systems have to rely heavily on intelligent data management. An integrated rule–frame system is an ideal environment for intelligent data management. In general, it is more convenient to define knowledge management issues within frames and inference issues within rules. However, the integration of rules and frames often raises practical issues about whether to use frames that call rules or rules that call frames in particular situations.

We may freely combine rules and frames within computations in a hybrid system such as the one we have presented. This system provides a powerful and flexible method for building knowledge-bases, but it also places a responsibility on the knowledge engineer or expert to ensure that there is a clear conceptual distinction between inference and retrieval processes. This distinction can then be used to guide in choosing which knowledge to describe in frames, which knowledge to describe in rules, and how to link the rule and frame representations together.

One may, in fact, go to the extreme of performing all inference as side effects from within a frame structure by using attached predicates. However, this results in a tangled architecture for an expert system, which is not only difficult to understand and maintain but is also inefficient. In our view, attached predicates should be devoted to the purpose of storing and retrieving data. Nondatabase actions and reasoning should be carried out with logic. This separation between knowledge maintenance and reasoning provides conceptual clarity in knowledge representation, resulting in knowledge bases that are easier to understand, maintain, and work with.

5.8.1 Rules that Act on Frames

One advantage of linking frames and logic is that the frame system can be customized to taste or to the demands of a particular application by writing addition predicates if an alternative syntax was preferred. To specify that the age of Ralph is 24, we write:

(Age of Ralph) : = 24.

But a user familiar with the syntax used in other frame systems such as FRL (Roberts and Goldstein, 1977) may wish to create a different syntax to say:

put slot Ralph, Age, 24

by defining a put slot predicate with

If

          put slot 'Frame', 'Slot', 'Value'

          ('Slot' of 'Frame') : = 'Value';

Thus rules may be used to customize the syntax of the frame system. However, rules that operate on frames do much more than modify syntax. The logical and extralogical predicates defined in Chapter 3 may be effectively used to perform a number of operations on frames. In such applications the control quantifiers discussed in Section 3.8.1 are particularly useful.

For instance, consider the definition of the predicate show descendants, which shows all descendants of a particular frame:

<pre>
            show descendants 'Frame'
If
            for-every 'X' is-a 'Frame'
            do write 'X', " is a descendant of ", 'Frame' ;
</pre>

We may in fact show all frames by proving the goal "show descendants Thing." Similarly, we may show all slots of a frame with:

<pre>
            show slots 'Frame'
If
            for-every 'Frame' has-a 'X'
            do write 'X', " is a slot of ", 'Frame' ;
</pre>

"For-every" statements may refer to each other. For instance, to find all frames which have a slot with the value 'Value,' we may define:

<pre>
            show values 'Value'
If
            for-every 'Frame' is-a Thing
            do search for value 'Frame', 'Value' ;

            search for value 'Frame', 'Value'
If
            for-every 'Frame' has-a 'Slot'
            do check for value 'Frame', 'Slot', 'Value' ;

            check for value 'Frame', 'Slot', 'Value'
If
            ('Slot' of 'Frame') = 'Value'
and
            write 'Frame', " includes the value ", 'Value', " in ",
            'Slot' ;
</pre>

These are just some examples of how logic may be used to operate on frames. In principle, any variable in a rule may refer to a frame, and we may freely use the inference engine to operate on the frame and inheritance structure.

5.8.2 Frames that Trigger Rules

As an example of how frames may activate rules, consider how we may dynamically create a set of frames that trigger rules as part of a rule-based simulation system. In this example, we illustrate the essential elements of a rule-and-frame-based simulation of a business where a number of "customers" are *serviced* by a number of "servers."

A top-level frame *Simulation* manages the base simulation data:

Frame: Simulation
Parent: Thing
Slot: Current Time   Value:
Slot: Customer-Total   Value:
Slot: Customers-Active   Value:
Slot: Server-Total   Value:
Slot: Servers-Active   Value:

We represent generic servers and customer with the following frames:

Frame: Server
Parent: Thing
Slot: Customer AssignmentValue:
Slot: Status   Value:
        If-Needed: provide trace Server, Requested Service
        If-Added: check status Server, New-Value

Frame: Customer
Parent: Thing
Slot: Requested Service   Value:
Slot: Status   Value:
        If-Needed: provide trace Customer, Requested Service
        If-Added: check status Customer, New-Value

To identify distinct customers, we assign a number to each customer. We can make customer names such as Customer–1, Customer–2, . . . , Customer-N by concatenating a number to the string "Customer-":

        make a new customer 'N', 'New Customer'
    If
        concatenate "Customer-", 'N', 'New Name'
    and
        new-frame 'New Name', Customer;

where 'N' is the customer number and concatenate is a built-in predicate that concatenates strings, e.g., *concatenate a, b, 'X'* binds 'X' to *ab*. To simulate a business, we create customers with:

        create customer
    If
        generate a number 'N'
    and
        make a new customer 'N', 'New Customer'

and
>
> set characteristics 'New Customer' ;
>
> generate a number 'N'

If
>
> 'Total' : = (Customer-Total of Simulation)

and
>
> 'N' : = 'Total' + 1

and
>
> (Customer-Total of Simulation) : = 'N' ;

Here *(Customer-Total of Simulation)* refers to a value in the frame Simulation, which manages the simulation environment as a whole. The predicate set characteristics sets the characteristics of a customer by selecting a type of service at random or based on some statistical formulas.

In this example, the attached predicate *provide trace 'Customer', 'Requested Service'* provides a trace of the system activity as customer status values are checked. The attached predicate *check status 'Customer', New-Value* is used to modify the state of the system as the status of a customer changes. The fact that these attached predicates are inherited by all frames makes the simulation much easier to manage.

The simulation activity can be simply managed by an event manager that, at given intervals, creates customers, advances time by modifying a slot value, and then proves a goal of the form:

>
> perform activities

If
>
> For-every 'Customer' needs service
> do perform service 'X' ;

which is invoked at given time intervals. Here *'Customer' needs service* is defined by:

>
> 'Customer' needs service

If
>
> 'Customer' is-a Customer

and
>
> 'Status' : = (Status of 'Customer')

and
>
> not 'Status' = Service-Completed;
>
> perform service 'Customer'

If

      'Request Type' : = (Requested Service of 'Customer')

and

      <u>find server for</u> 'Request Type', 'Server'

and

      <u>perform function</u> 'Request Type', 'Server';

The predicates <u>find server for</u> may be similarly defined to find a frame server that can perform the required service, and the predicate <u>perform function</u> may be defined to assign that server to the customer for a certain amount of time. These predicates may be defined in different ways by the user to experiment with different scheduling methods.

This example also illustrates how the same concept may be represented in different ways. We may choose to deal with time either with a set of clauses of the form:

Server–1 <u>deals with</u> Customer–5, Time–1, Time–2

which are managed in a factbase and are updated with assertions and retractions. Alternatively, we may add the slots *Begin-Time* and *End-Time* to the frames Customer and Server. The choice of which knowledge representation method is more appropriate depends on the application for which the simulation is constructed.

■ 5.9 EVALUATING THE INTEGRATED RULE AND FRAME SYSTEM

We have presented a hybrid knowledge representation method based on rules and frames. We have, however, kept rules and frames as two distinct components that can be combined in a number of ways.

In Chapter 4 we discussed the essential features that a good method of knowledge representation should have. We will now evaluate the integrated method of representing knowledge in terms of rules and frames using these guidelines. The guidelines covered four general issues:

    a. The quality of basic knowledge structures.
    b. The quality of storage mechanisms.
    c. The quality of retrieval mechanisms.
    d. The quality of the knowledge representation environment.

Each of these general issues leads to a number of evaluative questions:

A. *The Quality of Basic Knowledge Structures*
    1. What is the basic vocabulary of the knowledge representation?
        The basic vocabulary is defined by the user, who can define predicates and frames as deemed appropriate. Thus the basic vocabulary is exten-

sible and can be customized to the needs of the user. Further, the syntax is English-like and readable.

2. How modular is the representation?

Rules are generally recognized as being fairly modular structures, while the hierarchical organization of frames assists the developer in ensuring that the right information gets stored in the right place. Part of the art of building a frame system is in storing information as high in the hierarchy as possible so that changes get propagated through the relevant frames, but not so high that unrelated frames are improperly affected.

Modularity of rules is an important issue, but it is more the style in which rules are used rather than the basic nature of the rules themselves that determines their modularity.

3. Can knowledge be represented at multiple levels of detail?

Hierarchies of frames are flexible knowledge structures that can represent knowledge at any level of detail that is required.

4. Is the basic form of the knowledge structure easily understood by someone reading through the coded knowledge?

Frames and rules correspond closely to the manner in which people think. Frames, for instance, are closely related to the schemas or packages of information that have frequently been observed in human long-term memory. Rules, on the other hand, have frequently been observed in the way that experts describe the way in which they solve problems. The syntax we use for frames and rules may be easily read through and understood by nonprogrammers.

The integrated system thus scores highly on the issues relating to the adequacy of the basic knowledge structures.

B. *The Quality of Storage Mechanisms*

1. Can new knowledge be linked to old in a way that is consistent with the overall structure of the knowledge?

The frame system we have discussed allows for the dynamic addition of new frames and slots. Frame hierarchies encourage the interpretation and storage of new knowledge in terms of existing knowledge.

We may use procedural abstraction, as discussed in Section 3.7, to extend the definition of concepts expressed as rules.

2. What mechanisms are available for organizing knowledge?

The use of parent-child relationships between frames can create arbitrarily complex networks and hierarchies. Rules may be gathered and organized in rule sets or be managed with a hierarchy of frames that trigger them.

3. Can the structures that are used to organize the knowledge be updated reasonably easily?

Frames can be updated by creating new slots, changing the information within a slot, or even removing frames and creating new ones. A major feature of frames is that they can be modified during reasoning by having rules operate on them directly.

4. Is it possible to distinguish between permanent and temporary knowledge?

   The logical predicates retract-all-new (Section 3.5) and delete-new-frames, (Section 5.7) achieve this goal. The distinction between permanent and temporary knowledge may also be maintained by the designer of the knowledge-base. Permanent knowledge within frames can be protected from removal or alteration by writing if-added predicates that prevent modification except under special circumstances.

   The storage mechanisms thus provide all the ingredients expected from a knowledge representation method.

C. *The Quality of Retrieval Mechanisms*

1. What kind of retrieval is possible?

   Direct retrieval of information, default retrieval with attached predicates, exceptions, and inheritance are all implemented in the frame system. Further, we may retrieve information stored with predicates by pattern matching.

2. Can the knowledge structures be browsed over or reviewed during the updating or debugging of the knowledge-base?

   A knowledge-base editor with a *master scope* may be used to find frame definitions dynamically, as well as using standard methods of tracing or visual examination.

3. Can rules that need knowledge during inference call the knowledge-base directly to get it?

   Section 5.8 illustrates this point by discussing how frames and rules may interact.

   Retrieval is therefore a strong feature of our hybrid knowledge representation method.

D. *The Quality of the Knowledge Representation Environment*

1. Can the knowledge representation method handle the size of knowledge base that the application demands?

   The rule-based system relies on dynamic indices for efficient storage and retrieval. The frame-based system uses a virtual frame management system, which also uses dynamic indices, as well as cached storage. This provides highly efficient performance even on microcomputers.

2. Can the knowledge representation method itself be modified or extended?

   In Section 5.8 we showed how the frame system may be extended by defining additional predicates.

3. How efficient is the representation?

   As discussed in question 1 above, since the system is implemented in a conventional language, it enjoys a high level of efficiency in execution speed. Further, information is only stored in one place and is inherited as necessary, leading to space efficiency.

4. How easy is it to use the knowledge in reasoning?

   The examples presented in Section 5.8 show that frames may be easily called from rules and can trigger rules. It is thus very easy to use knowledge in reasoning.

Thus the system fares very well in terms of the guidelines. Further, the system we have described is not part of a hypothetical wish list. It has been fully implemented in the C programming language as part of the Intelligence/Compiler system and may be efficiently executed on microcomputers.

▪ 5.10 FRAMES, RULES AND RELATIONAL DATABASES

Technological advances have provided us with large amounts of disk space available at very low cost. Day and night, from the Silicon Valley to the far east, disk manufacturers are busy producing disks. Somehow, one of the laws of nature seems to dictate that: "Free disk space absorbs data." Thus, the amount of data in databases is rapidly increasing, matched only by the increase in the number of databases. The proliferation of laser disks will merely accelerate the data glut problem. Without intelligent and automated tools for data analysis, the percentage of large database owners who are unaware of the contents of their databases and the characteristics of the data will increase rapidly.

It is natural to try and apply the technology of expert systems to these large databases. There is a tremendous amount of valuable knowledge locked up in these databases that no one has the time to discover. To capture such knowledge we need to be able to interface expert systems with databases.

While the data glut problem is likely to continue for the foreseeable future, those who use intelligent tools to understand the data will be able to make more effective decisions. Data glut should therefore be viewed as an "opportunity" and not as a problem. Efforts should thus focus on intelligent programs which may be routinely used to analyze massive amounts of data.

There are two distinct avenues to pursue here:

a. Use expert systems which access the data in a large database.
b. Use intelligent programs which analyze large databases and discover knowledge, i.e., *machine learning*.

Case **a** is currently the most prevalent method for using expert systems in conjunction with databases. In many cases, an expert system is essentially acting as an intelligent retrieval system for the database. Case **b** is likely to capture attention soon, with the proliferation of machine learning technology.

The pay-offs from the machine learning approach of case **b** are likely to be significant. Even if we manage to provide a fraction of database users with hidden knowledge from their databases, we will achieve a substantial level of productivity increase within society as a whole.

To integrate expert systems and databases, we need a uniform approach to data management and knowledge management. In Section 5.10.1 we discuss how relational databases may be uniformly merged with our integrated rule and frame formalism.

5.10.1 Mapping Frames and Logic to Databases

As discussed in appendix D, the relational data model views the world in terms of *relations* which are essentially tables. We often use the term table, instead of relation. Each entry has a value for each attribute. Each table has a *schema,* which lists its *attributes* or *fields.* The relation, or table, is obtained by providing instances, entries or *records* for the schema. Further, each entry or record has a record number which uniquely identifies it.

A simple example of a table is the table shown in Figure 5.9. In this relation, *T1* is the table name, *Father* and *Child* are the two attribute names and *1, 2* and *3* are three record numbers. In this table, [John, Mary], [Paul, John] and [David, Paul] are records.

Thus the basic terms for describing relations are:

Schemas: which consist of a table name and a lists of attributes.
Records: which provide values for each attribute in a schema.
Record numbers: which uniquely identify records.

A schema is sometimes also called a *view.* As discussed in appendix D, the *Relational Algebra* provides operations on views. Some such operations (e.g. joins) modify both schemas and tables, while others, (e.g. select) only modify the table contents.

Relational databases are closely related to predicate logic (Gallaire and Minker, 1978; Kowalski, 1981; Warren, 1981; Parsaye, 1983a, b, c). Predicate logic views the world in terms of *clauses* which include *predicates* and *arguments,* as discussed in Chapter 3. A predicate is a verb or concept which relates its arguments.

A *clause schema* consists of a predicate name and an integer, indicating the number of arguments of the predicate. Each argument in a clause may be a constant or a variable. A clause whose arguments are all constants is called a

T₁

	Father	Child
1	John	Mary
2	Paul	John
3	David	Paul
	...	...

Figure 5.9   A simple relational table.

fact. Two facts have the same predicate schema if they have the same predicate name and the same number of arguments.

Viewed in this way, each clause schema may have a number of instances or facts. Each fact has a value for each argument. Each fact also has a fact number which uniquely identifies it. For instance, we may have:

Clause schema: <u>father</u> Argument₁, Argument₂

Facts:

<u>father</u> John, Mary
<u>father</u> Paul, John
<u>father</u> David, Paul

Thus the basic terms here are:

Clause schemas: which have a predicate name and a list of arguments.
Facts: which are a list of values for each argument in a clause schema.
Fact numbers: which uniquely identify facts.

The analogy with relational databases should now be clear. Predicates correspond to table names, arguments to attributes and facts to records.

Earlier in this chapter, we used the notation *John is-the father-of Mary* rather than *father John, Mary*. Both notations are acceptable. We have chosen the second notation in this section in order to illustrate the correspondence between predicates and tables.

We may operate on clauses by using rules. Thus the rule:

P(A1, . . . , An)

If

Q(A1, . . . , Am) and
R(B1, . . . , Bm);

means that P is true if both Q and R are true. If Q and R are two tables, the rule defines a *virtual table* for P. This point was discussed before in Section 3.8.1 and was illustrated in Figure 3.6. In this sense, rules provide us with *virtual relations*. Thus rules may be viewed as a generalization of relations.

By using rules in conjunction with databases, we may perform logical operations such as integrity checking on the database. For instance, to ensure that each person has at most one father, we may write:

has duplicate father 'X'

If

father 'X', 'F1'

and

father 'X', 'F2'

and

not 'F1' = 'F2' ;

As discussed in Section 3.8.1, we should also be able to interface rules to conventional languages and database systems. To do so, we use a built-in (or user defined) predicate which interfaces to a database system. For instance, to use a commercial product such as dBASE-III™, ORACLE™ (or any other relational database management system), we use a predicate *dbase* or *oracle* which reads dBASE-III or ORACLE databases. For instance, if the names of father are in a dBASE database, we define:

father 'A', 'B'

If

dbase fathers, father-field, child-field;

where the clause *dbase fathers, father-field, child-field* retrieves data from a dBASE file such as father.dbf.

Relational databases are related not only to logic, but to frames. As discussed earlier in this chapter, frame, or object oriented systems, view the world in terms of objects or *frames*. A frame is a conceptual entity which has a number of *slots*. Each slot in a frame may have a value. We call the slots in a frame the *frame schema*. A slot and its value may be *inherited* from a parent.

Each frame may have a number of *instances*. An instance of a frame is another frame which has the same slots as the frame and has a value for each slot. An instance has an instance identifier, or instance number. An instance will inherit all value present in its parent frame, unless explicitly over-ridden.

Note that the concept of *instance* is specifically used to separate instances from frames. Thus while frames may have children, instances cannot. To display instances, we use a notation very similar to our frame notation and use an instance identifier to distinguish between instances. For example, the following is a simple frame with some instances:

Frame: Person
Parent: Thing
Slot: Name   Value:
Slot: Father   Value:

Instance: 1
Parent: Person
Slot: Name   Value: Mary
Slot: Father   Value: John

Instance: 2
Parent: Person
Slot: Name   Value: John
Slot: Father   Value: Paul

Instance: 3
Parent: Person
Slot: Name   Value: Paul
Slot: Father   Value: David

Thus the basic concepts here are:

Frames: which include slots and values.

Instances: which are a list of values for each slot in a parent frame.

Instance identifiers: which uniquely identify frame instances.

Again the relationship between frames and relational databases is clear. Frame names correspond to table names, slots to attributes and instances to records.

Further, we now have a three way mapping (Figure 5.10) between tables, predicates and frames as follows:

Relational Databases	Frames	Logic
Schema	Frame schema	Clause schema
Attribute	Slot	Argument
Value	Value	Value
Record	Instance	Fact

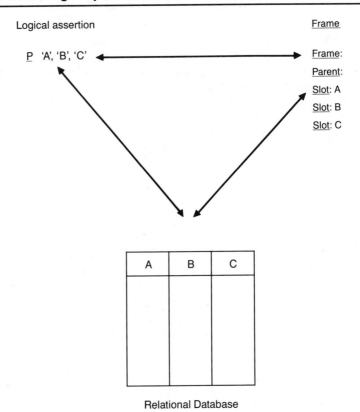

Figure 5.10 The relationship between logic, frames and relational databases.

Just as rules extend relational databases by providing virtual tables, frames extend relational databases by providing virtual attributes and virtual values. When an instance inherits a value, the value is kept only once in the parent frame, but is shared among all records.

Further, we may use attached predicates to perform logical operations on databases. An obvious application is the use of attached predicates as database integrity guardians.

> Frame: Employee
> Parent: Thing
> Slot: Name   Value:
> Slot: Department   Value:
> Slot: Manager   Value:
>   If-Added: check department Name, Department, New-
> Value

For instance, to ensure that an employee's manager has the same department as the employee, we may write rules of the form:

If
<u>check department</u> 'Name', 'Dept', 'Manager'

and
'M-dept': = (Department of 'Manager')

or
'M-dept' = 'Dept'

<u>write error message</u> 'M-dept', 'Dept' ;

<u>write error message</u> 'M-dept', 'Dept'

If

and
<u>write</u> 'Dept' " conflicts with ", 'M-dept'

<u>fail</u> ;

Again, we should be able to use this symbolic computation technology with existing databases. One way to do this is to define frames as *parents* of existing database files with the use of a special frame (say dBASE, or ORACLE) which knows about the relevant database operations. For instance:

<u>Frame</u>: Employee
<u>Parent</u>: Thing
<u>Parent</u>: dBASE
<u>Slot</u>: database-File   Value: <u>EMP.DBF</u>
<u>Slot</u>: Name   Value:
<u>Slot</u>: Department   Value:
<u>Slot</u>: Manager   Value:
       If-Added: <u>check department</u> Name, Department, New-Value

In this way, we may use the frame and inheritance structure to refer to a large number of database entries. However, note that this is an "alternative" to the use of a predicate such as *dbase* in conjunction with rules. We may thus combine databases and logic with rules and connect databases to frames with attached predicates and inheritance.

■ 5.11 SUMMARY

Frames can be used to organize conceptual entities into packages that facilitate storage, retrieval and management of knowledge. Frames are a powerful way of representing knowledge that subsumes a variety of related techniques. We have outlined a hybrid knowledge representation and inferencing system that combines desirable features of logic and frames.

The combination of frames and logic is well suited to the task of building expert systems. While frames are a powerful form of knowledge representation, predicate logic provides a simple and direct way of controlling the reasoning process. Thus the combination of frames and predicate logic functions effectively when the fundamental knowledge structures are built with frames and rules of logic are used to reason with the frames.

UNCERTAINTY

■ 6.1 INTRODUCTION

We live in an uncertain world. Nevertheless, we reason and make decisions in the face of this uncertainty. Investment decisions, patient diagnoses, nuclear power plant constructions, and the like continue to be made, although the information that leads to each decision, and the eventual outcome, may be uncertain. Expert systems that aim at mimicking human behavior should operate with real-world situations and reason with uncertain information.

In some knowledge domains, of course, there is a great deal more certainty than there is in others. For instance, computer hardware architectures involve well-established information such as "the memory board fits the card cage" or "the cable has a 25-pin female connector." On the other hand, an investment advisor must face a great deal of uncertainty in dealing with the vagaries of the stock market.

Often, in dealing with uncertainty, we are not completely sure of a fact, but we have reason to believe that it is "probably" true. Rather than taking such uncertain information and arbitrarily categorizing it as either certainly true (truth value = 100), or certainly false (truth value = 0), we need a way of dealing with uncertain information in its own right.

Coping with uncertainty in reasoning is a complex area within the field of artificial intelligence. As with other issues, the techniques actually used for uncertain reasoning in expert systems are only a subset of a large class of methods that may be considered.

There are two general ways in which uncertainty may be dealt with in an expert system. One aspect of uncertainty stems from the incompleteness of informa-

211

tion; i.e., it is not that the information is inherently uncertain, it's just that we don't have the information we need. The other aspect of uncertainty arises in those cases where the knowledge itself is inherently imprecise. Many expert systems assume that their knowledge base is fairly complete and that any symptoms of incompleteness should be debugged and rectified. Thus the treatment of uncertainty in expert systems has often focused on the problem of imprecise information.

Consider how human experts deal with uncertainty. Two examples of human experts who routinely deal with uncertainty are the detective and the physician. Both types of expert attempt to derive conclusions from uncertain information. For instance, the popularity of detective stories may be due to the manner in which fictional detectives such as Sherlock Holmes can apparently transform uncertainty into certainty and the challenge that they pose to the reader in so doing. The mechanism for transforming uncertainty into certainty is of course the collection of pertinent facts that confirm the hypotheses, hunches, or whatever that were initially generated by some type of uncertain reasoning. Thus the physician may order a laboratory test or exploratory surgical procedure that will provide conclusive evidence for or against the hypothesis.

Several methods have been proposed for dealing with uncertain information in expert systems. We shall review a few prevailing methods in this chapter. However, while there are a number of definitions of uncertainty, the issue of how to *use* uncertainty in an expert system is quite another matter. A major question is "How does one specify just how uncertain a piece of knowledge is?"

Once we know what uncertainties to attach to knowledge within the knowledge base, we can focus on methods for taking the uncertainties into account during inference. It should be clear, though, that the quality of uncertain reasoning will depend to a great extent on how well the basic uncertainties are quantified, as well as methods for combining uncertainties during inference.

We begin with an overview of methods for dealing with uncertainty during inference, namely, probabilities, fuzzy logic, and certainty theory. We outline the theoretical and practical issues involved in using these methods. This is followed with a discussion of inexact and semi-exact reasoning that blends in with our treatment of logic in Chapter 3. We then focus on the issue of quantifying inexactness and discuss how uncertainty may be assessed in graphical form or in terms of ranking and sorting methods.

■ 6.2 INEXACTNESS

Although today there are several schools of thought on the use of inexactness in expert systems, until one or two decades ago the concept of *inexactness* was synonymous with the notion of *mathematical probability*.

The roots of mathematical probability lie in the attempts by French and Italian noblemen of the seventeenth and eighteenth centuries to quantify the odds encountered in games of chance. Their attempts to gain an advantage in gambling resulted in the creation of mathematical models for different processes that could be used to predict the probabilities of different events. Card games and other events that did not conform easily to a predictive model came to be modeled by using the methods of *combinatorics*. Combinatoric methods are generally based on the following idea:

Definition 6.1: The chance that a particular event will occur is equal to the number of ways the event can occur divided by the number of ways all possible events (including the particular event of interest) can occur.

Such chances of event occurrence came to be known as *probabilities*. For instance, by using combinatorics, we can determine that the probability of throwing two successive heads with a fair coin is .25 because there is only one way of getting two heads but there are a total of four possible outcomes, i.e., Head-Head, Head-Tail, Tail-Head, and Tail-Tail.

Since its early days as a gambling aid, *mathematical probability* has developed into a sophisticated method of quantifying uncertainty. However, when applied to diverse applications from high-energy physics to horse racing, probability theory often retains a fundamental assumption about the domain it deals with. Specifically, it assumes that there are long run observations of events from which we select by combinatoric methods. Further, this implicitly assumes that we have a basic model of how processes interact in the system we model, e.g., that we know the structure of a horse race.

In many expert system applications, on the other hand, we simply do not have a good causal model of the processes that underlie uncertainty. As Shortliffe and Buchanan (1975) have pointed out, vast portions of areas such as medical experience suffer from having so few data and so much imperfect knowledge that a rigorous probabilistic analysis is not possible.

Probability is a good way of dealing with uncertainty when it is applicable, but it requires detailed domain knowledge of a type that is seldom available. This knowledge will include either a detailed causal model of the processes that lead to the uncertain events or a good statistical record of data covering previous instances of the events of interest. Thus, several alternatives to probability theory have been proposed. Further, within probability theory itself, there are different schools of thought regarding what probabilities are and how they should be dealt with. The major alternatives to probability theory that we will consider are *fuzzy logic* and *certainty theory*.

However, regardless of which method of dealing with inexactness we discuss, the basic method of representing inexactness is the determination of a *likeli-*

hood, probability, degree of truth, certainty, or *confidence factor,* which may be essentially viewed as the process of selecting a point on a scale, say, an integer between 0 and 100. After such values have been assigned to a set of basic events, we may use some methods of *likelihood calculation, probability combination, truth value propagation,* and *inexact reasoning* to reflect the uncertainty associated with compound or complex events. In dealing with inexactness, there are two basic steps (Figure 6.1):

   a. Determining the uncertainty of a basic set of events.

   b. Combining the values obtained in **a** to arrive at the uncertainty of compound or complex events.

Different methods of inexactness usually focus on **b.** However, in dealing with expert systems it is essential to carry out both **a** and **b** effectively.

6.2.1 Practical Issues in Inexact Reasoning

It is possible to develop a large number of interesting mathematical theories to deal with inexactness in expert systems. However, from a practical point of view, before getting carried away with complex formulas, we must consider what *actually* happens when inexact values are used in an expert system.

To begin with, experts provide some inexact rules to describe the nature of their decision making and then supply inexact values for step **a** above. The formulas of step **b** are then used to combine these values to produce eventual results for the system. Almost always, the system will not exhibit the desired results the first time it is tested. But what happens now? We have three choices:

   i. Change the values supplied in step **a** above.

   ii. Change some rules in the system.

   iii. Change the theory used in step **b** above.

After an inexact inference engine has been implemented (and purchased), option **iii** is generally not even considered. Thus, now the blame will be placed on

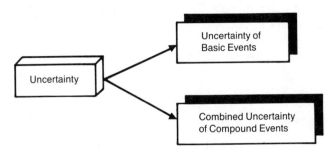

Figure 6.1 Issues in dealing with uncertainty.

the expert for not having supplied the correct values in step **a**, or for having supplied the wrong rules. Thus the expert will have to adjust the earlier estimates or change the rules. This process usually continues over time as the expert system is being developed and turns into a feedback process in which the original estimates and rules provided by the expert are modified repeatedly to the point that they no longer resemble the original knowledge-base.

These changes may take place irrespective of which theory is used in step **b** above, and regardless of the theoretical defenses that may be raised in favor of one theory or another. Thus experts often bypass the theory to obtain the results they need. This fact suggests design criteria for practical inexact reasoning systems. A practical system should:

a. Allow experts to adjust uncertainties associated with classes of events without difficulty.

b. Allow different methods of combining uncertainties for dealing with different problems or subproblems.

In some sense, the practical strategic issues involved in a theory of inexact reasoning resemble those in the design of a programming language. Returning to our analogy in Section 1.5.1, each theory of inexactness provides a *paradigm* for inexact programming. If the paradigm is not well suited to the task, we shall struggle to express our concepts just as we may struggle if we attempt to express rule-based concepts with FORTRAN Do-Loops or if we try to do matrix inversion in a forward chaining rule based language such as OPS–5.

■ 6.3 PROBABILITY

Since the early 1900s, logicians had considered multivalued logics as extensions of two-valued logic, and elaborate systems of multivalued logic were constructed (e.g., Chang and Keisler, 1973). However, such methods were more algebraic than numeric and were pursued for theoretical reasons rather than for practical decision making. Until recently (ca. 1965) probability theory was the only formal method for quantifying uncertainty.

Probabilities are a way of turning opinion or expectation into numbers. People often express uncertain information in terms of likelihood or odds, for instance, in thinking of a horse race:

> The odds are two to one in favor of Horse-1.

or

> Horse-1 is twice as likely to win as it is to lose.

This second version of the statement expresses the likelihood that Horse-1 will win the race. The mathematical equivalent of the intuitive notion of likelihood is probability. A *probability* is thus a number between 0 and 1 that reflects the likelihood of an event. An impossible event has a probability of 0, while a certain event has a probability of 1.

We write P(A) for the probability of the event A. The probability that both event A and event B will occur is then represented by P(A and B). The probability that one or both of events A and B will occur is represented by P(A or B). In a given situation, a set of independent events (sometimes called the *sample space*) such as $(A_1, A_2, \ldots, A_n)$ may represent all possible outcomes. The probabilities of all events must sum up to certainty, i.e.,

$$P(A_1) + P(A_2) + \ldots + P(A_n) = 1$$

In everyday conversation, the term "probability" is used rather loosely. A soldier going to war might consider the possibility of his death "highly probable" if it is greater than .5. A weather forecaster might consider the probability of rain "high" if it is greater that .75. A student might consider the possibility of getting an A in a particular course as "high" only if the probability is greater than .9.

Information, although imprecise, may still be useful in reasoning. Consider the example of a biased coin. A fair coin has equal probabilities of landing heads (probability = .5) or tails (probability = .5) when tossed. If we know that a biased coin has a .7 chance of landing heads each time it is thrown, we should use that information in deciding how to approach decisions that depend on the toss of the coin. It would be a mistake to try to treat each toss of the coin as if it involved certain information (i.e., the coin *must* land heads), but it would also be a mistake to ignore the information that was available just because it carries some uncertainty.

Lotteries and casinos provide examples of the value of information. When a casino sets up a game, there is a fairly good chance that the house may lose on any one roll of the dice, hand of cards, or spin of the wheel. Over the course of time, however, the house can *expect* to make a good profit with close to certainty.

Casinos stay in business because they rely on a favorable *expected value* for their gambling operations. The expected value of a game, or situation, is the long-run payoff that can be expected given a certain set of outcomes with associated values and probabilities of occurrence.

Probability theory allows one to behave rationally in the face of uncertain situations. One makes decisions on the basis of maximizing the expected value of the outcome. Consider a bet (using a biased coin that is more likely to turn up heads) where we win $10 if the coin lands Heads and we lose $10 if the coin lands Tails. We may lose on any one toss of the coin, but over a long sequence of tosses we will be almost certain to win.

The lawful behavior of sequences of uncertain events can be demonstrated using a standard coin tossing example. When we toss a fair coin twice we are just as likely to get both coins showing the same face as we are to get both coins showing a different face. When we toss 100 fair coins, however, the chances of getting all 100 coins showing the same face are so small as to be effectively zero. Thus, in sequences of trials where uncertainty can be quantified exactly, we may actually be fairly certain about features of the overall pattern of outcomes that will be observed.

This comforting feature of long-run sequences is not always applicable for expert systems. First, the degree of uncertainty about a piece of knowledge may itself be uncertain. Second, most expert systems do not deal with sequences of similar events, and they may encounter fairly unique situations.

Traditionally, there have been two approaches to the mathematical definition of probability, the classical and the Bayesian views. The classical definition of mathematical probability involves an *expectation* of what will be the outcome of an activity based on the *frequency* of the different possible outcomes that have occurred in prior instances of the activity. Thus, if we toss a coin 100 times and it comes up Heads in 70 of those tosses, the probability that it will turn up Heads on the next throw is 70/100, i.e., .7. According to this *frequency* view of probability:

Definition 6.2:   In the long run, the relative frequency of an event approaches its probability.

This definition captures the more intuitive notion that most people have of the *law of averages*. Research evidence (Peterson and Beach, 1967) has shown that people can judge relative frequencies and proportions very accurately.

In contrast to the traditional frequency view of probability, the *Bayesian* view holds that:

Definition 6.3:   A probability is a degree of belief held by a person about some hypothesis, event, or uncertain quantity.

Thus the Bayesian view of probability, although formulated mathematically, contains a subjective component reflecting human opinion. This has led to some controversy as to the validity of the Bayesian approach and its merits as compared with the relative frequency approach. In expert systems, however, the Bayesian approach is more dominant since the fundamental assumptions of mathematical probability involving frequencies are not applicable to some knowledge domains.

6.3.1 Conditional and Joint Probabilities

In the real world, the probability of one event is hardly ever independent of other events. Notions of probability and uncertainty, however, must deal with *combinations* of events. The probability of an event is often affected by the conditions in which it occurs.

A *joint probability* is the probability of the occurrence of two events. If two independent events A and B have probabilities P(A) and P(B), the joint probability of both A and B occurring is written as P(A and B) and is defined by:

$$P(A \text{ and } B) = P(A) * P(B)$$

For instance, suppose that we toss two fair coins separately. Let P(A) be the probability of getting Heads on the first coin and P(B) the probability of getting Heads on the second coin. Since the coins are assumed to be fair, it follows that P(A) = P(B) = .5. The probability of getting Heads on both coins is .5 * .5 = .25. The probability of getting Heads on *one or both* of the coins, i.e., the *union* of the probabilities P(A) and P(B) is expressed as P(A or B) and is defined by:

$$P(A \text{ or } B) = P(A) + P(B) - P(A) * P(B)$$

Thus the probability of getting Heads on one or both of the coins is (.5 + .5 − .25) = .75, as in Figure 6.2.

In tossing two coins, we generally assume that the way the first coin lands will not affect the way the second coin lands. In other situations, though, there

Possible Outcomes

HH

HT

TH

TT

Joint - P(H & H) = 1/4

Union - P(H or H) = 3/4

Figure 6.2 Joint and union probabilities.

does seem to be a linkage between different events. For example, if a physician suspects that a patient may have malaria, that belief will increase if it is discovered that the patient recently returned from a country where malaria is relatively common. In general, the surrounding conditions influence the probability of an event.

A *conditional probability* relates the probability of one event to the occurrence of another. Thus one's estimate about a probability will change as the context provided by related information changes. For instance, suppose that we were to determine the probability of a person being male, given that the person's age is 80. We will have to consider how the proportion of males in the population changes as age increases. In the case of guessing a person's gender, age changes the characteristics of the sample, since women generally tend to live longer than men. Thus the proportion of males in the general population tends to decrease with age. In fact, a significantly greater number of male babies are born, but male babies have a higher probability of dying in the first year of life than do females. Even if they survive to adulthood, males will have a shorter life expectancy than females.

Say that the probability of any one person chosen at random being male is about .50. The probability that a given person chosen at random is 80 years old may be .005, say. The probability that a given person chosen at random is both male *and* 80 years old may be .002. Now the probability that an 80-year-old person chosen at random is male might be more like .4, as shown below.

The conditional probability of event A, given the occurrence of event B, is written as $P(A \mid B)$, and is defined by:

$$P(A \mid B) = P(A \text{ and } B) / P(B)$$

For instance,

P('X' is male | The age of 'X' is 80) = P('X' is male and The age of 'X' is 80) / P(The age of 'X' is 80)

In the example above, .4 = .002 / .005.

Mathematical probability is based on a model that assesses the frequencies of sequences of events. Conditional probabilities provide a refinement of the concept so that particular features of a situation are taken into account when probability is assessed. If we rely on a frequency view of probability, however, the more features of a situation we consider, the more unique it is and thus there are fewer previous cases to draw on in estimating the probability. This, in turn, reduces our confidence in the accuracy of the probability assessment.

6.3.2 Bayesian Probabilities

The Bayesian approach to probability relies on the concept that one should incorporate the *prior probability* of an event into the interpretation of a situation.

Consider the case of a female patient who visits a physician complaining of severe abdominal pains. The physician may already have seen a number of patients with stomach flu in the past few days and may thus assign a high prior probability to that condition. Another hypothesis may be ectopic pregnancy whose proof requires an ultrasound screening that may itself not be entirely conclusive. Thus the physician provisionally decides on the stomach flu explanation, with the option of reconsidering the other alternative (after checking that the patient is, in fact, pregnant) if the apparent symptoms of the stomach flu do not disappear after 24 hours as they have with the other patients.

In this case the physician used prior personal beliefs about the relatively likelihoods of ectopic pregnancy and stomach flu to guide the initial diagnosis. Bayes' theorem provides a mathematical model for this type of reasoning where *prior beliefs* are combined with *evidence* to form estimates of uncertainty.

Bayes' theorem relates the conditional probabilities of events; i.e., it allows us to express the probability $P(A \mid B)$ in terms of the probabilities of $P(B \mid A)$, $P(A)$ and $P(B)$. This is often important, since the probabilities which are available are often $P(B \mid A)$, $P(A)$, and $P(B)$; but the desired probability is $P(A \mid B)$.

For instance, consider the case of a geology expert system that has to determine the likelihood of the existence of a mineral in a given location. Let us represent the hypothesis that the mineral is, in fact, present with the event H and the evidence available to us (e.g., geological samples) with the event E. Thus $P(H)$ represents the prior probability of the existence of the mineral, $P(E)$ represents the prior probability of the pattern of evidence obtained, and $P(H \mid E)$ represents the probability of the existence of the mineral, given the evidence, otherwise called the *posterior probability*.

Now a problem arises since we do not have a good estimate of the likelihood of the existence of minerals given a certain pattern of evidence, i.e., $P(H \mid E)$. However, we may have a good estimate of the likelihood of a pattern of evidence given that the mineral is indeed present, i.e., $P(E \mid H)$. Bayes' theorem allows us to convert $P(H)$, $P(E)$, and $P(E \mid H)$ to an estimate of $P(H \mid E)$, as in Figure 6.3. The formal definition of Bayes' theorem is:

$$P(H \mid E) = P(H) * P(E \mid H) / P(E)$$

In this equation, E represents the evidence (or symptoms) and H represents the set of hypotheses. The proof of the simple case of Bayes' theorem is

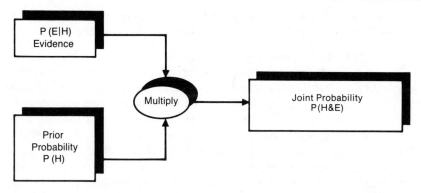

Figure 6.3 Illustration of relationship between conditional and joint probability.

straightforward. The joint probability of two events H and E can be expressed (as illustrated in Figure 6.3) as:

$$P(H \text{ and } E) = P(H) * P(E \mid H) = P(E) * P(H \mid E) = P(E \text{ and } H)$$

from the mathematical definition of conditional probability, since:

$$P(E \mid H) = P(H \text{ and } E) / P(H)$$

Bayes' theorem can thus be derived directly by taking the equivalence:

$$P(H) * P(E \mid H) = P(E) * P(H \mid E)$$

and rearranging terms. A more general form of Bayes' theorem deals with multiple hypotheses, e.g., $H_1, _2, \ldots, H_n$, and has the form:

$$P(H_i \mid E) = \frac{P(E \mid H_i) * P(H_i)}{P(E \mid H_1) * P(H_1) + \ldots + P(E \mid H_n) * P(H_n)}$$

Some expert systems use Bayesian theory to derive further concepts. For instance, the Prospector system (Duda, Nilsson, and Raphael, 1979) uses the concept of *likelihood ratio* based on the definitions:

$$LS = P(E \mid H) / P(E \mid \text{not } H)$$

and

$$LN = P(\text{not } E \mid H) / P(\text{not } E \mid \text{not } H)$$

to express sufficiency and necessity. The term LS represents the likelihood of sufficiency, while LN represents the likelihood of necessity for a rule.

Bayes' theorem can be used to answer questions involving conditional probabilities. As it stands, Bayes' theorem is derived directly from the axioms of mathematical probability. Controversy arises, however, when we give a *subjectivist* interpretation to Bayes' theorem. Many statisticians feel uncomfortable about using probability to express uncertainty about events that cannot be regarded as having been generated by a random process, such as subjective judgments of uncertainty. The alternative *subjectivist* view is that probability statements can be made with reference to any potentially verifiable proposition, irrespective of whether one can regard it as having been generated by a random process. The argument for why subjective judgments should be used in probabilistic analyses was made by Lindley (1982).

The use of subjective probabilities does not mean that we are no longer interested in accuracy. Subjective probabilities should be *calibrated*; i.e., if one predicts that an event has a probability of 50% then it should occur 50% of the time in such situations.

The interpretation of subjective estimates of uncertainty *as if* they were probabilities rests on the assumption that they are fairly accurate predictors of the probabilities of events. The use of the Bayesian approach to expert systems development rests on this assumption. In other situations the Bayesian approach loses its mantle of probabilistic respectability and becomes just another method for handling uncertainty in expert systems.

Practically speaking, applying Bayesian probabilities using a strictly probabilistic point of view is difficult for a number of reasons:

a. The application of Bayes' law requires the availability of all relevant prior and conditional probabilities. Obtaining this information can be very difficult in practice.

b. Bayes' law is mathematically correct only if all possible outcomes are disjoint. Although one may reformulate concepts, this often results in a model that does not correspond to the intuitive concepts of the expert. For instance, modeling a patient with multiple diseases requires a reformulation of the physician's concepts to conform to Bayesian theory.

c. As the knowledge-base size grows, it becomes virtually impossible to change one probability without causing a ripple effect that incorrectly changes other probabilities required to retain mathematical assumptions such as $P(H_1) + P(H_2) + \ldots + P(H_n) = 1$.

In practice, some expert systems use Bayesian reasoning, while inevitably violating the mathematical principles used to derive it. However, as our discussion in Section 6.3.1 suggests, one may view Bayesian probabilities as simply a method of combining inexact values, rather than as a probabilistic approach to uncertainty.

■ 6.4 FUZZY LOGIC

Fuzzy logic was invented in the mid 1960s as an alternative to two-valued logic and probability theory by offering alternatives to traditional notions of set membership and logic (Bellman, Kabala, and Zadeh, 1964; Zadeh, 1965). Fuzzy logic views two-valued logic and set theory as special cases of a more general multi-valued theory. In this approach mathematical probability is viewed as inappropriate and is replaced with an alternative theory referred to as *possibility theory* (Zadeh, 1978a).

In contrast to frequencies that tend to use the record of previous events in assigning probabilities, fuzzy truth values deal with the *likelihood* or *certainty* that a fact or rule is true. When we refer to the certainty of a future event such as:

The certainty that a democrat will be elected as president in the next election,

it will probably be misleading to base our assessment on the previous distribution of presidents, as might be done in using the frequency definition of probability. The state of the economy, the national mood, the performance of the current president, and other factors will probably be better predictors than will a simple statistical model based on previous elections. Thus each election is in some senses unique and it is more appropriate to assess uncertainty using a different model.

Zadeh (1965) described the mathematics of fuzzy set theory and fuzzy logic. The main idea behind fuzzy systems is that *truth values* (in fuzzy logic) or *membership values* (in fuzzy sets) are indicated by a value in the range 0–1; with 0 representing absolute Falsity and 1 representing absolute Truth.

Various ranges of numbers may be used to express uncertainty with equivalent results. In our own discussions of uncertainty we use a range of 0–100 to express the degree of uncertainty, but this scale can be transformed directly into the range [0, 1] with 50 mapping to .5, etc.

Fuzzy sets are intuitively very appealing. Natural language abounds with vague and imprecise concepts, such as "Helen is tall" or "It is very smoggy today." In formal two-valued logic, the "Law of the Excluded Middle," states that every proposition must either be True or False. But even the ancient Greeks were aware of the need for inexact concepts. One paradox they considered was based on a property of a *large* heap of stones, namely:

If we remove one stone from a large heap, the heap remains large.

By applying this concept again and again, we may ultimately reduce each large heap to a heap with just one stone. Thus the following question arises:

When does a large heap become a small heap?

The answer, of course, is obtained by viewing largeness as a relative property, which is true of all heaps to some degree. Thus the fact that a heap is large is a *vague* or *inexact* fact.

Fuzzy set theory deals with the mathematical theory of sets. In traditional set theory an object can be a *member* of a set. For instance, 2 is a member of the set of even numbers, while 3 is not. Similarly, George Washington is a member of the set of the presidents of the United States. But how about the set of large stones, or the set of large numbers? Is 134532 a member of the set of large numbers? As the preceding paradox suggests, subtracting 1 from a large number should leave us with a large number. Thus, being a member of the set of large numbers is also inexact and should be treated as a degree of membership in the *fuzzy set* of large numbers.

Expressing inexact concepts such as large or old in fuzzy logic is straightforward. For example, consider the statement:

Helen is old.

If Helen's age is 75, we may assign the statement the *truth value* of .95, or the *certainty* .95. The statement could be translated into set terminology as follows:

Helen is a member of the set of old people.

This statement would be expressed in the symbolic notation of fuzzy sets as:

mOLD(Helen) = .95

where m is the membership function, operating in this case on the fuzzy set of old people (denoted OLD), which returns a value between 0 and 1.

There is an important distinction between fuzzy systems and probability. Both operate over equivalent numeric ranges. However, the probabilistic approach yields the natural-language statement:

There is a 95% chance that Helen is old.

while the corresponding statement in fuzzy logic is:

Helen's degree of membership within the set of old people is .95 .

Although these two statements seem similar, they actually carry different meanings. The first view supposes that Helen either is or is not old (still assuming the Law of the Excluded Middle) but that we are uncertain about which set she is in. By contrast, fuzzy logic supposes that Helen is "more or less" old and that the uncertainty is an inherent part of Helen's state rather than being reflective of uncertainty in the information that we have about Helen's state. We can simultaneously assign a membership function expressing Helen's degree of membership in the set of young people, e.g.,

mYOUNG(Helen) = .05

In addition to defining the basic notion of uncertainty, fuzzy logic provides operators for combining uncertain information, just as AND and NOT combine truth values in two-valued logic.

The similarities between different methods of uncertain reasoning tend to be obscured by notational differences. For instance, the fuzzy logic statement:

mOLD(Helen) = .95

may be represented as an inexact fact in a reasoning system as:

Helen is old   CF = 95

Similarly, the degree to which Helen is middle-aged may be:

Helen is middle aged   CF = 10

Note that in fuzzy logic these membership values do not have to sum to 1, in contrast to probabilities that are constrained by a summation axiom. Thus, in fuzzy logic we may use any form of inexact value assignments without fear of upsetting the underlying mathematical model.

6.4.1 Formal Definitions for Fuzzy Logic
In this section we give a brief introduction to the syntax and operation of fuzzy logic. More extended treatments are provided by Zadeh (e.g., 1965, 1978a).

Let X be a set of objects, with elements represented as x, i.e., X = (x). A *fuzzy set* A in X is characterized by a membership function mA(x) that maps each object in X onto the interval of real numbers between 0 and 1 (written as [0, 1]).

Thus in the previous example A may be the set of old people and Helen is one of the people in the general set of people, X, who is mapped onto the real interval [0,1] according to her degree of membership in A.

As mA(x) approaches 1, the "grade of membership" of x in A increases. A is *empty* if and only if for all x, mA(x) = 0. A = B if and only if for all x: mA(x) = mB(x). We may now define the basic set theoretic operations and relations of complement, subset, union, and intersection with:

Definition 6.4: m(*complement* of A) = 1 − mA (i.e., the measure of a set's complement is one minus the measure of the set).

Definition 6.5: A is a *subset* of B if and only if mB(x) > = mA(x), for all x in X.

Definition 6.6: C is the *union* of A and B, if mC(x) = MAX[mA(x), mB(x)], for all x in X.

Definition 6.7: C is the *intersection* of A and B if mC(x) = MIN[mA(x), mB(x)], for all x in X.

The operations involving union and intersection represent a major departure from probabilistic theory. Operationally, the differences are as follows:

For independent events, the probabilistic operation for AND is multiplication. For example, let us presume that x = Bob, S is the fuzzy set of smart people, and T is the fuzzy set of tall people. Then, if mS(x) = .9 and mT(x) = .9, the probabilistic result (assuming independence) would be:

$$mS(x) * mT(x) = 0.81$$

whereas the corresponding fuzzy result would be:

$$MIN[mS(x), mT(x)] = 0.9$$

The probabilistic calculation yields a result that is lower than either of the two initial values, which when viewed as "the chance of knowing" makes good sense. However, in fuzzy terms the two membership functions would read something like "Paul is very smart" and "Paul is very tall." If we presume for the sake of argument that "very" is a stronger term than "quite" and that we can correlate "quite" with the value 0.81, the semantic difference becomes obvious. The probabilistic calculation yields the statement:

> If Paul is very smart, and Paul is very tall, then Paul is a quite tall and smart person.

The fuzzy calculation, however, yields:

> If Paul is very smart, and Paul is very tall, then Paul is a very tall and smart person.

Another problem arises as we incorporate more factors into our equations (the fuzzy set of heavy people, etc.). We find that the ultimate result of a series of ANDs using the probability method approaches 0.0, even if all factors are initially high. Fuzzy set theory implies otherwise: five factors of the value 0.90 (let us say, "very") ANDed together yield a value of 0.90 (again, "very"), not 0.59 (perhaps equivalent to "somewhat").

6.4.2 Fuzzy Hedges

One intuitively appealing application of fuzzy logic concerns the quantification of uncertainty and imprecision in natural language (Zadeh 1983b). Linguistic *hedges* (e.g., "very", "quite," and "moderately") can be naturally mapped into fuzzy values. One can then translate some natural language statements into a fuzzy logic form. These transforming operations are provided in an effort to maintain close ties to natural language and to allow for the generation of fuzzy statements through mathematical calculations. Definition of hedges is a subjective process and may vary in different contexts.

Vagueness and ambiguity make it more difficult to represent meaning formally, yet people using natural language do not appear to have any problem in making statements such as "John is short". The inherent ambiguity of such statements should be recognized, though. At 6 feet, John might be considered fairly short as a basketball player, but he might be considered fairly tall in general.

We can model the linguistic notion of *hedge* as a set theoretic operation that modifies a membership function. Consider an example in which one transforms the statement:

> Helen is old

to

> Helen is *very* old

In fuzzy logic, the hedge "very" is usually defined as follows:

$$m\text{"very"}A(x) = [mA(x)]^2$$

Thus, if mOLD(Helen) = 0.95, then mVERYOLD(Helen) = 0.903.

Other common hedges are "more or less", typically defined as SQRT[mA(x)], "somewhat," "rather," "sort of," and so on. Their definition is subjective, but their operation is consistent. Thus they serve to transform memberships and truth values in a systematic manner according to standard mathematical functions.

Algorithmic procedures can thus be devised that translate "fuzzy" terminology into numeric values, perform reliable operations on those values, and then return natural-language statements.

■ **6.5   CERTAINTY THEORY**

The basic difference between the different methods of inexact inference stems from how uncertainty is conceptualized and manipulated. We can think of uncertainty as reflecting the probability that a fact or rule is true. This is the approach taken in Bayesian methods. Or, we can represent uncertainty as a degree of belief in the fact or rule, which is what fuzzy logic does, and what, more generally, *certainty theory* does.

The starting point for any nonprobabilistic method of inexact inference is a method for expressing the degree to which each fact or rule is true. One then needs a method for propagating uncertainty as rules are applied during the inference process. Certainty theory relies on the use of *certainty factors*.

Each certainty factor can be regarded as updating the belief in a hypothesis based on evidence. The precise manner in which certainty factors should be used in calculating uncertainty has attracted some debate (Buchanan and Shortliffe, 1984). However, the discussion in Section 6.2.1 regarding the practical issues involved in inexact reasoning should also be kept in mind.

In certainty theory, as in fuzzy logic, we assume that each statement has a certainty factor, *degree of truth*, or a *confidence factor* (CF), which is a number between 0 and 100. Absolute truth corresponds to 100, while certain falsehood is represented by 0. We write CF(A) for the certainty factor of A. These certainty factors are, however, not probabilities and the degrees of truths of all statements in a given context do not need to sum up to 100.

To reason with certainty factors we need to be able to calculate degrees of confidence for statements connected by ANDs and ORs. We need formulas that calculate CF(A AND B) and CF(A OR B) in terms of CF(A) and CF(B).

The formula we use to calculate CFs for conjunctions (i.e., ANDs) assumes that a chain is as strong as its weakest link. We therefore take the *minimal* CF in a conjunction. On the other hand, in a disjunction we have a choice between two propositions and may rely on the strongest level of confidence. We therefore use the maximal CF in a disjunction. Formally, this means that:

$$\text{CF(A AND B)} = \text{minimum[CF(A), CF(B)]}.$$
$$\text{CF(A OR B)} = \text{maximum[CF(A), CF(B)]}.$$

The definitions are the same as the corresponding definitions for AND and OR in fuzzy logic. For instance, given that:

> CF(Stock12 is hightech) = 90
> CF(Stock12 is in demand) = 60

we have:

> CF(Stock12 is hightech AND Stock12 is in demand) = 60
> CF(Stock12 is hightech OR Stock12 is in demand) = 90

We cannot only assign a CF to facts but may also allow rules to be inexact by assigning a CF to each rule. The CF associated with a rule tells us how certain we can be about the conclusion drawn from that rule. For instance,

Rule₁:

> CF = 60
>
> If X is volatile
>
>   X is hightech
>
> and
>
>   X is in demand;

has a CF of 60. This means that we can only be 60% sure about the CF that we obtain from the premise of this rule. Thus to calculate the CF for the conclusion of this rule, we *multiply* the rule CF with the CF obtained from the premise of the rule. For instance, if we apply Rule₁ to Stock12, we have:

> CF(X is volatile) =
> CF(Stock12 is hightech AND Stock12 is in demand) * .6
> = 60 * 60 / 100 = 36

Note that now we divide the multiplication by 100 to maintain the scale of 0 to 100. In general, if we <u>only</u> have one rule, e.g.,

General rule:

> CF = c
>
>   Conclusion
>
> IF
>
>   Premise;

which supports the hypothesis *Conclusion*, we have

$$CF(Conclusion) \ = \ CF(Premise) \ * \ c \ / \ 100$$

However, if several rules support a hypothesis, we need to combine the confidence obtained from all these rules in support of the hypothesis.

6.5.1 Combining Evidence

Each rule whose conclusion matches a hypothesis may be viewed as a *piece of evidence* that supports the hypothesis. To calculate the final confidence in the hypothesis, we need to combine the certainty factors provided by these rules.

However, we cannot simply accumulate confidence by adding certainty factors. For instance, if two rules support a hypothesis H, each with a certainty factor 60, our combined confidence in H cannot be 60 + 60 = 120. We need a *subtraction factor* to allow for the fact that the certainty factors are being added. The definition first used in the expert system MYCIN used a subtraction factor equal to the product of the certainty factor obtained from each rule, i.e.,

$$A \ + \ B \ - \ A \ * \ B$$

This is, in fact, reminiscent of the definition of probabilistic union, defined in Section 6.3.1 above. But now, rather than using probabilities, we use certainty factors.

Let CF(H, E) denote the confidence in H based on evidence E. If we have two rules, say, $Rule_1$ and $Rule_2$, which support H, then CF(H, $Rule_1$ and $Rule_2$) denotes the result of combining CF(H, $Rule_1$) and CF(H, $Rule_2$).

Returning to the example in Section 6.5 above, suppose that we have another rule

$Rule_2$:

$$CF = 70$$

If

       X is volatile

or

       X is a new issue

       X is heavily traded;

which also supports "Stock12 is volatile." From the facts:

$$CF(Stock12 \text{ is a new issue}) \ = \ 80$$
$$CF(Stock12 \text{ is heavily traded}) \ = \ 40$$

we can calculate the confidence provided by $Rule_2$ for "Stock12 is volatile" as:

$$CF(\text{Stock12 is volatile}, Rule_2) = \max(80, 40) * 70 / 100 = 80 * 70 / 100 = 56$$

The eventual confidence in "Stock12 is volatile" is then calculated as

$$CF(\text{Stock12 is volatile}, Rule_1 \& Rule_2) = 36 + 56 - (36 * 56) / 100 = 92 - 20 = 72$$

The formula for combining evidence may thus be formally stated as

$$CF(H, Rule_1 \& Rule_2) = CF(H, Rule_1) + CF(H, Rule_2) - (CF(H, Rule_1) * CF(H, Rule_2)).$$

Thus, in general, given the rules

$Rule_1$:

CF = c
> H IF A AND B;

$Rule_2$:

CF = c'
H IF C OR D;

The CF for H based on each rule is obtained by multiplication with the certainty factor for the rule, i.e.,

$$CF(H, Rule_1) = \min[CF(A), CF(B)] * c = \text{say, } c_1$$
$$CF(H, Rule_2) = \max[CF(C), CF(D)] * c' = \text{say, } c_2.$$

Then, as in Figure 6.4, we combine these two pieces of evidence that support H by:

$$CF(H, Rule_1 \& Rule_2) = c_1 + c_2 - (c_1 * c_2)$$

If more than two rules support the hypothesis, we apply the same formula incrementally. If A and B are the CFs obtained from two rules supporting hypothesis H, the *combined certainty,* Combine(A, B) is defined as:

$$\text{Combine}(A, B) = A + B - (A * B).$$

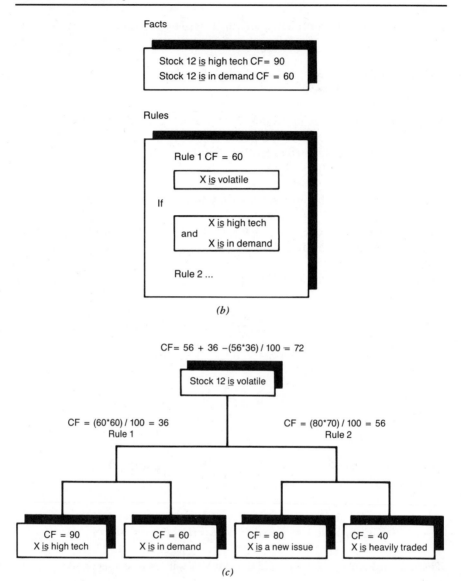

Figure 6.4 (a) Combining evidence—rules. (b) Combining evidence—the procedure.

If H is also supported by a third rule that provides us with a third CF, say C, the final confidence in H is obtained in the same way:

Combine(C, (A&B)) = C + Combine(A,B) − (C * Combine(A, B))

It is important to note that:

$$\text{Combine(C, (A \& B))} = C + A + B - (A * B) - (C * (A + B$$
$$- (A * B))$$
$$= (A + B + C) + (A * B * C) - (A * B + A * C + B * C)$$
$$= \text{Combine(A, (C \& B))} = \text{Combine(B, (A \& C)).}$$

Thus the order in which we combine evidence does not affect the eventual outcome.

In calculating certainty factors, we may wish to discard statements whose certainty falls below a certain *threshold*. For instance, we may wish not to consider any statement with a certainty less than 20.

■ 6.6 INEXACT AND SEMI-EXACT INFERENCE

Probabilities, fuzzy logic, and certainty theory are some among many definitions for dealing with inexactness. According to the discussion in Section 6.2.1, a practical inexact reasoning system should be abe to adapt to various paradigms for viewing inexactness. We discuss an approach to inexact reasoning that naturally fits into our discussion of logic in Chapter 3 and that can be adapted by a user to perform customized inexact reasoning.

As discussed in Section 6.2, to discuss inexactness in general, we need to address two basic issues:

a. How do we determine the uncertainty of a basic set of events?

b. How do we manipulate the values obtained in **a** to arrive at the uncertainty of compound or complex events?

To use inexactness in practical expert system applications, we also need to deal with another issue:

c. How can we use exactness and inexactness together?

Question **a** is addressed at length in Section 6.7, where we discuss methods of eliciting judgments and obtaining confidence factors. Questions **b** and **c** are answered if we modify the basic concepts of two-valued logic discussed in Chapter 3 to represent *inexact predicate logic*.

Intuitively, we associate knowledge with truth. To know something is to have information about a state of affairs that is true. We deal with two forms of logic:

Two-valued, or *exact*, logic
Multivalued, or *inexact*, logic.

We combine exact and inexact logic by defining the truth values for two-valued logic to be the two numbers 0 and 100. Thus two-valued logic has two truth values:

  100 meaning true.
  0 meaning false.

Thus, in general, a *truth value* is either 100 (definitely true), 0 (definitely false), or an integer between 0 and 100, such as 80 (meaning 80% sure). A special inexact truth value *unknown* may be used to reflect the fact that we have no idea about a truth value.

We again use the term "*confidence factor*" (CF for short) to refer to truth values. The truth value for "5 > 3" is 100, while the truth value for "2 > 3" is 0. The truth value for *John goes to school* may be 100, while the truth value for *John likes wine* may be 70.

Truth values for two-valued logic predicates are 100 or 0; e.g., the truth value for *write Hello* is 100. If a two-valued clause returns a truth value of 100, we say that the clause has *succeeded*. If the clause returns a truth value of 0, we say that the clause has *failed*. This naturally extends our discussion of logic in Chapter 3.

Let A and B be clauses. To perform inexact reasoning, we need to define four basic formulas for:

  CF(not A)
  CF(A and B)
  CF(A or B)
  Combine(A, B).

In general, the developer of an expert system should be able to *decide on* the definitions for these formulas. For instance, the following definitions are based on fuzzy logic and certainty theory:

  CF(not A) = 100 − CF(A)

  CF(A and B) = minimum[CF(A), CF(B)]

  CF(A or B) = maximum[CF(A), CF(B)]

  Combine(A, B) = CF(A) + CF(B) − (CF(A) * CF(B) / 100)

However, in some situations one may wish to define:

  Combine(A, B) = (CF(A) + CF(B)) /2

to take the average of confidence factors. However, in doing so, great care must be taken to preserve *continuity* and avoid sudden changes in truth values. For instance, consider a possible (but sometimes inappropriate) definition for CF(not A) and CF(A and B):

CF(not A) = 100 − CF(A)
CF(A and B) = (CF(A) + CF(B)) /2 if CF(A) > 0 and CF(B) >0

CF(A and B) = 0 if CF(A) = 0 or CF(B) = 0

In this case, if CF(A) = 99 and CF(B) = 89, CF(not A) will be 1. Therefore, CF(not A and B) will be (1 + 89)/2 = 45.

Note that in this definition, we have defined CF(A and B) to be 0 if either CF(A) or CF(B) is 0 in order to conform to the definitions of two-valued logic. Therefore, if CF(A) increases by just 1%, i.e., if CF(A) = 100, then CF(not A and B) will be 0. Thus in this case a 1% change in our confidence in A will result in a 45% change in the confidence in CF(not A and B). This type of behavior is not desirable when confidence factors may themselves be subject to variation.

We will, therefore, usually use the fuzzy logic definitions for ANDs and ORs and the Combine definition used in certainty theory. It is easy to see that these definitions naturally correspond to the definitions of ANDs and ORs in two-valued logic when truth or falsity are known with certainty:

(not A) = true when (A = false); (not A) = false when (A = true),
(A and B) = true only when (A = true) and (B = true), else (A and B) = false.
(A or B) = false only when (A = false) and (B = false), else (A or B) = true.

We can easily check this with the definitions given above:

CF(not A) = 100 when CF(A) = 0 ; CF(not A) = 0 when CF(A) = 100

CF(A and B) = 100 only when CF(A) = 100 and CF(B) = 100, else CF(A and B) = 0

CF(A or B) =0 only when CF(A) = 0 and CF(B) = 0, else CF(A or B) = 100

Although certainty factors represent inexactness, in some applications, we may wish to reflect the fact that we are totally uncertain about a fact. The special truth value *unknown* may be used when we have no idea about the truth value of an inexact fact. Thus an inexact truth value may be any number between 0 and 100, or the value may be *unknown*.

In general, the value unknown will propagate indeterminacy. For instance, if CF(A) = 60 and CF(B) = unknown:

> CF(not A) = unknown
> CF(A and B) = unknown
> CF(A or B) = unknown
> Combine(A, B) = CF(A)

However, if CF(C) = 100, and CF(D) = 0, we have

> CF(D and B) = 0
> CF(C or B) = 100

since *regardless* of the value of B, CF(D and B) will be 0 and CF(C or B) will be 100. The truth value unknown combines with other inexact truth values as follows:

> (unknown and X) = (X and unknown) = unknown if X > 0
> (unknown and 0) = (0 and unknown) = 0

> (unknown or X) = (X or unknown) = unknown if X < 100
> (unknown or 100) = (100 and unknown) = 100

> Combine(X, unknown) = Combine(unknown, X) = X

Thus, combining a truth value with an unknown value has no effect on the truth value. The reason for forcing all other operations involving unknowns to become unknowns is that we cannot predict how the results are to be interpreted. For instance, given:

> CF = 100
>   A
> If
>   B
> or
>   C;

If CF(B) = 70 and CF(C) = unknown, it may, at first glance, seem reasonable to interpret CF(A) as 70 since we can in all cases be "at least" 70% sure about A, regardless of C. However, what we may be really looking for may involve the negation of A, e.g.,

$$CF = 100$$
$$D$$
If
$$\text{not } A \; ;$$

In this case, interpreting D as 30% true may lead to confusion, since C may be 90, resulting in 10% confidence in D.

6.6.1 Inexact Rules

Theories of inexact reasoning are interesting for expressing and propagating uncertain information, but to use them in practical inference tasks, we should utilize them within an inference engine. To perform inexact inference, as in backward chaining, we provided an inference engine with a specific clause called a *goal*. However, rather than simply succeeding or failing, inexact goals will have a certainty factor, which is a number in the range 0–100. Inexact inference finds confidence factors, or CFs, for goals by matching them with the factbase and conclusion of other rules.

We thus extend the concept of two-valued rule to the concept of an inexact rule. In either forward or backward rules, the certainty factor of the conclusion is based solely on the certainty factor of the premise; i.e., the conclusion is true if the premise is true. Inexact rules, however, also allow for the concept of *rule certainty*.

The certainty factor for the conclusion of a single inexact rule is based on both the rule certainty and the certainty factor of the premise. The certainty factor or, confidence factor, for the conclusion is thus calculated by:

$$CF(\text{conclusion}) = CF(\text{premise}) * \text{rule-certainty} / 100$$

In backward chaining, we look for *some* method of success; i.e., if a goal can be proved with one rule, we stop the backward chaining process without attempting any other rules. In inexact reasoning, however, we always try *all matching rules* for a goal and combine the certainty factors obtained from them. Thus the purpose of inexact reasoning in an expert system application is to come up with the most likely conclusion or explanation on the basis of the available facts.

For instance, suppose that we had the following rules:

Rule₁:

$$CF = 70$$
$$\text{Investor-1 } \underline{\text{should invest}} \text{ in 'X'}$$

> If
>
> > Broker-A <u>recommends</u> 'X'
>
> and
>
> > Broker-B <u>recommends</u> 'X'
>
> and
>
> > not 'X' <u>is</u> overpriced;

Rule₂:

> CF = 50
>
> > Investor-1 <u>should invest in</u> 'X'
>
> If
>
> > Broker-A <u>recommends</u> 'X'
>
> and
>
> > 'X' <u>is</u> undervalued;

Rule₃:

> CF = 100
>
> > 'X' <u>is</u> undervalued
>
> If
>
> > not 'X' <u>is</u> overpriced;

and the facts

> Broker-A <u>recommends</u>   Gold CF = 75
> Broker-A <u>recommends</u> Silver   CF = 50
> Broker-B <u>recommends</u> Silver   CF = 90
> Gold <u>is</u> undervalued   CF = 80
> Silver <u>is</u> overpriced   CF = 90

Consider what an inference engine will do to find the certainty factor for the goal *Investor-1 should invest in* Gold.

First, we check to see whether *Investor-A should invest in Gold* matches a fact in the factbase and find that it does not. We now try to find *all* rules whose conclusion matches *Investor-A should invest in Gold*. First, we find the first rule, binding 'X' to Gold. We try to find the certainty factor for the premise of this rule. The premise has now become:

> Broker-A <u>recommends</u> Gold and
> Broker-B <u>recommends</u> Gold and
> not Gold <u>is</u> overpriced;

We try to find a certainty factor for each clause in the premise as a goal. The certainty factor for the premise will then be the minimum of the certainty factors for these three clauses.

The goal *Broker-A recommends Gold* is in the factbase and has a certainty factor of 75. The goal *Broker-B recommends Gold* does not match the factbase or the conclusion of any rule; it will have a certainty factor of 0. This means that the certainty factor for the premise will have to be 0. We do not even need to attempt to find a certainty factor for the third clause. The certainty factor for the first rule is therefore 0.

Since inexact inference considers all rules whose conclusion matches a goal, we now try to match with the second rule and succeed by binding 'X' to Gold. We try to prove the premise of this rule. The premise has now become:

> Broker-A recommends Gold and
> Gold is undervalued;

Both clauses in the premise may be found in the factbase; the first has a certainty factor of 75 and the second has a certainty factor of 80. Thus the certainty factor for the premise of the second rule is minimum[75, 80] = 75. The certainty factor for the rule is then obtained by multiplication with the rule certainty factor:

> CF for the second rule = 75 * 50 / 100 = 37.5

Since the certainty factor for the first rule is 0, we do not really need to combine certainty factors; but if we had, the certainty factor for *Investor-1 should invest in Gold* would be

> Combine(0, 37.5) = 0 + 37.5 − (0 * 37.5) / 100 = 37.5

Now what would the inference engine do if we tried to prove the goal *Investor-1 should invest in* Silver?

First, we again try to match *Investor-1 should invest in Silver* with the factbase; however, no match is possible. We try to find all matching rules and again match with the first rule first, binding 'X' to Silver. The premise now becomes

> Broker-A recommends Silver and
> Broker-B recommends Silver and
> not Silver is overpriced;

We try to find a certainty factor for each clause in the premise as a goal. The certainty factors for the goal *Broker-A recommends Silver* and *Broker-B recommends Silver* are found in the factbase as 50 and 90, respectively. We then try to find the certainty factor for the goal *not Silver is overpriced* and to do so, we try to find the certainty factor for *Silver is overpriced*. This clause exists in the factbase and has certainty factor = 90. Therefore, *not Silver is overpriced* has certainty factor = 100 − 90 = 10.

Having found the certainty factors for all the clauses in the premise, we now find their minimum; i.e., the certainty factor for the premise is minimum(50, 90, 10) = 10. Then, as before, we multiply the certainty factor for the premise with the rule certainty factor:

$$\text{CF for the first rule} = (70 * 10) / 100 = 7$$

We now try to match the top-level goal *Investor-1 should invest in Silver* with the second rule and succeed by binding 'X' to Silver. We try to prove the premise of this rule. The premise has now become

Broker-A recommends Silver and
Silver is undervalued;

The first clause in the premise may be found in the factbase and has a certainty factor of 50. The second clause does not match the factbase but matches the third rule. The certainty factor for the goal *Silver is undervalued* on the basis of the third rule is obtained by

$$\text{CF(not Silver is overpriced)} = 100 - \text{CF(Silver is overpriced)}$$
$$= 100 - 90 = 10.$$

$$\text{CF(Silver is undervalued)} = 100 \ \text{CF(not Silver is overpriced)} / 100$$
$$= 10$$

since the rule-confidence (certainty factor) for the third rule is 100.

Thus the certainty factor for the premise of the second rule is minimum(50, 10) = 10. The certainty factor for the second rule is then obtained by multiplication with the rule certainty factor:

$$\text{CF for the second rule} = 10 * 50 / 100 = 5$$

We now combine the certainty factors obtained from the first and the second rule to obtain:

$$\text{Combine}(7, 5) = 7 + 5 - (7 * 5) / 100 = 10.8$$

The eventual confidence in *Investor-1 should invest in Silver* is thus 10.8, which can roughly be interpreted as about 10 percent confidence.

■ **6.7 QUANTIFYING UNCERTAIN KNOWLEDGE**

At first glance, quantifying uncertainty seems to be deceptively easy. We can, for instance, represent the confidence in a fact or decision with a number between 0 and 100. But in many cases, jumping to conclusions on the basis of readily obtained confidence factors will be misleading.

Experts typically do not have predetermined numbers representing the uncertainty of a particular fact or rule at hand. Instead, they guess or estimate such numbers in some way, e.g., on the basis of remembered information. In such situations there are a number of cognitive biases that may affect the accuracy of their judgment. One of the best known of these biases is the *availability heuristic*.

People use the availability heuristic when their judgment of the probability of an event is affected by how easy it is to recall a similar instance (Tversky and Kahneman, 1973). Thus one might assess the probability or likelihood of divorce among a certain class of people in terms of how many relevant cases of divorce one knows about. Like most rules of thumb, this is a "good bet," but it is not always accurate. Thus people tend to overestimate the likelihood of being in an airplane crash because such incidents are sensational and it is easy to remember various incidents (i.e., they are available for recall) from news media accounts.

The basic idea behind the availability heuristic is that:

People will generally assign a higher probability or certainty to information that is easy to remember.

Consider the following problem:

Estimate whether there are more English words that begin with the letter "r" or whether there are more that have "r" in the third position of the word.

In attempting to solve this problem, people tend to generate examples of both types of word and then base their answer on which type of word generated the most cases. In this situation, however, it is much easier to retrieve words that begin with "r" than corresponding words where "r" is the third letter, because we seem to organize our mental dictionaries on the basis of which is the first letter of each word. Thus the availability heuristic predicts that people generate more examples of words that began with "r" and thus incorrectly estimate that such words are more common.

Another cognitive bias is known as the *representativeness heuristic*. The basic idea of this heuristic is that:

People base their assessment of the probability that an object belongs to a particular class on the extent to which the object seems to be *typical* or *representative* for that class.

Consider the following example:

1. A group of 100 people contains 70 engineers and 30 lawyers. One person is chosen at random from the group. What is the probability that the person is an engineer?
2. Another person is chosen randomly from the same group, who has been described by a friend as follows:

Jack is a 45-year-old man. He is married and has four children. He is generally conservative, careful, and ambitious. He shows no interest in political and social issues and spends most of his free time on his many hobbies, which include home carpentry, sailing, and mathematical puzzles. What is the probability that Jack is an engineer?

In a study by Kahneman and Tversky (1973), the average subject gave a .7 probability estimate on question 1 and a .9 probability on question 2. In the first case the people in the experiment respond to the *prior odds* or *base* rates in determining their estimation. In the second case they appeared to increase their estimate of the probability on the basis of their perception that the description of Jack seemed to be more typical or representative of an engineer.

The strength of the representativeness heuristic was shown when the proportions of physicians and lawyers in the hypothetical sample was reversed. In this case people still responded with the estimate of a .9 probability that Jack was an engineer. Thus, even though the basic statistical information now pointed toward lawyers (the base rate answer would have been .3), the subjects in the experiment still appeared to be focusing on the representativeness and typicality of the description of Jack. Experiments such as this show that representativeness is a fairly powerful effect in uncertainty assessment.

When experts assess their own knowledge, they have to be aware of the cognitive biases that may occur. It is often harder to quantify one's thoughts and impressions alone than when assisted by another person. In such cases, the expert may benefit from trying to explain ideas to someone else, who may be another expert, an apprentice, or a knowledge engineer. The reaction of the other person, or the expert's attempts to clarify the issues, may lead to better quantification.

When knowledge engineers deal with experts, one approach to dealing with cognitive biases is to try to prevent their occurrence by carefully wording the questions that are posed to experts and allowing them to think about the implications of their initial assessments. Guiding questions may help experts to express their uncertainty (Behn and Vaupel, 1982).

A useful approach described in Section 6.7.2 is to force the expert to compare different uncertainties against each other. This overcomes the need to generate numbers "out of one's head." Instead, one can give judgments of uncertainty in terms of how uncertain one fact or rule is in relation to other facts and rules. Yet another approach is to use a visual or graphic representation, as discussed in the next section.

6.7.1 Graphical Representation of Uncertainty
Although experts can usually provide confidence factors as numbers such as 75% sure, we can give them further assistance by allowing them to "see" the confidence factors in a graphic form and visually compare and sort confidence factors. This can be done by providing a graphic representation of inexactness by using a set of horizontal scales.

Each end of the horizontal scale represents one end of the spectrum of certainty; i.e., one end means absolutely false, while the other end means absolutely true. The expert's confidence is represented by placing a marker somewhere on the scale, as shown in Figure 6.5.

If the expert places the marker toward the "No confidence" portion of the scale, the lack of confidence is indicated. Similarly, if the expert places the

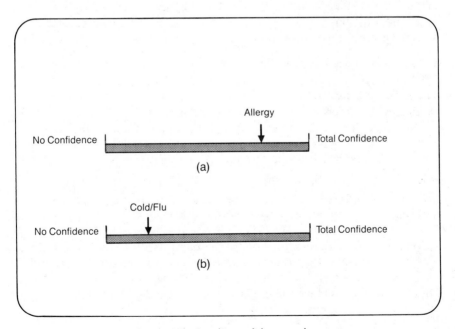

Figure 6.5 Graphic confidence scales.

marker towards the "Total confidence" end of the scale, a high level of confidence is indicated. Placing the marker in the midpoint between the two ends indicates a 50% confidence.

For instance, in Figure 6.5 graph *a* indicates that the expert has a good deal of confidence in the diagnosis "Allergy" for a patient. On the other hand, graph *b* suggests that the expert has little confidence in the diagnosis "Cold/Flu."

Graphical scales such as these can be stretched to give the expert more room to make judgments and can also have additional *anchors*; e.g., the midpoint of the scale could be designated as neutral or assigned a truth value of 50.

Generating a number, or even indicating a point on a graphic scale, will not necessarily lead to well-calibrated and exact uncertainty assessments. One problem is that few people have experience in generating numbers or marking graphical scales in this way. Experts who work with uncertain knowledge may not even think in terms of multiplying or combining measures of uncertainty when carrying out their reasoning, even though they appear to be taking account of the uncertainty in some way in their behavior.

However, by correlating a number of horizontal scales and dynamically sorting them according to the level of certainty, we may help experts visualize relationships between levels of uncertainty. In this way, experts may not only express confidence factors but may see a relative ordering that dynamically changes as they manipulate confidence factors. For instance, if they increase the confidence in Cold/Flu, this selection will move its position with respect to the others. This is a form of *sorting*, which is pursued further in the next section.

6.7.2 Uncertainty Assessment with Ranking

Often, experts may not have complete insight into their own expertise. Even when experts do have such insight, there may be problems associated with expressing that knowledge in an accurate fashion. An investment analyst, for instance, may not be able to fully express the levels of uncertainty dealt with every day. Thus, it is often unwise to asks experts to simply "pull numbers out of their heads" in response to a particular question.

In general, people perform rather well if they are faced with familiar physical quantities such as height but are not so good at estimating weight (which require more dimensions to judge) and are fairly poor at assessing traits like "friendliness of a smile." So, if there is not an obvious physical quantity involved, we may have reason to doubt the numbers that people use when expressing confidence since we are not sure how they are being produced. In many cases, it is difficult to assess uncertainty because there is no obvious physical property that can be used to assist in making judgments.

One method of helping experts to better express uncertainty is *ranking*. Ranking is a simple technique that requires the expert to order a set of facts or rules in terms of their uncertainty. Ranking has been studied in psychometrics for a number of years (Guilford, 1954). The simplest form of ranking is to present the expert with all the facts or rules and ask this expert to place them in order, running from the most uncertain at one end to the least uncertain at the other.

This basic technique becomes difficult to work with if there are large numbers of facts and rules to consider. However, there are alternative ranking methods that are more suitable for uncertainty assessment as the number of objects increases. We will describe the basic types of ranking method that can be used for uncertainty assessment and will then focus on augmented conceptual ranking, a method that we regard as a particularly promising tool for quantifying uncertain knowledge (Chignell and Patty, 1987).

Generally, all ranking methods can be classified in terms of one or more of three basic ideas:

Ranking by selection.
Ranking by insertion.
Ranking by exchanges.

Figure 6.6 shows these approaches for a set of three blocks. Selection techniques pick out the objects in order, using the general rationale of "select the next smallest" until the list of objects is exhausted and an ordered set of selections is obtained. Insertion techniques take the ith object to be sorted and insert it into the ordered list created from the i-1 previous insertions. This process is continued for all N objects. Finally, exchange methods successively compare pairs of objects in the list, swapping as necessary until the entire list is ordered.

6.7.3 Augmented Conceptual Ranking

Ranking methods that require a person to judge all the available objects simultaneously are difficult to use since they violate well known limitations in human working memory (e.g., Baddeley, 1976). Another drawback of such methods is that even if experts can cope with a large number of objects at the same time, they still tend to take a long time adjusting and readjusting the ordering of the objects. These problems can be overcome with methods for efficient ranking such as shellsort (Whaley, 1979), unshuffle (Kagel, 1986), and augmented conceptual ranking (ACR, Chignell and Patty, 1987).

Consider a problem where an expert must assess the uncertainty of each fact in a set of facts. We can illustrate the process of uncertainty assessment with the ACR method.

In ACR the expert begins by placing a set of objects (where each object represents one of the facts) in a rectangular array. The expert then carries out the following steps:

A) Ranking by Insertion

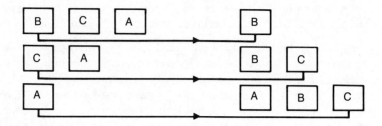

B) Ranking by selection

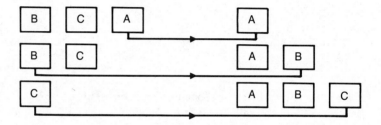

C) Ranking by exchange

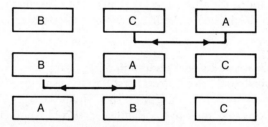

Figure 6.6 Three approaches to ranking.

Step 1. Rank the facts in the first (top) row, so that the fact with the largest certainty value is at the right most location in the row and the fact with the smallest value as at the leftmost end of the row. Continue this step with successive rows from top to bottom, sorting each row into left to right increasing order until the bottom row is reached.

Step 2. Rank the facts in the first (left most) column, in top to bottom increasing order. Continue the sorting with successive columns until the right most column is completed.

Step 3. Rank the facts on each of the diagonals running northeast to southwest in the array into top right to bottom left ascending order (as shown in Figure 6.7). Continue ordering successive diagonals finishing with the diagonal in the bottom right-hand corner.

Step 4 (optional). Assign scale values for each object on the basis of its position in the final array. For the facts in row i and column j, the assigned value is "$2i + j - 2$". This method for assigning scale values can be used for any rectangular shape.

A) Sort by rows

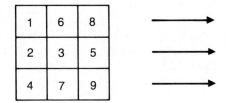

B) Sort by columns

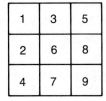

C) Sort by diagonals

Original value	Scaled value
1	1
2	2
3	3
4	3
5	4
6	5
7	5
8	6
9	7

Figure 6.7 An illustration of the augmented conceptual ranking procedure.

In the case of an 8 × 8 array (64 facts), for instance, there are 22 different scale values assigned. If necessary, ties can then be broken by asking the expert to rank the subsets of facts that have been assigned the same scale values. Figure 6.7 gives a visual representation of the ACR procedure.

Once the final array has been reached, there are a number of ways to convert that array into a set of certainty values for the facts. One method is to use step 4 above to derive scale values that can then be transformed into numbers between 0 and 100 using a linear transformation of the general form:

$$Y = a X$$

where Y is the resulting certainty value, X is the scale value assigned from the array, and a represents a parameter whose value is determined by the number of facts being ranked. For instance, assuming that certainty factors should be uniformly distributed on the range 0–100, and that there are M rows and N columns in the array, simulations suggest that there will be (2M + N − 2) unique scale values (Chignell and Patty, 1987). Each scale value can be converted into a certainty factor using the formula:

$$Y = (100 / (2M + N - 2)) X$$

Thus if there were 20 different scale values, this method would convert a scale value of 1 to a certainty factor of 5, a scale value of 2 to a certainty factor of 10, etc. Alternative transformations can be used if different ranges of certainty factors are desired. Other methods may be preferable, such as placing the facts in order according to their scale values in the array and then asking the expert to assign certain values such as 0, 5, 10, . . . to appropriate points in the row.

Augmented conceptual ranking is an approximate ranking procedure in that it is not guaranteed to yield the exact ordering of uncertainties. However, in most cases the uncertainty induced by the method is probably a great deal less than the uncertainty inherent in the experts' judgments. One can get some feeling for the approximate nature of the method by setting up an array with objects of known values and then seeing how well they are ranked by the method. Consider the following grid of 25 objects:

12	6	1	24	23
9	17	15	22	20
18	3	21	19	5
11	10	13	7	16
2	25	4	8	14

The reader can perform this experiment with a set of 25 cards, each representing one of the numbers and then laying the cards out on a grid on a table top.

How closely do the scale values assigned by the method match the true order of the numbers? One can continue to test the method by shuffling the cards and creating a new array that is then ranked, again comparing the order assigned to the cards with the orders of their actual values. The process of simulating the performance of a method like this and then collecting related statistics is generally referred to as *Monte Carlo simulation*. Extended simulations of this type have been used to establish the adequacy of the ACR method (Chignell and Patty, 1987).

The use of numbers, as shown above, highlights the approximate nature of the method. However, the method is designed for use in those cases where the values of objects are difficult to establish by other techniques.

■ 6.8 SUMMARY

Uncertain inference can be implemented in many different ways. When viewing uncertainty, there are two issues to deal with: the assessment of uncertainties for basic events and the use of methods for combining these to obtain uncertainties for compound and complex events.

We reviewed three basic approaches to uncertainty: probabilities, fuzzy logic, and certainty theory. We outlined the theoretical issues underlying each approach and gave some practical advice on the use of inexact inference methods. In general, a practical system should allow the developer the choice of using different methods of dealing with inexactness to represent different problems and subproblems. We showed how two-valued logic and two-valued rules may be extended to inexact reasoning.

We then discussed the issue of uncertainty assessment. We illustrated that care should be taken in deriving estimates of uncertainty from experts since they can be prone to cognitive biases often observed in human assessments of uncertainty. Graphical presentations and methods of ranking, such as augmented conceptual ranking, can be used to eliminate some of the bias from uncertainty assessment.

7

THE INFERENCE PROCESS

■ 7.1 INTRODUCTION

In Chapter 3 we discussed logic and outlined the basic ideas of inference. We pointed out that logical deduction forms the basis of the inference process used in expert systems. In Chapter 6, we extended the logical notions presented in Chapter 3 to deal with inexact inference.

To be useful, inference must be controlled. In general, the same methods of controlling inference will apply with both certain and uncertain knowledge, but with additional procedures added in the case of uncertain knowledge to take into account the need to propagate uncertainty through the inference tree. The goal of this chapter is to give a detailed account of inference, focusing on general methods for controlling inference that apply to both certain and uncertain information.

Inference begins with a well-defined goal. We must be able to recognize a successful outcome to reasoning if it occurs. Thus reasoning must be goal-directed in some way. As we pointed out in Chapter 3, a goal is a clause whose truth value should be determined. Computation within an inference engine relies on trying to prove goals, i.e., finding the truth value for goals. In this chapter we show different methods of achieving this.

We begin by discussing the inference process in general terms. We then focus on backward chaining and discuss issues relating to backtracking. Forward chaining is then contrasted with backward chaining and mixed-mode reasoning issues are discussed. Next we discuss algorithms for inexact and semiexact reasoning.

■ 7.2 THE INFERENCE PROCESS

We discussed inference in Chapters 2 and 3 and gave a number of examples of how facts and rules combine to form conclusions. The process of combining facts and rules was referred to as *inference*. It is often useful to view inference in terms of a *tree of possibilities*. This provides a diagrammatic way of representing the structure of knowledge and helps in visualizing inference as a dynamic process.

As discussed in Section 3.5.1, each rule consists of a premise and a conclusion. We can thus construct a tree whose *nodes* are the clauses used in the rule and whose *branches* are arrows connecting the clauses. When clauses are joined by an AND connective, we have an "AND node"; whenever clauses are joined with the OR connective, we have an "OR node." The branching in such trees reflects the structure of a set of rules. Such trees are called *AND/OR* trees.

These trees often provide good intuition about the structure of the rules. By using these trees, we can visualize the process of inference as a movement along the branches of the tree. This is called *tree traversal*. To traverse an AND node, we must traverse all of the nodes below it; i.e., we have to prove every clause in the AND node. To traverse an OR node, it is sufficient to traverse just one of the nodes below, i.e., to prove just one of the OR conditions.

The root of the tree is the *top-level goal* to be proved. To prove the goal, we have to traverse part of the tree by traversing the AND and OR nodes as described above. The parts of the tree that we traverse to prove the goal form a *path* along the nodes called a *proof path*. The proof path itself is a subtree below the top-level goal. We call this path the *inference tree* or the *proof tree* for the goal.

Different methods of inference traverse the tree in *different order,* although they may produce the same proof tree. As discussed in Section 2.5.1, we may draw an analogy between this form of tree traversal and the selection of connecting flights when traveling between cities.

In backward chaining inference, we start at the root of the tree and follow the branches toward the leaves until we find facts in the factbase. In forward chaining inference, we start from the leaves and work our way toward the root until we find a chain of branches that leads to the top-level goal. Consider the two rules:

If
    A
and
    B
Then
    C;

If

  C

or

  D

Then

  E

These rules are diagramatically shown in Figure 7.1. In this figure, each rule is represented as a conclusion with the relevant premises nested beneath the conclusion. We have also indicated the type of links that connect the nodes. ANDs are represented by links with arcs. ORs are represented as links without connecting arcs. The rules are linked by the clause C, which is a conclusion in the first rule and a premise in the second rule.

Suppose that we are to prove the goal E. Even with the simple inference tree shown in Figure 7.1, we have a choice as to how to control the inference process. One method is to take the goal and see what is needed to prove it true. To prove the goal E, for instance, we need to prove C OR D, and in order to prove C, we then need to prove clauses A AND B. This strategy is referred to as *backward chaining inference.*

Another strategy is to see what facts are present and then draw whatever conclusions are possible, continuing until one of the conclusions turns out to be the goal, or until no more new facts are available. Thus when facts A and B are present, this inference method deduces C. Once C is known, the goal E is recognized as being true.

It is tempting, but unwise, to attempt to draw blanket conclusions about the relative efficiency of forward and backward chaining inference. Each method will work best in different situations, as discussed in Section 2.5.1. The expertise of the expert is used to construct the tree so that its traversal will lead to efficient inference. Thus, as discussed in Section 1.4, one of the main lessons learned in the late 1960s and early 1970s was that success in building expert

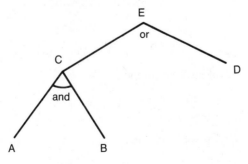

Figure 7.1   An inference tree.

systems often results from the construction of *smart trees*, whose structure makes inference easier to perform.

■ 7.3 BACKWARD CHAINING INFERENCE

In backward chaining inference, the system is provided with a specific clause called a *goal* to prove. To prove a goal, backward chaining inference begins with and focuses on the *conclusions* of rules. This is not as counterintuitive as it may seem. In medical diagnosis, for instance, the task of the physician is to find a plausible explanation of the observed symptoms. This is typically done by reasoning backward and asking "What could have caused this pattern of symptoms?"

Backward chaining inference proves two-valued goals (True or False) by matching them with the factbase and conclusions of backward rules. For instance, suppose that we had the facts

> Broker-A recommends Gold
> Broker-A recommends Silver
> Broker-B recommends Gold
> Gold is overpriced
> Silver is undervalued

and the two rules:

Rule 1:

> Investor invests in 'X'
> If
> Broker-A recommends 'X'
> and
> Broker-B recommends 'X'
> and
> not 'X' is overpriced;

Rule 2:

> Investor invests in 'X'
> If
> Broker-A recommends 'X'
> and
> 'X' is undervalued;

Let us trace what a backward chaining inference engine does to prove the goal *Investor invests in Silver.*

First it checks to see whether *Investor invests in Silver* matches a fact in the factbase. This fact is not in the factbase. It therefore tries to find a rule whose conclusion matches *Investor invests in Silver;* it finds the first rule, binding 'X' to Silver. It tries to prove the premise of this rule. The premise has now become:

> Broker-A recommends Silver and
> Broker-B recommends Silver and
> not Silver is overpriced;

The inference engine tries to prove each clause in the premise as a goal. The goal *Broker-A recommends Silver* is in the factbase and is true. The goal *Broker-B recommends Silver* does not match the factbase or the conclusion of any rule. We therefore fail to prove the premise of the first rule.

The inference engine now tries to match with the second rule and succeed by binding 'X' to Silver. It tries to prove the premise of this rule. The premise has now become:

> Broker-A recommends Silver and
> Silver is undervalued;

Both of the clauses in the premise are found in the factbase, so the rule is proved and we succeed.

Now, if we had tried to prove a goal with an unbound variable, e.g., *Investor invests in 'Y'*, what would the inference engine do?

First, it tries to match *Investor invests in 'Y'* with the factbase; no match is possible. It tries to find a matching rule and match with the first rule, binding 'X' to 'Y'. The premise now becomes:

> Broker-A recommends 'Y' and
> Broker-B recommends 'Y' and
> not 'Y' is overpriced;

We try to prove each clause in the premise as a goal. The goal *Broker-A recommends 'Y'* matches the factbase, binding 'Y' to Gold. The premise now becomes:

> Broker-A recommends Gold and
> Broker-B recommends Gold and
> not Gold is overpriced;

The goal *Broker-B recommends Gold* exists in the factbase and is true. The inference engine then tries to prove the goal *not Gold is overpriced,* and to do so, it tries to find the truth value for *Gold is overpriced.* This clause exists in the factbase and succeeds by returning a truth value of true; therefore, *not Gold is overpriced* fails and returns a truth value of false.

This means that the inference engine needs to go back and try alternative bindings. The process of going back to get a new binding or checking whether a goal can be proven another way is called *backtracking*.

We go back and undo the binding of 'Y' to Gold and try to prove *Broker-A recommends 'Y'* again. This time, the next fact in the factbase matches, binding 'Y' to Silver. The inference engine again tries to prove *Broker-B recommends Silver* and fails as before.

We go back again and undo the binding of 'Y' to Silver and try to prove *Broker-A recommends 'Y'* again. This time, no new facts match the goal. The inference engine therefore fails to prove the premise of the first rule.

We now try to match the top-level goal *Investor invests in 'X'* with the second rule and succeed by binding 'X' to 'Y'. We try to prove the premise of this rule. The promise has now become:

> Broker-A recommends 'Y'
> 'Y' is undervalued

We try to prove each clause in the premise as a goal. The goal *Broker-A recommends 'Y'* matches the factbase, binding 'Y' to Silver. Both clauses in the premise may now be found in the factbase, so the rule is proved and we succeed with the binding 'Y' = Silver.

7.3.1 The Backward Chaining Algorithm

In the preceding section we showed how backward chaining works with a simple example. The process of backward chaining can now be expressed in terms of a formal algorithm. To prove a goal by backward chaining, an inference engine follows the basic steps shown in Figure 7.2 and explained below:

a. *Is the Goal a Built-in Clause?* If the goal is a built-in clause, we evaluate it according to the semantics of the built-in predicate. In general, built-in clauses will be extralogical features such as input-output (I/O) predicates (read, write, etc.) or mathematical operators.

b. *Match with the Factbase.* Check that the goal does not match the factbase. If it matches a fact, succeed and return true. If the goal matches an askable fact (i.e., the system knows that the information can be requested from the user), the user is asked about the truth of the goal.

c. *Match with Rules.* Try to match the goal with the conclusion of a rule in the knowledge-base. If there is no matching rule, fail and return false.

d. *Prove the Rule Premise.* If a matching rule may be found, try to prove each clause in the premise of the rule. If all clauses succeed, return true.

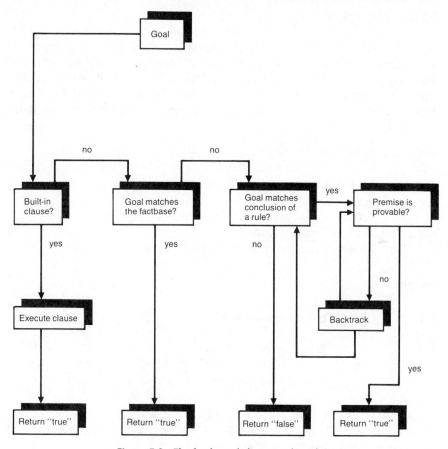

Figure 7.2 The backward chaining algorithm.

e. *Backtrack within a Premise.* In performing **d** above, if a clause fails, go back to the previous clause, i.e. *backtrack*, and try to find new bindings for variables in that clause, with the hope that these might succeed.

f. *If Necessary, Try Another Rule.* If the rule under consideration is of no use in proving the goal, we should consider the next matching rule in the rule-base, i.e., if no new bindings may be found in the current rule, try to find another matching rule for the goal. This means that the inference engine will try the next sequential rule whose conclusion matches the goal.

If no further matching rules may be found, the goal fails and returns false. Step **e** above is important in the operation of a backward chaining inference engine since it allows for the "rebinding" of variable values.

7.3.2 Backtracking

When a clause fails in the premise of a rule during backward chaining, *backtracking* takes place. Backtracking is the process of going back over clauses in a rule premise to find other ways of proving them. The process of backtracking is equivalent to backing up to a previous node in the inference tree (discussed in Section 7.2) and trying a new path. Trying to find a new way to prove a clause in the premise that failed requires finding another binding for a variable.

For instance, consider the facts:

> Broker-A <u>recommends</u> Platinum
> Broker-A <u>recommends</u> Silver
> Broker-A <u>recommends</u> Gold
> Broker-B <u>recommends</u> Gold
> Broker-B <u>recommends</u> Foreign Currency

and the rule:

> Investor <u>purchases</u> 'X'
>
> If
>
> Broker-A <u>recommends</u> 'X'
>
> and
>
> Broker-B <u>recommends</u> 'X';

In trying to prove the goal *Investor <u>purchases</u> 'A'*, we first try to prove *Broker-A <u>recommends</u> 'Y'*. We match *Broker-A <u>recommends</u> 'Y'* with the factbase and first get a binding 'Y' = Platinum.

When we fail to prove *Broker-B <u>recommends</u> Platinum*, we *backtrack* to the previous clause, i.e., *Broker-A <u>recommends</u> 'Y'*. We get another binding, i.e., 'Y' = Silver. Again, when we fail to prove *Broker-B <u>recommends</u> Silver*, we *backtrack* to the previous clause, i.e., *Broker-A <u>recommends</u> 'Y'*. We then get another binding, i.e., 'Y' = Gold. This time we succeed in proving *Broker-B <u>recommends</u> Gold*.

Thus the basic idea behind backtracking is:

Definition 7.1:   If a clause in the premise of a rule fails, go back to the previous clause (if any) and try to prove it in a new way, e.g., by getting a new binding or by matching with the conclusion of a new rule.

Backtracking may thus be used to find new solutions for goals.

7.3.3 Computing with Backtracking

Since backtracking generates new bindings for clauses, it may be used as a means of computation. We can use backtracking for computations that would otherwise require iteration or recursion. Backtracking may thus be viewed as a *computing paradigm*, as discussed in Section 1.5.1.

Often backtracking can be used as an effective method of computation if we use the built-in predicate fail, which always fails.

For instance, consider the facts

> Broker-A recommends Platinum
> Broker-A recommends Silver
> Broker-A recommends Gold
> Broker-A recommends Oil
> Broker-B recommends Gold
> Broker-B recommends Oil

and the rule:

> If   show recommendations 'X'
>
> and   'X' recommends 'Y'
>
> and   write "I think ", 'X', " recommends ", 'Y'
>
>   fail;

Now let us see what happens if we try to prove the goal *show recommendations Broker-A*. We first bind Broker-A to 'X' and then try to prove the clause *Broker-A recommends 'Y'*. The first fact in the factbase matches, binding 'Y' to Platinum. With these bindings, we then try to prove the goal *write "I think," Broker-A," recommends," Platinum*. This goal succeeds and writes

> I think Broker-A recommends Platinum

to the screen. We then try to prove the next goal, i.e., fail. This goal will obviously fail, so we backtrack and try to prove the goal *write "I think," Broker-A," recommends," Platinum* in a different way. But there is no new way for proving a built-in write goal.

So now we backtrack again to prove the goal *Broker-A recommends 'Y'* in a new way. This time we succeed in getting a new binding for 'Y', i.e., 'Y' =

Silver. Again we succeed in proving the goal *write "I think," Broker-A," recommends," Silver* by writing

I think Broker-A recommends Silver

but fail when we get to fail. Backtracking will continue in this mode until no further solutions can be found for *Broker-A recommends 'Y'*.

The top-level goal *show recommendations Broker-A* will thus fail. But before failing, the attempt to prove this goal has written 4 lines to the screen as follows:

I think Broker-A recommends Platinum
I think Broker-A recommends Silver
I think Broker-A recommends Gold
I think Broker-A recommends Oil

The backtracking process has thus acted as a method of computation. If we had wanted the goal *show recommendations Broker-A* to succeed, we could have defined it with two rules:

show recommendations 'X'

If

'X' recommends 'Y'

and

write "I think", 'X', " recommends ", 'Y'

and

fail;

show recommendations 'X'

If

true;

Then after all the possibilities for the first show recommendations rule have been exhausted, the second rule will be tried and will succeed immediately.

Backtracking with fail may even be used to call other rules, e.g., if we have the facts:

Broker-A recommends Platinum
Broker-A recommends Silver
Broker-A recommends Gold
Broker-A recommends Oil
Broker-B recommends Gold
Broker-B recommends Oil

and the rules:

> If
>
> Investor <u>purchases</u> 'X'
>
> and
>
> Broker-A <u>recommends</u> 'X'
>
> and
>
> Broker-B <u>recommends</u> 'X';
>
> If
>
> <u>show purchases</u> 'X'
>
> and
>
> 'X' <u>purchases</u> 'Y'
>
> and
>
> <u>write</u> 'X', " should purchase ", 'Y'
>
> and
>
> <u>fail</u>;
>
> If
>
> <u>show purchases</u> 'X'
>
> <u>true</u>;

then the goal *show purchases Investor* will write

> Investor should purchase Gold
> Investor should purchase Oil

and will succeed. Each time the goal *Investor <u>purchases</u> 'Y'* is called, the rule with the conclusion *Investor <u>purchases</u> 'X'* will match and will generate a binding for a purchase that both Broker-A and Broker-B recommend. After all possibilities are exhausted, the first <u>show purchases</u> rule fails, but the second <u>show purchases</u> rule will immediately succeed.

According to our discussion of the control quantifiers in Section 3.8.2 and later in Section 7.3.6, this form of backtrack/fail computation can also be achieved with quantifiers such as "for-every do." For instance, to define <u>show purchases</u>, instead of the two rules above, we can also write

> If
>
> <u>show purchases</u> 'X'
>
> <u>for-every</u> 'X' <u>purchases</u> 'Y'
> <u>do write</u> 'X', " should purchase ", 'Y' ;

to achieve a far more readable syntax.

7.3.4 Avoiding Backtracking

Sometimes one does *not* want to do any backtracking. Thus we need a facility that we refer to as *no-backtrack* to terminate backtracking. This concept is also used in the programming language Prolog (Clocksin and Mellish, 1987), where it is called the *cut*.

This facility can be used to disable backtracking in backward chaining. The clause no-backtrack succeeds the first time it is tried during backward chaining. However, one can never backtrack through a no-backtrack. An attempt to backtrack through a no-backtrack will fail the clause in the conclusion of the rule *altogether*, even if there are other rules within that clause as their conclusion.

If we have a rule of the form:

$$
\begin{array}{ll}
& A \\
\text{If} & \\
& B \\
\text{and} & \\
& C \\
\text{and} & \\
& D;
\end{array}
$$

then, if D fails, we go back to prove C. However, if we have a rule

$$
\begin{array}{ll}
& A \\
\text{If} & \\
& B \\
\text{and} & \\
& C \\
\text{and} & \\
& \text{no-backtrack} \\
\text{and} & \\
& D;
\end{array}
$$

and D fails, we fail A altogether, since one can never backtrack through a no-backtrack. Thus no-backtrack is like a one way street: the first attempt to prove it always succeeds, but we can never go back in the opposite direction. It is important to note that A fails altogether; i.e., if we have the two rules:

$$
\begin{array}{ll}
& A \\
\text{If} & \\
& B \\
\text{and} & \\
& C
\end{array}
$$

and

no-backtrack

and

D;

A

If

true;

and D fails, A will still fail, since the second rule will not even be tried.

This is an important point, and no-backtracks should be used very carefully. For instance, consider the following two rules:

'X' likes 'Y'

If

'X' knows 'Y'

and

no-backtrack

and

'X' trusts 'Y';

'X' likes 'Y'

If

'Y' seems nice;

First suppose that we have a factbase with only one fact:

Mary seems nice.

If we try to prove the goal *John likes Mary,* the first rule will be tried first. The clause *John knows Mary* fails, so we try the second rule and succeed with *Mary seems nice.* Now suppose that we have a factbase with two facts:

Mary seems nice
John knows Mary.

Again this time the first rule is tried first. The clause *John knows Mary* now succeeds, so we try to prove the next clause, i.e. no-backtrack. After immediately succeeding with no-backtrack, we try to prove the next clause, i.e., *John trusts Mary.* We shall, however, fail to prove *John trusts Mary,* so we try to backtrack. The attempt to backtrack through no-backtrack will then result in the total failure of the parent goal, i.e., *John likes Mary.* This means that now the second rule will not even be tried.

To illustrate this point further, as in Figure 7.3, consider how the placement of a no-backtrack changes the inference process in the following two rules:

If
    A

    <u>no-backtrack</u>

and
    B

and
    C

and
    D;

If
    A

    B

and
    C

and
    D

and
    <u>no-backtrack</u>;

Which of these two situations is more severe in restricting the number of alternatives that might be considered? It turns out that the second situation is more restrictive because the <u>no-backtrack</u> predicate is at the bottom of the premises and thus there is no possibility of backtracking once the first bindings for B, C, and D are made.

In the first situation backtracking is possible as far back as the <u>no-backtrack</u> predicate, but no further. This means that all the possible combinations of B, C, and D can be tried, but that if all of these fail, it will not be possible to try a different method of proving the parent goal A. Thus in the first situation we are committed to the first predicate that matches the parent goal, but we are free to try any of the possible bindings for the premises. In the second situation, we are committed not only to that particular predicate for proving the parent goal but also to the first set of bindings that are tried.

Placing the <u>no-backtrack</u> predicate somewhere between the beginning and the end of the list of premises will produce an intermediate effect where backtracking is possible for the premises below the <u>no-backtrack</u> but not for those above. Regardless of where the <u>no-backtrack</u> is placed within the rule, however, it will still commit the inference procedure to that particular strategy for satisfying the parent goal. Figure 7.3 illustrates the effect of placing the <u>no-backtrack</u> predicate in different positions with the premises.

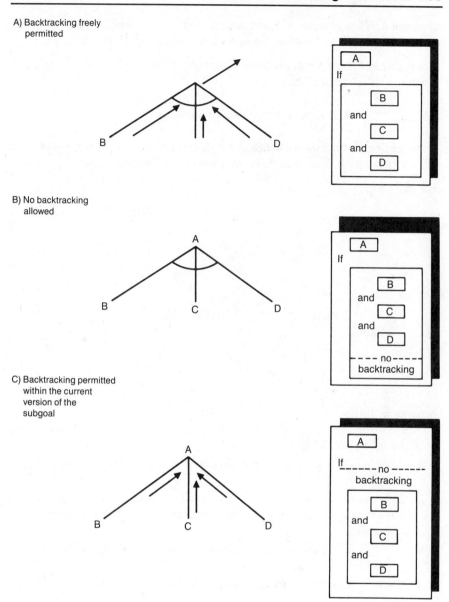

Figure 7.3 The effect of no-backtrack in a rule.

7.3.5 Reversing Backtracking

Backtracking is a way of backing up an inference tree to try and find a new set of bindings that will lead to a method of satisfying the goal. The reverse of backtracking, in some sense, is to allow the existing set of bindings to be used again. Thus instead of backtracking and finding a new path in the tree, by reversing backtracking we can continue to work down the same path.

The predicate repeat always succeeds, even on backtracking, and thus provides a method of iteration. Thus:

> repeat always reverses backtracking.

Thus, unlike no-backtrack, which ends backtracking with failure, repeat ends backtracking with success and resumes backward chaining again.

For instance,

$$\text{If} \quad \begin{array}{l} \text{print sequence 'N'} \\ \text{'X' := 0} \end{array}$$

and

repeat

and

write 'X'

and

'X' := 'X' + 1

and

'X' = 'N' ;

behaves as follows:

a. First, we set 'X' to 0.

b. Then repeat succeeds for the first time and we write the value of 'X', namely, 0.

c. Then we increase 'X' by 1. Note that at this time 'X' has the value 1 anywhere in the rule, since it has been involved in an assignment (:=) operation.

d. If 'N' is 1, we exit the rule; otherwise, the goal *'X' = 'N'* fails and we begin backtracking.

e. Backtracking passes by the clauses *'X' := 'X' + 1* and *write 'X'* with no effect.

f. We reach the repeat goal. At this point repeat will succeed and ends backtracking, thus beginning backward chaining again.

When we resume backward chaining, we write the new value of 'X', i.e., 1. Then, 'X' is increased to 2 and we compare it with 'N' again. If 'N' is 2, we exit the rule, or else we begin backtracking until we reach repeat, which will end backtracking and will again force us to begin backward chaining. This process will continue until we reach 'N' by increasing 'X'. Of course, if 'N' is 0 or negative, we will loop forever.

If this example reminds you of a FORTRAN loop, it is intended to do so. This example illustrates how we can write FORTRAN-like rules in a logic programming language. Such computations may, of course, be used for purposes other than simply printing numbers, since the clauses involved in a repeat rule may be any logical clauses. Using such iterative rules is often more efficient than recursions.

7.3.6 Superlogical Quantifiers

The no-backtrack and repeat predicates can be used to control the flow of reasoning, but people often seem to have difficulty in using them correctly. We need a set of higher-level predicates to control the flow of reasoning within rule-based systems. The extralogical quantifiers that we defined in Section 3.8.2 achieve this purpose.

These high-level, or *superlogical,* quantifiers facilitate the expression of iteration and looping constructs. These predicates are essentially shorthand notations for programs with repeats, fails, and no-backtracks, but make rules much more readable.

The first quantifier we discuss implements *exhaustive actions.* It finds every possible combination of pattern matches for a clause and then performs a specified action for each match. The predicate:

> for-every Clause$_1$
> do Clause$_2$

will find all possible pattern matches or proofs for Clause$_1$ and for each such match or proof will perform Clause$_2$. This predicate is essentially equivalent to

> . . .
>
> and
> > Clause$_1$
>
> and
> > Clause$_2$
>
> and
> > fail
>
> or
> > no-backtrack;

First, therefore, all possible pattern matches for Clause$_1$ are found and for each Clause$_2$, are proved. Then, after no other match is possible, the second branch of the "or" is tried and succeeds. For instance, the goal

for-every 'X' is a Container
do write 'X'," may contain liquids"

combined with a factbase that contains the three facts:

Container-1 is a Container
Container-2 is a Container
Container-3 is a Container

leads to the three written statements:

Container-1 may contain liquids.
Container-2 may contain liquids.
Container-3 may contain liquids.

This is essentially equivalent to proving

. . .

and

'X' is a Container

and

write 'X'," may contain liquids."

and

fail

or

no-backtrack;

Other examples of the use of this predicate were illustrated in Sections 5.8.1 and 3.8.2.

However, sometimes we are not interested in exhaustive information, but only in carrying out a procedure until a certain condition is reached. The "do until" quantifier achieves this purpose. This construct corresponds to the do-until loops used in procedural languages and is useful in directing an end to computation when a condition becomes true. The statement:

do Clause$_1$
until Clause$_2$

performs Clause$_1$, until Clause$_2$ becomes true. In general,

do Clause$_1$
until Clause$_2$

is essentially equivalent to:

>   . . .
> and
>   repeat
> and
>   Clause₁
> and
>   Clause₂
> and
>   . . .

That is, it will prove Clause$_1$, then try to see whether Clause$_2$ is true and if so, will succeed; otherwise, it will retry Clause$_1$, or go back to repeat and then retry Clause$_1$, until Clause$_2$ becomes true. Note also that if Clause$_2$ always fails, then the program will loop.

Consider the predicate <u>print sequence</u> defined in the previous section as

>   <u>print sequence</u> 'N'
> If
>   'X' := 0
> and
>   <u>repeat</u>
> and
>   <u>write</u> 'X'
> and
>   'X' := 'X' + 1
> and
>   'X' = 'N' ;

The <u>do until</u> quantifier may be used to achieve a more readable form of <u>print sequence</u> by writing

>   <u>print sequence</u> 'N'
> If
>   'X' := 0
> and
>   <u>do print number</u> 'X', 'N'
>   <u>until</u> 'X' = 'N' ;

>   <u>print number</u> 'X', 'N'
> If
>   <u>write</u> 'X'
> and
>   'X' := 'X' + 1 ;

A third quantifier may be used for *meta-level* reasoning. The predicate:

> <u>for-all</u> Clause₁
> <u>is-true</u> Clause₂

will succeed if whenever Clause₁ is true, Clause₂ is also true. From the point of view of execution, this is equivalent to:

> Clause₁
> and
> not Clause₂
> and
> <u>no-backtrack</u>
> and
> <u>fail</u>
> or
> <u>true</u>

This means that the <u>for-all</u> will succeed as long as we don't encounter a situation in which

> Clause₁ and not Clause₂

becomes true. If such a situation is encountered even once, we will prove the <u>no-backtrack</u> clause, then fail to prove <u>fail</u>. Since we can not backtrack through <u>no-backtrack</u>, the entire rule will fail. This quantifier is also discussed in Section 3.8.2. As another example of its use, consider

> <u>for-all</u> 'X' <u>is-a</u> 'Frame–1'
> <u>is-true</u> 'X' <u>is-a</u> 'Frame–2'

which checks whether every child of 'Frame–1' is also a child of 'Frame–2'. This is essentially equivalent to

> 'X' <u>is-a</u> 'Frame–1'
> and
> not 'X' <u>is-a</u> 'Frame–2'
> and
> <u>no-backtrack</u>
> and
> <u>fail</u>
> or
> <u>true</u>

The use of higher-level quantifiers greatly simplifies the programming task and makes the rules much more readable.

■ 7.4 FORWARD CHAINING INFERENCE

In some senses, forward chaining is the opposite of backward chaining since it focuses on the premises of rules rather than their conclusions. If the clauses in the premise of a forward rule are proved, the conclusion of the rule is added to the factbase.

Forward rules can be grouped into *rule sets.* A rule set is simply a partitioned set of rules. Each rule set has a name. The rules in a rule set are repeatedly proved, until either a given goal, or *hypothesis,* is proved or no new facts can be discovered. To begin forward chaining with a rule set (without a hypothesis), we may prove the goal:

> invoke rule-set-name.

We may provide the rule set with a hypothesis that terminates forward chaining by using:

> invoke rule-set-name, hypothesis

where hypothesis is a clause. For instance, consider the facts:

> Broker-A recommends Silver
> Broker-A recommends Gold
> Broker-A recommends Oil
> Broker-B recommends Gold
> Broker-B recommends Oil

and the rule-set Set–1; defined as follows:

Rule 1:

> If
>> Broker-A recommends 'X'
> and
>> Broker-B recommends 'X'
> Then
>> Investor invests in 'X';

Rule 2:

> If
>> 'X' invests in 'Y'
> Then
>> 'X' owns 'Y';

Consider what the inference engine does with this rule set. The first rule is tried first. We try to match the premise of this rule with the factbase. The first fact in the factbase; i.e., *Broker-A recommends Silver* matches this rule, binding 'X' to Silver. We then try to prove the next goal in the premise of the same rule; i.e., *Broker-B recommends Silver. Broker-B recommends Silver* does not match a fact in the factbase.

Remember that, in forward chaining, a rule can be applied or invoked only if *all* the clauses in its premise can be shown to match facts in the factbase. So the inference engine will continue searching for a match. Before considering the second rule, we find that there is a match for the first rule once we choose an appropriate binding for the variable 'X'. The two matching facts are:

> Broker-A recommends Gold
> Broker-B recommends Gold

When we try the goal *Broker-A recommends 'X'* in the first rule, we match the first of the two facts shown above, binding 'X' to Gold. Next we find a match for the second clause in the premise, i.e., *Broker-B recommends Gold.* Note that the binding of 'X' in the first clause of the premise has to match the binding of 'X' in the second clause of the premise, as it does when these two facts are used. Thus the two facts match successfully with the premise of the first rule. We now add the conclusion of the first rule to the factbase; i.e., we add the clause *Investor invests in Gold* to the factbase.

The inference engine will now try the second rule, whose premise is matched by the fact that has just been generated by the application of the first rule. Application of the second rule then produces the conclusion *Investor owns Gold*. Since there are no more rules in the rulebase, we return to the first rule again. We begin pattern matching with the factbase and look for a binding different from that used in the previous application of the rule. This search for new bindings in a forward chaining rule interpreter is analogous to the strategy of the backward chainer when it backtracks. In both cases a search for new information is occurring.

In the second application of rule one, *Broker-A recommends Oil* matches the first clause in the rule premise, and after 'X' has been bound to *Oil*, the second clause of the premise is matched by *Broker-B recommends Oil*. The conclusion clause *Investor invests in Oil* is then added to the factbase. When we try the second rule again, the clause *Investor owns Oil* is added to the factbase.

Now, when we go back to the first rule, no new matches for *'X' recommends 'Y'* may be found. We therefore fail to prove the first rule again. The same applies to the second rule, since its premise cannot have any new matches either. The forward chaining process thus stops.

In this example the forward chainer had no specific *hypothesis* to prove. We could have also invoked the same rule set with a hypothesis, by proving:

invoke Set-1, Investor owns Gold

In this case, as soon as the hypothesis *Investor owns Gold* was added to the factbase, forward chaining would have stopped. Similarly, we may have used the hypothesis *Investor owns 'X'* to stop forward chaining as soon as a matching fact is proved.

In this forward chaining example we applied each rule in the rule set in turn; i.e., we proved "all" the rules before going back to the first rule. There are, however, other forward chaining strategies, as discussed in the next section.

7.4.1 Conflict Resolution

Backward chaining generally proceeds down one path as it tries to prove a succession of goals and subgoals. In contrast, forward chaining invokes rules based on the facts that are encountered. At each step in the forward chaining process a rule is invoked if its premise matches the facts in the factbase. What happens if more than one rule matches the current facts? We have to make a decision as to which rule to apply first.

When multiple rules match the factbase, we need a strategy for deciding which rules to apply. Such a strategy is called a *conflict resolution* strategy. The need for conflict resolution thus arises when several rules match the factbase during forward chaining.

Conflict resolution can be better understood if we view forward chaining as a three-step cycle:

1. *Match.* Match all the rules against the factbase and determine the successful matches.
2. *Resolve Conflicts.* If more than one rule matches the factbase, choose either one, some, or all the matching rules based on a conflict resolution strategy.
3. *Act.* Add the conclusion(s) of the selected rule(s) to the factbase.

Various conflict resolution strategies have been defined for forward chaining systems. Some strategies are:

Do One. Choose the first rule that matches the factbase.

Do All. Apply all the matching rules in one batch, i.e., add all new facts at once.

Do in Sequence. Apply of the matching rules one by one in sequence so that a new fact proved by a rule can be used to establish the premises of rules further down the sequence.

Do the Most Specific. If there are two matching rules, and the premise of one rule is a more specific case of the premise of the other, this strategy favors the more specific rule.

Do the Most Recent. If there are two matching rules, select the one that matched a fact that has more recently been added to the factbase. This strategy, of course, requires the management of time-tags in the factbase.

Suppose that we have a factbase that contains the facts:

> A
> C
> D.

Consider a rule set with the following three rules:

Rule 1:

> If
> > A
> and
> > D
> Then
> > F;

Rule 2:

> If
> > F
> Then
> > G;

Rule 3:

> If
> > A
> and
> > C
> and
> > D
> Then
> > E;

The *Do One* strategy applies Rule 1, and then tries to apply it again. When it fails, it moves to Rule 2. The *Do All* strategy applies all three rules at once, but succeeds in proving only Rule 1 and Rule 3. The next time around, the Do All strategy proves Rule 2, since now the conclusion of Rule 1 is available as a new fact. The *Do the Most Specific* strategy matches all the rules and discovers that both Rule 1 and Rule 3 match. But Rule 3 is more specific since its premise includes the premise of Rule 1. Hence Rule 3 is applied. The philosophy behind the *Do the Most Specific* strategy is that it is best to select the rule that relies on the most information in arriving at its conclusion. In this case, Rule 3 relies on D, while Rule 1 does not. Similarly, the *Do the Most Recent* strategy will select between Rule 1 and Rule 3, depending on the recency of the addition of the facts.

Naturally the question "What is the best conflict resolution strategy?" comes to mind. However, the answer is most often dependent on the application. Attempting to answer such a question will suffer a similar fate to attempts to mandate a single method for general problem solving, as discussed in Chapter 1. While the method of matching and applying rules is relatively fixed, there is considerable flexibility in conflict resolution and there may not be one best strategy for handling conflict resolution.

7.4.2 Combining Forward and Backward Chaining

Variation in controlling inference can be created by developing strategies for *mixed forward and backward chaining*. The idea here is to find some way of switching between forward and backward chaining methods so as to produce an overall pattern of inference that is as efficient as possible.

In a medical diagnostic system, for instance, the overall diagnostic reasoning might be implemented with backward chaining inference, while forward chaining might be used to process and interpret the symptoms for subsequent use by the diagnostic system. In a monitoring system, the main monitoring activity may be controlled with forward chaining, while reasoning to interpret signals may be done by backward chaining.

A logical approach to inference allows for the integration of forward and backward chaining. Forward rule sets are invoked by the predicate invoke using the form:

> invoke rule set-name, hypothesis

and will succeed if the hypothesis can be proved. Thus a forward rule may be easily invoked from within a backward rule.

Alternatively, backward rules may be freely called from within forward rules. The premise of each forward rule consists of a set of clauses. To prove one such clause, we may either match it with the factbase or prove it with a backward rule.

Thus during forward chaining, backward chaining is attempted if a clause in the premise of a forward rule does not match the factbase but matches the conclusion of a backward rule. In such a case, backward chaining inference is initiated with the clause in the premise of the forward rule as a goal.

For instance, consider the facts:

> Broker-A recommends Oil
> Broker-A recommends Silver
> Broker-A recommends Gold
> Broker-B recommends Oil
> Broker-B recommends Silver
> Broker-B recommends Gold
> Investor–1 can afford Silver
> Investor–2 can afford Silver

the forward rule:

> If
> > 'X' is a suitable investment
> and
> > 'Investor' can afford 'X'
> Then
> > notify 'Investor', 'X';

and the backward rule:

> > 'X' is a suitable investment
> If
> > Broker-A recommends 'X'
> and
> > Broker-B recommends 'X' ;

In performing the forward chaining, the clause *'X' is a suitable investment* may itself be proved with the backward rule. Thus we call the backward rule from within the forward rule and first get the binding Oil for 'X'. We then resume forward chaining and attempt to prove *Investor-1 can afford Oil*. However, we will fail in matching this fact with the factbase. We therefore go back in the premise of the forward rule and try to find another binding for 'X'.

This now automatically initiates backtracking in the backward rule, and we obtain the binding Silver for 'X'. We then return to the forward chaining system again and resume the proof of the premise of the forward rule. Now the clause *Investor–1 can afford Silver* will match the factbase, and we succeed in proving the first rule.

Thus when we go backward within the premise of a forward rule, we may automatically begin backtracking within the backward rule used to obtain bindings for variables. This further requires that when the forward rule is invoked again in the forward chaining cycle, the backward rule resumes proof from where it had left off before. This means that in the preceding example, when the forward rule is called for a second time, the binding Gold should be provided for 'X' by the backward rule.

7.4.3 Proving Forward Rules

To prove a single forward chaining rule, the premise of the rule must be proved true. A goal in the premise of a forward rule is true if:

 i. It is a built-in clause that succeeds.
 ii. It matches a fact in the factbase.
 iii. It is an askable fact and is confirmed by the user.
 iv. It is proved true by backward chaining.

When the premise of a forward rule is proved true, its conclusion is added to the factbase. The steps to prove a clause in the premise of a forward rule are as follows:

 a. *Built-in Clause.* If the goal has a built-in predicate, prove it on the basis of the semantics of the predicate.
 b. *Match with Factbase.* If the clause matches a fact, succeed. If the clause is askable, ask the user.
 c. *Backward Chain.* If **b** above does not succeed, try to prove the clause by backward chaining. If backward chaining succeeds, return 100.
 d. *If Necessary, Backtrack Within the Premise.* If a clause fails, go back to the previous clause within the premise, i.e., backtrack, and try to find new bindings for variables in that clause, with the hope that these might succeed.

Each time a proof is attempted on a clause, the first option (if applicable) will be an attempt to find and use a built-in predicate. Then the factbase will be searched, and if not successful, we search for a matching backward rule. Backtracking will automatically occur within the premise of a forward rule when a clause fails. We backtrack to a previous clause within the premise to try and get a new binding.

If we backtrack to a clause within the premise of a forward rule that is proved by backward chaining, as in step **c** above, we begin backtracking within the backward rules used to prove that clause. Backtracking should take place uniformly across forward and backward rules.

Once again there are choices that will change the nature of the inference process. Instead of backtracking to a previous clause within the rule and looking for new bindings as described, we could have moved on to another rule. In this second strategy the system will not "remember" the bindings that have already been tried with the first rule. Thus repetition may not be avoided later.

7.4.4 The Forward Chaining Algorithm

We now describe a basic forward chaining algorithm based on the *Do in Sequence Strategy* for conflict resolution described in Section 7.4.1. Given a rule set of the form:

> If Premise$_1$ Then Conclusion$_1$;
> If Premise$_2$ Then Conclusion$_2$;
> If Premise$_3$ Then Conclusion$_3$;
>
> . . . .
>
> If Premise$_n$ Then Conclusion$_n$;

We first try to prove each rule individually. We begin by proving Premise$_1$, if it succeeds, Conclusion$_1$ will be added to the factbase. Then we try Premise$_2$, etc. until all the rules have been tried. Then we repeat the cycle again by going back to Premise$_1$. When the forward chaining process begins, the forward chainer may be given a hypothesis. The hypothesis is just another clause that will be proved. The basic forward chaining cycle can then be described as in Figure 7.4.

The forward chaining algorithm for Do in Sequence is as follows:

a. *Prove a Rule.* Prove the premise of the first (next) rule in the rule set. If the premise succeeds, add the conclusion to the factbase.

b. *Check Hypothesis.* Check to see if the hypothesis (if any) has been proved. If so, stop and succeed.

c. *Prove another Rule.* Repeat **a** and **b** for the next rule in the rule set until all rules in the rule set have been tried.

d. *New Assertions or Bindings?* Check whether there are any new assertions or new bindings due to this cycle of the forward chainer. If there is nothing new, stop. If there has been a new binding or new assertion, repeat the cycle from **a** again.

If there is no hypothesis, setp **b** may be bypassed. Thus, whenever there is no hypothesis, the forward chainer simply continues until no new facts or bindings can be obtained.

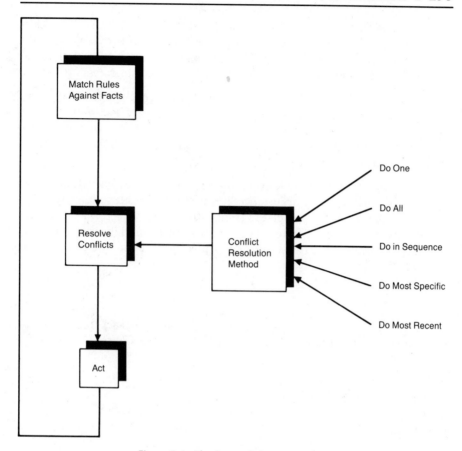

Figure 7.4 The forward chaining cycle.

7.5 Inexact Inference

In Chapter 6 we discussed the general issues involved in uncertainty, and in Section 6.6 we dealt with inexact reasoning in detail. In inexact reasoning, as in backward chaining, inference is initiated with a specific clause called a *goal*. However, rather than simply succeeding or failing, inexact goals will have a truth value, or confidence factor, which is a number in the range 0–100.

Inexact inference finds confidence factors (CFs) for goals by matching them with the factbase and conclusions of other rules. In backward chaining, we look for *some* method of success; i.e., if a goal can be proved with one rule, we stop the backward chaining process without attempting any other rules. However, in inexact reasoning, we try *all matching rules* for a goal and combine the CFs obtained from them.

Inexact inference thus aims to determine the truth for a goal. The premises of inexact rules include clauses whose truth value is a number between 0 and 100. Such clauses may indeed be two-valued clauses which have either 0 or 100 as truth values. Thus exact and inexact inference may be integrated.

During the inexact inference process, we may also prove backward chaining goals that return 0 or 100. In general any goal provable by backward chaining may be invoked from within an inexact rule. We may even invoke the forward inference engine from an inexact rule by proving a clause with the invoke predicate, as discussed in Section 7.4.

It is also important to be able to access inexact values from within a two-valued reasoning system. For instance, it is useful to be able to directly access the truth value for an inexact clause from within a two-valued rule. To do so, we may define a number of predicates that relate exact and inexact reasoning. One such predicate is the two-valued CF = predicate and has the general form

$$CF = \text{'X', Clause}$$

where Clause is a clause whose truth value is found by inexact reasoning. The CF = predicate then binds 'X' to this truth value. For instance, if we have the inexact fact

$$\text{Silver is overpriced} \qquad CF = 75$$

proving the goal

$$CF = \text{'X', Silver is overpriced}$$

will succeed and will bind 'X' to the value 75. We may use this predicate in a number of ways. For instance, we may extend the inexact reasoning system defined by certainty theory to allow rule certainty factor to be dynamically determined during inference. For example, we may rewrite

$$CF = 70$$
   'Investor' should invest in 'X'

If

   Broker-A recommends 'X'

and

   'X' is undervalued ;

to allow the value 70, which may be dependent on Broker-A, to be dynamically determined on the basis of the characteristics of any broker. The rule may thus become

CF = 'A'

    'Investor' <u>should invest in</u> 'X'

If

    'Broker' <u>recommends</u> 'X'

and

    'X' <u>is</u> undervalued and

and

    <u>CF =</u> 'A', 'Broker' <u>is</u> reliable ;

In this rule, the rule confidence is dynamically determined by our confidence in the reliability of 'Broker'.

7.5.1 The Inexact Inference Algorithm

As in backward chaining, inexact inference begins with and focuses on the *conclusions* of rules. The basic steps followed in the inexact reasoning algorithm (Figure 7.5) are as follows:

a. *Is the Goal a Built-in Clause?* If the goal is a built-in clause, we evaluate it according to the semantics of the built-in predicate and return 0 or 100.

b. *Match with the Factbase.* Check whether the goal matches the factbase. If it matches a fact, return the certainty factor in the factbase. If the goal matches an askable fact, ask the user.

c. *Match with a Backward Rule.* Check whether goal matches a two-valued backward rule. If it does, prove the goal and return either 0 or 100.

d. *Match with Rules.* Try to match the goal with the conclusion of inexact rules in the knowledge-base. Find a certainty factor for each matching rule.

e. *Combine Confidence.* Combine the certainty factors obtained from the matching rules. In step **d** above, the certainty factor for each matching rule is found by:

  d1. *Finding a Certainty Factor for Each Clause in the Premise.* Find a certainty factor for each clause in the premise by using this algorithm recursively.

  d2. *Finding the Certainty Factor for the Premise.* Use minimum for ANDs and maximum for ORs to find a certainty factor for the premise.

  d3. *Finding the Certainty Factor for the Rule.* Multiply the certainty factor for the premise with the rule certainty factor to obtain the eventual certainty factor for the goal based on the rule.

■ 7.6 SEMIEXACT INFERENCE

We can extend the range of possible inference methods by allowing the combination of exact and inexact inference during reasoning. *Semiexact inference* is the process of combining exact, i.e., two-valued, and inexact inference. Semi-

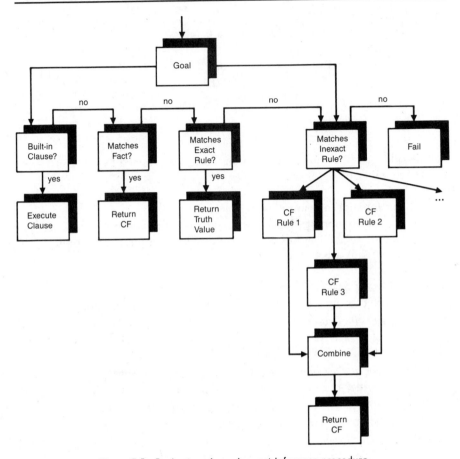

Figure 7.5 Basic steps in an inexact inference procedure.

exact inference relies on the use of inexact inference to find *the best value* for use within exact inference.

For instance, consider the rule:

> Diagnosis is 'Disease'
>
> If
>
> 'Disease' is likely
>
> and
>
> 'Disease' can be confirmed;

To prove the goal *Diagnosis is 'Disease'* with the unbound variable 'Disease', we try to prove the first clause *'Disease' is likely* by pattern matching with the factbase. Normally, 'Disease' will be bound to the *first* matching fact in the factbase.

However, likelihood is not an exact concept, but a vague one. What if we wished to find the *most likely* disease? We would have to consider *'Disease' is likely* an inexact clause and choose from among a number of options for diseases by selecting the option for which the *'Disease' is likely* has the highest confidence.

We may achieve this form of *semiexact* inference with a special two-valued predicate select-best-of, which evaluates an inexact clause on a number of selections and returns a binding based on the selection with the highest confidence.

For instance, suppose that we have a factbase consisting of:

> Disease-1 is likely   CF = 70
> Disease-2 is likely   CF = 50
> Disease-3 is likely   CF = 90
> Disease-1 can be confirmed
> Disease-2 can be confirmed

which offers three likely diseases. The exact rule above may then be rewritten as:

> Diagnosis is 'Disease'
>
> If
>
> select-best-of 'Disease' is likely
>
> and
>
> 'Disease' can be confirmed;

Let us now see what happens when the inference engine tries to prove the goal *Diagnosis is 'Disease'*. First, we match confirmed with 'Item' and the premise of the rule becomes:

> select-best-of 'Disease' is likely and
> 'Disease' can be confirmed;

Now we try to prove each clause in the premise as a goal. To prove the first clause, i.e. *select-best-of 'Disease' is likely* we invoke semiexact reasoning. There are three possible selections: Disease-1, Disease-2, and Disease-3. We need to find a CF for each of these clauses. The confidence factors for these clauses are found in the factbase as:

Disease-1 is likely	CF = 70
Disease-2 is likely	CF = 50
Disease-3 is likely	CF = 90

At this point select-best-of selects the clause with the highest CF; i.e., *Disease-3 is likely.* The exact goal *select-best-of Disease-3 is likely* then succeeds with a truth value of 100.

We now try to prove the second clause in the premise of the exact backward rule; i.e., *Disease-3 can be confirmed.* However, this goal fails and forces backtracking. We therefore have to go back and retry the goal *select-best-of 'Disease' is likely.*

When we retry this goal, the next selection will be the clause with the next-highest CF; i.e., *Disease-2 is likely.* Thus now 'Disease' is bound to Disease-2 and we need to prove *Disease-2 can be confirmed.* This clause matches the factbase and succeeds.

The top-level goal *Diagnosis is 'Disease'* thus succeeds, binding 'Disease' to Disease-2. In this example, rather than simply using the sequential listing of facts in the factbase, we used a set of inexact rules to find a binding for 'Disease'.

In this example, although the confidence factors for *'Disease' is likely* were found in the factbase, in general they may be computed by any sequence of inexact rules. Semiexact reasoning thus provides us with an alternative to the sequential selection method often used in backtracking in logic programming languages such as Prolog (Clocksin and Mellish, 1987).

7.6.1 The Semiexact Inference Algorithm
Semiexact inference begins with an attempt to prove a goal of the form

> select-best-of Clause

where *Clause* may be proved by inexact reasoning. To perform semiexact inference, as in Figure 7.6, we follow the following basic steps:

a. *Find CFs for Selections.* Find a CF for each selection.

b. *Select the Highest CF.* Choose the selection with the highest CF.

c. *Match with Clause.* Try to match the selected clause with *Clause*, the argument to select-best-of.

d. *Bind Arguments and Succeed.* Following the pattern matching at step **c**, the goal succeeds with a truth value of 100.

However, if another goal later fails and we need to backtrack and retry a select-best-of predicate, we need to:

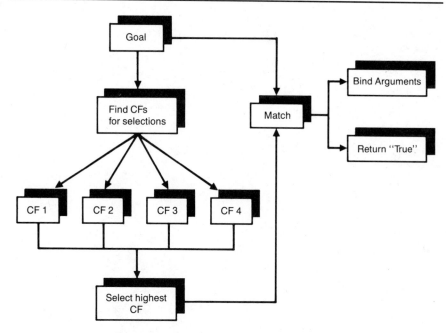

Figure 7.6 The semiexact inference algorithm.

e. *Backtrack to the Next CF.* To retry the select-best-of predicate, we simply choose the next-highest CF from the selection file. If no other selection exists, we fail with a truth value of 0.

Thus semiexact reasoning allows us to combine exact and inexact inference.

■ 7.7 SUMMARY

This chapter discussed the inference process in detail. We reviewed the algorithms for forward, backward, inexact, and semiexact reasoning and contrasted their similarities and differences.

Our treatment of these reasoning methods shows that we may uniformly combine them as control paradigms for controlling inference. We may also integrate them with the knowledge structures discussed in Chapters 4 and 5.

8

BUILDING EXPERT SYSTEMS

■ 8.1 INTRODUCTION

Knowledge of *what* an expert system is does not guarantee that one knows *how* to build an expert system. The goal of this chapter is to provide practical information about the process of building an expert system.

Expert system technologies constitute a new paradigm that extends the capabilities of traditional programming techniques to deal with knowledge-oriented tasks. In this sense expert system construction can be viewed as an advanced form of software construction and knowledge engineering as an advanced form of software engineering.

As we pointed out in Section 1.5.1, expert systems represent a new step in the evolution of programming paradigms. The key features of the expert systems paradigm correspond to the way that knowledge is represented and the way that reasoning is carried out. We discussed the following lineage of control paradigms:

The Goto or Jump Paradigm.
The For-Loop Paradigm.
The Recursion Paradigm.
The Backtrack-Fail Paradigm.
The Do-Whenever Paradigm.

and the following data and knowledge structuring paradigms:

Arrays.

Records and Fields.

Dynamic Data Structures.

Built-in Databases.

Frames.

Although expert systems can be seen as a step in the evolution of programming paradigms, like all new technologies, they require new social structures and methods for their use.

In this chapter we discuss the issues involved in building expert systems. We begin with a discussion of why expert system construction often requires a change of attitude toward the software development process as a whole. We then discuss the expert system lifecycle and describe its phases. Next we focus on tools for building expert systems and outline the criteria for evaluating such tools. To illustrate expert system architectures, we then describe the structure of some expert system examples.

■ 8.2 ATTITUDES FOR THE KNOWLEDGE AGE

Expert systems are the technology for use in the *knowledge age,* just as early computers were the technology for the *information age.*

We can draw a number of parallels between expert systems as a new technology and the development and the evolution of other technologies throughout recent history. The industrial revolution, for instance, created a new set of social structures based on the factory and the associated labor force. One feature of this technology is that one could predict with some accuracy the amount of time that it would take for a person working with a given machine to produce a particular output (Taylor, 1911; Barnes, 1980).

The social structures that grew around the technology included a number of fundamental, yet implicit, assumptions. For instance, one such assumption suggests that there is an almost linear relationship between manpower and output, e.g., that two coal miners can dig almost twice as much coal as one coal miner. Thus one can generally increase output by adding personnel along with the appropriate tools or machines.

The computer brought with it the information age and a new set of technologies. To begin with, the social organizations supporting these technologies inherited the implicit assumptions of the earlier technologies; e.g., some people began to assume that two programmers could produce almost twice as much software as one programmer in the same amount of time. However, the old rule about the linear relationship between labor resources, machine resources, and output no longer applied. If it took one programmer 6 months to complete a job, it was not generally possible to get two programmers to complete the job in 3 months.

As Fredrick Brooks (1975) has pointed out, software developers, and business and industry in general are still grappling with the problem of identifying and implementing the new social structures that are needed in the information age. Still, to this date, one can hear statements of the type: "Is the software project late? Why don't we hire some more programmers?" Of course, those with more experience now generally accept the axiom: "The most certain way to further delay a late software project is to add new programmers to it."

This is merely one example of the need for adapting social structures to new technologies (Toffler, 1981). The history of technological change is replete with similar examples. Society's response to new technologies inevitably lags behind their development (Figure 8.1). It is common for old organizational structures and ideas to be inappropriately applied to new technologies. The earliest cars were modeled after horse-drawn carriages. Today's computer key-

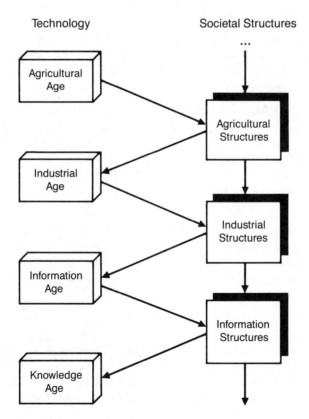

Figure 8.1 The asynchrony between technology and societal structures.

boards have a layout that was determined by the mechanical properties of early typewriters. People tried to apply the principles of industrial labor productivity to software programming and failed.

One challenge in building expert systems today is to determine what organizational methods are required by the technical paradigms and what current practices are simply hangovers from earlier technologies.

In the current climate where the rate of technological progress is accelerating, the new technology of expert systems has arrived well before any understanding about how to organize it within a larger social context. Some methods of building expert systems have been grafted onto the new technical paradigm in order to meet the needs of the moment. Society has not yet absorbed the full meaning of expert systems, and their ultimate role remains to be defined.

The situation is further complicated by the asynchrony in the development of related subtechnologies within a technology, e.g., the development of inference tools and knowledge acquisition systems. In such cases, the inadequacies introduced by the social inertia are compounded by this technical asynchrony. For instance, one outcome of the information age has been the development of computer specialists who act as *intermediaries* between users and computers. A whole range of roles of this general type exist, ranging from the systems analyst and the information systems specialist to the search intermediary who helps people find information online. The current relationship between experts and knowledge engineers is often modeled after this intermediary concept.

In many cases, such relationships are constructed as quick fixes to a more fundamental problem, i.e., the lack of knowledge acquisition tools to match the inference tools provided by the early work in expert system technology. In the early days, it was natural that the computer scientists who knew how expert systems worked acted as intermediaries, since others did not understand the language of the knowledge base, especially when it was written in Lisp or an early expert system shell.

This led to the focus of attention on the knowledge engineer as an essential component for building expert systems and on knowledge engineering as a discipline. In the rush to build expert systems quickly, this interaction paradigm, based on the role of the intermediary, has gained its own inertia and has led to stereotypes about expert system development.

However, just as the social structures suggested by this intermediary approach are solidifying, knowledge acquisition tools whose shortage gave rise to these structures are advancing to a point as to make the intermediary approach inappropriate in many situations. Ironically, the development and implementation of knowledge acquisition tools may now be overlooked and in some cases hampered by the stereotypes created by the intermediary approach.

The knowledge engineer is, in fact, a classic example of the type of intermediary that is seen so often in the *information age* paradigm. Intermediaries are probably not an inherent part of the *knowledge age* (of which current expert systems are just a beginning) any more than the labor productivity methods of industrial age apply to the information age.

This discussion should not be seen as an attempt to mandate a particular approach to building expert systems. Instead, we intend to emphasize the fact that a change of *attitude,* away from traditional views of information processing is essential to expert system development. We need to replace some of the attitudes of the *information age* with attitudes more suited to the *knowledge age.*

To make this discussion more concrete, we illustrate the point with two examples. First, consider the concept of a *prototype.* Prototypes are now popular within the software industry. Prototypes are often useful since they help demonstrate some basic features of a system. After a prototype has been constructed, it can often be extended to a fully functional system while its basic structure is preserved. It is generally considered that a prototype has succeeded if its structure is preserved in the final system.

Restructuring the basic ideas followed in a prototype is often unacceptable from a management or organizational context. The funding agency or higher-level management often will not contemplate throwing away something on which effort has been expended. It is thus generally expected that a project begins with a prototype demonstration and then extends the ideas developed in the prototype. This is despite the fact that the structures developed in a prototype reflect the resources allocated to it. Again, ironically, such resource are often limited because of the fact that the prototype "is" a prototype.

This *attitude* toward prototypes may succeed in cases where increasing the complexity of some parameters in the prototype does not dramatically alter the overall structure. For instance, a good indexing strategy for a database may be extended to deal with a larger file size in a reasonable manner.

On the other hand, in knowledge-intensive tasks, changing one parameter may require a total redesign of all structures in a prototype and may necessitate a new approach altogether. For instance, it is well known that a method that solves a problem in a restricted domain (e.g., a 4 × 4 chessboard) may not scale up to solve a related, but larger, problem (e.g., the same problem on an 8 × 8 chessboard or a hypothetical 16 × 16 chessboard).

In general, knowledge-related problems have the disconcerting feature that a *linear* increase in the definition of the problem leads to an *exponential* increase in the amount of knowledge needed to deal with it (where knowledge is broadly defined). Thus the success of a prototype expert system on a restricted portion of the domain may be extremely misleading in terms of predicting how useful the methods used in the prototype will ultimately prove to be.

Thus it should be fully acceptable to discard a prototype in a knowledge-intensive task altogether and start all over again, with the added experience gained in building the prototype (Figure 8.2). This, however, requires a fundamental change in organizational policies. In fact, there seems to be little alternative. Not discarding the prototype and insisting that its structure be preserved increases the likelihood of total project failure, at a much higher expense. In practice, this often acts as a much more elaborate prototype construction scenario in which, after the failure of the project, the development team joins other organizations where the prototyping experience is put to good use.

As another example, consider how the normal law of supply and demand does not always apply in the expert system paradigm. Normally, demand is expected to produce a supply. However, in expert systems the *expertise dilemma* generally causes those who need to automate expertise most to be the last to achieve automation of expertise. There are many anecdotes about cobbler's children not having shoes and behavioral psychologists who own unruly dogs, but when things are in extremely short supply, there is a tendency to ''eat one's seed,'' i.e., consume resources without thought for the future.

This typically happens when an expert system is constructed (too late) ''because'' experts in the domain are in short supply and as a result are over-

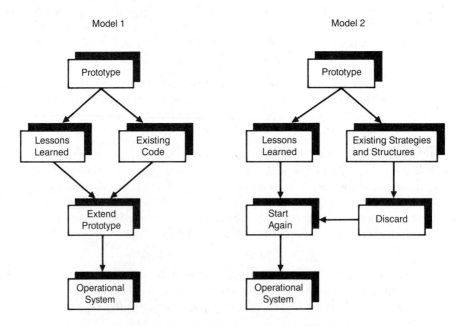

Figure 8.2 Two models of prototypes and their use.

worked and inaccessible. In such cases it is difficult to perform knowledge acquisition with any continuity since experts are often interrupted to "put out fires" and have so many problems on their minds that they cannot focus on the knowledge acquisition tasks. Thus the more valuable an expert is, the more difficult it is to capture that expert's expertise; i.e., demand adversely affects supply.

Isolating the expert from day-to-day activities for a period of time will, of course, result in short-term losses that may have to be incurred for the sake of long-term gain. Not adapting such an attitude will result in a failed expert system, as well as the loss incurred in partially taking the expert away from the day-to-day activities.

Thus, in dealing with expert systems, we need new attitudes about the nature of expertise, the relationship between knowledge and problem complexity, and the organization and utilization of expertise.

■ 8.3 BUILDING EXPERT SYSTEMS

Where should one start in building an expert system? Generally, one begins building an expert system with a set of questions in mind:

Why are we developing this expert system?
Will the effort in building the system be justified?
What will the return on investment be?
How are we going to build it?
Who is going to help us?
What tools are available?
Can the system be built in the way that we envisage?
What can go wrong?
When do we stop development?
How do we maintain the system after it has been built?

The first question, as in any software development effort, is "why are we doing this?" with the associated questions "will the effort in building the system be justified?" and "what will the return on investment be?"

The issue of *why* is quickly followed by *how*. If we think that the expert system can be justified and will produce a return on investment, how are we going to build it? In general, one will also ask "who is going to help us?" The development of most large expert systems is a joint, rather than an individual effort. Joint efforts have one advantage in that there are more people who are knowledgeable about the system and who can potentially support it after it is built.

The development of knowledge acquisition tools, as discussed in Chapter 9, makes it feasible for experts to take on some, if not all, of the knowledge engineering task. In general, the need for a knowledge engineer is often inversely proportional to the quality of the knowledge acquisition tools that are available.

Apart from domain experts and knowledge engineers, a third type of person who should be consulted is the user. In some cases, experts will use the expert system themselves. In other cases there will be a different class of user. The user should be involved early in the process so that the input-output characteristics of the system, and its interface, can be molded to personal needs.

The way in which expert systems should be built; i.e., the *how* of building expert systems, is strongly affected by *what* tools are available. At one extreme the choice of tools to be used in building the expert system is predetermined by organizational policy. At the other extreme, one has total freedom in the choice of the hardware and software to be used for expert system development. However, most situations lie somewhere between these two extremes and compromises need to be made.

We will discuss the features to look for in an expert system shell later in this chapter. Other important tools include knowledge acquisition tools and programs for testing and validating the knowledge base. An interface building toolkit will also be useful in testing early prototypes. Such a toolkit would allow a variety of screen design utilities, windowing and menu options, etc. This toolkit may be built into the expert system shell or added by linking external routines.

Another major question is "can it be done?" One way to get a better perspective on this question is to think through the possible failure modes and construct a "fault-tree," as it were. An expert system development project can fail for a number of reasons such as:

The knowledge required and the difficulty in acquiring it is underestimated, or the expert finds it difficult to express how the knowledge is structured.

During the project key members of the development team depart without leaving behind sufficient documentation of their activity. The system never fully recovers from the resulting internal chaos.

The project has insufficient financial backing, or because of internal policy or management changes, the level of resources originally promised is not fulfilled.

The inference engine is too slow when the system is fielded, producing unacceptably poor real-time performance.

Users cannot use the system because they do not understand how to operate it due to either poor interface design or to the lack of appropriate instructions.

No one is available to update and maintain the system as the knowledge in the domain changes. Consequently, the system falls out of step with the knowledge domain.

A serious attempt should be made at the beginning of the development process to think through the stages of building the expert system and anticipate any flaws or pitfalls that may be encountered. A sufficiently serious flaw may lead one to suspend the project, while in other cases it may produce a modified strategy.

Like any software development effort, building an expert system requires some discipline in the methods and processes that are used. Enforcing discipline can be difficult as a result of social issues that interfere with building expert systems. These social issues are often different from the issues involved in conventional software development, as discussed in Section 8.2.

A final feature of expert system development can be overlooked: Knowing when to stop. An expert system can always be refined, rewritten in a new shell, and so on. Deciding when development stops and the system becomes operational can be a difficult decision. Stopping early can lead to an immature system that is rejected by users. Stopping too late is wasteful at the least; and after a certain point the ratio of return to effort becomes unfavorable.

8.3.1 The Expert System Lifecycle

An expert system is a piece of software. Expert systems are similar to conventional software in some respects but different in others. To build expert systems, we must merge new ideas with traditional ones. Often an expert system is only one part of a larger software system. Thus the development of the expert system has to be coordinated with other software development efforts.

Thus, some software engineering methods also apply to expert systems and features of the *software lifecycle* can also be observed in expert systems. We can draw analogies between the phases in expert systems construction and corresponding phases in software development.

The process of expert system development can be compared with the traditional software lifecycle by identifying six phases in the expert system construction process (Figure 8.3). These phases are as follows:

i. *Feasibility Analysis.* The *domain* in which the expert system is to operate (e.g., medicine, engineering, finance) and the *task* which will be performed by the expert system (e.g., diagnosis, monitoring, cash-management) are studied and analyzed by the expert system builder.

Identification of an appropriate task is a vital step in the development of any expert system. The vague sense that an expert system might be useful in a

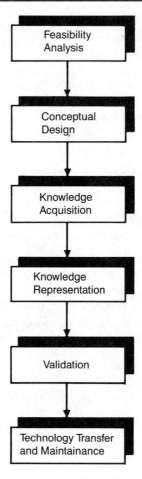

Figure 8.3 The expert system lifecycle.

particular knowledge domain is not, in itself, sufficient reason for justification of the effort required in building an expert system. The decision about whether to build an expert system should be based on a specification of what tasks will be performed by the expert system and whether or not they meet appropriate needs.

    ii. *Conceptual Design.* The conceptual structure of the system is defined, along with a specification that describes the way in which the expert system will carry out the task.

In general, the next step, namely, knowledge acquisition, is facilitated by having a good idea of the overall structure of the system. A good conceptual design tells the knowledge engineer what to look for and can be used to decide which issues are important and which are not.

iii. *Knowledge Acquisition.* The knowledge required for performing the task is acquired from a human expert, case histories, reference sources, etc.

This phase deals with the task of obtaining knowledge and formalizing it so that it can be included in the expert system's knowledge-base. Since expert systems rely heavily on the quality of the knowledge they possess, knowledge acquisition is a crucial part of the expert system construction process.

iv. *Knowledge Representation.* The knowledge is formalized and represented within a symbolic program so that it is executable by the inference engine.

Knowledge must be expressed in the knowledge representation method and the language of the expert system tools used for building the expert system. This task is facilitated when the form of the knowledge that is captured from the expert corresponds fairly closely to the knowledge structures that are available in the expert system tool.

v. *Validation.* User's views, expert opinions, or operational criteria are used to determine whether the expert system has achieved an acceptable degree of success.

Intuitively, the aim of a validation effort for any system is to answer the question: *"Does the system work?"* In the case of complex systems, however, one should first ask: What does it mean to ask, *"does the system work?"* The basic axiom relating to the validation of complex systems states: *"Complex Systems cannot be evaluated or validated by using simplistic criteria."* The expert system should thus be evaluated using a range of validation guidelines.

vi. *Technology Transfer and Maintenance.* The expert system is moved to an operating business or an industrial environment, and its structure and use are gradually modified through maintenance.

Many tasks involved in maintaining a functioning expert system often are analogous to tasks in traditional software maintenance. Categories of maintenance tasks include

Adapting user interfaces.
Porting the system to other hardware or software environments.
Reflecting new user requirements.
Fixing bugs and errors.
Enhancing performance.

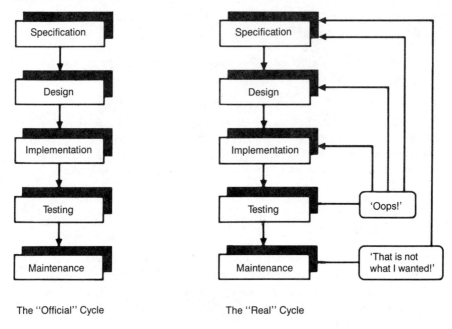

The "Official" Cycle   The "Real" Cycle

Figure 8.4 Two versions of the software development lifecycle.

In practical expert systems good maintenance makes the difference between an interesting piece of machine reasoning that is not used and a fully functioning expert system that is an integral functioning part of an operational environment.

Like the lifecycle for traditional software (Figure 8.4), the phases outlined above are not always distinct and sometimes involve some overlap. For instance, in doing knowledge acquisition one may uncover unknown characteristics of the task and the domain, leading to an overlap between knowledge acquisition and feasibility analysis.

8.3.2 Feasibility Analysis
One way of avoiding failure in expert system construction is to choose a manageable task. The task should not be too difficult (at present, tasks such as playing chess and innovative engineering design fall under this category), nor should it rely on large amounts of common sense (since expert systems rely on focused knowledge). It also helps greatly if there is a good model of how the task is performed. In the development of a medical expert system, for instance, it helps to have a good idea a priori about what types of disease exist and how they can be classified into a hierarchy.

When expert systems development is a commercial enterprise, additional factors arise that are associated with the development of any product. Like any new product, an expert system should be at least as good as the alternatives that it supplements or replaces. For instance, building an expert system as an alternative to the simplex method of linear programming would not be wise in cases where linear programming is appropriate since the existing product already does the job very well.

We can summarize the requirements for feasibility analysis in expert systems with questions such as the following:

Is the Task Lacking an Adequate Existing Software Solution? There is no point in duplicating something that already works well.

Does the Task Have a Narrow Focus? It is important to realize that often the best expert system tasks are rather limited in nature and have a narrow focus. Trying to develop an expert system that attempts to solve all of mankind's problems at once will result in failure.

Are Experts Demonstrably Better than Amateurs? It is generally difficult to attempt a task that has proved equally difficult for experts and novices. This generally suggests that the task is inherently difficult to deal with.

Will the Rules of the Game Change Overnight? It is important to know whether the criteria for performing the task are likely to stay stable; otherwise, it will be difficult to capture knowledge.

Is a Human Expert Available and Committed? It is essential to have an expert who will be dedicated to the project and who will patiently provide knowledge.

Is the Skill Taught or Documented? Teaching material or internal documentation and guidelines for performing the expert system task often serve as an invaluable source of information.

What Will the Criteria for Success or Failure Be? It is important to know what will constitute success for the expert system. Does the expert system have to be 100% right all the time, or will a reasonable rate of success or partial correctness be acceptable?

In some cases, even if the system succeeds 50% of the time, it will still be of great help. For instance, consider a system that successfully diagnoses computer crashes 50% of the time and says "I don't know" otherwise. Such a system may still be a success if it acts as a problem filter that handles routine cases and passes the most difficult problems to the human expert.

8.3.3 Conceptual Design

Once the task is well formulated and it is clear that expert system development is appropriate, the task of conceptual design can begin. A useful side effect of deliberately carrying out conceptual design as a separate phase in the lifecycle is that it allows experts to explore the structure of their knowledge. Conceptual design often focuses on a restricted but manageable portion of the knowledge domain that is representative of the concepts and structure present in the overall domain.

Conceptualization is an exploration by the expert, possibly with the assistance of others, into the main concepts and relations that make up that expert's problem solving knowledge. General constraints on problem solving are also explored during conceptualization. For instance, in hazard analysis, some of the constraints in aerospace applications will come from a variety of military standards that may affect not only the safety aspects of the system but also its performance and effectiveness. Part of the expertise is knowledge about what levels of decreased performance are acceptable for a given improvement in safety.

An approximate understanding of how the expert system will work, gained during the process of conceptual design, may help experts to frame their knowledge in an appropriate way. Thus we see an expanded role for the expert in knowledge engineering. The interaction between a knowledge engineer and an expert can be a partnership and a joint search for knowledge.

As well as specifying how the knowledge will be organized, the conceptualization should also trace the general features of the remaining components of knowledge, i.e.: naming, describing, relating, and constraining. These issues are supplemented with other information about the task to create the following list of issues that should be addressed in conceptual design:

> What are the major objects, concepts, or entities in the knowledge domain?
> How should the objects, concepts, and entities be described?
> What are the important relationships that exist between the objects?
> How are these relationships further constrained in the knowledge domain?
> What are the general characteristics of the problem that will be dealt with?
> How will the expert system obtain information about the current problem?
> How will the system interact with the user?

A final advantage of conceptual design is that it forces the experts to structure their knowledge and bring this knowledge out in the open. This process of knowledge explication will continue in the knowledge acquisition phase. The outcome of conceptual design is a conceptualization of the components and organization of expertise.

8.3.4 Knowledge Acquisition

Although there may be disagreement among different schools of thought regarding the best strategy or methodology for knowledge acquisition and representation, almost everyone agrees that these tasks are *the* bottleneck in expert system construction.

Since expert systems rely heavily on knowledge, the quality of knowledge acquired for an expert system will often be the determining factor in its success. Thus the ratio of effort expended to results achieved for the expert system as a whole is often decided by the knowledge acquisition process and the level of success achieved there.

Knowledge can be surprisingly difficult to recognize when it has to be extracted from a noisy background of hints and possibly relevant events. Knowledge acquisition can be likened to a distillation process where the essential facts and rules must be isolated from information that contains many impurities. Instead of being embedded in various handbooks and manuals, the knowledge in many domains is available only to experts and may never have been written down in a structured form. In such cases, the task of building an expert system must begin by acquiring or capturing the expert knowledge.

Chapter 9 is devoted to a further analysis of knowledge acquisition, where we discuss the various approaches and tools for knowledge acquisition.

8.3.5 Knowledge Representation
We discussed knowledge representation in Chapter 4. In Chapter 5 we showed how knowledge can be expressed in terms of knowledge structures such as facts, rules, and frames. Once we acquire knowledge, we use the knowledge representation system to transform it into the language of the knowledge-base.

One feature of practical knowledge representation is the need to subdivide knowledge into contexts as the amount of knowledge increases. Knowing how to organize and partition knowledge during the knowledge representation process may be particularly challenging in domains where the knowledge is complex but where different types of problem are encountered that generally deal with different contexts of knowledge.

A full discussion of knowledge representation is provided in Chapter 4; criteria for evaluating a knowledge representation system are discussed in Section 4.5. An evaluation of the integrated rule-frame system in terms of these knowledge representation guidelines is provided in Section 5.9.

8.3.6 Testing and Validation
During the validation phase the requirements for the expert system and the criteria for success or failure are verified. Criteria that can be used in performing expert system validation include the following:

> *Conclusions.* Validating conclusions is an obvious method for increasing the confidence in the expert system's behavior. This is essentially equivalent to evaluating the input-output behavior of the expert system, as in traditional software testing.

Reasons. Validating the reasons for arriving at conclusions is just as important as validating the conclusions themselves. This increases our confidence in the expert system and our belief that it is, indeed, a clone of the expert.

Reasoning Methods. We should validate reasoning and inference methods as well as reasons. This provides insight into how the knowledge is operated on and tests the operation of the inference engine.

If the evaluation is by human peers, the importance of psychological factors affecting the evaluators should not be ignored. It has been experimentally observed that in the evaluation of expert systems, some evaluators criticize the computer's inability to comprehend concepts when they know that the task is performed by a machine. The criticisms stop once reports are reformatted so that the evaluators cannot determine whether the task was performed by a machine or a human.

We can also assess the overall validity of an expert system, i.e., whether its appearance and performance are acceptable to those who will be using it. In making this type of acceptability judgment, care should be taken to account for subjective factors which relate more to the appearance than to the performance of the system. Some overall validity criteria include the following:

Face Validity. Does the expert system look and feel good in terms of its knowledge-base, inference structure, and output?

Naturalness. How well does the system do in giving the user a feeling of dealing with an expert rather than with a machine?

Coverage. How well does the expert system cover the range of important problems in its knowledge domain?

Robustness. How sensitive is the expert system to minor changes in the way that the problem is described?

Performance. How well does the performance of the system match reality? For instance, does an investment adviser give profitable investment advice?

Precision. How precise are the predictions made by the system? For instance, does a fault diagnosis system provide a detailed fault description or simply an idea of the general location of the fault?

Reliability. What proportion of the advice or predictions of the system can be classified as being in error?

Validation increases one's confidence in the future behavior of the system, but there can never be total certainty about the correctness of any nontrivial software system. This concept is well known to those involved in program verification efforts.

Even with the best attempts at validation, an expert system may inevitably make mistakes in unexpected situations. Of course, human experts also make mistakes, and we tend to tolerate them—except when they lead to catastrophe. The key questions to ask in tolerating the mistakes of an expert system are how often the mistakes are made and what price one must pay for each mistake.

8.3.7 Maintenance

It is important not to forget about possible problems in maintaining an expert system when one is focusing on the prior problem of building it. Once the expert system becomes available to users outside the original development team, the problem of maintenance emerges.

For instance, the user interface will need to be adapted to the needs of the users. Significant modification of the interface will tend to occur over the life of an expert system for two reasons:

1. Over time it will become much easier to modify the interface than to modify the basic knowledge-base and inference engine used in the expert system.
2. User evaluation and acceptance of the system will be heavily influenced by the quality of the interface. Some users may even prefer a less competent expert system if it has a better interface. This effect can occur in medicine where a good bedside manner may outweigh other considerations in determining the acceptability of a physician for patients.

Portability of expert system software is often necessary because the type of hardware and software environment used in developing and rapid prototyping of the system may not be available or appropriate for versions of the system in the field. Expert systems for aiding the aircraft pilot, for instance, will have to run on hardware that conforms to the constraints of an environment where weight and space are critical.

One feature of early expert systems was that they could only run on a certain type of expensive machine. The current trend toward implementing expert system shells in conventional languages, notably the C programming language, is leading to much more portable expert systems. While the knowledge-base and inference engine will be fairly portable, however, the user interface is likely to continue to be somewhat machine dependent.

New releases of an operational expert system are inevitable as the system is updated to cope with erroneous knowledge, missing knowledge, and a changing environment that creates new knowledge. New releases are problematic in that they may create new bugs or old code may not be "upwardly compatible" with them. The problem of new releases may be particularly severe in expert systems where the systems are developed by small teams of highly skilled people who may have little patience with irritating bugs or site-specific problems.

This points up the fact that an expert system will also require support. This is, in fact, a good argument for developing in-house expertise on the expert system so that there is not an undue reliance on the few individuals who originally built the system.

■ 8.4 TOOLS FOR BUILDING EXPERT SYSTEMS

A program used to build an expert system is usually called an *expert system shell.* In the same way that a word processor is not a letter or document, but a shell that aids in the creation of the text file, an expert system shell aids in the creation of an expert system.

The expert system shell can be considered as a reasoning system out of which all the knowledge has been emptied. When knowledge about a new domain is entered into the shell appropriately an expert system is created. The original shell can then be used to create a new expert system in similar fashion.

An expert system shell performs three major functions:

1. Assists in building the knowledge-base by allowing the developer to insert knowledge into knowledge representation structures. There is a close analogy here between using the word processor to insert text into a text file and using an expert system shell to insert knowledge into a knowledge-base.
2. Provides methods of inference or deduction (which we described in Chapters 3 and 5) that reason on the basis of information in the knowledge-base and new facts input by the user.
3. Provides an interface that allows the user to set up reasoning tasks and query the system about its reasoning strategy.

Of the three functions of the expert system shell, the construction of the knowledge-base places the greatest burden on the developer. The inference methods and interface are standard features of the shell that do not change greatly across different expert systems. But the knowledge-base is unique to each expert system and the shell gives no assistance in collecting and organizing the knowledge, it only provides a framework in which to express the knowledge.

An expert system shell should therefore be distinguished from a *knowledge acquisition tool,* which helps in the elicitation and organization of knowledge. Knowledge acquisition tools are discussed further in Chapter 9.

Many different shells are available today, each with a different set of features. However, at a minimum, an expert system shell should be expected to have:

1. A production rule system, preferably capable of varying inference strategies, as discussed in Chapter 7.

2. A method of organizing the knowledge in the database (frames, objects, etc.) as discussed in Chapter 4.

3. A method for reasoning with uncertain information, as discussed in Chapter 6.

It is generally advantageous to implement an expert system using a shell rather than directly in Lisp, Prolog, or another language. In a direct implementation, the bulk of the programming task will in fact be repetition of effort as facilities such as explanation, forward chaining inference, and so on are developed, essentially replicating a shell.

The relative attractiveness of Lisp and Prolog as expert systems development languages is diminishing as more and more features are added to expert system shells. Although early shells were built in Lisp, today many modern shells are implemented in conventional languages such as C and Ada, with consequent improvements of speed and portability.

The ability to implement symbolic reasoning is an essential feature of an expert system shell. Expert system shells are designed for reasoning. One should not use a shell to carry out tasks, such as mathematical programming, that are performed well by numerical reasoning languages.

A good shell includes special-purpose interfaces to make the construction and operation of expert systems as smooth as possible. Some shells can be used as very high level programming languages, and the functionality of other languages that excel in numerical reasoning, for instance, can be emulated by providing "hooks" so that predicates in the expert system shell actually call subroutines written in a conventional language (e.g., see Section 3.8.3).

The expert system shell should also have a built-in ability to construct explanations. Human experts are often asked to explain their views, recommendations, or decisions. If a physician suggests an operation to a patient, the patient may wish to ask why the operation is necessary. If expert systems are to mimic humans in performing highly specialized tasks, they need to justify and explain their actions.

A good explanation facility is particularly useful in developing a large expert system that includes more facts and rules than can be easily remembered. Often, a new rule added during expert system development will interact with other rules and data in unanticipated ways and will make the expert system display strange behavior. A good explanation facility can then help the system designer to identify and remedy such anomalies.

The proliferation of expert system shells coupled with the advance of micro-computer technology means that expert systems can be effectively built and delivered on personal computers. This, in turn, has led to an unprecedented capability for experts to build their own expert systems on a relatively small budget given the assistance of effective knowledge acquisition tools.

8.4.1 What to Look for in an Expert System Tool

The effectiveness of an expert system shell can be evaluated independently of the effectiveness of the expert systems that are created using it (although we expect that good expert system shells lead to good expert systems, provided that they are used properly).

We develop a set of guidelines for evaluating shells in terms of their ability to express knowledge, organize and display knowledge, reason with and validate knowledge, and operate with knowledge.

8.4.1.1 *Expressing Knowledge*   Expressing knowledge is not just a problem in expert systems development. It is a fundamental problem for the teacher, the author, and anyone who is trying to communicate knowledge. The two components in expressing knowledge are

The conceptual model.

The language.

The *conceptual model* includes the basic way in which knowledge is represented in the system along with an interpretation that organizes the knowledge in a form that is appropriate for the current context. The *language* then transforms the components of the conceptual model into a standardized description that can be recognized by other agents who speak the same language.

The same conceptual model can be used with multiple languages, as is shown by the speaker who can express the same idea in a number of different languages. Another analogy concerns data modeling for databases. The *relational data model* can be used to capture the structure of a database, while being used with a variety of query languages.

Issues involving the expression of knowledge in expert system shells generally revolve around the adequacy of the knowledge representation language and the ease with which concepts can be transformed into the language. The adequacy of the knowledge representation language is captured in the notion of descriptive power:

> *Descriptive Power.* An expert system shell should be capable of describing a wide variety of knowledge domains. Thus the knowledge structures used to represent knowledge should be sufficiently general to cover many knowledge domains, and the inference engine should not be specialized to a restricted class of knowledge domains.

This criterion should be tempered with the understanding that, in contrast to general expert system shells, it is possible to develop specialized shells to cope with the special features of restricted classes of knowledge domain.

The transformation of concepts into the knowledge structures of a language is a difficult task, which is made easier when the way in which concepts are expressed and organized appears to correspond to appropriate terms and structures in the language. We refer to this criterion as "ease of translation":

> *Ease of Translation.* An expert system shell facilitates easy translation if users can learn it easily and write code that is relatively free of both syntactic and semantic errors.

Paradoxically, perhaps, natural language may not facilitate easy translation as far as expert systems are concerned because it often leads to the blurring of distinctions that are important in reasoning as was discussed in Chapter 4. This leads us to the notion of readability:

> *Readability.* Unless security issues are involved expert system code should be highly readable. Readability makes it easier to update and maintain code. Readability makes it easier to build explanation facilities that point to the rules being used in describing what is going on to the user.

Readability also allows the expert system to function as a succint representation of the expertise that is useful in both training and archiving knowledge.

The fourth criterion relating to the expression of knowledge concerns the ease with which representations in the language can be modified to reflect changes in the conceptual model:

> *Flexibility.* In traditional computer programs, complex models are written using deeply nested logic and specially tailored data structures. As a result, these models tend to be difficult to change, particularly when changes affect the fundamental structure of the program or data.

An expert system shell should facilitate the graceful introduction of additional facts and rules. This type of flexibility permits dramatic modification of expert system behavior without major reprogramming.

Another important issue is whether experts can use the shell themselves. Although factors such as speed will be obvious to experts, they will be particularly concerned with the quality of the user interface and whether it allows them to enter and review their knowledge in a natural way.

8.4.1.2 *Organizing and Displaying Knowledge*

The ability to organize and display knowledge helps the developers as well as the user of the expert system.

The management of rules and data can be difficult if there are no immediate structuring principles that can be used in displaying the organization of the knowledge to the user.

A knowledge editor is needed to display the current knowledge representation when it is being modified. This editor should be intelligent in that it knows how the knowledge-base is organized so that related knowledge structures are presented to the user and changes in one version of a particular knowledge structure will also be reflected in related versions of the knowledge structure.

The functions of the intelligent editor will generally be a subset of a more general system for managing knowledge. The *knowledge manager* should include a number of facilities for viewing the knowledge and checking new entries. Features for browsing over knowledge in some fashion are particularly useful. One way of implementing a browsing facility is to have the overall knowledge structure displayed as a hierarchy or network, with the ability to zoom in on a node in the network which in turn expands into a new network. A useful way of displaying a rule is to show the inference tree that will be generated when the rule is invoked.

Another useful concept is the Masterscope. The masterscope is an interactive program that contains facilities for analyzing rules to determine which other rules are called by it or it calls, as well as how and where the variables are bound or referenced. As with any method of displaying knowledge, the masterscope can also be useful in validating and debugging the system.

8.4.1.3 *Reasoning with and Validating Knowledge*

For expert systems, a large part of validation will be concerned with the knowledge in the knowledge-base. Knowledge can be surprisingly difficult to validate. The evaluation and validation of expert systems requires a wide range of criteria and methods.

Validation methods should address the validity of conclusions, the reasons for arriving at conclusions, and the basic reasoning methods themselves. Inference itself is a method for establishing valid arguments and can be used to determine whether there are inconsistent rules in the knowledge-base. Explanations can be used to check whether the utilization of knowledge makes sense. Case histories can also be used in validating knowledge by assessing the output of the expert system against the actual outcomes of previous cases.

Section 9.10 discusses expert system validation and how it can be automated. Chapters 3, 6 and 7 discuss logic, reasoning and inference.

8.4.1.4 *Operating with Knowledge*

Basic issues about the speed and performance of the expert system should be carefully considered. Users may not accept a system that reasons too slowly or cannot handle the size of knowledge-base that their application requires. An expert system should be compact and should operate speedily in most cases.

There are many different ways in which to assess the speed of an expert system shell. One way is to measure the time to execute a rule in a standard application. Other speed related criteria are as follows:

Time to retrieve a fact.

Time to delete a fact.

Time to access a frame slot.

Time to assign a value to a slot.

Time to add or delete a slot.

Time to access a slot through inheritance.

Other issues that are of concern include the size of the knowledge-base, e.g.; will the application outgrow the expert system shell as more and more knowledge is added?

The integration of the expert system with conventional software and links to the outside world should be considered. Relevant questions include the following:

Does the shell provide an interface to applications such as spreadsheets and databases?

Does the shell provide an execution/runtime version? As well as accelerating the performance of the system, this allows developers to field the expert system without losing control of the source code.

Does the shell communicate with external interfaces such as the RS232 port? This is important in systems that need to acquire data online, control devices, or interact with other computer systems.

The efficiency of an expert system is determined largely by the shell in which it is implemented. The processing time of an expert system should not increase exponentially with a linear increase in the number of rules, for instance.

▪ 8.5 AN ANALYSIS OF EXPERT SYSTEM ARCHITECTURES

The apparent uniformity with which facts, rules, and frames may be used for knowledge representation should not disguise the diversity of expert system architectures that can be constructed for different knowledge domains. Aside from the choice of whether to use forward chaining inference, backward chaining inference, or some combination of the two, there are many ways to organize the knowledge-base as we will show using different expert system examples.

There are a variety of tasks for which an expert system may be constructed. These tasks may be categorized into well-defined classes that require different approaches and methodologies. Some basic classes of expert system tasks are as follows:

Diagnosis and Repair. This is the identification of faulty parts in a system and the suggestion of remedies or repairs (e.g., identifying faulty parts in a computer).

Monitoring and Control. This is the task of continuously interpreting signals or data and the setting of alarms or the suggestion of corrective action (e.g., controlling instruments in a power plant).

Design and Configuration. This is the task of making decisions regarding the selection of components and their interconnections to achieve specified requirement (e.g., configuring computers based on customer orders).

Instruction. This is the task of educating a student about a subject domain (e.g., teaching a medical student how to diagnose blood infections.

8.5.1 Diagnosis and Repair

Diagnosis (troubleshooting) has probably been the task that expert systems have handled most successfully to date. The task of a diagnostic expert system is the identification of a malfunctioning component of a complex system. Often the expert system also must suggest a method of remedy or repair. Sometimes it is difficult to separate the tasks of diagnosis and repair.

Consider an expert system that diagnoses hardware faults in a minicomputer. The major task of such a system is the determination of a piece of faulty hardware that can be replaced in the field, i.e., a field-replaceable unit, or FRU. The expert system needs to diagnose faults only up to the granularity of a FRU; in other words, the level of detail may vary according to the availability of field-replaceable parts, e.g., a board in a computer. It does not matter which part of the FRU the fault has occurred on. Thus the form of available repair affects the method of diagnosis.

In most cases one cannot directly observe the internal structure of a malfunctioning system, such as a human patient or a crashed computer, but can observe only *symptoms.* Diagnosis may thus be viewed as the task of discovering relationships between symptoms and faults. The diagnosis task can be difficult for two reasons:

a. A single symptom, at a given level of granularity, may be the result of many interacting faults; e.g., there can be many interacting reasons for fever in a patient.

b. A single fault may produce many symptoms; e.g., a computer may write many strange things on a tape just as it is crashing.

Although diagnosis is recognized as a difficult task for humans, expert systems do fairly well at it, at least in some knowledge domains.

8.5.2 Monitoring and Control

In contrast to diagnosis, where symptoms change relatively slowly, monitoring and control involves the management of the components of a real-time system by interpreting and classifying incoming data and recommending, or taking, suitable actions. Monitoring requires time varying, almost real-time, analysis of data. Monitoring and control often involves five subtasks:

Measurement. This involves the measurement of real-time data and its analysis as to being correct or erroneous. It is important that the system be able to realize and deal with measurement errors.

Interpretation. This involves understanding and interpreting the significance of the data.

Model Analysis. This aims at understanding the behavior of the overall system in terms of an underlying model and the interpreted data.

Planning. This allows the expert system to have long-term goals. A monitoring and control expert system should be much more than a simple feedback loop. It often relates to long-term planning just as it is dealing with short-term actions.

Expectations. These represent the system's view of future events. The setting of expectations allows the system to both better interpret data and discover whether it has misunderstood a situation with respect to the underlying model.

Monitoring and control is a very attractive area for the application of expert system technology. As industrial systems become more and more complex, the response time and the amount of thinking needed to monitor and control a large number of instruments far surpasses the capability of the human operator.

Modern industrial process control systems, e.g., the process control system for a large power plant, involve a staggering number of alarms and dials that require constant monitoring. In some cases, when an abnormal condition exists, hundreds of alarms can go off at once. A single human operator cannot immediately predict the internal state of the plant by correlating a large number of events. Further, some industrial control systems are so large that no single human operator possesses all the knowledge required to deal with them. There is some evidence that while the operator is more adept at monitoring a complex system, engineers who understand the design of the system are better at troubleshooting problems once they have occurred (e.g., Wickens, 1984).

8.5.3 Design and Configuration

Design and configuration is the task of selecting a suitable aggregate from a given set of components based on a given set of constraints to satisfy a goal. Note that this definition of design does not cover innovative or conceptual design that may involve the use of new components.

Configuration is a highly structured task in which approaches that select a locally suitable solution may eventually produce globally acceptable solutions. The system R1, discussed in Section 8.6.4, illustrates this point. The high level of structure within the configuration task may be exploited to direct the inference process.

Design, on the other hand, is a highly unstructured task that relies on very few fixed rules. In some sense, attempts at developing expert systems for design essentially eliminate the concept of *design* by formalizing the design process. This is illustrated by the concept of a silicon compiler, which to some extent replaces the designer, but which may be nothing more than a "compiler," which does very little "design."

8.5.4 Instruction

Education involves the communication of knowledge to students. Since expert systems deal with knowledge, it seems natural to use them in conjunction with teaching and instruction. The use of expert systems in instruction has two distinct facets:

a. One can use the knowledge and inference mechanisms available within an expert system to teach a student about a domain; e.g., the knowledge of a medical expert system may be used to educate medical students.

b. One can build an expert system that includes knowledge about instruction, e.g., teaching rules and models of student behavior.

Computer-aided instruction is an attractive area for expert system applications since qualified teachers in highly specialized areas are often in short demand.

An "intelligent tutoring system" generally includes four specific components:

Domain Knowledge. This includes knowledge of the domain of instruction and may be based on the knowledge-base of an expert system for the domain.

Operational Knowledge. This includes operational knowledge about the performance of a task, such as diagnosis, and may be based on the inference engine of an expert system for the domain.

The Student Model. This incorporates a model of student behavior and the methods used for presenting the knowledge to the student.

The Tutoring System. This includes the rules of tutoring and the strategies used to teach the student.

Expert systems for instruction are very different from simple computer-aided instruction programs, which typically follow a regimen of presenting material and then testing the student's retention of that material. Expert systems may include deep knowledge about the topic they are teaching, and the logic of teaching may be captured in the expert system. The student's progress can be carefully monitored and models of student behavior may be constructed.

■ 8.6 EXAMPLES OF EXPERT SYSTEMS

In this section we examine the structure of some expert system examples to highlight their architectural distinctions.

8.6.1 MYCIN: A Diagnostic System
MYCIN was one of the first successful expert systems to demonstrate the feasibility of developing intelligent programs with performance rivaling that of a human expert. The development of MYCIN (Shortliffe, 1976) followed the early success of the DENDRAL project at Stanford University, which produced an expert system for identifying chemical structures by analyzing mass spectrograms.

MYCIN was designed to interact with a physician, collect all the relevant information about a patient, and examine this information for evidence on which to base a diagnosis and recommend a treatment regimen. MYCIN attempts to model the chain of reasoning that a human expert would use when confronted with a case. The human expert relies heavily on clinical judgment and experience, and MYCIN embodies this knowledge in the form of production rules. Many of these rules are designed to handle uncertain information so that, like an actual medical expert, MYCIN forms tentative hypotheses and then tries to find evidence that will confirm them.

MYCIN is a rule-based system of about 500 rules. It pioneered the rule-based approach to expert systems and its success gave rise to the development of a good number of other systems with a similar architecture. MYCIN's task is the diagnosis of infectious diseases and the suggestion of suitable therapies. The problem is essentially the identification of the bacterial organisms that may be causing the infection and the selection of a suitable combination of antimicrobial agents as a remedy. In analyzing each case, MYCIN answers four basic questions:

1. Is the infection significant?
2. What is the identity of the organism causing the infection?
3. What are the potentially useful drugs?
4. Which drug is best for this patient?

The problem with which MYCIN deals can often be quite difficult. No single antimicrobial agent is effective against all bacteria, and drugs that are effective against some agents may be very ineffective against others. Using ineffective drugs can lead to problems, since time may be an important factor in treating the infection.

The average physician may perform rather poorly in MYCIN's domain. A study of patients in a community hospital (Roberts and Visconti, 1972) suggested that 66% of therapies selected by physicians were contraindicated and of these, over 62% used inappropriate combinations of antimicrobial agents to treat the patient's condition.

General knowledge about infectious diseases is represented in MYCIN in terms of facts and rules with degrees of confidence. Knowledge about specific cases is represented in terms of *contexts, parameters,* and *values.* A context is a basic conceptual entity, and a parameter is a distinguishing element of a context. Intuitively, a context may correspond to a frame, while a parameter corresponds to a slot. The parameters can have values, just as slots have values. The following are simple examples of contexts in MYCIN:

Context: *patient*   Context: *organism*

Parameter: *age*   Parameter: *identity*

Value: *28*   Value: *E-Coli.*

Each fact in MYCIN is represented as a list consisting of a context, a parameter, a value, and a degree of confidence, or *certainty factor.* MYCIN's knowledge-base may contain several values for a parameter with different degrees of confidence. For instance, both of the following facts may be present in the knowledge-base at the same time:

(Organism-1 identity E-Coli 80%).
(Organism-1 identity Pseudomonas 15%).

This means that the identity of Organism-1 is most probably E-Coli (Escherichia coli), but there is also slight evidence that it may be Pseudomonas.

Contexts are hierarchically related within a *context tree,* an example of which is shown in Figure 8.5. The root of a MYCIN context tree is usually the diagnosed context, e.g., the patient. The context tree helps relate the contexts involved in a diagnosis.

As the consultation proceeds, MYCIN builds up information about contexts (entities) such as offending organisms or the culture from which they were obtained. In every consultation there is one context of type PERSON (i.e., the current patient) that has no "parent context" and that serves as the root node of the context tree that is built during the consultation.

MYCIN creates each context as the need for it is discovered. A consultation begins by putting an instance of the context type PERSON at the top of a new

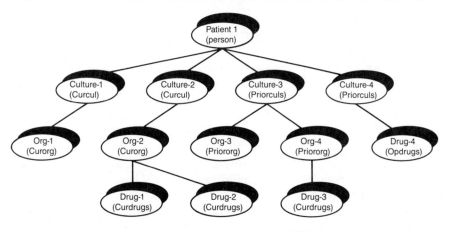

Figure 8.5 A context tree in MYCIN.

context tree. Each new instance of a context type is automatically assigned a unique name (e.g., CULTURE-1). Each context type has an associated set of clinical parameters. The parameters associated with the PERSON context include NAME, AGE, and SEX. The most important parameter, however, is REGIMEN. This is the recommended treatment for the patient and it is associated with the PERSON context. Some of the clinical parameters are supplied directly by the user, while others are deduced by MYCIN using rules that link an unknown value of a parameter to the values of other parameters.

The basic operation of MYCIN is controlled by a backward chaining *rule-interpreter*. During operation, the rule-interpreter, or inference engine, attempts to establish values for parameters by backward chaining.

An actual MYCIN rule in its English-like translation is as follows:

RULE035 (English Form):

IF:

     1. The gram stain of the organism is gramneg, and
     2. The morphology of the organism is rod, and
     3. The aerobicity of the organism is anaerobic

THEN:

     There is suggestive evidence (.6) that
     the identity of the organism is bacteroides.

To establish the value of the parameter *identity* for a context such as organism-2, the rule-interpreter follows the following steps:

    1. Rule035 is retrieved from the knowledge-base, since its right hand side deals with identities of contexts.

2. The rule variable CNTXT in Rule035 is matched with the context organism-2. The occurrences of CNTXT on the left-hand side of the rule now refer to organism-2.

3. The rule-interpreter now has three new goals to prove, namely, the three goals on the left-hand side of Rule035. These are again proven by backward chaining.

MYCIN interacts with the user during inference if it encounters parameters whose values are not known. MYCIN recognizes that information is not always certain and uses certainty factors to indicate the degree to which a fact is assumed to be true. In making judgments, MYCIN combines various hypotheses and actions to arrive at a diagnosis. The action (conclusion) in each rule has a number assigned to it on a scale ranging from -1.0 to $+1.0$, where -1.0 indicates complete confidence that a proposition is false and $+1.0$ indicates complete confidence that it is true. Certainty factors can either be computed or entered by a physician.

MYCIN is a good demonstration of many of the fundamental components of expert systems. It has a well-defined knowledge-base, inference engine, and user interface. It also handles uncertain information. MYCIN uses the certainty factors associated with facts and rules to determine the certainty of the conclusions it arrives at. MYCIN includes a user interface with explanation facilities including both *how* and *why* explanations.

8.6.2 CATS-1: A System for Troubleshooting and Diagnosis

CATS-1, the computer-assisted troubleshooting system, is an interesting diagnostic expert system that contrasts with MYCIN in that it combines forward and backward chaining, has been reimplemented in a nontraditional AI language (viz., Forth), and uses a videodisk for interaction with the user.

CATS-1 (Bonisonne and Johnson, 1984) was developed at the General Electric Research and Development Department in order to assist in the diagnosis of malfunctioning diesel locomotive engines. A first version of CATS-1 was developed in Lisp to demonstrate its feasibility. A later version was reimplemented in Forth on a PDP-11 and was joined to a videodisk for interactive display of system components.

CATS-1 is a rule-based system with approximately 500 rules, of which 300 are diagnostic rules. The other 200 rules support features such as the help facility. The help facility itself is just another part of the rulebase.

The architecture of CATS-1 (Figure 8.6) consists of the following components:

The *Factbase,* which stores all the known facts.

The *Knowledge-base,* which stores the rules used by the system for diagnosis or help.

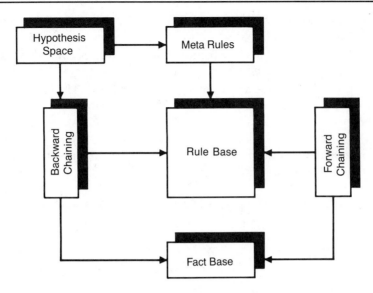

Figure 8.6   The architecture of CATS-1.

The *Metarulebase,* which stores metarules used for selecting the rules relevant to each diagnosed case.

The *Hypothesis-space,* which holds the current diagnostic hypotheses of the system.

An interesting feature of CATS-1 is that its factbase always explicitly includes *all* the facts that the system can possibly derive.

CATS-1 represents facts by using predicate functions applied to arguments. These predicates are quite easy to deal with:

EQ and NE. These measure equality (EQ) and inequality (NE).

NC. This predicate deals with confirmation. NC (not confirmed) evaluates its arguments and returns a true value if the argument was either proved false or was unknown.

ND. Similarly, ND (not disconfirmed) evaluates its arguments and returns a true value if the argument was either proved true or was unknown.

Eval-all. This predicates attempts an exhaustive evaluation of all possible values for its arguments and returns a true value if at least one case succeeds.

Procedural knowledge in CATS-1 is represented as a combination of several forms of rules. CATS-1 uses the following forms of rules:

a. *IF Rules.* These have the usual form of If A Then B, which specifies that B logically follows A.

b. *IFF Rules.* These have the form (A Iff B), which is equivalent to If A Then B, and If B Then A.

c. *WHEN Rules.* These are action rules, e.g., When A Then B, which specifies that the action B should be performed whenever the condition A becomes true.

d. *Metarules.* These are not directly executed by the inference engine but are used to index the other three kinds of rules mentioned above to select appropriate rules for each specific diagnostic task.

The following is an example of a CATS-1 rule, where comments appear in italics:

IF:

EQ (ENGINE SET IDLE)

Is the engine at idle?

EQ (FUEL PRESSURE BELOW NORMAL)

Is the fuel pressure below normal?

EQ (FUEL-PRESSURE-GAGE USED IN TEST)

Did you use the locomotive gage?

EQ (FUEL-PRESSURE-GAGE-STATUS OK)

Is the locomotive gage known to be accurate?

THEN:

WRITE (FUEL SYSTEM FAULTY)

Established that there is a fuel system fault.

CATS-1's inference system is split into two separate modules: the *Backward chainer,* which proves hypotheses from the knowledge-base; and the *Forward chainer,* which is used for discovering consequences of new facts.

A diagnosis in CATS-1 begins by the operator inputting a set of facts about the case. The basic operation of CATS- is then as follows:

a. *Rule and Hypothesis Selection.* The metarules are used to select which rules are appropriate for the case being diagnosed. This reduces the number of rules that will be active in the rulebase. The metarules also select a set of hypotheses which are placed in the hypothesis space. The metarules are not used any more in the computation after this point.

Thus, metarules in CATS-1 are just used to select an appropriate knowledge-base and hypothesis base.

b. *Backward Chaining.* The backward chainer does most of the inference in the system. It selects a hypothesis from the hypothesis space and tries to prove it by backward chaining. Either the system succeeds in proving the hypothesis, or it encounters an *askable* fact.

c. *New Fact Discovery.* At this point CATS-1 asks the user for further input; e.g., it may ask: "Is there rust on the engine?". The information provided by the user is entered in the factbase. When a new fact is entered in the factbase the forward chainer is called.

d. *Forward Chaining.* CATS-1 stores all the facts it can know *explicitly*. Thus when a new fact is entered in the factbase, the forward chainer is called to find *all* the consequences of the new fact and add them to the factbase. The forward chainer is run until no further facts can be found at all. At this point the control goes back to the backward chainer.

If the selected hypothesis is not successful, CATS-1 tries another hypothesis from the hypothesis-base and continues the steps above. CATS-1 also includes a help facility that helps the user with explanations and makes it possible to view components on a videodisk.

8.6.3 VM: A System for Monitoring and Control

The Ventilator Manager (VM) is an expert system developed to aid in monitoring patients immediately after cardiac surgery. VM was developed in Lisp and was influenced by the MYCIN system, although it later incorporated major changes.

In VM (Fagan, 1980), the patient has just had cardiac surgery, is in the Intensive Care Unit, and usually needs breathing assistance with a mechanical ventilator that delivers air. The ventilator is essential for the survival of many of these patients. Data about the patient is gathered with electrocardiogram (ECG) leads and other implanted monitoring sensors. The ventilator/patient airway is monitored to collect respiratory flow rates and pressure. These measurements are usually available at bedside through special computer terminals.

Over 30 measurements of the patient's condition are provided to VM by the measurement system. The measurements are collected every 2–10 minutes and are communicated to VM for interpretation. The interval for measurement is dependent on the patient's condition and is shorter for more critical cases.

VM generally has to deal with three kinds of problems in managing the patient of the ventilator:

a. Changes in the patient's recovery process which require changes to the life support equipment,

b. Malfunction of the life support equipment requiring repair,

c. Failure of the patient to respond to therapeutic interventions within the expectations of the clinician in charge.

The task of VM consists of five basic steps:

1. Detect possible errors in measurement.
2. Recognize oncoming events and suggest corrective short-term action.
3. Summarize the patient's condition.
4. Consider long-term goals and suggest long-term therapies.
5. Develop a set of evaluations and expectations about the patient's future condition.

Unlike MYCIN, which is designed to be an interactive consultation program, VM aims at minimizing interaction with the physician since it is a real-time system.

8.6.4 R1/XCON: A System for Configuration and Design

R1 (McDermott, 1982) was an expert system for configuring VAX™ mini-computers at Digital Equipment Corporation (DEC). It was developed at Carnegie Mellon University in cooperation with DEC and was later fully transferred to DEC. It is in commercial use now and has been renamed XCON to reflect this change of environment. XCON is now quite successful in configuring 97% of VAX orders at DEC.

R1 was originally implemented in the language OPS4, a predecessor to OPS5, and was later moved to OPS5 (Forgy, 1981). R1 originally had about 700 rules, but at last count XCON had been extended to well over 4000 rules and is constantly growing. Of course, a good number of these are *rules reflecting changes in hardware,* and rules for performing a number of other tasks, rather than the basic configuration task. The system we describe here is essentially R1, rather than XCON.

The configuration problem within DEC was known for quite some time before R1 was developed. Several internal development attempts at building a program to configure VAXes were made at DEC. These approaches based on conventional programming techniques failed, and it was claimed that on the basis of conventional algorithmic approaches, the problem had no reasonable solution. However, R1 succeeded by using the *do whenever* style of forward chaining rules rather than the *do while* style of traditional programming.

The input of R1 is in terms of orders received for computer equipment. The task of R1 is two-fold:

a. Determine whether the order is complete.

b. Determine the spatial relationships among the components on order.

There can easily be over 3000 pieces of information about components. Not only does R1 help in performing the configuration task; it also indirectly helps in the maintenance process. The orders configured by R1 are quite uniform, since it has no intentions of expressing originality in doing the configuration. The human configurers generally added a twist to the configuration for the sake of originality, often making future maintenance difficult.

The original knowledge of R1 came from one domain expert and two VAX configuration manuals. Later, the expert gradually educated the knowledge engineer who transcribed the rules as the system evolved. The development was continuous and the system was under constant testing.

An example of an R1 rule is as follows:

ASSIGN-POWER-SUPPLY-1

IF:

THE MOST CURRENT ACTIVE CONTEXT IS ASSIGNING A POWER SUPPLY

AND

AN SBI MODULE OF ANY TYPE HAS BEEN PUT IN A CAB-INET

AND

THE POSITION IT OCCUPIES IN THE CABINET (ITS NEXUS) IS KNOWN

AND

THERE IS SPACE AVAILABLE IN THE CABINET FOR A POWER SUPPLY FOR THAT NEXUS

AND

THERE IS NO AVAILABLE POWER SUPPLY

AND

THE VOLTAGE AND FREQUENCY OF THE COMPONENTS ON THE ORDER IS KNOWN

THEN:

FIND A POWER SUPPLY OF THAT VOLTAGE AND FRE-QUENCY AND ADD IT TO THE ORDER

R1 does not explicitly use any inexact logic. During its development, it did not even have to deal with faulty configuration. Whenever there was a problem, the expert would simply produce more rules on how to avoid the bad path.

R1 stores knowledge of components in a database that also contains *cabinet templates* describing the space available in a cabinet type. These help R1 to know what space is available and help it assign specific coordinates to each component in a cabinet. This database is not where inference takes place, however. R1 operates by matching patterns in the working memory of the OPS5 interpreter, which is used as an active factbase. The active components are objects in the OPS5 working memory represented as *component tokens.*

R1 retrieves values and information about components from the database as needed. The basic operations that R1 performs for retrieving elements fall into three classes: those that generate tokens, those that retrieve information about some component, and those that add information to existing templates. Apart from component tokens, the working memory includes information about the following:

Subtasks. These determine which subtask is currently being solved. A subtask symbol in R1 includes the subtask name and indicates whether it is active.

Partial Configurations. These are partially determined arrangements of relationships. Typically, these indicate that either one component is to be connected to another by a cable or, in case one is a container, the spatial relationship between the container and each component.

Results of Computations. These include a symbol that names some computation and one or more values indicating the result of that computation.

Initially, when the operation of R1 begins, the working memory, i.e., the factbase, is empty. As the configuration goes on, partial configurations are formed in working memory as new components are added to the configuration.

Part of R1's success comes from the fact that its subtasks may be performed independently. The configuration task in R1 can be viewed as a hierarchy of subtasks with strong temporal dependencies. The actions in a subtask can be highly variable depending on particular combination of the components that are on order, and the way the components have been configured in the previously solved subtasks. The approach of R1 to solving subtasks is quite straightforward and relies on the fact that the subtasks may be performed in any order:

1. It will do all it can within a subtask before leaving that subtask.
2. It chooses between rules by choosing the more specific rule.

To achieve this, R1 has several rules that determine when a new subtask should be initiated, on the basis of various kinds of component information. When one of these rules fires, it adds a new subtask symbol to the working memory, with an indication of when this was done. Thus, this becomes the most active subtask.

Each R1 rule has two conditional elements that are sensitive to subtask symbols and ensure that only those rules that are relevant to the most current active subtask will fire. Each subtask also has an associated rule that deactivates it. This rule has only the two subtask elements and will fire last as a result of the conflict resolution style of OPS.

8.6.5 Guidon: An Expert System for Instruction

We shall illustrate the features of an instructional expert system using Guidon. Guidon (Clancey, 1983) is a tutoring expert system developed at Stanford University in close connection with MYCIN. Guidon uses the knowledge obtained during the construction of the MYCIN system to teach medical students about infectious diseases.

Guidon was originally conceived as an extension of the explanation facility of MYCIN, with the hope that the explanations provided could teach medical students to diagnose blood infections. However, the explanation system and the nature of MYCIN's operation proved unsatisfactory from an instructional point of view.

The MYCIN rules and their execution were unsatisfactory for teaching because the form of the rules was somewhat counterintuitive and the method of diagnosis did not closely correspond to the way humans think. It was found that the basic inference mechanism of MYCIN did not fully reflect the diagnosis strategy of a human expert. Further, the knowledge of infectious diseases and the general knowledge of diagnosis strategies were combined in the MYCIN knowledge-base and had to be separated. As a result, MYCIN had to be reformulated into a new, pedagogically directed, expert system called Neo-MYCIN.

The expert system Neo-MYCIN was created by rewriting the rules of MYCIN. There were two major steps in developing Neo-MYCIN:

a. The rules were re-written in a forward chaining mode, as opposed to MYCIN's backward chaining style.
b. Neo-MYCIN further separated the domain knowledge of MYCIN, i.e., knowledge about infectious diseases, from its knowledge of diagnostic strategy.

Guidon was then built in conjunction with Neo-MYCIN. Guidon also includes its own tutorial knowledge-base, but explicitly separates Neo-MYCIN's knowledge, e.g., knowledge of both diagnosis and infectious diseases, from tutoring knowledge.

Guidon uses the Neo-MYCIN knowledge-base to represent its medical knowledge and its own knowledge-base to represent tutorial knowledge. To represent the student's knowledge, Guidon uses the *overlay student model,* in which the knowledge of the student is modeled as overlaying sets of understood and misunderstood concepts available in the MYCIN knowledge-base.

Guidon uses two kinds of rules: domain rules (*d-rules*) and tutorial rules (*t-rules*). The d-rules essentially come from the Neo-MYCIN knowledge-base and refer to medical knowledge. The t-rules, on the other hand, reside in Guidon's own knowledge-base and represent tutorial knowledge. Guidon has three forms of t-rules:

1. Rules that select a discourse pattern, i.e., a conversation pattern, with the student. These rules guide the discussion of the d-rules, respond to student's hypotheses, and choose question formats.
2. Rules that choose domain knowledge. These rules provide orientation for pursuing new goals and measure interestingness of d-rules.
3. Rules that maintain the continuity in the communication model with the student. These rules update the overlay student model when d-rules are invoked, modify the overlay model when hypotheses are evaluated, and create a plan for the lesson.

The following are two examples of t-rules in Guidon:

T-RULE 9.01 (English form):

IF:

1. The d-rule is not on the lesson plan for this case, and
2. Based on the overlay model the student is ignorant about the d-rule

THEN:

Affirm the conclusions made by the d-rule by simply stating the key factors and values to be considered.

T-RULE 6.05 (English form):

IF:

1. The hypothesis does include values that can be concluded by this d-rule, as well as others, and
2. The hypothesis does not include values that can only be concluded by this d-rule, and
3. Values concluded by the d-rule are missing in the hypothesis.

THEN:

Define the belief that the rule was considered as $-.70$.

T-rules are gathered together in terms of *packets,* which are of two types: t-rules that are used for accumulating belief and t-rules that are used for selecting a suitable discourse procedure to follow.

Guidon uses the *case-method* of instruction, in which the student follows through the diagnosis of an actual case study of a patient. In each lesson, the student is presented with a case to diagnose, where only the patient's identity has been changed.

The student must ask questions in order to arrive at a diagnosis. One of the major problems in teaching this subject was that it is generally not possible to order the collection of evidence which needs to be gathered, since there is no agreed-on order for performing the task among the experts.

Guidon uses three levels or *tiers* of structured knowledge:

a. The *performance tier,* which consists of all the rules and tables used by MYCIN for performing inference and collecting the initial data about the patient.

b. The *support tier,* which consists of annotations to the rules and the factors used by them. These include, for instance, "canned text" descriptions of laboratory tests in the MYCIN domain and remarks about how the tests should be performed.

c. The *abstraction tier,* which represents patterns in the performance knowledge-base, i.e., tier **a** above. For instance, descriptions of "kinds of rules" and preconditions that appear in their premises are included. At each point during the interaction, the d-rules of Neo-MYCIN are forward chained to perform inference. Guidon then responds to the student's hypotheses, updates the overlay student model and informs students of the rules they did not consider.

To keep the interaction with the student focused, Guidon uses a *focus record* to guide the direction of the dialog. For each interaction, Guidon has a case-lesson plan and uses a focus record to focus on the subject being taught.

The operation of Guidon is thus guided by three components: the overlay student model, which represents the knowledge of the student; the case-lesson plan, which decides what should be presented in the lesson; and the focus record, which maintains continuity in the dialog.

■ 8.7 SUMMARY

The organizational structure required for dealing with expert systems currently lag behind the technology of building expert systems. Experts are beginning to be more directly involved in the development of expert systems.

The expert systems lifecycle corresponds generally to the software development lifecycle, but the emphasis on knowledge in expert systems is a mixed blessing for the developer. On one hand, a knowledge-base is much more adaptive and flexible than a conventional program (e.g., it allows for rapid prototyping and updating of expert systems); on the other hand, the validation of knowledge and the assessment of expert system performance can be extremely difficult.

Tools available for developing expert systems can be of great assistance, when compared with programming languages. These tools generally fall into two classes: expert system shells and knowledge acquisition tools. We discussed criteria for selecting expert system shells in this chapter. Knowledge acquisition tools are described in Chapter 9.

9

KNOWLEDGE ACQUISITION AND VALIDATION

■ 9.1 INTRODUCTION

In the previous chapters we presented a formal theory of inference and knowledge, discussed the expert system lifecycle, and outlined the process of constructing an expert system. Building expert systems is not, however, simply a matter of selecting an expert system shell, and obtaining a set of facts, rules, and frames and transforming them into the syntax of the knowledge representation language. In most cases the facts, rules, and frame structures are not initially available or well identified, and must be sought out.

The process of seeking out the knowledge required by an expert system is referred to as *knowledge acquisition*. The knowledge must be acquired either through a process of knowledge transfer from one or more agents or experts, who already possess the expertise, or through some type of learning process that observes examples and distills knowledge.

The knowledge acquisition task is often complicated by the fact that human experts have not analyzed the contents of their thoughts, so that they are not explicitly aware of the structure of their knowledge. As a result, the intermediate steps in their reasoning seem obvious to them and they cannot eloquently provide an overall account of how their decisions are made at the level of detail required by a machine reasoning process.

Expert systems rely heavily on knowledge. The quality of knowledge often determines the success of an expert system. Thus the ratio of effort expended to results achieved for the expert system as a whole is often decided by the knowledge acquisition process and the level of success achieved there.

327

As we pointed out in Chapter 8, with improving expert system tools, experts will be able to carry out the knowledge engineering process themselves, provided they have the necessary skills and an appropriate shell to work with. From a different perspective, the focus of knowledge representation and acquisition *languages* should evolve to knowledge acquisition and knowledge representation *environments*, just as the focus of programming *languages* has now turned to programming *environments*. The evolution of languages to interactive environments is a trend that will eventually impact almost all areas of computer science (Parsaye, 1985).

In this chapter we discuss several knowledge acquisition methods and consider a number of strategic issues. We begin with manual approaches such as interviewing and protocol analysis and then focus on automated knowledge acquisition. Repertory grids and automated tools for knowledge acquisition in classification tasks are then presented. In addition to methods of acquiring knowledge, we also discuss the automation of knowledge-base validation.

■ 9.2 KNOWLEDGE AND EXPERTISE

Knowledge acquisition is the process of capturing knowledge and *expertise*. Expertise is fairly easy to recognize, although it may be difficult to define. First, expertise is inherently *task-specific*. Most of the expert's knowledge cannot be transferred between different domains, and the expert must learn about each new domain almost from scratch. Second, expertise is relatively inflexible so that the experts may not be able to cope with new situations that do not conform to their past experience. Third, expertise tends to focus the reasoning of the expert so that only one type of solution is considered.

Johnson (1983) defines an expert as follows:

> An expert is a person who, because of training and experience, is able to do things the rest of us cannot; experts are not only proficient but also smooth and efficient in the actions they take. Experts know a great many things and have tricks and caveats for applying what they know to problems and tasks; they are also good at plowing through irrelevant information in order to get at basic issues, and they are good at recognizing problems they face as instances of types with which they are familiar. Underlying the behavior of experts is the body of operative knowledge we have termed expertise.

Expertise is a two-edged sword, with expertise being effective in routine situations but relatively inflexible in the face of unfamiliar situations. Yet experts are remarkably effective most of the time and they are usually respected and rewarded highly. The essential characteristics of experts are as follows:

They possess appropriate specialized knowledge.
They know how to use that knowledge effectively.

They are able to recognize the boundaries of their knowledge.

They do not attempt to solve problems where their specialized knowledge does not apply.

They provide their solutions in a timely fashion.

Consider the nature of expertise in medicine. Because of the breadth of issues that they must address, general practitioners are not experts in all areas of medicine. When a patient walks into the physician's office, the first task is to collect all the data on symptoms relating to possible medical conditions. On the basis of the symptomology, the physician may come up with a diagnosis and a suggested course of treatment. But if the condition is unusual or outside the physician's knowledge, an appropriate specialist must be consulted. Thus a physician may be confident in prescribing a treatment regimen to deal with high blood pressure but may refer someone suffering from a set of chest symptoms to a heart specialist.

As an example of how a knowledge domain is divided up among a set of experts, consider the case of a young child with defective vision. A pediatrician may be able to detect a problem in a child's vision, but will then direct the child to an ophthalmologist for a more detailed analysis of the problem. In certain cases the ophthalmologist may refer the case to an even more specialized expert such as a pediatric ophthalmologist. The first expert, the general practitioner, handles the routine cases and refers the other cases to the next level of expert. Experts in the next level again handle what they can and pass the remaining cases either to other experts at their level or to even more specialized experts. Extremely unusual cases that do not fall neatly into a single area of expertise may actually bounce around between the various experts.

Although experts are often easy to recognize, it must be pointed out that in some situations, exactly what an expert is and does may be very vague and difficult to quantify. Such situations typically occur when the nature of the task mostly involves extensive interaction within a complex environment. The need for specialization and focusing on narrow domains has led to one definition of an expert as someone who "learns more and more about less and less." In vague and inexact circumstances, however, it is sometimes difficult to find any other definition for an expert than that of someone who can "charge more and more for doing less and less."

The *knowledge acquisition bottleneck* (Feigenbaum, 1980) was encountered in the early days of expert systems (in the late 1970s) when knowledge engineering was an art that depended greatly on the skill and availability of knowledge engineers with only pencils, paper, and tape recorders to guide them. Initially, the knowledge acquisition bottleneck and the shortcomings of existing knowledge engineering tools gave rise to gloomy estimates about the number of expert systems that could be built, reflecting the limited availability of knowledge engineers.

One is reminded of similar types of gloomy estimate made about other emerging technologies. Many people thought that early cars should be banned because they frightened the horses on the street. Similarly, for those who could not imagine automated switching equipment, the number of telephone calls that could possibly be made was limited by the number of telephone operators required to manually switch the calls, as well as the amount of time it took to manually switch a call. The advent of automatic call switching forced a revision of the early estimates of how many telephone calls could be made. In the same way, automated knowledge acquisition tools, along with machine learning techniques, are minimizing the effect of the knowledge acquisition bottleneck.

■ 9.3 A SOFTWARE ENGINEER'S VIEW

We said in Chapter 8 that expert systems may be considered as an evolution of conventional software paradigms. Thus, we should be able to draw some analogy between expert systems and other types of software. As discussed in Chapter 8, we may view an expert system shell as a very high level programming language and an expert system implemented in an expert system shell as an application that has been written in a programming language.

When we are writing a program to manage payroll or a database, what needs to be done is often clear. But even in traditional software applications, the specification of what needs to be done can sometimes be vague. In building expert systems, specifications are usually vague. Many traditional programs have well-defined input–output behavior, allowing us to define what a program should do in terms of a set of input–output specifications. This is illustrated by black box models of software engineering, where each programmer writes a module whose inputs and outputs will match the corresponding inputs and outputs of other modules that interact with it. This modular programming activity allows multiple programmers to work on a software project with each programmer treating the modules being worked on by other programmers as black boxes of which only the input–output behavior is of concern.

Do we have equivalent types of specification and software engineering strategies for the task of building expert systems? The answer is: "far less frequently than in the case of traditional programs." Even when we identify an expert who may serve as a model for the program, it may not be clear what the expert does or how that expert does it. Even when we try and simplify the problem of specification by focusing on input–output behavior, we may encounter difficulties. It is often not clear what the inputs and outputs for the expert system will eventually be.

In a medical expert system, for instance, we might be able to say that the inputs will be patients presenting sets of symptoms and the outputs will be diagnostic decisions, but it can be extremely difficult to convert these general notions into detailed specifications. Each patient is in some sense unique. Categorizing patients is much harder than categorizing prime numbers. For instance, experience has shown that moving an expert system from one hospital to another may render the system ineffective. Different hospitals have different methods of routing patients through their wards and in doing so, screen and classify patients and route them differently. A "patient" has a different meaning at different wards within different hospitals. Thus a specification of the "input" patient may involve a complex set of attributes, which do not directly relate to the expert system.

Part of the task of knowledge acquisition is determining the mappings between the inputs to and outputs from an expert. Of course, the conceptual design task discussed in Section 8.3.3 helps in determining some issues, but often a good number of features and characteristics are not uncovered until knowledge acquisition is well under way.

So how does knowledge acquisition fit in the analogy between expert systems and traditional software? One aspect of knowledge acquisition is that it must carry out some of the functions that are normally considered as "specification" in conventional software development methodologies. Although knowledge acquisition may be viewed as a black box model of expertise, we cannot be concerned merely with mimicking the input–output behavior of the expert. Our confidence in the behavior of the expert system may partially depend on the reasons and reasoning methods used by the expert system for arriving at conclusions.

In traditional software, the issues of design and implementation may be far more readily separable than are knowledge acquisition and knowledge representation. In many case, knowledge acquisition is a form of specification and design mixed together. You have to find out not only how to do things, but also what needs to be done. It is generally a good idea to separate these two functions in knowledge acquisition at an early stage, although one will, in practice, oscillate between the two over the course of knowledge acquisition.

■ 9.4 THE NEED FOR KNOWLEDGE

Knowledge acquisition is a topic that is receiving a great deal of attention because the need for knowledge expressed in a structured and explicit form currently exceeds the ability to acquire and represent that knowledge and will continue to do so in the forseeable future. This demand for knowledge serves to reemphasize its importance.

Why has knowledge acquisition come to be regarded as not only important, but also difficult? Because the acquisition of knowledge merely increases our thirst for more knowledge. By learning to solve problems that seem hard today, we simply change the definition of "hard." Thus knowledge acquisition will remain difficult for a long time to come. However, the range of problems for which knowledge acquisition is relatively easy will grow rapidly as tools and methodologies for automated knowledge acquisition improve.

One changing factor, however, will be the expanded role for experts in the task of building expert systems. This may also be seen in terms of the analogy with traditional software systems. In the early days of programming, business-people and managers had to rely on programmers and other intermediaries (discussed in Section 8.2) to build and operate information systems, databases, and the like. The development of a variety of "off-the-shelf" application software packages, coupled with the availability of personal computers, allowed managers and other professionals who were not programmers to build and design their own databases and information systems.

In the early days of computing, programmers were needed to both write code and interpret it for nonprogrammers. As expert systems tools have become easier to use and their source code easier to read and understand, experts can build some expert systems themselves without difficulty. So, for some problems, knowledge acquisition now becomes an easy programming task using very high level languages.

This does not, however, mean that the need for knowledge engineers will suddenly disappear. On the contrary, as the usefulness of expert systems becomes widely accepted, knowledge engineers will be used to deal with the "hard" problems, with the definition of "hard" evolving over time, as automated knowledge acquisition technology advances. This may be seen in terms of an analogy with the relation between mainframes and personal computers.

In the early days of personal computers, it was sometimes conjectured that the proliferation of personal computing would lower the demand for mainframe use. In fact, exactly the opposite has happened, in some cases increasing the demand for mainframe processing by as much as 70 percent. In many corporations, databases and spreadsheets used on personal computers access data on a mainframe via a micro-mainframe link and can be used to pose more complex queries to mainframe databases, thus increasing the load on the mainframe's central processing unit, rather than off-loading the processing task.

■ 9.5 PROBLEMS IN KNOWLEDGE ACQUISITION

One problem in approaching knowledge acquisition is that there is a natural tendency to underestimate the difficulty of acquiring implicit knowledge. The concept of gravity, for instance, which is familiar to every educated person, was misunderstood or ignored for thousands of years. Similarly, when we look at knowledge that has already been codified and packaged into the knowledge-base of an expert system, it may be difficult to recognize how much effort went into structuring the knowledge in that form.

To acquire knowledge, one may either capture the surface level, or shallow knowledge that an expert has already formalized, or try to emulate models of processes using deep knowledge (as discussed in Section 4.2.2). Many expert systems typically use task-oriented shallow knowledge. In knowledge acquisition it is sometimes necessary to carry out excursions into deep knowledge in order to understand and validate the associated shallow knowledge. This is another argument in favor of providing experts with a larger role in knowledge acquisition, since they are in a position to understand the deep knowledge and its relation to the shallow knowledge.

The key question asked by someone who is new to knowledge acquisition is: "How do I acquire knowledge?" The answer often depends on the domain and task for which the expert system is to be constructed. For some domains, such as heuristic classification (discussed in Section 9.9), well-identified knowledge acquisition strategies can be outlined. Other domains are currently more difficult to deal with. However, one can facilitate the knowledge acquisition process in any domain by being aware of possible problems and standard pitfalls.

One commonly made mistake that can adversely affect ultimate performance of the expert system is to collect knowledge from the first available or most convenient source. In most problems, relevant knowledge is scattered across multiple sources, and it may be necessary to be fairly aggressive in pursuing the different sources.

The world is full of books, manuals, and reports that contain information relevant to various knowledge domains. Since knowledge is so frequently available in textual form, why incur the time and expense of dealing with a busy expert to capture the knowledge? The brief answer is that the expert contains the knowledge in a well-packaged form that is specially designed for efficient reasoning. Going to the books may lead to the incorporation of knowledge that is either not a part of practical reasoning or that has exceptions that the expert has had to discover and work around.

Knowledge can be surprisingly difficult to recognize when it has to be extracted from a noisy background of hints and possibly relevant events. Knowledge acquisition can be likened to a distillation process where the essential facts and rules must be isolated from information that contains many impurities. Knowledge in many domains is available only to experts and may never have been written down in a structured form. In general, since experts are known to perform tasks well, we assume that their knowledge is correct. Occasionally, however, there may be some justification for supplementing gaps or errors in an expert's knowledge if they can be demonstrated and alternative sources of the correct knowledge are available.

Experience with knowledge acquisition indicates the need for a broad perspective on knowledge. One pitfall in knowledge acquisition is not collecting knowledge from a variety of perspectives. The use of books alone may not provide the practical knowledge that is required while reliance on a single expert may not give full and accurate coverage of a knowledge domain.

We illustrate the acquisition and verification of knowledge dispersed among multiple sources with an example involving an instrument landing system (Chignell and Higgins, 1987). The intelligent instrument landing system (IILS) is designed to monitor the status of the approach and detect the occurrence of hazardous situations during instrument landings in aircraft.

The need for expert systems that assist the flight crew during instrument landing is indicated by the facts that approximately two-thirds of aviation accidents appear to be caused primarily by the flight crew (Billings and Reynard, 1984) and about half of all accidents occur during the landing phase of flight.

Even the most critical of system parameters may be improperly monitored by a pilot in a particular situation, as is seen in the case of a United Airlines DC-8 that crashed on the night of December 28, 1978 (Hurst and Hurst, 1982). The aircraft ran completely out of fuel so that a dead-stick landing (i.e., landing without the engines running) had to be made. The accident investigators determined that the pilot did not properly monitor the fuel state because his attention had been diverted to a landing gear malfunction. Meanwhile, the first officer and the flight engineer did not fully comprehend the development of a critically low state of fuel.

Early prototypes of IILS were based on Air Force and FAA manuals outlining the prescribed model of pilot behavior that should occur during an instrument landing (U.S. Department of the Air Force, 1984; U.S. Department of Transportation, 1980). In keeping with the principle of collecting knowledge from multiple sources, however, this knowledge was then checked against the behavior of experts. The technique used to collect examples of expert behavior will be explained in the section on verbal protocol analysis (Section 9.8.1.2).

Analysis of the behavior of pilots during instrument landings in a flight simulator provided a test of several aspects of the expertise that had been extracted from the instrument flight manuals and the recollections of a former pilot. During the instrument landings the pilots were concerned mostly with the control of *pitch* (tilt of the aircraft's nose) and *heading* (direction of horizontal travel). This suggested that rules concerned with the control of pitch and heading should be given more weight in the knowledge-base. This was in contrast to the knowledge derived from the manuals where equal weighting was assigned to attributes such as pitch, heading, and *vertical velocity* (how fast the aircraft's altitude is decreasing or increasing).

A second pitfall in knowledge acquisition concerns the collection of irrelevant knowledge. Although the expert knows and can talk about many different things, the knowledge engineer must determine which knowledge is actually relevant for the expert system. One way of identifying which knowledge is really relevant is by comparing the knowledge of people with different levels of expertise on the task. Critical knowledge will be indicated when it is known by experts but not by those with less expertise.

In studying the behavior of pilots in a flight simulator, we compared the behavior of pilots with different levels of expertise to find some of the critical components of expertise. An interesting distinction between absolute and relative changes in such physical parameters as fuel flow and pitch was found. The excerpts indicated that the most experienced pilot controlled the relative, whereas the less experienced pilot controlled the absolute amount of fuel flow and pitch. This also led to a reevaluation of some of the rules in IILS. As it turned out, the behavior of the expert pilots could be justified in terms of control theory applied to systems with inherent lags, but it was important to observe this behavior as part of practical expertise.

A third pitfall in knowledge acquisition is not sufficiently exploring the range and flexibility of the expert's knowledge. A working expert system can be expected to encounter many different situations in the field. Thus it is essential that its knowledge-base contain as many exceptions and unusual cases as possible. Creative methods of knowledge engineering can help in eliciting this more *unusual* knowledge from the expert.

In the study of the pilots, for instance, experiments were used to confirm that hypothesized elements of expertise really were important. The results suggested that monitoring certain instrumentation, such as the vertical velocity indicator, and the command steering bars, may not be as critical during instrument landing as is suggested in the instrument flight manuals. Further explorations of critical expertise can be carried out by designing experiments to assess pilot behavior under unusual conditions such as wind shear, instrumentation failures, and so on.

Another pitfall concerns the difficulties inherent in observing behavior. It is obviously desirable that we observe typical situations, unaffected by our observation. But psychologists have for a long time known about *experimenter effects* where people's behavior tends to change when they know they are being observed in experiments. Similarly, people have noticed the presence of the *brass effect* in the aerospace industry, where machinery and systems tend to break down in the presence of high-ranking officials.

There are a whole host of social psychological issues about knowledge acquisition without biasing or disturbing typical behavior. It is not clear, for instance, to what extent experts who are acquiring knowledge about their own expertise are more or less biased than nonexperts. Total solutions to the problems of observational bias are not immediately available. However, some simple methods may be used to reduce bias. These include the use of techniques that are less obtrusive, e.g., "observe the expert in a natural setting," and that do not influence the experts' behavior or descriptions with our own preconceptions about the nature of their expertise, i.e., "don't lead the expert."

■ 9.6 APPROACHES TO KNOWLEDGE ACQUISITION

A number of approaches to knowledge acquisition have been suggested (Figure 9.1). The three basic approaches are as follows:

a. *Interviewing.* In this approach a knowledge engineer obtains knowledge from the human expert through a series of interviews and encodes it in the expert system. Here the knowledge engineer plays a central role in the knowledge acquisition process, and the quality of the expert system greatly depends on the skills of the knowledge engineer.

b. *Learning by Interaction.* This approach often relies on computer-assisted knowledge acquisition. Experts directly interact with a computer program that helps to capture their knowledge. The need for a knowledge engineer can be significantly diminished here and the program often helps experts clarify their own thoughts.

c. *Learning by Induction.* In this approach a computer program distills knowledge by examining data and examples. Here the dependence on both the expert and the knowledge engineer is again diminished. The main problem here is the identification of the suitable characteristics or attributes on which induction would be performed.

Historically, interviewing has been the most prevalent method of knowledge acquisition. It is, however, highly dependent on the knowledge engineer and is often time-consuming and expensive. Approach **b** focuses on specific interaction methodologies and interactive interviewing techniques that help experts discover the structure of their own knowledge in selected tasks. Approach **c** focuses on algorithms that analyze data and examples and then generalize them to obtain the required knowledge. These three approaches can, however, be combined into an overall knowledge acquisition strategy.

The distinction between supervised and unsupervised learning reflects the difference between being told something (approach **b**) and learning it for oneself (approach **c**). In reality, by far the majority of human learning is, in fact, supervised in one way or another. In reading a book, for instance, we are guided by the author and the author's arguments even though the author is not physically present. Unsupervised learning is sometimes referred to as *trial-and-error* learning. Here the person tries something out and sees if it works. Generally, supervised learning is much more efficient when it is an available option.

However, the increasing size of databases and the amount of data in each database suggest fruitful possibilities for unaided discovery from large data-

Interviewing:

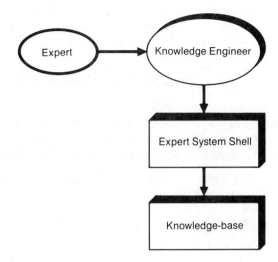

Learning by Interaction:

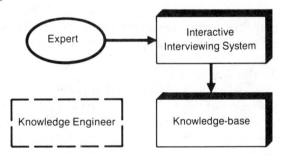

Learning by Induction:

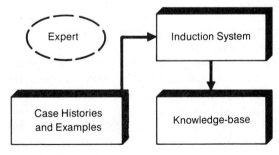

Figure 9.1   Approaches to Knowledge Acquisition.

bases. With the increasing availability of unused processing power (many computers are not used at 3 a.m.), come new opportunities for directly obtaining new knowledge by examining structures and patterns within large databases (Blum, 1982; 1986; Walker, 1987).

■ 9.7 THE COMPONENTS OF KNOWLEDGE REVISITED

In building the knowledge-base for an expert system one must transform expertise into the components of knowledge representation discussed in Section 4.3. Once knowledge is expressed in this form, it is then available for reasoning, in conjunction with an appropriate inference engine.

Thus, to describe the relevant knowledge for an application, we must deal with the following processes:

Naming.
Describing.
Organizing.
Relating.
Constraining.

One can then develop structures, rules, and procedures for implementing these components of knowledge in order to emulate the relevant expertise.

9.7.1 Naming

The key objects in the knowledge domain should be identified and named. Identification of these objects is a first critical step in knowledge acquisition. There will be a host of objects and concepts in any knowledge domain, and it is up to the developer, in consultation with the expert, to determine which of these potential objects are really necessary in the description of expertise. Once the objects are chosen, the names that are assigned to the objects should be unique so that we do not become confused as to who or what we are talking about. It will generally be appropriate to describe each key concept or object in a frame.

The process of naming objects within a knowledge domain should not be taken for granted. In view of the need to avoid interesting but irrelevant knowledge, the process of choosing and naming the critical components of expertise can set a knowledge acquisition effort on either the right or the wrong path. There are some arguments for requiring experts to name and organize objects at the same time. This is because many concepts may actually be synonymous and these synonyms can often be weeded out when they are observed to fall into similar categories.

The level to which theoretical development has occurred in the knowledge domain will often determine whether the relevant objects that constitute expertise are already known. In some cases one can refer to an encyclopedia, handbook, dictionary, glossary or even the index to a text to find an initial set of objects. In other cases, one may have to rely on getting the objects from the expert. In this latter situation there is the problem of dealing with limitations in memory where the expert may simply forget to mention important concepts and objects. In such cases it will be necessary to stimulate the expert's recall using a variety of problem scenarios and hypothetical situations.

Once a list of names has been obtained, the names should be screened to remove synonyms and their meanings should be clarified. The remaining objects should then be described. Again one is faced with choosing the information that is relevant to the task. In the same way that there are many objects that are potentially part of a knowledge domain, there are many properties that potentially describe each of these objects. The developer must establish which of these properties are important to understanding and performing the task. Substances, for instance, have many different properties, including color, density, and molecular structure, but their boiling points and flash points are the most important properties in determining combustibility and flammability.

9.7.2 Describing

There are, of course, many ways of describing objects, but we should describe only those characteristics that have an impact on subsequent reasoning and that actually influence the decision making process. In general, the characteristics of interest will *discriminate* between objects. For instance, in selecting among programming languages, one characteristic is that they all work on computers, but we take that for granted. Instead, we look for characteristics such as *portability* that (a) discriminate between languages and (b) have a bearing on the task of interest.

The assignment of attributes to objects often depends on the context in which the objects are discussed. Thus a beetle may be ''large'' in comparison to other insects, but ''small'' in comparison to mammals. As well as being context-sensitive, attribute labels may also be ambiguous. Expressing attributes as traits can be useful in avoiding ambiguity since the antonym of the trait indicates the sense in which it is being used. Thus the attribute ''light'' may be ambiguous, whereas the trait ''light–dark'' is not.

One way of overcoming these problems of context and meaning in attribute identification is to construct the concept out of examples. This can be done by taking a small number of objects and pointing to those that have high loadings on the attribute and then identifying those objects with low loadings on the attribute. For instance, the attribute ''small'' distinguishes a Volkswagen Rabbit from a Rolls Royce or a Cadillac because the Rabbit has a high loading on the attribute while the other two objects have low loadings. In Section 9.8.3 we introduce repertory grids as a method of achieving this.

Repertory grid analysis performs two tasks: (1) the attributes are identified and (2) values on each of the attributes are assigned in examples. This process of assigning values to attributes is referred to as "scaling" in psychometrics. There are a number of techniques other than repertory grid analysis developed for the purpose of scaling that may also be profitably applied to the task of describing knowledge. These include a variety of clustering and data reduction methods (Hartigan, 1975; Marriott, 1974) and techniques such as ranking and multidimensional scaling (Kruskal and Wish, 1978).

9.7.3 Organizing

Some of the most important properties of objects refer to the types of thing that they are (i.e., how they should be classified). A particular person is a member of the human species, a member of a family, an employee of a company, a citizen of a country, and so on all at the same time. Which of these implied organizing structures is relevant to the performance of the task? We must be able to identify the organizations of objects that are relevant to the problem solving knowledge.

Sorting is one technique that can be used to discover the organization of knowledge that an expert uses. Sorting is one of the simplest and most direct methods for discovering organization. Suppose that we want to build a hierarchy (tree) reflecting an expert's view of the knowledge domain. We can obtain it from the expert using a sorting task. In this task the expert is presented with the names of the most important objects, concepts, or terms in the knowledge domain and is then asked to group them according to which ones are similar or belong together. These groups can themselves be grouped until eventually a tree is formed. We have found the sorting task to be useful not only as a method for constructing classifications and hierarchies directly but also as a way of structuring interviews. The expert who is grouping the objects together can be asked what the basis of each grouping is, what the relations between different groups are, and so on.

There are numerous variations on the basic sorting technique. One variation, which is sometimes referred to as *clumping*, is to allow groups to overlap so that the same object may belong to more than one group. This reflects the prevailing condition in many knowledge domains where the important concepts may not be strictly nested, i.e., where the organization of knowledge constitutes a network rather than a hierarchy.

9.7.4 Relating

Knowledge acquisition is a complex process because there are a number of components of knowledge to be described and potentially many different ways of describing a knowledge domain. At some point in knowledge acquisition one generally encounters the distinction between shallow and deep knowledge that was introduced in Section 4.2.2.

To what extent should we attempt to capture the causal structure that is implied in the way that the expert performs the task? There is no simple answer to this question. Most expert systems do not explicitly model causality because it can be difficult to capture knowledge about causality unless it can be described in terms of fairly simple relations between objects.

The description and organization of knowledge does not, by itself, provide the task-oriented knowledge required for reasoning. Some way of identifying the rules that are used to express relations and constraints is also needed. Three major tools are available for this purpose. These are verbal protocol analysis, interviews, and repertory grids. Although repertory grids are methods for describing and organizing objects, they can also be extended into a general procedure for automated knowledge acquisition as discussed in Section 9.8.2.

9.7.5   Constraining

One class of relations between objects constrain the patterns of properties that can be observed within or between objects. The class of flammability or combustibility that is assigned to a substance, for instance, constrains the range of boiling points and flash points that the substance can have. This is an example of constraining the relations between the properties within an object. Rules that describe how containers of flammable substances should be stored depending on the availability of automatic sprinkler systems are examples of constraining relationships.

The final component of knowledge is the general strategy for carrying out reasoning. This is generally implemented in expert systems as a set of rules that identify courses of action based on the characteristics observed in the objects that are relevant to the problem. These courses of action or strategies may be critically important to the ultimate success of the expert system, but they are generally difficult to capture.

■   9.8   STRATEGIES FOR KNOWLEDGE ACQUISITION

As with inference, there are two distinct ways of looking at the knowledge acquisition problem. In the first method, we begin with what the expert does and work backward to identify the structures the expert uses. For example, in dealing with the expertise of a pilot, you may observe the pilot and gather rules on the basis of how this person carries out the task. You can then gradually formalize what the pilot does in terms of facts, rules, and frames.

The alternative methodology begins by formulating an analytical model based on the components of knowledge. One then attempts to fit the knowledge and behavior of the expert into the model. In the case of the pilot, this methodology would begin by going through the flight manuals to determine what the important knowledge structures are. This static knowledge is then converted into the expertise exhibited in on-task behavior by asking pilots to identify when they do what during the task.

The second approach, based on first building a normative or analytical model of the task, lends itself to automation much more easily because of its early focus on task specific structures which can often be expressed in terms of existing textbook representations of the systems. In many cases, though, it is the first approach that simulates what pilots think they are doing. In cases where the answers given by the two methodologies are clearly different, one may have to decide whether it is appropriate to second-guess the expert in building the expert system—that is, favoring an idealized view of how the task should be carried out over what the expert actually does. In some cases this type of second-guessing may be warranted, but there is always the danger that the expert actually jettisoned features of the analytical model that experience showed to be defective.

The first approach is labor-intensive and time-consuming in that it requires interaction between the expert and an external observer (who may, in fact, be an expert). The second approach is more conducive to the use of knowledge acquisition tools. Later in this chapter we show how and why knowledge acquisition tools are used with the second approach.

9.8.1 Manual Knowledge Acquisition

Eliciting expertise from human experts is generally recognized to be a difficult process. Hawkins (1983) analyzed the nature of expertise and emphasized its severe limitations and dependence on critical assumptions that are often implicit.

Bainbridge (1986) reviewed the difficulties of verbal debriefing and noted that there is no necessary correlation between verbal reports and mental behavior. Another discouraging study was that of Collins (1985), who investigated knowledge transfer processes among scientists and suggested that some knowledge may not be directly accessible through experts, not only because they cannot express it, but also because they may not be aware of its significance to their activities.

The technological lag in knowledge acquisition is underscored by the fact that the chief tools of early knowledge acquisition were not computers and software, but pencil, paper, and audio tape recorders. Each knowledge acquisition method developed in the late 1970s and early 1980s has been a variant on the general theme of ''talking to the expert.''

Currently, the two most popular methods of knowledge elicitation are interviewing (generally carried out manually) and repertory grids (for which automated techniques exist). The questioning that occurs during interviewing is a relatively simple way to elicit knowledge, but there is little in the way of methodology to guide the interaction between expert and knowledge engineer. Interviews are sometimes supplemented or replaced with verbal protocols that are essentially descriptions of how the expert carries out the task.

9.8.1.1 *Interviewing* In developing a knowledge-base, there are usually a number of opportunities for face-to-face meetings between the developers and experts. While verbal protocol analysis (Section 9.8.1.2) uses the task to structure the communication with experts, face-to-face meetings allow experts to talk more generally about the task and the nature of their expertise. Ideally, these more general discussions should be planned so that the developer has specific objectives and questions in mind. Unfortunately, because of the problem-specific nature of expertise, there is no established methodology to guide one in conducting interviews with the expert. Instead, communication, interpersonal, and analytic skills need to be used to lead the expert down fruitful lines of inquiry and then interpret the responses appropriately.

There are, however, a few guidelines that may be of use in conducting interviews. These include being as specific as possible so that the expert has something to facilitate recall, speaking the language of the expert so that it is possible to concentrate on the task rather than having to figure out how to explain it in particular, allowing the expert to complete thoughts without interruption, and recording the interview in as complete a fashion as possible so that it can be thoroughly analyzed at a later time.

In general, the goal of the interview is to provide a context within which experts can explore and explain their knowledge, accompanied by methods for obtaining a full record of their descriptions and explanations. Where possible, videotaping may be used so that body language and the use of props can also be recorded. As is the case with verbal protocol analysis (discussed in the next section), the interviewing process is facilitated if a good basic understanding of the expert's model of the knowledge domain is available, so that it can be related to what the expert says.

Since interviewing is a subjective and poorly defined process, it is particularly important that the interpretations of the expert's comments be validated by checking back with the expert. The expert should have the opportunity to query or modify the interpreted data. For instance, an expert might forget important information during the interviews but may be able to recall the missing information when confronted with intermediate results based on the interviews. This feedback process also has the beneficial side effect of showing that the hours of interviewing really were productive and that the effort expended is resulting in something of use. Experts are often surprised at how their knowledge is reconstructed in a knowledge-base. Sometimes the results provide new perspectives and ideas for them that help to justify the time that they have spent during interviewing.

One pertinent technique of questioning focuses on critical incidents that represent interesting or difficult cases. Interesting or important cases are by their nature more memorable and stimulating. Focusing on an interesting case can provide information quickly and form a basis for further discussion. To the extent that critical incidents are unusual they have to be supplemented with more routine cases to provide more complete information on the knowledge domain.

In summary, interviewing is an important part of knowledge acquisition and is unlikely to be completely superceded by the more efficient automated knowledge acquisition methods described below. Interviews place a heavy burden on the developer, however, and it is essential that interview results be subjected to careful validation and analysis.

9.8.1.2 *Verbal Protocol Analysis* Verbal protocol analysis is a method of identifying rules quite popular among cognitive psychologists who are concerned with finding out how people think and reason. Although often aimed at theoretical distinctions, verbal protocol analysis can be adapted to play a role in knowledge acquisition for expert systems.

Verbal protocol analyses (Ericsson and Simon, 1984) attempt to track the process of expert reasoning "as it occurs." In verbal protocol analysis the expert is asked to "think out loud" while performing the task. Although this method has been useful in some cases, there are serious scientific questions about its overall validity. It has, for instance, been argued that verbal protocols are an example of an introspective process that requires that the subject act as though observing behaviors that are in many cases unobservable (Nisbett and Wilson, 1977). In brief, this type of argument runs along the line of

Definition 9.1: If you ask someone to tell you what they are thinking as they are thinking it they will tell you something, but it won't be a valid representation of that thought process because they don't have access to that information.

Some researchers have referred to verbal reports and descriptions disparagingly as "soft data," in contrast to "hard data," which would include measures such as reaction time and proportion of errors. In machine reasoning, however, we have a pragmatic concern with actual reasoning. The hard data that is available may be impressive in terms of its hardness (quantifiability), but it does not necessarily provide usable knowledge that can support reasoning. We can either take numbers that we are confident in, when we are really trying to derive data for symbolic reasoning, or we can collect somewhat dubious symbolic information in hopes of being able to construct a useful knowledge-base.

However, many practitioners view a total reliance on numbers and hard data as analogous to the old Sufi story of the person who loses a key in the dark and looks for it in a different place (under a lamp) because it is easier to see there. It is undoubtedly true that verbal protocols leave something to be desired as data, but in many cases they contain information that is needed.

We can test the quality of facts and rules derived from protocol analysis by evaluating how they affect machine reasoning. Verbal protocols suggest knowledge that is then evaluated, debugged, and refined until a satisfactory knowledge-base is achieved. Needless to say, this is a difficult and time-consuming process.

Verbal protocols should use questions that check that experts really know what they are talking about and that explore the reasons behind the conclusions that they reach. Consider the following examples:

> QUESTION: Do you know the name of the disease that exhibits the observed symptoms?
>
> ANSWER: Yes.

In this first example we have to trust the expert if we want to infer that this person actually knows the name of the disease.

> QUESTION: Which of these three diseases, malaria, typhoid, or cholera, exhibits the observed symptoms?
>
> ANSWER: Malaria.

In this second example it is possible that the expert guessed, based on the selection that we offered.

> QUESTION: Name the disease that exhibits the observed symptoms.
>
> ANSWER: Malaria.

In this example, it is unlikely that the person could generate the correct name unless it were accessible from memory. While the answer could have been a lucky guess, the odds are against it.

> QUESTION: Do you know the name of the disease that exhibits the observed symptoms?
>
> ANSWER: Yes.
>
> QUESTION: How did you arrive at your answer?
>
> ANSWER: First I focused on the fact that there was high fever and it appeared to be a tropical disease. Then I realized that the recurring episodes of the disease were consistent with malaria and that

the patient had lived in a country where malaria is still fairly common. I was then confident that malaria would be a good diagnosis.

The fourth example verifies that the subject has the name in memory together with some redundant information about it that gives him confidence in the answer. Asking the two questions in the final example gave us not only the answer but also information about the reasoning process that led to the answer.

There are a number of ways in which we might modify the basic idea of protocol analysis to work in a particular situation. One method is to split the task so that the critical expertise or knowledge that we are interested in becomes more apparent. In building the IILS system, for instance, the task was divided up between two pilots where one pilot told the other pilot what to do (Higgins and Chignell, 1987). The idea of this modification is to separate the knowledge of interest from the manual skills not relevant to the system. Thus the verbal protocols were collected as a side effect of this *division of labor* technique where pilot A operated the controls and pilot B gave verbal instructions to pilot A about how to operate the controls. These verbal instructions were then used directly as a verbal protocol of the task.

Verbal protocols can also be supplemented with more general interviews. In addition to asking the expert to think aloud during the task, we can also ask that expert general questions about the task and the solution strategy, such as, "what is the most important piece of information that you use in solving this problem?" This type of knowledge acquisition is important but remains an art.

9.8.2 Automated Knowledge Acquisition

One disadvantage of manual methods such as interviewing and verbal protocol analysis is that they consume large portions of the time of people who are in short supply, namely, experts and experienced developers.

Interviewing is usually productive only if a skilled knowledge engineer is available. There is always the possibility that the interview may not fully elicit important aspects of the knowledge domain. Even when experts do have access to explicit representations of their expertise, the process of knowledge acquisition is time-consuming and they may prefer to go out and exercise their expertise rather than talk about it.

Obtaining the cooperation of experts who know how they perform the task is necessary but by no means sufficient for building the knowledge-base. An expert may forget to mention critical concepts during the interviews, leading to incomplete structures in the knowledge-base. If they are not careful, developers may have insufficient understanding of the knowledge domain to interact smoothly with the expert.

Similar situations have been observed in the interaction between subject experts and online intermediaries during online information retrieval, as occurs in large libraries. In the case of online retrieval, one person has the domain expertise while the other has the search expertise. Some users of online retrieval systems prefer to carry out the search themselves, without the aid of an intermediary, because they find it difficult to communicate their information needs to someone who does not fully understand their knowledge domain.

Similarly, knowledge elicitation can be a frustrating experience when the knowledge engineer has insufficient understanding of the knowledge domain of the expert. In some cases, as with end-user searching in online retrieval, the domain expert may be better off interacting with an automated knowledge elicitation tool directly.

The disadvantages and uncertainties of interviewing and verbal protocol analysis have paved the way for new methods of knowledge acquisition. Tools are now available that provide a structure for the knowledge acquisition process and bypass the knowledge engineer as facilitator and intermediary. Automated knowledge acquisition is the process of using these tools.

Recently two major vectors of research directions for automated knowledge acquisition have emerged, one focusing on *knowledge elicitation*, and the other on *machine learning*. Knowledge elicitation techniques such as repertory grids have been developed to capture the basic description of objects in terms of their properties.

In contrast, machine learning methods assume that object descriptions are already available. Given the object descriptions, machine learning techniques seek to discover rules about how different object configurations explain task-relevant behavior. Thus the objective of one machine learning task is to analyze the traits of different cancer cells and determine rules for detecting different types of cancer cell on the basis of a defined profile of trait values being present.

In terms of components of knowledge (Section 4.3), these two vectors of knowledge have focused on two subsets of knowledge acquisition:

  i. Knowledge elicitation focuses on naming, describing, and organizing.
  ii. Machine learning focuses on relating and constraining.

The history of automated knowledge elicitation goes back to the definition of repertory grids by George Kelly (1955). He was concerned with acquiring knowledge about personality traits of patients long before the advent of expert systems (before the field of artificial intelligence had been named in fact). Gaines and Shaw (1980) proposed that Kelly's personal construct psychology could be adapted to the requirements of building expert systems. Shaw and Gaines (1983) then formulated and tested methods for using repertory grids in knowledge engineering which led to a series of experimental programs such as PLANET (Shaw, 1982) and to further industrial studies about the use of repertory grids in knowledge engineering (Boose, 1984, 1985; Bradshaw and Boose, 1986; Wahl, 1986). Boose (1985) developed the ETS system for knowledge acquisition using repertory grids and noted that repertory grids are generally better suited for analysis tasks than for synthesis tasks. The AQUINAS system (Boose, 1986) introduced hierarchical repertory grids. Auto-Intelligence™ (Parsaye and Murphree, 1987) was the first commercial knowledge acquisition tool to combine repertory grids with rule induction techniques to perform both tasks **i** and **ii** above.

The topic of automated knowledge acquisition continues to advance rapidly. Research efforts are currently being directed at finding more powerful knowledge acquisition tools. The MORE system (Kahn, Nowlan, and McDermott, 1985), for instance, is an automated knowledge acquisition system that helps refine an existing knowledge-base. SALT (Marcus, McDermott, and Wang, 1985) is one of the first automated knowledge acquisition methods to address synthesis (rather than analysis) problems. SALT consists of two subsystems that share a knowledge-base. One subsystem interviews the expert to elicit three kinds of knowledge (method, constraint, and fix schemas) and builds up a representation of that knowledge. The rule generator then translates this representation into rules that can then be used in the knowledge-base.

Our focus in the rest of this chapter will be on automated knowledge acquisition techniques that are well understood and available. At present this restricts us to systems that carry out knowledge acquisition for analysis problems, such as diagnosis, classification, and decision making. Automatic knowledge acquisition is, however, not a single technique but a collection of tools and methods (Figure 9.2).

To automate the knowledge acquisition process, we need to provide tools that:

    a. Help experts without a knowledge engineer capture their own expertise.

    b. Allow knowledge engineers to capture knowledge more effectively in very complex applications.

    c. Provide methods of *automatic induction* that capture knowledge usually unobtainable without computer assistance.

Ideally, a system for automated knowledge acquisition should consist of at least five modules, as shown in Figure 9.3:

The interview manager.

The structure discovery system.

The example manager.

The induction system.

The expert system generator.

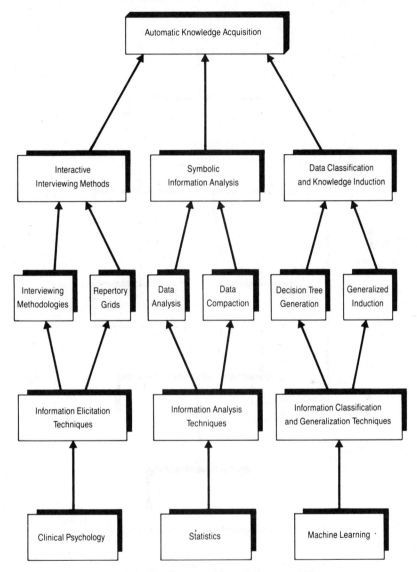

Figure 9.2 The lineage of knowledge acquisition.

The role of each of these modules is as follows. The interview manager is responsible for interacting with the expert and capturing knowledge. The interview manager would include the knowledge acquisition tools for naming and describing the objects.

The structure discovery system captures the structure of the knowledge and helps to identify the key components used by the expert in making decisions.

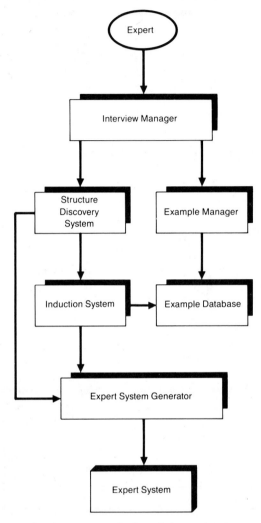

Figure 9.3 The structure of a knowledge acquisition system.

This system would be responsible for finding the right organization for the objects.

The example manager keeps track of data and examples and helps the expert in bookkeeping tasks. The task of the component is necessary because people generally have difficulty in keeping track of many different pieces of information.

The induction system both classifies and generalizes data and examples provided by the expert, using one of a number of machine learning methods or statistical methods such as discriminant analysis, factor analysis, or cluster analysis.

Finally, the expert system generator generates a working expert system based on the knowledge generated by the other modules. This component of automated knowledge acquisition is not fully a reality at present. In general, the rules that are generated automatically still have to be screened, edited, and augmented before they constitute part of an adequate knowledge-base for an expert system (Figure 9.4).

9.8.3   Repertory Grids

Repertory grids are used to identify traits and attributes and to describe objects in terms of those traits and values. Repertory grids were developed as a result of the work of George Kelly on Personal Construct Theory (Kelly, 1955), which has been very influential in recent approaches to knowledge elicitation.

Kelly developed a theory of human cognition based on the notion of *constructs*. These are the templates that a person creates and then attempts to fit over the realities of which the world is composed. He developed this personal construct theory in the context of clinical psychology and hence was concerned with having techniques that bypassed cognitive defenses and elicited the construct systems underlying behavior.

Kelly's approach can be directly applied to eliciting knowledge from an expert. The repertory grid technique is a way of representing personal constructs as a set of distinctions made about elements relevant to the problem domain.

9.8.3.1   *Terminology for Repertory Grids*   The terminology used in describing the properties of objects has sometimes been inconsistent, largely because of the influence of the many different disciplines (e.g., pattern recognition, psychometrics, numerical taxonomy) that are concerned with describing and classifying objects. We shall use the following terminology.

A *decision making task* or a *selection task* is one in which an expert makes decisions or selections. In such tasks the expert chooses from among a set of alternatives. For instance, given a set of possible investments, an investment adviser *selects* one as the best investment, or given a set of possible faults for a car that does not start, a mechanic *selects* one as the most likely fault.

Decision making is the process of *selecting* from among a set of alternatives. When we make a decision, we favor one selection over others. For instance, to make a recommendation for investment, an investment adviser makes a decision by *selecting* one investment instead of others. In each instance of the application of an expert system, decisions are made on specific *cases*. A case is essentially an input to an expert system for analysis. Thus, when a mechanic diagnoses a car, the *car* is the *case* for the diagnosis. Thus a decision making expert system *makes a selection*, i.e., provides recommendations, for *a given case* by analyzing the characteristics of that case.

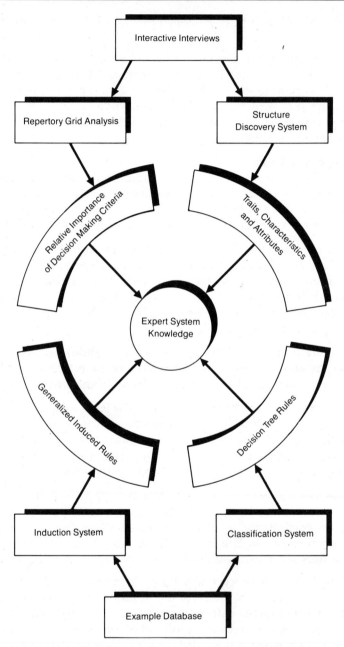

Figure 9.4 The components of a knowledge acquisition system.

When a large number of selections are possible in an application, experts often make a number of *intermediate selections*. For instance, to select an investment, an investment adviser first decides whether the investment should be long-term or short-term, *then* he decides on a particular long- or short-term investment.

When the number of eventual selections is large, the decision making will have a *hierarchical form*. Thus the expert will have a hierarchy of selections or a tree of selections and subtopics. This form of selection is called *hierarchical decision making*.

A human expert has usually observed many cases in the past and can relate the characteristics and traits of the cases to the features of selections. We call the cases that the expert has observed in the past and that serve as training instances *examples*.

Examples help the expert to relate the abstract concepts to concrete terms and become more accurate. Without examples we may never really know whether we have captured the right knowledge. By asking the expert to compare examples and case histories, one can often identify distinguishing traits and characteristics that could otherwise not be easily discovered.

During decision making, experts make selections by considering characteristic *features* that distinguish selections. For an investment adviser, the *feature* "Liquid" distinguishes between the selections "Stocks" and "Real Estate." Features are thus general characteristics and properties of selections. Experts use such characteristic properties of selections to make decisions. To identify features, we ask the expert to compare selections and examples and to indicate how they are similar or different.

Since features reflect the characteristics of selections, usually each feature has an *opposite* feature. The opposite of a feature reflects the opposite properties of the selection. For instance, for an investment, the opposite of "Heavy" is "Light"; the opposite of "Liquid asset" is "Tied-up money," etc.

A feature and its opposite provide two *poles* for matching a property. For instance, "Heavy" and "Light" are two poles of a feature. Here are some examples of features and their opposites:

Feature	Opposite
Heavy	Light
Reliable	Unreliable
Serious illness	Minor problem
Long-term	Short-term

By asking experts to identify the opposite for a feature we help them to focus on the two extreme poles of a characteristic or property. This facilitates discovery of their preferences for selection.

Just as experts use features to distinguish selections, they also think of characteristic traits of examples. During decision making, experts make selections by considering characteristic *traits* that distinguish between examples. For instance, for a mechanic the *trait* "Dim Lights" distinguishes between the selections "Dead Battery" and "Engine Trouble." To identify traits, we ask the expert to compare examples and to say how they are similar or different. For instance, by comparing a few patients who have allergies or colds and/or flu with other patients, we identify the trait "Sneezing."

Since traits reflect the characteristics of examples, usually each trait has an *opposite* trait. The opposite of a trait reflects the opposite properties of an object. For instance, the opposite of "Young" is "Old," the opposite of "Bright" is "Dim," the opposite of "Tall" is "Short," etc.

To represent specific values for a trait, we use an *attribute*. For instance, the attribute "Inflation Rate" may have a value between 1 and 20. A value of 1 for "Inflation Rate" may be viewed as low inflation, while the value of 14 may be viewed as rather high. Using an attribute helps us be more specific about how an object matches a property. For instance, it is much more accurate to find the value for "Inflation Rate" than a judgmental match for "High Inflation." In fact, by capturing a relationship between the trait "High Inflation" and the attribute "Inflation Rate," we help to capture some of the expert's judgmental knowledge.

Here are some traits, their opposites, and the attributes characterizing them:

Trait	Opposite	Attribute
Young	Old	Age
New	Used	Date of Purchase
Tall	Short	Height
Heavy	Light	Weight
Rich	Poor	Amount of Money

When should we use a trait, when should we use an attribute? This question is best answered by the expert. The choice of using a trait itself, an attribute with symbolic or numeric values should be made to make the expert feel most comfortable about expressing knowledge.

The criteria for decision making fall into two distinct categories:

The characteristic *features* of the selections.

The characteristic *traits* or attributes of the case.

For instance, in recommending an investment, an investment adviser makes a decision by matching the characteristic *features* of each selection (i.e., investment) with the characteristic traits of each case or example (i.e., investor), e.g.,

Selection Features	Investor Traits
Risky Business	Risk-taker
Large Investment	Wealthy
Tax Shelter	Has High Tax Bracket

It is important to distinguish between features and selections, since the space from which selections (such as investments) are drawn is often distinct from the space from which cases (such as investors) are selected.

9.8.3.2 *Using Repertory Grids*

Traits and features are characteristics of objects, examples, or cases that distinguish among instances. It is important that the meaning of the traits used in a repertory grid be clearly (unambiguously) understood. This requires that the problem under investigation is defined prior to the grid elicitation so that the trait names are applied in a constrained and unambiguous context.

Take a trait name such as "Light," for instance. In the context of margarine, it might refer to the percentage of unsaturated fats, in photography it might refer to the brightness of the surroundings; in wrestling, it might refer to the weight of a wrestler; while in business, it might refer to the amount of information contained in a report. Since natural language is inherently ambiguous, we should treat trait names as predicates having a clearly defined meaning within the particular context of the knowledge domain under consideration.

Experience has shown that repertory grids should be constructed separately for selections and examples. The formation of a particular repertory grid proceeds in two steps. First, the traits are elicited. Comparisons among small groups of selections (typically made in *triads*, i.e., three at a time) is one method that can be used to elicit the traits.

Experts can usually identify some traits by comparing selections. However, much better results are often obtained by asking the expert to think of concrete examples and then perform the comparison. Traits are thus identified by comparing typical examples with respect to a set of selections. This allows the expert to think carefully about how examples are different. Thus to identify structure of examples, we ask the expert to give a trait that differentiates one example from another.

For instance, in medical diagnosis, we ask a physician to provide *traits* by saying how two patients are similar or different; e.g., patient John Smith has the trait "Looks Pale." We may also ask a physician to provide *features* by saying how two diseases are similar or different; e.g., the selection "Cold/Flu" has the features "Sneezing" and "Causes Fever."

9.8.3.3 *Identifying Traits and Features*

In using Kelly's original method to identify traits, the expert is asked to study the examples (such as Sara Davidson, John Smith, and Jane Simpson) and decide how one of them is different from the other two by asking the question:

> What is a trait that two of
>
>> Sara Davidson
>> John Smith
>> Jane Simpson
>
> share, but the third does not?

The expert may now select John Smith and identify the trait "Young" as distinguishing him from Jane Simpson and Sara Davidson. We may then ask:

> What is the opposite of Young?

to obtain the opposite trait "Old." This form of triadic comparison continues until a number of traits are identified and is used in most implementations of repertory grids, e.g., AQUINAS (Bradshaw and Boose, 1986), Kitten (Shaw and Gaines, 1986). However, while this method easily provides descriptions it does not directly provide discriminating rules; i.e., it performs "describing," but not "relating."

A method, first developed within the Auto-Intelligence system (Parsaye and Murphree, 1987) relies on relationships between features and traits and utilizes form-filling methods to extend the repertory grids to perform interactive rule derivation. As well as "describing," this performs "relating" and "constraining" interactively.

In this method, features may be identified either by Kelly triads, as above, or by comparing two selections with respect to an example. Good results are often obtained by simply allowing an expert to *"fill in blanks"* in automatically generated *forms*. For instance, we present the expert with the following form:

> For *Samantha Davis* I selected *Real Estate* and NOT *Stocks*
>
> because Real Estate is/has/does: _____
>
> but Stocks is/has/does not.

The expert may complete this form by filling in the blank with the feature *Tax Shelter*. Similarly, traits may be identified by providing a form such as:

> I selected *Real Estate* for *Samantha Davis*, but NOT *David Cooper*
>
> because *Samantha David* is/has/does: _____
>
> but *David Cooper* is/has/does not.

The expert may complete this form by filling in the blank with the trait *Long-Term Investment Goal*. Opposite traits may be obtained with the form:

The opposite of *Long-Term Investment Goal* is: _____

to which the expert may respond: *Short-Term Investment Goal*.

By asking experts to fill in blanks in dynamically generated forms, a surprising amount of information can be obtained rapidly. Further, the ability to dynamically switch between this method and the traditional Kelly triads (described above) helps to provide flexibility and avoids interview-related fatigue.

However, the forms must be generated intelligently; i.e., the content of each form must be determined by the answers the expert has provided before. In Auto-Intelligence this is achieved with a set of "interviewing rules."

Multistep relations (i.e., rules) are obtained with forms such as

Both *Stocks* and *Certificates of Deposit* are *Short-Term*
but for *Anthony Walden* I selected *Certificates of Deposit*
because *Certificates of Deposit* is/has/does:
but *Stocks* is/has/does not.

The expert may complete this form by filling in the blank with the trait *Low-Risk*. This suggests the rule:

Investment <u>is</u> Certificates of Deposit
If
Investment <u>should be</u> Short-Term
and
Investment <u>should be</u> Low-Risk;

Although this form of rule may be obtained from the expert interactively, without machine induction, other rules may also be obtained by induction as discussed in the next section.

Traits and features may be related by using forms such as:

For *David Cooper* I selected *Stocks* because

Stocks is/has/does *High-Risk Investment* and

David Cooper is/has/does: _____

The expert may complete this form by filling in the blank with the trait *Risk-Taker*. This relates the feature *High-Risk Investment*, which applies to selections (i.e., investments) to the trait *Risk-Taker*, which applies to examples (i.e., investors). In this way we obtain a mapping between the domain of selections and the domain of examples.

9.8.3.4 Confidence Factors for Repertory Grids   To identify the structure of a decision making process, we may proceed by identifying features for selections and traits for examples. However, before we go further, we can relate these entities, i.e., see to what extent they match each other.

In using repertory grids we need to scale or calibrate the relevant cases and selections in terms of their traits and features. Consider the following example. Suppose that you are an expert in the use of programming languages for different applications. The goal of the knowledge acquisition process is to identify the rules that you use for selecting a specific programming language for an application. We might start by considering a set of applications (i.e., examples) you have dealt with before, such as a compiler, a user interface, a database management system, and a knowledge representation language. Say that your expertise covers the following languages:

Lisp.
Prolog.
Fortran.
Pascal.
Smalltalk.

These languages constitute the selections that you will consider. The features that will be important in selecting one programming language rather than another will be those which differentiate these languages. Differentiating features and traits can be found by comparing the languages and applications, as discussed before. Suppose that you identify the following features and opposites:

Feature	Opposite
Symbolic	Numeric
Graphic	Character-Based
Real-Time	Batch-Oriented
Functional	Relational
Easy to Learn	Difficult

Each language may *match* each feature (or its opposite) to some extent. Such a match may be expressed as a number in a scale, e.g. 0–10 or 0–100. The expert is thus asked to directly indicate the degree of matching, which is in some way equivalent to the operation of scaling. For instance, matches for Pascal may be:

Symbolic: *30*
Graphic: *60*
Real-Time: *80*
Functional: *40*
Easy to Learn: *60*

Here 100 means a complete match, while 0 means no match at all. On the other hand, matches for Lisp may be:

Symbolic: *100*
Graphic: *20*
Real-Time: *0*
Functional: *100*
Easy to Learn: *50*

The expert may actually provide this information *graphically* by moving a pointer along a scale, as discussed in Section 6.7.1. The system may automatically manage and order the confidence factors by using a visual display format that makes it very easy to understand the order relation between the different items.

After the matches have been provided, a grid may be constructed with the features as rows and the selections as columns (or vice versa), as in Figure 9.5.

Traits

Symbolic	Graphic	Real-Time	Functional	Easy to Learn	
100	20	0	100	50	Lisp
100	60	0	0	80	Prolog
20	10	80	0	70	Fortran
30	60	80	40	60	Pascal
70	100	80	80	50	Smalltalk

Languages

Figure 9.5 A repertory grid.

The entries in such grids reflect the degree to which selections and features match each other. Such grids may be extended to match examples with selections and traits with examples (Figure 9.6).

The information in the grid may in itself be used to provide a first prototype of an expert system by pattern matching with values and choosing the closest match. For instance, an application that does not require a symbolic language but involves graphics and real-time code may match Pascal better than Lisp. However, this is a very rough match, and we can provide much better results by further analysis and induction as discussed in the next sections.

9.8.3.5 *Attributes and Induction*   Traits are used to distinguish between examples. Attributes are used to characterize *examples* by using values. Each trait may lead to an attribute; e.g., the pair of traits "Young" and "Old" lead to the attribute "Age." For instance, a patient may be characterized with a set of attributes such as age, sex, and weight:

Attribute	Value	Type
Age	24	Numeric
Weight	140	Numeric
Height	6	Numeric
General Health	Good	Symbolic
Depressed	30	Confidence

Each attribute has a type (numeric, symbolic, etc.). Attributes with symbolic and enumerated values are sometimes very useful. For instance, we may use an attribute with the enumerated values (Good, Average, Poor).

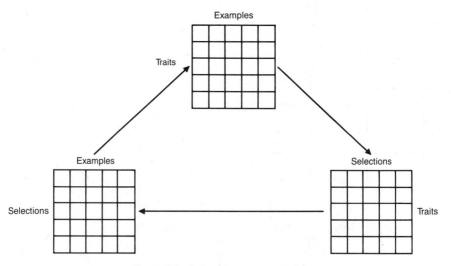

Figure 9.6   Extending repertory grids.

After the attributes have been identified, the expert may provide values for
the attributes of each example, e.g.,

Patient: John Smith

> Age: *24*
> Sex: *Male*
> Temperature: *Normal*
> Sneezing: *80*
> History of Allergy: *Yes*

After these values have been obtained, we ask the expert to provide confidence
in the suitability of each selection. For instance, in the case of a medical diagnostic system that chooses between Allergy-Related, Cold/Flu, Serious
Causes, and Simple Headache we may have:

Patient: John Smith

> Allergy-Related: *80*
> Cold/Flu: *50*
> Serious Causes: *10*
> Simple Headache: *20*

Here 100 means total confidence, while 0 means no confidence at all. Again
the expert may actually provide this information *graphically* by moving a
pointer along a scale, as discussed in Section 6.7.1.

These confidence factors reflect the suitability of each diagnosis for John
Smith. Similarly, we obtain values and confidence factors for other patients.
After the values and confidence factors have been obtained for each example,
we have a good deal of information from which we can distill knowledge.
The process of discovering knowledge from examples is called *induction*. With
induction we generate rules that classify new cases. The structure of components of automated knowledge acquisition is shown in Figure 9.7.

When the expert system is presented with a new case (i.e., patient), there are
two possibilities: (a) exactly the same example has already been classified by
the expert (this rarely happens in practice); (b) the case is new and does not
exactly match any of the examples provided by the expert (this usually happens
in practice). In case a, the answer is clear. In case b, we need to *guess* which
one of the selections the expert would have made in the new case.

It is, in general, theoretically impossible to be "always right" when we guess.
If we have to make a guess, there must be more than one plausible choice so
that our guess can go wrong; otherwise, we would not be guessing. However,
despite the theoretical arguments, in practice, some guesses are much better

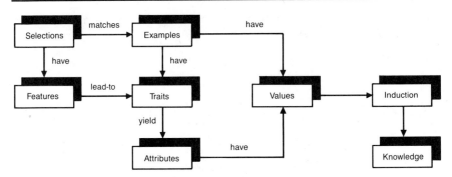

Figure 9.7 Automated knowledge acquisition terminology.

than others. The main goal of induction is thus to provide "very good guesses."

Early machine learning systems would simply make a guess based on an induction algorithm and could not provide justifications of how they made the guess. Thus early machine learning systems suffered from the fact that often knowledge seemed to appear from within a vacuum with no clear basis. This obviously had a negative affect on the quality of the induced knowledge. In a modern induction system the expert may view the gradual formation of rules during induction. The expert is often one of the best judges for whether induction is moving in the right direction.

We may actually perform several layers of induction, each becoming more general than the next, thus allowing the expert to gradually observe the formation of rules. This greatly helps the experts to better understand the information they have provided. For instance, we may use four *induction levels*, each using a less conservative induction method, thus producing more general results.

First-level induction classifies the examples for selecting the best selection without using inexact values or ranges. This is a very conservative, but often accurate method of removing redundancy from the example set. For instance, we categorize information about cases where Age = 12 and when Age = 20, but we do not jump to conclusions about the ages in between, e.g., 17.

Second-level induction generalizes values of attributes but does not leap far beyond the example set, thus performing a semiconservative generalization. For instance, now we generalize from Age = 12 and Age = 20 to 12 < Age < 20 but do not jump to conclusions about the cases where Age is less than 12, e.g., Age = 4.

Third-level induction fully generalizes the examples and attempts to produce as general a rule set as possible without conflicting with counterexamples. Now we actually generalize to as wide an age range as possible, e.g., to the unbounded range Age > 20.

Fourth-level induction, performs fuzzy induction producing very general rules with inexact results. Now rather than selecting any specific diagnosis, we provide inexact confidence values for each diagnosis.

After the induction process, we produce rules such as:

> Diagnosis is *Allergy-related*
> If
> History of Allergy = Yes
> and
> Sneezing > 60
> and
> Temperature = Normal ;

These rules can then be executed to diagnose new patients. Further, such rules may be embedded within other large-scale expert systems. Often, one may wish to modify the rules with an editor and then transport, recompile, and execute them within another environment.

■ 9.9 AUTOMATIC ACQUISITION OF CLASSIFICATION KNOWLEDGE

Two basic types of task can be carried out by expert systems: *analysis* and *synthesis*. Analysis generally involves the interpretation of data in terms of patterns and components. Problems in classification and diagnosis, for instance, are examples of analysis. Analysis is sometimes thought of as the reduction of complex phenomena into simpler elements. In medical diagnosis a complex set of symptoms is reduced into a diagnosis from a set of diagnostic categories. Synthesis works the other way, building a larger, more complex structure out of a basic set of components. Design is the preeminent example of a synthesis task.

Analysis is often easier to automate in an expert system since it is easier to recognize basic components in a complex structure than it is to build that complex structure out of the basic components. In contrast to analysis, where a restricted number of outcomes (hypotheses) usually must be considered, synthesis has too many components and too many possible outcomes. We see this phenomenon in chemistry, for instance, where the analysis of complex compounds into their basic components is considerably easier than the synthesis of complex compounds.

Many expert systems perform some type of *classification* such as diagnosis or investment recommendation. Classification tasks are a type of analysis and differ from *synthesis* tasks that combine objects. Thus fault diagnosing of a computer is an analysis or classification task, while the design or configuration of a computer is a synthesis task.

Knowledge can often be expressed as relations between objects. A relation can generally be expressed as a constraint on the properties that one object may have given the properties that exist for the other objects that affect it. Finding these relations can be difficult, depending on the type of expert system that is being constructed.

One reason for the proliferation of classificatory expert systems is that classification can be based on properties of objects and does not usually have to consider complex relations between objects. Classification expert systems form a very high proportion of practical expert system applications.

Classification problems are very common. Some examples are as follows:

a. Given a new patient, diagnose the condition on the basis of attributes such as age, sex, and blood pressure.

b. Given a new investor, find an investment based on the investor's age, tax bracket, financial status, etc.

c. Given a car that does not start, diagnose the fault by considering the brightness of the lights, noise from the engine, etc.

In a classification application the task of knowledge acquisition is composed of the following components:

a. Identify the basic criteria used by the expert in making decisions. This helps the expert study the problems piece by piece and then integrates the resulting knowledge. This is very important, since experts often do not know how their own expertise is structured.

b. Discover the importance of the criteria used by the expert in decision making and analyze the interrelationships between these criteria. This actually helps experts to clarify their own thoughts on the relative merits of the criteria used in forming decisions.

c. Analyze data and examples for redundancy and inconsistency and generate knowledge by capturing the rules that classify and generalize the data. Knowledge is distilled by performing induction on examples.

In terms of the terminology of repertory grids, this translates to the following:

a. *Identify Selection Topics.* Identify the basic selections and decisions used by the expert in making decisions.

b. *Identify the Features of Selections.* Identify which features distinguish between the possible selections.

c. *Identify Traits and Attributes.* Perform comparisons that help to identify the traits and the criteria used in decision making. Objects or cases are then described in terms of the traits and attributes. Features discovered in **b** may also lead to traits.

d. *Capture Examples and Values*. Ask for case histories or examples that illustrate the decision making process.

e. *Induce Knowledge*. In this phase, the system uses induction to discover rules.

As discussed in Section 9.8.3.2, in automated knowledge acquisition for classification the discovery of structure can be facilitated by utilizing special question generation techniques to help experts to study problems *locally* and piece by piece, thus gradually revealing their expertise. Often experts have not analyzed their own decision making process to a great extent and may not be aware of which traits or characteristics are important in the selection process. However, experts are usually very good at saying why they made a *particular* decision or why two specific selections are different from each other.

The discovery of the appropriate attributes is a critical part of knowledge elicitation and it can be facilitated by presenting good examples to the experts. The use of examples helps the expert to relate the abstract concepts to concrete terms. Often after using examples, an expert may discover inaccuracies in previous discussions. Thus it is important to ask experts for *representative* examples or case histories that show how the identified traits work in practice. In a representative example set each selection has at least one example in which it is a good choice and one example in which it is a poor choice.

■ 9.10 MEASURING EXPERT SYSTEM PERFORMANCE

After we have acquired knowledge and built an expert system, how do we know either that it works or *how well* it works? Obviously, one way would be to ask an expert. But by simply relying on an expert's *feelings* about the resulting knowledge, we do not get good scientific answers to questions relating to the quality of a knowledge-base.

Intuitively, the aim of a validation effort is to ensure that the expert system behaves "correctly." But what does this mean for systems that produce inexact results? Can we ever be 100% sure that the knowledge is correct? From a philosophical viewpoint, the answer is *no*. Even in the case of traditional programs, one can never be 100% sure about a verification effort in all cases, since as the program size grows, the size of the verification program will also grow and at some point the verification system may be more complex, and error-prone, than the program itself. Thus a verification effort can increase our confidence in the future behavior of the expert system, but may not always confirm it with 100% confidence.

From a different perspective, it is important to realize that expert systems will inevitably make mistakes. Of course, human experts also make mistakes, and we tend to tolerate them—especially because they *are* experts. Thus the key questions in tolerating the mistakes of an expert system are: "*What is the price to be paid for each mistake?*" and "*How often are the mistakes made?*" Rather than aiming to *verify* the behavior of an expert system, we should try to *measure* its performance.

Validation can be done either by judging the ultimate performance of the expert system as a black box or by focusing on the quality of the expertise itself, i.e., by looking inside the box. Aside from measuring the performance of the resulting expert system, logical and empirical analysis of the expertise within the knowledge-base may indicate inconsistencies and errors. In some cases this approach to validation may be preferable because it can be used to test sections of the knowledge-base before a complete expert system prototype has been constructed.

However, in many cases input–output behavior will determine the success or failure of the expert system, and black box validation cannot be overlooked. Black box validation is also often more objective than other methods since it is less affected by feelings, biases, etc. Issues involved in automating this form of validation for classification expert systems are discussed in the next section.

Validation of expert systems is a crucial issue for applications in which one has to "get it right the first time." In such situations debugging the performance of the expert system will be inappropriate because failures cannot be tolerated, as in systems dealing with civil defense, earthquake response, troubleshooting in a nuclear power plant, and cockpit aids. Thus there is a need for methods of experimentation that can construct scenarios to test both the performance of the expert system and the validity of the expert knowledge that it embodies prior to its operation.

Some of the techniques for verifying and validating simulation models (Sargent, 1982) are also useful in testing and simulating the operation of an expert system. These include the use of historical data to test the expert system, assessment of the face validity of the system by experts, and extensive use of the expert system within a simulated environment.

Suwa, Scott, and Shortliffe (1982) focus on verifying the completeness and consistency of a knowledge-base by considering all possible combinations of attributes used in the premises of rules and the corresponding attributes used in the conclusions of rules. Tables obtained in this way are then checked for conflicts, redundancy, subsumption, and missing rules. Nguyen, Perkins, Laffey, and Pecora (1987) extend such a method to include checks for circular rules, unreachable conclusions, and dead-end goals.

These types of validation approach are a powerful way of checking the logical structure of the facts and rules in the knowledge-base, but they don't fully address the issue of whether the individual rules themselves are correct. We should remember that logical validity is not the same thing as truth, since a logically valid argument may be based on faulty assumptions.

Expert systems that produce vague or inexact results are difficult to validate since it is often hard to simply guess how well the results match those produced by an expert. Manual methods of performing comparisons are simply too laborious and inaccurate to be practical or effective. Further, as different versions of an expert system are developed through gradual refinement, it becomes exponentially harder to dynamically compare different versions. Automated tools for validation produce improvements in helping us to determine the quality of the knowledge in a knowledge-base.

9.10.1   Automating Expert System Validation
As the need for using knowledge-based systems increases, two fundamental questions need to be answered:

a. How do we acquire knowledge?
b. How good is the knowledge we have acquired?

However, with a view to automation, these questions can also be asked as follows:

i. How do we automate knowledge acquisition?
ii. How do we automate the measurement of the quality of the knowledge we have acquired?

It is important to ask questions **i** and **ii** rather than **a** and **b** since nonautomated methods have little chance of keeping up with the increasing demand for knowledge-based systems. It is also important to ask question **ii** whenever we ask question **i**; i.e., the efforts to accelerate the knowledge acquisition process should always be accompanied by the development of adequate tools for measuring the quality of the acquired knowledge.

We now discuss the use of automated tools for validating classificatory expert systems. In such systems, when the expert system is presented with a new case to classify, it will assign a confidence factor to each selection. By comparing these confidence factors with those provided by an expert, we can measure the accuracy of the expert system on a single case. By performing comparisons on many cases, we can arrive at an overall measure of the performance of the expert system over a set of test cases. We are, however, considering only the validation of the input–output behavior of expert systems here.

From a strictly scientific point of view, when performing such measurements, it should be kept in mind that the expert system has been tested and measured only with respect to a specific set of test cases and a specific expert. Measurements on other test cases and experts may produce different results. It is thus imperative to also measure the quality of the test cases on which the measurements are performed. Use of a representative set of cases will provide a more meaningful set of results.

It should also be noted that the approach described here may be used not only to measure an expert system against a human expert but also to measure and compare the performance of two expert systems, or to compare two human experts, for that matter.

9.10.1.1 Yardsticks for Knowledge To automate the processes of knowledge validation, we need to provide tools and facilities for managing a database of test cases and evaluating them to measure the quality of the captured knowledge with respect to a set of validation criteria.

To measure the behavior of an expert system, we need to first compare specific test cases. Given a specific test case, we use the term *"recommendation"* to refer to the vector of confidence factors provided for a set of selections. For instance, let us consider the diagnostic expert system discussed in Section 9.8.3.5. which performs classification by choosing between the selections:

Allergy-Related
Cold/Flu
Serious Causes
Simple Headache

For instance, for a given patient, the system may provide the following classification:

> Patient: John Smith
>
>> Simple Headache: 50%
>> Cold/Flu: 70%
>> Allergy-Related: 60%
>> Serious Causes: 40%

while the expert recommends:

> Patient: John Smith
>
>> Simple Headache: 30%
>> Cold/Flu: 80%
>> Allergy-Related: 70%
>> Serious Causes: 40%

We thus have two recommendations:

System recommendation: 50, 70, 60, 40

Expert recommendation: 30, 80, 70, 40

We can ask several questions here:

a. Was the *order* of the recommendations provided by the expert system right, i.e., were the confidence factors assigned to the selections in the same order both by the expert and the system?

b. *How many* selections were misclassified?

c. What were the *numeric differences* between the confidence factors provided by the system and the expert?

d. How *important* was each misclassification?

e. On a large set of test cases, how *often* do these misclassifications take place?

f. How *good* were the examples on which the measurements took place?

On the basis of these questions, we can develop a theory of how the results provided by the expert system can be measured. This theory is based on the following fundamental consideration:

Definition 9.2:   No single measure of accuracy is uniformly applicable to all application areas and tasks for which expert systems may be built. We should therefore be able to adjust various parameters from expert system to expert system and should be able to measure several forms of accuracy as called for by different applications.

Thus, one (the human expert, or the person performing the measurements) will need to define one's own method of measurement based on social, industrial, and other factors to determine what constitutes "good" performance for the expert system. Many such measures may be defined.

To begin with, we can compare recommendations on a single case based on order. We say that two recommendations are *order-compatible* if the orders of the highest to the lowest confidence factors for the selections are the same in both cases. We can quantify this notion of order compatibility using statistical measures of the correlation between ranked data such as Spearman's rho (ρ) or Kendall's tau (τ) (Snedecor and Cochran, 1967).

Sometimes we may be interested in more than just the order of different attributes. For instance, if we assume that the numbers are *ratio-scaled*, i.e., that a case having a value on an attribute of 40 really does have twice as much of that attribute than a case whose corresponding value was only 20, the absolute values of the numbers become important.

In such cases, being order-compatible may not really mean very much. For instance, consider:

> 80, 70, 40, 30
> 4, 3, 2, 1.

These recommendations are order-compatible but are not really conveying the same information. There are a number of ways that we can express the lack of compatibility between sets of numbers that are ratio-scaled. In general, these types of measure are referred to as *distance measures*. Thus we can introduce a distance measure for recommendations. If A and B are two recommendations, then *distance(A, B)* measures the distance between A and B as measured on all confidence factors, i.e., the sum over j of:

$$(CF(A_j)^2 - CF(B_j)^2)^{1/2}$$

This distance measure is referred to as the *Euclidean distance*.

Thus we now have two measures: distance and order. But which is better? Consider the following examples:

a.
> 81, 79, 60, 70
> 80, 78, 20, 30

b.
> 78, 80, 20, 30
> 80, 78, 20, 30

Which of these two recommendation sets are closer together, pair **a** or pair **b**? In case **a** the order of the top two recommendations is right, but the lower recommendations are really off the mark. In case **b** the order of the top two recommendations is wrong, but the top two recommendations are so close that this may not be significant. Perhaps this was a borderline case, anyway.

Which are we to choose as better, **a** or **b**? The answer is thus that in different situations, different measures of accuracy are preferred. For instance, in some cases order is all that matters, while in other cases the absolute values of confidence factors are important.

9.10.1.2 Confusion Matrices One approach to measuring the performance of an expert system is to examine cases where the system gave the wrong answer. In humans, giving the wrong answer is sometimes referred to as *confusion*; e.g, when we incorrectly hear a word, we confuse the word that we thought we heard with the word that was actually said.

Human confusion can be measured using a *"confusion matrix."* Confusion matrices are used in a variety of fields including psychology (Moates and Schumacher, 1980) and the nuclear industry (Stampelos and Apostolakis, 1985). When a human makes a decision or selection relating to a set of objects, the confusion matrix measures how different objects are confused. For instance, in psychology confusion matrices are used to measure how well a person can distinguish sounds, e.g., how often a person confuses a "t" with a "d." In the nuclear industry confusion matrices measure the cost of operator errors—e.g., what is the probability that the operator can confuse "action a" with "action b" and if this confusion does occur, what will the consequences be?

We can adapt the use of confusion matrices for measuring the performance of expert systems. First, let us define a confusion matrix to measure how well the expert system classifies test cases. This matrix applies to a specific set of test cases and measures how often two selections were confused.

The confusion matrix is a two-dimensional matrix whose rows and columns are *selections*. The entry in row i and column j reflects the relative frequency of confusing selection i for selection j. The entries in a confusion matrix are thus numbers between 0 and 100. An entry of 100 means that the two entries have been confused in every single case (i.e., 100% of the time), while 0 suggests that they have never been confused (i.e., total accuracy).

For instance, if we have 10 test cases and in 3 of them Cold is confused for Allergy, then the entry for Cold/Allergy will have the number 30. Figure 9.8 shows such a confusion matrix in which Allergy is confused for Cold/Flu 25% of the time and Cold/Flu is confused for Allergy 30% of the time.

All errors made by an expert system may not be equally serious. We therefore define a *confusion cost matrix* to measure the importance or cost of confusing one selection with another.

The confusion cost matrix is also a two-dimensional matrix whose rows and columns are selections. The entry in row i and column j reflects the cost of confusing selection i for selection j. The entries in a confusion cost matrix may be any numbers chosen by the expert. A natural method will be to use numbers

		Diagnosis Made			
		Headache	Cold/Flu	Allergy	Serious Causes
Actual Problem	Headache	—	20	25	0
	Cold/Flu	20	—	30	30
	Allergy	10	25	—	20
	Serious Causes	0	10	10	—

Figure 9.8 A confusion matrix.

between 0 and 100 as relative costs. An entry of 100 suggests that confusing one element for the other is extremely costly or extremely serious, while 0 suggests that the confusion is really not important.

However, other entries, such as "infinite cost," may be used in some situations to indicate totally unacceptable mistakes. Obviously, the cost of confusing A for B in general differs from the cost of confusing B for A.

The values in the confusion cost matrix should be defined by the expert or the person performing the measurements. These values are independent of any test cases or example sets. Figure 9.9 shows a confusion cost matrix that suggests that the cost of confusing a simple headache for a cold is not very high (30). The cost of confusing a cold for serious causes is higher (70) but is less than the cost of confusing serious causes for a cold (100).

Now by multiplying the number of confusions for each case with the cost for the error or confusion, we arrive at some measure of how well the system performs. Thus we get the *eventual confusion matrix*, as shown in Figure 9.10.

By summing the rows and columns of this matrix, we get a measure of how confused the system is with respect to classifications in general. For instance, in the preceding example the total for the classification confusion is 122. Since there were 12 filled cells in the matrix, the average confusion is 10%. Similar measures may be used to weight distance measures.

9.10.1.3 *Measuring the Yardsticks*   Since the results obtained from a confusion matrix are dependent on the set of test cases presented to the expert system, it is important to know how good the test cases are. Therefore, in validating the expert system, we should:

i. Allow the measurements to reflect what the expert or the user consider as important.

ii. Perform measurements on the test cases as well as the results.

Diagnosis Made

	Headache	Cold/Flu	Allergy	Serious Causes
Headache	——	30	50	70
Cold/Flu	50	——	50	70
Allergy	70	70	——	70
Serious Causes	100	100	100	——

Figure 9.9   A cost confusion matrix.

Diagnosis Made

	Headache	Cold/Flu	Allergy	Serious Cases
Headache	——	6	12	0
Cold-Flu	10	——	15	21
Allergy	7	17	——	14
Serious Causes	0	10	10	——

Figure 9.10 An eventual confusion matrix.

There is one quality about test cases that is difficult to measure numerically, namely, the quality of being *typical* cases encountered by the expert everyday. The test cases should be selected by the expert to reflect this quality as well as the requirements listed below the paragraph that follows.

We say that two selections are *well distinguished* by a test case if their confidence factors are well separated and one of them is the best selection for the case. The test cases should be chosen so that:

a. Each attribute is exercised in the full range of its values.
b. Each confidence factor is varied between 0 and 100.
c. Each selection will have both a high and low confidence factor within the test set.
d. Each pair of selections is well distinguished by at least one test case, i.e., a clear-cut case.
e. Each pair of selections is poorly distinguished by at least one test case, i.e., a borderline case.

This immediately suggests that a large set of test cases is considered better than a small set. Although there is no doubt that using different test cases may produce different measurement results for the expert system, the key question in performing validation on an expert system is: "To what extent will changes in the test cases produce large differences in the measured quality of the expert system?"

For instance, suppose that we have 30 test cases. We can divide them into three sets of overlapping test cases each with 20 entries. Now, will the results of the measurements be very different for these three sets? If so, our confidence in the measurements should be low. Otherwise, we may begin to take the measurements seriously.

In fact, this form of *divide and test* strategy may be repeated on a test set many times to increase our confidence in the test results. Of course, an automated tool will again be much better in performing this task than a human.

The performance measures discussed above allow us to assess how well an expert system is performing. Confusion matrices go further in yielding diagnostic information about distinctions that are being ignored by the system. Thus, in situations where two selections are being confused with each other in a number of cases, there is prima facie evidence that either the current rules for distinguishing the selections are incorrect or additional rules are needed to capture aspects of the distinction that are currently being overlooked.

■ 9.11 SUMMARY

It is helpful to think of knowledge acquisition in terms of the five components of knowledge that were discussed in Chapter 4. Naming and describing are generally straightforward tasks, and good progress has been made in developing automated knowledge acquisition methods for describing objects in terms of their attributes. In addition, it is usually easy to collect knowledge about how the relevant objects are organized using methods such as sorting, but it may take some effort to identify the best way for organizing the objects, particularly when multiple perspectives are possible. In medical diagnosis, for instance, it may be possible to classify diseases according to either their severity, the bodily functions that they affect, the organ or system of origin, or their etiology.

When coupled with appropriate machine learning systems, the knowledge acquisition methods outlined in this chapter provide a uniform approach for interactive and deductive knowledge acquisition. Experience with this type of integrated system has taught us that a careful approach that builds on previous work but couples it with innovation can provide dramatic improvements in the productivity of the knowledge acquisition process.

Techniques for validating knowledge-bases and measuring their performance should supplement knowledge acquisition by providing information about the quality of the knowledge. As is the case with knowledge acquisition, the focus should be on automating such techniques.

10

SUMMARY

Our goal in writing this book has been to provide overall knowledge of expert system technologies and methodologies that experts need in order to play a larger role in the process of building expert systems. We see this expanded role for the expert as being especially important as the need for expert systems increases. We expect that among the readers of this book there will be a large number of experts who are interested in replicating their expertise.

In Chapter 1 we began by describing what expert systems are and how they fit into the general search for machine intelligence. We defined an expert system as a program which relies on a body of knowledge to perform a somewhat difficult task usually only performed by a human expert.

We traced the emergence of expert system languages through the evolution of programming paradigms for data structuring and control. We showed that the programming technologies used in developing expert systems are a new level of expression which permits us to represent and deal with knowledge. Thus expert system languages and environments may be viewed as higher level programming systems which approximate more closely the patterns of expression used by humans. They allow experts who are not computer scientists to transfer their knowledge and skills to computer systems.

We outlined the essential elements of expert systems in Chapter 2. We described how they work, what their structure is, and what techniques of knowledge and reasoning they use. We introduced facts, rules, and frames as straightforward but effective ways of capturing expertise within an expert system. It was shown that the two basic components of an expert system are the knowledge base, composed of facts, rules and frames, and the inference engine. We then recognized that the process of using the knowledge base and inference engine to make inferences is a reasoning process that has much in common with systems of formal logic.

We explored the nature of predicate logic in Chapter 3, where we viewed logic as a method for both knowledge representation and inference. In representing knowledge with predicate logic we showed how facts and rules can be expressed in terms of clauses and logical sentences. We also introduced a syntax for defining clauses which makes rules readable and easy to understand. Chapter 3 included a discussion of logic programming. We emphasized this topic, because, in addition to aiding our understanding of how expert systems work, logic programming provides a unified framework for knowledge representation and inference that we see as being particularly valuable.

We found that the concept of a rule provides a practical and intuitive method in which knowledge may be represented. Rules are also a natural way of expressing expertise. Facts and rules can be supplemented with frames or similar methods of knowledge representation to reflect the organization of knowledge in the knowledge domain and to assist the process of reasoning.

Chapter 4 discussed knowledge representation in general. Issues that were covered included the components of knowledge, the nature of knowledge representation, the evaluation of knowledge representation methods, and the comparison of different forms of knowledge representation. We identified five components that are essential to the process of describing knowledge: naming objects, describing objects, organizing objects, relating objects, and constraining relations. Later, in Chapter 9, these same five components were found useful in organizing and understanding knowledge acquisition methods. We outlined how the major knowledge representation methods can be conceptualized in terms of building blocks similar to nodes and arcs in a network.

In view of the many knowledge representation schemes that have been proposed, and the many more that could be proposed, we needed a way of evaluating different knowledge representation methods to guide us in selecting an appropriate one. We discussed the features that a good knowledge representation method should have. To begin with, representation of knowledge requires that relevant objects in the knowledge domain be named, described, and organized. Then, relationships are expressed, including constraining relationships that govern the storage and retrieval of object properties.

We developed and discussed a number of questions for evaluating knowledge representation methods. These questions covered four major categories, which were the quality of the basic knowledge structures, the quality of the storage mechanisms, the quality of the retrieval mechanisms, and the quality of the knowledge representation environment.

Chapter 5 dealt with frames. Frames represent systems of facts organized into packages that facilitate storage, retrieval and management of knowledge about objects, concepts, and entities. Other useful properties of frames include the use of inheritance and attached procedures. We have chosen to use a combination of frames and logic in representing knowledge. Although there are a number of alternative techniques, the combination of frames and logic appears to be well suited to the task of building expert systems. Our system of logic and frames fares well in terms of the evaluation guidelines discussed in Chapter 4.

In Chapter 6 we turned to the problem of uncertain knowledge. Coping with uncertainty in reasoning is a complex area within the field of artificial intelligence. As with other issues, the techniques actually used for uncertain reasoning in expert systems are only a subset of a large class of methods that have been considered. The three major strategies that we considered were certainty theory, Bayesian probability theory, and fuzzy logic.

We found that quantifying uncertainty was not as straightforward as it appears to be. Most people, including experts, do not have experience in generating numbers to reflect their uncertainty. There may be a number of cognitive biases that affect the accuracy of expert judgments. We showed how efficient methods of ranking may be used for uncertainty assessment.

Chapter 7 showed how the general ideas about logic and inference that were discussed in earlier chapters can be formalized into the procedures that can be used in an inference engine. We discussed forward, backward, inexact, and semi-exact reasoning.

Chapters 8 and 9 addressed the issue of how expert systems can be built. We approached the problem of building expert systems by recognizing that expert systems are a type of software, which, although possessing some unique properties, nevertheless share many of the features of conventional software. Thus many of the principles for building expert systems can be understood in terms of corresponding principles in building software in general.

However, we noted that expert system technologies constitute a new paradigm which extends the capabilities of traditional programming techniques to deal with knowledge-oriented tasks. We compared the process of expert system development with the traditional software lifecycle by identifying six phases in the expert system construction process. These phases were feasibility analysis, conceptual design, knowledge acquisition, knowledge representation, validation, and technology transfer and maintenance.

In Chapter 9 we showed that as knowledge acquisition tools improve, more of the knowledge acquisition task can be placed in the hands of the expert. Knowledge acquisition has already evolved in the few years since its first application. We expect knowledge acquisition to continue to evolve, and experts to be more involved in the knowledge acquisition process. We also discussed some of the issues involved in validating expert systems and pointed out that in general validating an expert system can be a difficult task, but that in some cases tools for expert system validation can lessen this burden.

The future of expert systems is likely to become intertwined with the future of the rest of the computer industry. Just as database systems have penetrated the mainstream computing environment, expert systems will be merged with and embedded within conventional software applications. However, once we view expert system technology as an evolution of programming paradigms, as in Section 1.5, this trend is not surprising.

■ APPENDIX A ■

SEARCH

■ A.1 INTRODUCTION

As discussed in Chapter 1, an early finding in artificial intelligence (AI) was that much of reasoning can be considered as a type of problem solving. We illustrate this with a simple problem involving three coins.

Given an initial state of three coins as shown in Figure A.1 (two coins, heads; one coin, tails), the goal is to flip one or more of the coins over so that the same side is showing for all three coins (either all heads—HHH or all tails—TTT). In this problem one can perform three possible operations corresponding to the three coins (i.e., turn Coin-1 over, turn Coin-2 over, or turn Coin-3 over). A move corresponds to choosing one of the three operators, and a solution is a sequence of moves that transforms the initial configuration into one of the goal states.

We can now create a network that encapsulates all the possible moves that can be made on the way to a solution. A state space for a problem generally consists of:

- A set of possible starting states.
- A set of operators.
        Operator-1: Turn Coin-1
        Operator-2: Turn Coin-2
        Operator-3: Turn Coin-3
- A set of goal states (two, in the case of the three-coin problem)

Intermediate states in the state space are created by applying the operators to the initial states. A solution to the problem is then a sequence of operators (moves) that transforms the initial state into the goal state.

Figure A.1 An initial configuration (state) for a three coin problem.

State space representations of problems can generally be formulated in terms of a tree structure where the root of the tree corresponds to an initial state and the leaves (tip nodes) of the tree correspond to goal states. If such a representation is appropriate, the problem becomes one of searching through the tree to find the goal. A computer can be programmed to generate the search space for a problem, but exhaustive enumeration of each node of the tree becomes increasingly difficult as the number of nodes in the tree increases. Figure A.2 shows a tree representation of the three-coin problem.

As the number of available operators in a problem increases, there is an explosion in the size of the solution tree. This combinatorial explosion is illustrated in comparing the state space representation for the three-coin and five-coin problems (Figures A.2 and A.3, respectively). The complexity of the state space representation increases by leaps and bounds with each new increment in the number of operators.

■ A.2 SEARCHING A TREE

Search problems are frequently encountered and early theoretical work in AI sought to develop methods for controlling the search process so that good solutions could be found without getting lost in a combinatorial explosion of possible pathways (e.g., Nilsson, 1971).

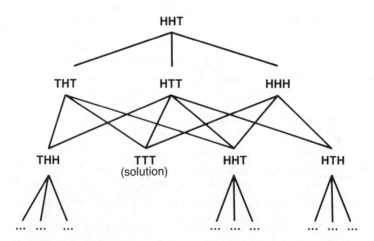

Figure A.2 A state space representation of the three coin problem.

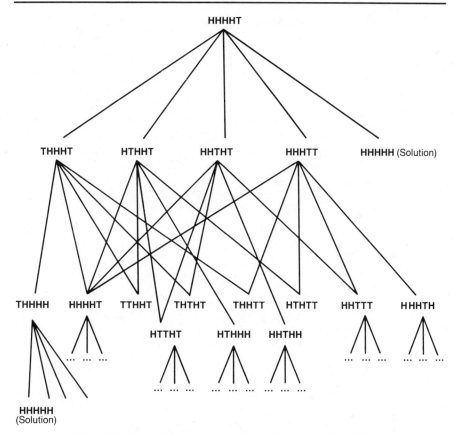

Figure A.3 A state space representation of the five coin problem.

Consider the abstract search problem shown in Figure A.4, where node H is the goal state and node A is the initial state. One way to represent the problem is as a network, but we can also create a tree of possible paths through the network (Figure A.5). If we want to find a solution and are not overly concerned with finding the most efficient path, we can begin searching the tree. Two basic approaches to search are breadth-first and depth-first search.

The distinction between breadth-first and depth-first search stems from the strategy used to pick the next node while moving through the tree. In Figure A.5, for instance, we might start by moving from node A to node B. If we then move across to C, we are doing breadth-first search. In breadth-first search we shuffle down through the tree examining all the alternatives at each level of the tree looking for the goal node.

Depth-first search burrows into a tree looking for the goal state. By convention, the leftmost alternative below the current node is chosen as the next node

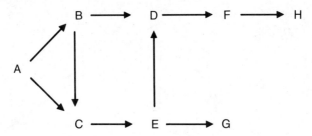

Figure A.4 An abstract search problem represented as a network.

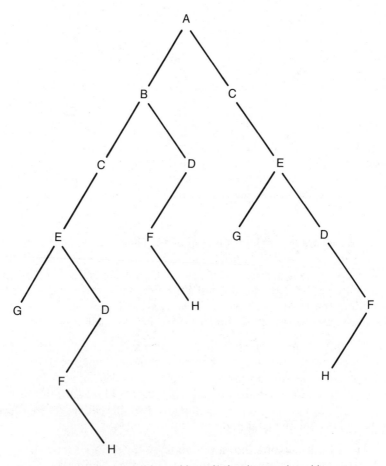

Figure A.5 A tree of possible paths for the search problem.

to move to. Thus depth-first search begins by examining the leftmost branch in Figure A.5 (A–B–C–E–G). Since a terminal node is encountered without reaching the goal, the search method then moves back up the tree (backtracks) to the next untried path. In this example, it moves back up one node to E and then continues in the pattern E–D–F–H, eventually finding the solution after going through the entire sequence:

A–B–C–E–G–E–D–F–H

In this example, breadth-first search takes considerably longer because all the versions of the goal node are relatively far down the tree. In the present example, the sequence of nodes examined by the breadth-first search procedure are:

A–B–C–C–D–E–E–F–G–D–G–D–H

Although depth-first search worked better in this example, it is not always better than breadth-first search. We could, for instance, add a new path to the tree from node A directly to node H (Figure A.6). If this were the rightmost branch of the tree, it would not help the depth-first search process, but now the breadth-first search would be much shorter:

A–B–C–H

We can characterize different types of search in terms of algorithms that form queues of nodes waiting to be examined. An example of such an algorithmic formulation is the following specification of depth-first search:

1. Put the top node in the queue.
2. If the queue is empty or the goal has been reached, go to 4.
3. If the first element is not the goal node, remove the first node from the queue and replace it with its immediate (i.e., children, but not grandchildren, etc.) successor nodes (in left-to-right order) at the front of the queue. Go back to 2.
4. If the goal node has been found, report that the goal has be reached; otherwise, report failure.

In the case of breadth-first search, step 3 of this procedure is altered so that the successor nodes are placed at the back of, rather than the front of, the queue, as shown in the following algorithm for breadth-first search:

1. Put the top node in the queue.
2. If the queue is empty or the goal has been reached, go to 4.
3. If the first element is not the goal node, remove the first node from the

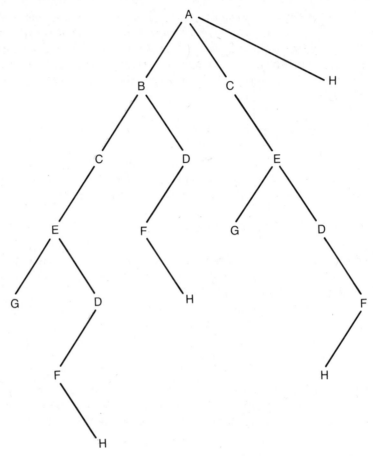

Figure A.6 A modified search problem (addition of one new path).

queue and place its immediate successor nodes (in left-to-right order) at the back of the queue. Go back to 2.

4. If the goal node has been found, report that the goal has been reached; otherwise, report failure.

■ A.3 FINDING AN EFFICIENT PATH

One (inefficient) way of finding the best path to the solution is to work through all the paths and select the best. This exhaustive procedure becomes tedious and impractical as the size of the search tree increases and the problem of combinatorial explosion becomes an issue.

Branch-and-bound search is a more efficient way of looking for the best path. During search, a number of alternative nodes can be reached from the set of current nodes. Each partial path that has been expanded so far will have an accumulated cost associated with it.

In branch-and-bound, the next node to be examined is at the end of the shortest incomplete path currently known. The procedure stops when the goal state is reached and the cost of each of the remaining incomplete paths is greater than the path to the solution.

Each node at the end of a partial path in a method such as branch-and-bound has a *heuristic function* associated with it. A heuristic function is an integer that is assigned to each node on the basis of its "suitability," i.e., the anticipated cost or distance of the path leading from the node to the goal.

Search methods that utilize heuristic functions are referred to as *heuristic search methods*. Aside from branch-and-bound, other well-known forms of heuristic search are *hill-climbing, A*,* and *beam search*. Hill-climbing is the simplest of the heuristic search procedures. Its name comes from the analogy where the problem space is a two-dimensional plane with the heuristic function defining the elevation of each point above the plane. Hill-climbing works by always choosing, at each step, the operator that leads to the best value of the heuristic function, at the end of that step (operation). If the heuristic function were expressed as a cost, the procedure would work its way down, rather than up, the hills.

The problem with hill climbing is that it can become trapped in a *local maximum* (or *local minimum* for cost-based search), which is like reaching the top of a small hill (or bottom of a valley) that is surrounded by one or more higher hills. Since the method only moves upward at each step, there is no way of going back down the hill and then climbing one of the larger hills.

■ A.4 SUMMARY

Many problems in AI can be formulated as tree search problems. This has tended to make search a central topic in AI. However, large amounts of domain knowledge can reduce the need for extensive search. The chess player who has a rule about what to do in a particular situation, for instance, can avoid lengthy search through a huge tree of possible continuations. In fact, the very best chess players, who may not have all the machine cycles (neuron firings), and who definitely do not have all the working memory necessary for extensive search, still beat specially designed chess machines that are custom-built to carry out vast amounts of search.

In expert systems, search problems appear in finding a line of reasoning in an inference tree. Heuristic methods cannot be applied in inference when there is no straightforward heuristic—this often happens to be the case. Detailed domain knowledge can, however, bypass the need for extensive search (as is probably the case with expert chess experts).

GENERAL-PURPOSE REASONING

■ **B.1 INTRODUCTION**

An interesting orientation that characterized early AI systems may be called the *generality principle.* The implicit assumption of programs built with this principle was that:

Definition B.1: If one captures the basic logical structure necessary for solving a problem then, *in principle,* one can use a powerful computer to compute a solution.

Further, the generality principle relies on the assumption that there are *general* methods of expressing and solving problems. As discussed in Chapter 1, although this may be true "in principle," when dealing with real problems, the amount of time taken in the computation becomes unacceptably long, even on extremely fast computers.

Many problems begin with an initial state and end when some goal has been achieved. One general strategy in problem solving is to carry out a succession of actions that bring one closer to the goal until the goal itself is finally reached. The *means–ends analysis* approach to problem solving uses this strategy by specifying what the ends (goals) are and then analyzing what means (actions or operators) are available to achieve those ends.

The GPS (general problem solver) is a problem solving method that provides a good example of the use of the generality principle. GPS is a software program (Ernst and Newell, 1969) that implements means–ends analysis in a general way, allowing it to be applied to a number of problem domains.

In this appendix we will discuss the GPS approach to problem solving and will illustrate some of its strengths and weaknesses with examples. Other programs in the GPS tradition include ABSTRIPS (Sacerdoti, 1977), MPS (Korf, 1985), and SOAR (Johnson-Laird, 1986).

■ B.2 GPS: THE GENERAL PROBLEM SOLVER

GPS begins its analysis of a problem by characterizing it as a journey from the initial state to the goal state. For instance, if we consider a game of chess as a version of this metaphor, the initial state is the starting configuration of the board at the beginning of the game. The goal state is then the placement of the opponent's king in checkmate, and the game is a journey from the start position to checkmate.

The means–ends analysis process of getting from the initial state to the goal state begins by detecting the *differences* between the *initial state* and the *goal state*. An *operator* is then selected to reduce the *distance*. In the case of chess, the operators correspond to moves. If the operator cannot be applied to the initial state, a subproblem is set up that will get us to a new *current state* from which the chosen operator will be applicable.

In nontrivial problems, we typically cannot get directly from the initial state to the goal state using a single operator. Instead, we must split up the problem into a manageable series of subproblems. Each of these subproblems is then solved through means–ends analysis. Thus means–ends analysis is a *recursive* procedure. Finally, the method needs a way of assessing the difference from the current state to the goal and a way of *assigning priorities* to the currently active operators based on the difference between the current state and the goal state.

GPS is in some ways an extension of the tree search methods introduced in Appendix A. However, GPS involves more than just search, since instead of taking an existing tree and choosing a suitable path on the basis of a search method, GPS has to *construct* the tree one node at a time. Given the current node, GPS examines the available operators to see which one will produce a state (node) that is closer to the goal. GPS continues down a path until it does not appear to be getting any closer to the goal, at which point it goes back up the tree (backtracks) until a promising new direction is encountered. Thus GPS aims to create a focused tree that considers only those nodes that are on possible solution paths.

The basic GPS method can be modified in a number of ways. GPS can, for instance, either work forward from the initial state, seeking to reduce the distance to the goal state as it goes, or backward from the goal state, seeking to reduce the distance to the initial state. We see another version of this dilemma (which direction to search in) when considering forward and backward chaining inference methods for rule-based systems (as discussed in Chapter 7).

In GPS, the important concepts are as follows:

- An initial state.
- A goal state.
- A method for calculating differences between states.
- A set of operators for reducing differences.
- A selection method for choosing operators according to their priority.

■   B.3   GPS AND THE THREE-COIN PROBLEM

We saw in Appendix A how the three-coin problem could be represented and solved as a search tree. GPS can also be used to solve this problem. We represent each node as a string of three letters (H if the coin in that position shows heads, T if it shows tails).

Consider the problem where the initial state is HHT. There are two goal states, either HHH or TTT. The distance from the current state to the goal state is given as

distance = the number of coins that are in the wrong position

It is easy to see that no state in the three-coin problem can be more than a distance of one from the goal. There are two operators in this problem, which can be applied separately to each of the three coins:

The H-T operator turns a coin over to show tails.

The T-H operator turns a coin over to show heads.

In the three-coin problem, no difference table is really necessary, because the same two operators are always applicable, and the choice of which operator can be used follows directly from seeing which face of the coin is currently uppermost.

On this very simple problem, GPS works as follows:

Initial-State HHT: Goal-State HHH or TTT

Current Distance = 1.

Coin 1 - available operator is H-T
resulting state is THT
distance to goal (TTT) = 1.

Coin 2 - available operator is H-T
resulting state is HTT
distance to goal (TTT) = 1.

Coin 3 - available operator is T-H
resulting state is HHH
distance to goal (HHH) = 0.

Thus the method finds the solution by turning one coin.

This easy problem shows that, under favorable circumstances, GPS not only builds a focused search tree but also works its way to the solution quickly. If we have an N coin problem, even with the most "difficult" initial states, GPS will never take more than N/2 moves to solve the problem. For an odd number of coins, the worst case is (N − 1)/2 moves, while for an even number of coins the worst case is N/2 moves.

If every problem were as easy (trivial) as the three-coin problem, we could use GPS for all problem solving tasks. However, most problems are much more difficult, and in these more difficult cases GPS is rarely very helpful in finding a solution.

■ B.4 GPS AND THE HOUSEHOLD ROBOT

Consider a slightly more difficult problem. Robin the robot is a state-of-the-art household model made by the Hood company of Chicago. Among other duties, Robin sets the table, mows the lawn, and does fetch-and-carry tasks. Some of Robin's capabilities are shown in the abbreviated list of operators in Figure B.1. Robin is able to find locations, move himself, shift objects, grasp objects, and so on. The circumstances under which these operators are used is defined in the difference table (Figure B.2).

The workings of Robin can be examined through a sampling of his activity. One Saturday morning, Robin finds himself in the garden shed holding a watering can in his gripper. He receives a request to bring the plant food located in the northeast corner of the garage back to the garden shed. This request jumps to the top of his priority list and becomes the current goal to be satisfied.

Since Robin uses GPS to solve his problems, he formulates the situation as follows:

Goal: plant food located at garden shed.

Current State: plant food located at NE corner of garage.
Robin holding watering can.
Robin located at garden shed

Difference - Goal: plant food located at garden shed
Current: plant food located at garage.

Robin now tries to find an operator that will get the plant food from the garage to the garden shed. He knows that he has a Move operator (Figure

Operators

```
Find
Move
Shift
Grasp
Open
Close
Ask
...
```

a) Model of the Move operator

Usage:	<u>move</u> 'Object,' from, 'Location-1', to, 'Location-2'
Preconditions:	Robot <u>at</u> 'Location-1' 'Object' <u>within grasp</u>
Result:	Robot <u>at</u> 'Location-2' 'Object' <u>at</u> 'Location-2'

b) Model of Grasp operator

Usage:	<u>grasp</u> 'Object'
Preconditions:	<u>Empty</u> gripper Robot <u>at</u> 'Location' 'Object' <u>at</u> 'Location'
Result:	'Object' <u>within grasp</u>

Figure B.1 Operators for Robin the robot.

	Map	Ask	Walk	Drive	Fly	Pick-up	Put-down
Find location	map available	map not available					
Move self			< 1 mile	>1 mile	>100 miles		
Grasp object						✓	
Empty Gripper							✓

Figure B.2 Part of the difference table for Robin.

B.1), which seems to be appropriate since the difference can be eliminated by grasping the object and moving it to the required location. The preconditions for the Move operator present a new problem, however. Before he can move the plant food from the garage, Robin must first have an empty gripper (holding more than one object at once was not one of his design specifications) and must be at the same location as the plant food (i.e., in the garage).

Robin empties his gripper using the Put-down operator. Robin's next goal is to move himself to the garage. First he has to locate the garage. He has two operators (Figure B.1) that allow him to locate a place. If a relevant map is not available, he uses the Ask operator. Fortunately, however, there is a map of the estate in the garden shed, and Robin uses this to find where the garage is. Getting to the garage can itself be considered as a GPS problem.

This example is starting to reveal some of the weaknesses of the GPS method. How does Robin learn and remember where new locations are so that he doesn't have to keep reading maps, asking people, or working out a route between where he is and where he wants to go as if it were always the first time he had traveled it? The basic version of GPS really has no answer, preferring to work from first principles and building any knowledge about how the world works into the definitions of the operators and the difference table.

Once Robin reaches the location of the plant food, he grasps the plant food using the Pick-up operator. He can now shift the plant food using the Move operator, since the preconditions of Move have been satisfied. After working out where the garden shed is and how to get there, he returns with the plant food, satisfying the goal that he had been set.

In this first example, we can criticize Robin for failing to learn and remember, but he got through the task without making any mistakes. We may not always be so lucky.

A day later it is Sunday morning, and Robin is asked to serve breakfast in bed. After moving to the kitchen, he begins to assemble the ingredients. He finds the cornflakes missing, so he creates the subgoal *Get cornflakes.* He knows that there are packets of cornflakes in the supermarket down the road. (This knowledge could be incorporated as a special version of the Get operator that deals with food and household products.)

Robin drives to the supermarket (since the distance is greater than a mile). He parks the car (as you may surmise, writing a GPS model for this may take considerable time, e.g., perhaps years), and moves to the supermarket. He then locates himself in the cereals section and grasps a box of cornflakes using Pick-up. Assessing his list of goals, he now realizes that he has to satisfy the current goal of having the cornflakes in the kitchen by returning home (shifting himself, with cornflakes in gripper, from supermarket to kitchen at home).

On the way out, however, he encounters a problem. He tries to go out a turnstile, but these appear to rotate in only one direction. He then saunters pass a checkout stand with the cornflakes in his gripper. On his way out he is confronted by the store detective, who deactivates him and calls his owner. What went wrong? Well, Robin's general-purpose knowledge wasn't strong enough to cope with the details of the environment. He knew how to fetch and carry, but he didn't know that he had to pay for an item before he took it out of a supermarket.

We may, of course, continue to add more and more domain knowledge to Robin's knowledge-base. However, using the GPS approach, there seems to be no end in sight for how much knowledge we need to add before Robin can function in a "common-sense" way. For instance, suppose, we add knowledge about store detectives etc. and send Robin back to the supermarket. What do you think will happen next?

He may begin taking goods out of other customer's baskets. We have just explained to him that the goods still belong to the supermarket until they pass the checkout. Now to explain to Robin that this is against social etiquette, we need to open a whole new Pandora's box about social interaction. The main point here is that as soon as we think we have explained something to Robin in detail, he will apply it inappropriately, since he will then be missing another piece of knowledge; e.g., we may have to explain that he may take tools out of a basket in the garage, but not in a hardware store, etc.

Another problem with GPS is that the goal state may be sufficiently ambiguous (although easily recognizable once it has been achieved) that it becomes difficult to assess the distance between the current state and the goal state. In chess, for instance, the goal state may take as many forms as the board positions in which checkmate is achieved.

To the extent that problem solving is carried out in a dynamic environment, the definition of the goal state may change radically during the course of problem solving, making it difficult to come up with meaningful estimates of the distance between the current state and the goal state. Returning to our chess example, a player who appears to be losing may change the goal state from that of winning the game to simply drawing the game. In this case the goal state may be redefined as the achievement of perpetual check or a stalemate position.

▪ B.5 PROCEDURE SYSTEMS

Production systems can be considered as general-purpose reasoning systems that also include specialized knowledge about a particular domain. In the case of the household robot, for instance, the definitions of the difference table and the operators can be converted into production rules. Thus the row in the difference table corresponding to the *Move self* subgoal would be equivalent to the following rules:

> If
>> the current subgoal is to move self
> and
>> the distance to move is less than a mile
> Then
>> walk the required distance;
>
> If
>> the current subgoal is to move self
> and
>> the distance to move is greater than a mile, but less than 100 miles
> Then
>> drive the required distance;
>
> If
>> the current subgoal is to move self
> and
>> the distance is greater than 100 miles
> Then
>> fly the required distance;

Current states are equivalent to the facts in working memory. Before Robin moved to the garage, we might have the fact:

> Robin is in the garden shed

in working memory. After the move this fact would be replaced by:

> Robin is in the garage

Reasoning begins by placing facts corresponding to the initial state into working memory. Then, instead of carrying out means–ends analysis, the production rule interpreter fires appropriate rules until the goal is reached. Careful formulation of the rules will accelerate this process of converging on the solution. Thus a GPS model can be implemented as a production system.

The difference between a general-purpose reasoning system and a production system can be likened in some ways to reasoning from first principles (GPS) versus following a set of well-defined (compiled) rules that guide the reasoning process. The difference tables and operators used in a GPS type of model for a domain represent an underlying theory of how the domain works, but the knowledge is not directly accessible until a means–ends analysis is carried out.

In a production system, the knowledge that is implicit in the difference tables and operators of the GPS model is made explicit. Thus the rules of a production system can be regarded as compiled versions of the underlying general-purpose knowledge, with means–ends analysis being equivalent to a type of compilation mechanism.

■ B.6 SUMMARY

General-purpose reasoning is interesting, but it turns out to be much easier to supply knowledge to solve a problem than to build a system that can figure the knowledge out for itself. Although GPS creates a conceptually attractive metaphor for problem solving, it is a difficult method to apply in practice. GPS is often not very good at dealing with highly specific world knowledge that may be critical to successful problem solving.

■══ APPENDIX C ══

PROPOSITIONAL LOGIC

■ C.1 INTRODUCTION

Chapter 3 discusses predicate logic. In this appendix we introduce propositional logic as a simple method for formal reasoning.

An obvious way of expressing or representing facts and thoughts is by writing them in a natural language such as English. However, English can often be vague, and a single sentence can usually be interpreted in more than one way, possibly inhibiting the development and use of formal reasoning to some extent.

In order to express facts and concepts in an unambiguous and well-defined way, we need to use a more formal language. The formal language should capture deeper regularities than those that exist in everyday language. The power of language as a descriptive system stems from the fact that it can "code" real-world concepts in terms of a well-defined symbol system. The major parts of speech in a sentence (nouns, adjectives, and verbs) describe objects, attributes, and relationships that exist in the portion of the world under discussion (sometimes referred to as "the domain of discourse"). The weakness of language from the perspective of formal reasoning is that it does not make clear distinctions between major logical entities such as those discussed in this appendix and in Chapter 3.

We can illustrate this lack of rigor with regard to the concept of implication. In logic, an implication can be represented in the form:

If P Then Q

This statement then has a clearly defined and unambiguous meaning. In language, however, the concept of implication is less clear-cut. Consider the following statements:

1. I was late because of the traffic.
2. I am late when the traffic is heavy.
3. Heavy traffic can make me late.
4. I am on time when the traffic is light.
5. I will be on time if nothing unusual happens.

Are these five statements all saying the same thing? On an initial reading, each of these five statements might *appear* to be saying the same thing. From a logical perspective, however, there are some important differences. Statement 2 is an example of the statement:

> If
>   the traffic is heavy
> Then
>   I will be late;

while statement 1 is an implicit syllogism of the form

> If
>   the traffic is heavy
> Then
>   I will be late;
>
> The traffic is heavy
> _____.
> I will be late

with a modification in the tense of the syllogism (i.e., "am" instead of "will be"). Statement 3 is an extended version of statement 2, with the added notion of uncertainty expressed by the word "can." Statement 4 is a reversal of the earlier implication. Finally, statement 5 is vague in that it does not specify the conditions under which lateness occurs. It is related to the other four statements only insofar as it mentions lateness and appears to involve some form of implication.

This type of example shows how the properties and use of language can obscure important logical distinctions. The English language statements are at the same time both richer and less rigorous than corresponding statements in formal logic.

▪ C.2 PROPOSITIONAL LOGIC

For the purposes of machine reasoning, we need a more formal language that is capable of expressing logical distinctions and can automatically deduce new facts based on a collection of statements that are known to be true. Formal logic is a language that provides these features. The essence of formal logic is as follows:

a. We know a number of things that are true (these are called *axioms* or *facts*).

b. These facts or axioms are combined to obtain new facts using the process of inference.

Thus logic consists of two basic steps: *logical representation* and *inference*. Logic representations are operated on using the rules of logic to make inferences about the state of the world implied by the logical assertions.

Propositional logic is a fairly simple version of formal logic that incorporates the important notions of truth and inference. *Propositions* are statements that reflect the state of the world. Each proposition makes an assertion about something being either true or false. For instance,

> Copper is a metal
> Wood is a metal

are both propositions, one being true, the other false.

Propositional logic is a language and a tool for determining the truth or falsity of propositions. We often represent propositions as symbols, e.g., P, Q, and R. Single propositions are called *atomic formulas*. Individual propositions function as facts.

Compound propositions are used when single facts or propositions alone are insufficient to support complex reasoning. One often needs to relate facts together. We combine and relate facts in propositional logic by using *logical connectives*. The logical connectives are:

> and
>
> or
>
> not

When logical connectives are used, the resulting combinations of facts are still called *propositions,* or *propositional sentences*. For instance, the following example is a propositional sentence. In this example we have used parentheses to make it easier to distinguish between the words that belong to individual propositions and the connective that separates the propositions.

(today is Saturday) and (the weather is fine)

A compound proposition involving an "and" is called a *conjunction*. A compound proposition involving an "or" is called a *disjunction*.

As in the usage of everyday language, a conjunction joining two propositions in a fact indicates that both propositions are true. A disjunction indicates that both propositions cannot be false. Thus

(today is Saturday) or (the weather is fine)

is true under the following circumstances:

(today is Saturday)—(the weather is fine)

(today is Saturday)—(the weather is not fine)

(today is not Saturday)—(the weather is fine)

but is false if today is not Saturday and the weather is not fine.

Propositions are negated by using *not*. For instance,

not (the weather is fine)

is equivalent to the statement "the weather is not fine," while

not (Wood is a metal)

is equivalent to the statement "Wood is not a metal."

In formal logic, the truth of an assertion is expressed as a truth value. In addition, the meaning of logical connectives can be expressed in terms of the situations under which they will be true. In two-valued logic any statement must be either true or false. It is not possible for the same proposition to be both true and false at the same time.

If A and B are propositions, the logical connectives determine the truth of compound propositions as follows:

(A and B) is true if both A and B are true.

(A or B) is true if either A or B is true.

not (A) is true if A is false.

■ C.3 THE PRECEDENCE OF LOGICAL CONNECTIVES

Since "and," "or," and "not" may combine with propositions and each other in a variety of ways, it is important to know which of these operators takes precedence in cases where there is an apparent conflict. The situation is analogous to the use of arithmetic operators, where an expression such as:

$$8 \times 7 + 2$$

can be disambiguated by supplying parentheses:

$$8 \times (7 + 2)$$

or by assuming that multiplication takes precedence over addition, in which case the effective interpretation is

$$(8 \times 7) + 2$$

As in the case of arithmetic operators, we need to disambiguate combinations of logical connectives by either adding parentheses or using a convention that establishes the order in which the connectives will be applied.

Where more than one connective is involved, as in:

A and B or C and D;

the proposition may be interpreted in a number of ways, e.g.,

A and (B or C) and D

(A and B) or (C and D)

((A and B) or C) and D.

In general, in order to disambiguate compound propositions such as these, we can use either parentheses or a "disambiguation convention." Although we sometimes use parentheses in disambiguating propositions, we also make use of a disambiguation condition that can be used instead of parentheses.

The logical connective convention that we use is:

not takes precedence over "and"

not takes precedence over "or"

i.e., of the three connectives (and, or, not), "not" is always applied first.

The precedence of "not" stems from the fact that it is an operator that modifies the meaning of a single formula (whether it is a simple or a compound proposition). In contrast, the connectives "and" and "or" modify the meanings of two or more formulas jointly by specifying allowable combinations of truth and falsity that can be observed among the formulas that they connect.

The conflict between "and" (conjunction) and "or" (disjunction) is resolved as:

> "and" always take precedence over "or"

i.e., conjunctions are always grouped together first.

Thus

> A and B or C and D

always means

> (A and B) or (C and D).

This convention is not restrictive since, if we wish to write

> A and (B or C) and D;

we use a new clause E, which stands for *(B or C)*. Then, with the implication

> If B or C Then E

we may write

> A and E and D

to achieve the same result.

An expression that represents a proposition, or a compound proposition, is referred to as a *well-formed formula* (WFF). WFFs in propositional logic can be defined recursively:

1. A simple proposition (such as "Today is Saturday") is a formula.
2. If A is a formula, then not (A) is a formula.
3. If A and B are formulas, then the following expressions are also formulas:
   a. (A and B)
   b. (A or B)
   c. (if A then B)

4. All formulas that are admissible in propositional logic can be generated by applying the first three rules of this definition.

▪ C.4 TRUTH VALUES

It is important to establish the truth of a statement before it is used to support reasoning. Philosophers and mathematicians have long known that no argument should be made without first establishing the truth of the axioms (i.e., the statements initially assumed to be true prior to deduction). If the axioms are false, then a valid method of inference will produce false conclusions. Sometimes a whole theory can turn on a single axiom. For instance, the difference between Euclidean and Riemannian geometry stems from a difference in one axiom.

The correspondence between the ideas expressed in a sentence and the objects and events existing in the domain of discourse is a reflection of the meaning and the truth of the sentence. Using the notion of truth, formal logic can often be used not only to represent natural language statements about the world, but can also provide the capability for abstract reasoning to check the validity of discussions.

A discussion is a group of statements, one of which (the conclusion) is claimed to follow from one or more of the others (the premises). Discussions can be characterized as "True" if the conclusion really does follow from the premises, as claimed, or "False," otherwise. In two-valued logic, an argument must be true or false, but if inexact reasoning is allowed (as in multivalued logic), then we can talk about arguments being "probably true" or "probably false."

The first three logical connectives (and, or, not) are useful in expressing combined ideas, but a fourth connective based on the concept of implication is needed to form the basis of reasoning.

Imagine that you are told that attending a seminar will increase your self-confidence. Under what conditions would you say that this was a lie? If you attended the seminar and became more self-confident then there would be no problem. If you attended the seminar and you didn't become more self-confident, you would clearly have been lied to. But what would happen if you didn't attend the seminar in the first place? Either you become more self-confident or you don't, but in neither case can you claim to have been lied to since you didn't attend the seminar.

Consider the following propositional sentences:

a. (Paul attends the seminar) and (Paul becomes more self-confident).
b. (Paul attends the seminar) or (Paul becomes more self-confident).
c. not (Paul attends the seminar).

These statements appear to cover the set of possible events that might occur in relation to Paul's attendance at the seminar and his subsequent financial status. In addition, though, we need some way of expressing the idea that Paul should attend the seminar if he wants to get rich. This notion of implication (one thing leading to another) can be expressed as a combination of the basic propositions and the connectives "or" and "not" as in:

   d. (Paul becomes more self-confident) or not (Paul attends the seminar).

The compound proposition **d** shown above conforms in some way to our intuitive notions of causation and correlation. Example **d** says that "either Paul becomes more self-confident or Paul does not attend the seminar." Another way of saying the same thing is "if Paul attends the seminar then Paul becomes more self-confident," which is the original claim made by the promoter of the seminar.

In formal logic, the relationship shown in example **d** above is referred to as *implication* and can be expressed by using a special implication operator that itself can be written in two ways. We could express the information in example **d** as:

   e. (Paul attends the seminar) implies (Paul becomes more self-confident).

or as:

   f. If (Paul attends the seminar) then (Paul becomes more self-confident).

More generally,

   (If A then B) is true if (not(A) or B) is true.

The equivalence of the two propositions can be shown by constructing a truth table for each, as will be shown in Section C.5. With the addition of implication, logic can be used to represent problems and then reason about their solution. We might, for instance, have the following information:

1. Today is Saturday.
2. The current season is fall.
3. If (today is Saturday) and (the current season is fall) then (there will be a football game this afternoon).

In this example, the individual propositions have been represented in the form of English phrases. Their logical structure is shown more easily by using an alternative symbolic form with the following assignments:

P: "Today is Saturday"

Q: "The current season is fall"

R: "There will be a football game this afternoon"

The information shown previously can then be represented as:

1. P
2. Q
3. If P and Q Then R

Using logical inference, we can then deduce

4. R

In this example, R (there will be a football game this afternoon) logically follows when implication 3 is applied to the facts P and Q.

Complex ideas can be expressed by building combinations of propositions and connectives in the form of implications. Thus the statement:

If (today is Saturday) and (it is the fall season) then not (it is advisable to use the freeway in the late afternoon).

can be represented as:

If (P and Q) Then (Not U)

where P represents "Today is Saturday," Q represents "it is the fall season," and U represents "it is advisable to use the freeway in the late afternoon."

There is a fifth logical connective (if and only if, or iff) that is defined in propositional logic:

A Iff B

This is equivalent to the joint effect of:

If A then B

combined with:

If B then A.

■ C.5 TRUTH TABLES

From the perspective of logic the meaning of propositions is embodied in the effect that they have on the truth or falsity of related propositions and the effect that the truth or falsity of related propositions has on them. Thus we need a method of demonstrating the truth or falsity of one target proposition given the truth or falsity of related propositions. Fortunately, a well-known demonstration method of this type is available and it is based on the concept of truth tables developed by Boole.

Truth tables are the ultimate arbiters of valid deduction and correct interpretation within two-valued logic. The meaning of a proposition can be represented unambiguously in the form of a truth table. If A and B are both WFFs, then the truth values of combinations of A and B, obtained by applying the logical connectives, are given in a truth table such as Table C.1.

Truth tables lie at the heart of formal logic. In the truth table shown in Table C.1, for instance, the meaning of the statement:

     If A then B

can be expressed (paraphrasing the truth table) as:

     not A or B.

Truth tables can be constructed for any combination of logical connectives and propositions. The truth value of any WFF, no matter how complex, can be ultimately evaluated in terms of the truth values of the component simple propositions.

Truth tables can also be used to establish the equivalence of logical statements expressed in different surface structures. For instance, the equivalence between:

     If P Then Q

and

     not P or Q

TABLE C.1   A Truth Table Showing the Logical Meaning of Four Connectives

A	B	NOT A	A AND B	A OR B	IF A THEN B
T	T	F	T	T	T
T	F	F	F	T	F
F	T	T	F	T	T
F	F	T	F	F	T

**TABLE C.2 Truth Table Constructed to Assess
the Logical Equivalence of Two Expressions**

P	Q	not(P)	if P then Q	not(P) or Q
T	T	F	T	T
T	F	F	F	F
F	T	T	T	T
F	F	T	T	T

is demonstrated by the fact that both of these statements have identical columns of truth values beneath them, when written in truth table form, as shown in Table C.2.

■ C.6 VALIDITY AND TRUTH

Propositional logic can be used to check whether an asserted proposition is *valid,* i.e. provable, given a known set of facts.

A formula is *true* (i.e., a tautology) if it has the truth value "T" (True) under all possible combinations of truth and falsity for its component propositions. Thus

> If
>> (P and Q)
> Then
>> (P or Q);

is a tautology. You can check this by constructing the appropriate truth table. You should find that all the values in the rightmost column of this table are true.

At the other extreme, a formula is *inconsistent* if it is false under all its interpretations. Thus:

> P and not (P)

is inconsistent.

Many formulas are untrue, but not inconsistent, as is the case for the following example:

> If P then not(P)

Although it seems counter intuitive, the previous implication is false only when P is true. Thus as far as logic is concerned, the statement:

if the earth is flat
then the earth is not flat

must be true as long as the earth is not flat, since the premise of the implication (i.e., the earth is flat) is false and its conclusion (i.e., the earth is not flat) is true.

A *theorem* is a statement that is *provable*. The provability of a statement can be established by using a consistent method of inference. In propositional logic it can be proved that validity (provability) is equivalent to truth. Thus every true proposition is provable (valid), and every valid proposition is true. This property is called *completeness*. This equivalence between truth and validity does not always hold in other forms of logic.

In summary, then, there is an important distinction between truth and proof. Assessment of truth is based on the assignment of truth values to the component propositions. A statement is true only if it is true under all possible assignments of truth and falsity to its component propositions. Proof, on the other hand, requires that a valid argument be shown to connect the axioms with the theorem (i.e., the statement to be proved). Provided the axioms are true, any statement that can be proved must be true, but in some forms of logic, not all true statements are provable.

One problem that arises in the application of logic is determining whether a statement is true, but unprovable, or simply false. This has been the case with many mathematical conjectures. For instance, for centuries, it was empirically known that every two-dimensional map containing enclosed regions could be colored with only four colors so that no two adjacent (sharing the same border) regions had the same color. Although the conjecture appeared to be true and no one could find a counterexample, it took many years for it to be *proved* to the satisfaction of most mathematicians.

■ C.7 PROVING ASSERTIONS

In formal logic, the most important way to deduce new information is by the construction of *syllogisms*. A syllogism uses implication to draw a conclusion (deduce a new fact). An example of a syllogism is:

If (today is Saturday) Then (I will not work today)
today is Saturday

_____.

I will not work today

In general, a syllogism takes the form:

> If A Then B
> A
> _____.
> B

A syllogism is just like the firing of a rule (see Chapter 3). Given a known rule (e.g., If A then B) and a known fact (e.g., A) that matches the antecedent of the rule, the consequent (B) is deduced.

This process of logical deduction is much more efficient if assertions and facts are expressed in a common form, which makes it relatively easy to construct syllogisms. The process of proving whether a given proposition is true is often aided by applying simplifying transformations to the proposition. Well-known equivalences (Table C.3) allow a number of transformations to be made.

■ C.9 SUMMARY

Propositional and predicate logic both utilize the logical connectives along with the notions of truth, validity, and proof. However, predicate logic is much more powerful because it introduces predicates that can contain variables, and these variables may be either existentially or universally quantified. In propositional logic, the fundamental reasoning tool is the syllogism. In predicate logic we deal with the more complicated form of inference necessitated by the introduction of variables. Many of the ideas present in propositional logic such as truth values and truth tables are also found in predicate logic. Predicate logic is discussed in Chapter 3.

TABLE C.3.   Well-Known Equivalences in Propositional Logic

modus tolens
    if A then B = not(A) or B
symmetry
    A or B = B or A
    A and B = B and A
associativity
    d. (A or B) or C = A or (B or C)
    e. (A and B) and C = (A and B) or C
distributivity
    f. A or (B and C) = (A or B) and (A or C)
    g. A and (B or C) = (A and B) or (A and C)
reversability
    h. not(not(A)) = A
de Morgan's laws
    i. not(A or B) = not(A) and not(B)
    j. not(A and B) = not(A) or not(B)

RELATIONAL DATABASES

■ D.1 INTRODUCTION

Since its formulation (Codd, 1970), the relational model has had a major impact on the management of data. Unlike earlier data models, i.e., the hierarchical and the network models, the relational model can be defined in terms of simple yet rigorous mathematical concepts. Further, its underlying structure lends itself to easy querying, modification, updating, and database restructuring.

In this appendix, we review the relational model. We also show queries with query languages such as SQL may be performed on relational databases. In Section 5.10 we showed how relational databases can be integrated with both logic and frames using the unified approach to expert systems discussed in this book.

■ D.2 THE RELATIONAL DATA MODEL

A *relational database* consists of a set of *tables*. Each table consists of columns (also referred to as *attributes* or *fields*) and rows of data records. A row in a table represents a relationship among a set of attributes. For example, consider the following table:

Cust-address

Name	Cust#	Street	City
Hughes	1712	Sepulveda	Culver
Aamco	2487	Washington	Venice
Shell	3445	La Cienega	WHlwd

411

Name	Cust#	Street	City
MGM	1464	La Brea	Hollywd
Gucci	3577	Rodeo	BevHls
SAG	2667	Stone Cnyn	BevHls

Note that customer numbers are used to identify customers uniquely in this table. In each table there will generally be one attribute that is referred to as the *index* or *primary key*. For instance, Social Security numbers are used to distinguish people since names cannot be guaranteed to be unique.

We will refer to each row in a table as a *record*. In relational databases, each record usually describes a single object. The attributes that describe records (i.e., the columns in the table) are referred to as *fields*. The fields of the table shown above are "Name," "Cust#," "Street," and "City."

Each field has a *domain,* or set of possible values; for example, "Cust#" must be an integer between 0 and 999999999. Domains may be defined less strictly, as a variable of a certain predefined data *type,* for example, we could define "Cust#" as an integer, with no specification of upper and lower bounds.

The definition of a table's fields and domains is called the database *schema.* The particular table shown above, and many others of the same type, are called database *instances.* For most purposes, the schema of a database is all a database designer may be concerned with from a logical point of view. The concept of a relation scheme may seem similar to a frame template with slots, as discussed in Chapter 5.

■ D.3 OPERATING ON RELATIONS

The *relational algebra* is a method for operating on relations. The five fundamental operations in the relational algebra are:

Selection.
Projection.
Product.
Union.
Set difference.

In addition, the *join* is another operation that may be defined in terms of the cartesian product and selection operations.

The selection and projection operations are *unary* operations, since they operate on one relation. The other three relations operate on pairs of relations and are, therefore, called *binary* operations. Joins can be performed on two or more tables.

D.3.1 Selection

Selection involves taking a table and *selecting* the rows that satisfy a predicate. For example, you can select all customers in Beverly Hills from the Cust-address table. The selection operator takes a table and a predicate (in this case, City = BevHls) as input and returns another table as output:

Name	Cust#	Street	City
Gucci	3577	Rodeo	BevHls
SAG	2667	Stone Cnyn	BevHls

D.3.2 Projection

Projection *removes* certain columns from a table. For example, you might want to see just the Name, Customer number, and City fields from the Cust-address table. The projection operator takes a table and a set of field names as input and returns another table as output. The resulting table contains the same number of rows but fewer columns. Thus:

> Project Name, Cust#, City (Cust-address)

produces the following table where only the columns referred to in the projection are included:

Name	Cust#	City
Hughes	1712	Culver
Aamco	2487	Venice
Shell	3445	WHlwd
MGM	1464	Hollywd
Gucci	3577	BevHls
SAG	2667	BevHls

D.3.3 Product

The third basic operator is the product. The product *multiplies* two tables so that if one table has N rows and the other has M rows, the product table will contain (N * M) rows. Thus if we take the product of the following two tables:

Cust-address

Name	Cust#	City
Gucci	3577	BevHls
SAG	2667	BevHls

Cust-credit

Name	Credit
Gucci	Good
SAG	Average

We obtain the following table with $2 \times 2 = 4$ rows:

Name	Cust#	City	Name	Credit
Gucci	3577	BevHls	Gucci	Good
SAG	2667	BevHls	Gucci	Good
Gucci	3577	BevHls	SAG	Average
SAG	2667	BevHls	SAG	Average

Where the first three columns are from the first table and the last two columns, from the second table. This new table does not look right as it stands. Why should we have a record that refers both to Gucci's location and SAG's credit record, for instance?

We can clean up the table by selecting those rows where the names in columns 1 and 4 match to obtain the following table:

Name	Cust#	City	Name	Credit
Gucci	3577	BevHls	Gucci	Good
SAG	2667	BevHls	SAG	Average

We can then project out one of the Name fields to get

Name	Cust#	City	Credit
Gucci	3577	BevHls	Good
SAG	2667	BevHls	Average

D.3.4 Union and Difference

The *union* of two tables with N and M rows, respectively, is obtained by concatenating them into one table with a total of (N + M) rows. Union will generally make sense only if the schemes of the two tables match, i.e., if they have the same number of fields with matching attributes in each field.

The *difference* operator can be used to find records that are in one relation, but not in another. The difference between A and B is often denoted by A − B. As an example of set difference, we can find all the part-names in the product-composition table (Table D.1) that are parts of the fastener but not of the adapter by specifying the following query:

> Project Part-name ((Select Product = fastener (Product-composition)) − (Select Product = adapter (Product-composition)))

The result of this query is then:

Part-name

Lever
Sprocket
Cog

Additional operators can be defined to simplify the process of building queries, but the essential elements of the relational algebra consist of the operators defined above along with intersection, which can be expressed by using differences and unions. The *intersection* between two relations A and B can be expressed as

$$A - (A - B)$$

and contains all records in A that are also in B.

TABLE D.1

Product	Part-name	Part#	Qty
fastener	lever	2021	1
fastener	sprocket	2197	3
fastener	cog	2876	4
fastener	spring	2346	6
adapter	spring	2346	5
adapter	pulley	2477	5
adapter	rivet	2498	21
transformer	pulley	2477	3
transformer	lever	2021	1
transformer	cam	2655	3
transformer	rivet	2498	12
processor	cpul	9876	1
processor	8k-chip	9801	4
processor	led	9701	4

D.3.5 Joining Tables

The *join* operator allows us to join several tables together. Although the join is not one of the basic five relational operators, it can often be very useful.

Given two tables, A and B, the join operator allows one to apply a predicate to all rows that are formed by concatenating rows from A and rows from B. Those rows satisfying the predicate are returned. For example, if we have 3 rows in A and 7 rows in B, we can form 21 possible rows to apply the predicate to (this is simply the product of the two tables).

Only some of the rows have any meaning. For example, if both tables contain data about customers, we must include in our predicate a test that the "Cust#" fields in A and B are equivalent. Thus the join operator is equivalent to a product followed by a selection that ensures that all the rows in the new table are meaningful.

For example, a manufacturer may have a database containing the following data:

> Cust-address:
>> Cust#, Name, Street, City
>
> Suppliers:
>> Sup-name, Part#
>
> Product-composition:
>> Product, Part-name, Part#, Qty
>
> Orders:
>> Order#, Cust#, Product, Qty, Status

How can we derive a table that includes all customers who returned Products that contained parts manufactured by the Ace Supply Company? We will need to use selection, projection, and the join to find the desired table. Such a table, constructed out of one or more tables by the application of the operators, is called a *view*.

To get the view, we need to do a number of operations. We need to join the Supplier and Product-composition tables together to obtain a table that relates Products to Parts-suppliers (we need to use a predicate that ensures that Part# is equal). Then we will select only those products that contain parts made by Ace supply company. After projecting out the important fields and eliminating duplicate records, we need to join the resultant table to the order table (after selecting only the returned products) to find the returned orders that contain Ace parts. (Here we need to use a predicate to ensure that Product# is equal.) The following tables show how the joins, selections, and projections would affect the Suppliers and Product-composition tables.

Product-composition

Product	Part-name	Part#	Qty
fastener	lever	2021	1
fastener	sprocket	2197	3
fastener	cog	2876	4
fastener	spring	2346	6
adapter	spring	2346	5
adapter	pulley	2477	5
adapter	rivet	2498	21
transformer	pulley	2477	3
transformer	lever	2021	1
transformer	cam	2655	3
transformer	rivet	2498	12
processor	cpul	9876	1
processor	8k-chip	9801	4
processor	led	9701	4
•	•	•	•
•	•	•	•

Suppliers

Sup-name	Part#
Ace	2021
Ace	2346
Ace	2477
Jackson	2197
Campbell	2876
Trueman	2498
•	•
•	•

W = Join (Product-composition, Suppliers, Part#)

W

Product	Part-name	Part#	Qty	Sup-Name
fastener	lever	2021	1	Ace
fastener	sprocket	2197	3	Jackson
fastener	cog	2876	4	Campbell
fastener	spring	2346	6	Ace
adapter	spring	2346	5	Ace
adapter	pulley	2477	5	Ace
adapter	rivet	2498	21	Trueman
transformer	pulley	2477	3	Ace
transformer	lever	2021	13	Ace

Product	Part-name	Part#	Qty	Sup-Name
transformer	cam	2655	12	Trueman
transformer	rivet	2498	1	Trueman
processor	cpul	9876	4	Bitstream
processor	8k-chip	9801	4	Electra
processor	led	9701	•	Electra
•	•	•	•	•
•	•	•	•	•

X   X = Select (W, Sup-Name = Ace)

Product	Part-name	Part#	Qty	Sup-name
fastener	lever	2021	1	Ace
fastener	spring	2346	6	Ace
adapter	spring	2346	5	Ace
adapter	pulley	2477	5	Ace
transformer	pulley	2477	3	Ace
transformer	lever	2021	1	Ace

Y = Project (X, Product, Sup-Name)
Y

Product	Sup-Name
fastener	Ace
fastener	Ace
adapter	Ace
adapter	Ace
transformer	Ace
transformer	Ace

Z = Unique (Y)
Z

Product	Sup-Name
fastener	Ace
adapter	Ace
transformer	Ace

Orders

Order#	Cust#	Product	Qty	Status
091	901	process2	25	return
092	805	adapter	12	ok
093	807	adapter	24	ok
094	675	adapter	144	ok
•	•	•	•	•
•	•	•	•	•

A = Select (Orders,
Status = return)

A

Order#	Cust#	Product	Qty	Status
091	901	process2	25	return
107	923	process3	20	return
161	801	adapter	17	return
228	801	adapter	23	return
274	805	adapter	12	return
281	917	process3	12	return
297	801	adapter	28	return
306	675	adapter	10	return
311	916	process3	12	return

B = Join (A ,Z ,Product)

B

Order#	Cust#	Product	Qty	Status	Sup-Name
161	801	adapter	17	return	Ace
228	801	adapter	23	return	Ace
274	805	adapter	12	return	Ace
297	801	adapter	28	return	Ace
306	675	adapter	10	return	Ace

∎ D.4 QUERYING THE RELATIONAL MODEL

The relational algebra provides a concise language for representing queries. However, database system products require query languages that may be easily used and interfaced to programs. Two major approaches are based on the languages SQL (Chamberlin, Astrahan, Eswaran, Griffiths, Lorie, Mehl, Reisner, and Wade, 1976) and QUEL (Stonebraker, Wong, Kreps, and Held, 1976). In this section we review the language SQL (Structured Query Language), which is the most widely used relational query language.

SQL is, in fact, more than merely a database query language. It includes features for defining the structure of the data, modifying the data, and specifying security constraints within the database. We shall present a "generic" version of SQL whose specific features may vary between different implementations.

SQL expressions are made up of three clauses: *select, from,* and *where.* A query in SQL has the form

> *select* Attribute$_1$, Attribute$_2$, . . . , Attribute$_n$
> *from* Relation$_1$, Relation$_2$, . . . , Relation$_m$
> *where* Predicate

In this notation, the list of attributes may be replaced with a star (*) to select all attributes of all relations appearing in the *from* clause.

The *select* clause in SQL (confusingly) corresponds to the projection operation described above for the relational algebra. In SQL, a select is used to list the attributes desired in the table produced by a query. The *from* clause specifies a list of relations to be used in executing the query. Finally, the *where* clause corresponds to the selection predicate of the relational algebra. If the where clause is omitted, no selection is made. If the where clause is present it consists of a predicate involving attributes of the relations that appear in the from clause.

The result of an SQL query is a relation. SQL acts as follows:

a. It forms the product of the relations named in the *from* clause.
b. It performs a relational selection using the *where* clause predicate.
c. It *projects* the result onto the attributes of the select (in the SQL sense) clause.

SQL can thus be viewed as an outgrowth of the relational algebra. It includes the basic relational algebra operators that we discussed earlier. Selection is represented in SQLs where clause, while projection is performed in SQLs select clause. Product is represented by the from clause of SQL. SQL also handles set operations, including the union, intersection, and set difference, and the logical connectives *and, or,* and *not.*

Some features of SQL are not available in the relational algebra. For instance, aggregate operators such as avg (average) operate on aggregates of records, providing statistical and related information, while sorting procedures can be used to order records according to their attributes. The flexibility of SQL can be further enhanced by linking it with general-purpose languages such as Pascal and C. This allows the development of customized routines to manipulate the database and makes the SQL language extensible.

Consider the following table:

Cust-account

Name	Cust#	Street	City	Amount
Hughes	1712	Sepulveda	Culver	10000
Aamco	2487	Washington	Venice	1700
Shell	3445	La Cienega	WHlwd	3200
MGM	1464	La Brea	Hollywd	7000
Gucci	3577	Rodeo	BevHls	15000
SAG	2667	Stone Cnyn	BevHls	1000

The query "Find the names of all the customers in the Cust-account table" can be expressed in SQL as

> Select Name
> from Cust-account

The result of this query will be a list of all the customer names in the table, i.e., Hughes, Aamco, Shell, MGM, Gucci, and SAG. In this example, each customer name appeared only once in the table. However, if there had been more than one record for a customer name, that name would have appeared as many times as there were relevant records in response to the query. In such cases, the duplication can be avoided by using the keyword distinct after the select instruction:

> Select distinct Name
> from Cust-account

We identify the customers located in Beverly Hills using

> Select Name
> from Cust-account
> where City = "BevHls"

To find those customers in Beverly Hills owing more than $5000, we then pose the following query:

> Select Name
> from Cust-account
> where City = "BevHls" and
> amount > 5000

It is possible to combine SQL statements into fairly complex queries. SQL statements may also be embedded in programming languages for general-purpose computation. Further details on SQL may be found in Ullman (1982), Korth and Silberschatz (1986), and Date (1986).

■ **D.5 SUMMARY**

The relational data model provides a simple yet rigorous model of viewing data. The basic concept underlying the relational model is a table template with a set of fields, called a *schema*. Each schema may have a set of records, which define a table. By use of the relational algebra, tables may be joined, projected, selected from, etc.

The language SQL provides a formal yet intuitively easy way of dealing with queries. It may be used to select items from tables based on characteristics expressed as field values, e.g., Amount > 1000 and City = BevHls.

Relational databases, frames, and logic may, in fact, be uniformly integrated by using our logical and frame-based approach to knowledge representation, as shown in Section 5.10.

BIBLIOGRAPHY

Ackley, D. H., and Berliner, H. J. The QBGK System: Knowledge Representation for Producing and Explaining Judgements. Technical Report CMU-CS-83-116, Carnegie Mellon University, Department of Computer Science, Pittsburgh, PA, March 1983.

Ackley, D. H., Hinton, G. E., and Sejnowski, T. J. A Learning Algorithm for Boltzmann Machines. *Cognitive Science,* Vol. 9, 147–169, 1985.

Adams, J. B. A Probability Model of Medical Reasoning and the MYCIN Model. *Mathematical Biosciences,* Vol. 32, 1976.

Aikins, J. Prototypical Knowledge for Expert Systems. *Artificial Intelligence,* Vol. 20, No. 2, 1983.

Aikins, J. S., Kunz, J. C., Shortliffe, E., and Fallat, R. J. PUFF: An Expert System for Interpretation of Pulmonary Function Data. Stanford University Computer Science Dept, Report STAN-CS-82-931, 1982.

Allen, B. P., and Wright, J. M. Integrating Logic Programs and Schemata. *Proceedings of IJCAI-83,* Karlsruhe, West Germany, pp. 340–342, 1983.

Allen, J. *Anatomy of LISP.* New York: McGraw-Hill, 1978.

Alter, S. L. Decision Support Systems. Reading, MA: Addison-Wesley, 1980.

Anderson, J. R. A Theory of Language Acquisition Based on General Learning Principles. *Proceedings of the Seventh IJCAI,* Vancouver, BC, pp. 97–103, 1981.

Anderson, J. R. Acquisition of Cognitive Skill. *Psychological Review,* Vol. 89, pp. 369–406, 1982.

Anderson, J. R. *The Architecture of Cognition.* Cambridge, MA: Harvard University Press, 1983.

Anderson, J. R. *Cognitive Psychology and its Implications.* 2nd ed., San Francisco: Freeman, 1985.

Anderson, J. R. Knowledge Compilation: The General Learning Mechanism. In R. S.

Michalski, J. G. Carbonell, and T. M. Mitchell (Eds.), *Machine Learning: An Artificial Intelligence Approach,* Vol. II. Los Altos, CA, Morgan Kaufmann, 1986.

Anderson, J. R., and Bower, G. H. *Human Associative Memory.* Washington, DC: V. H. Winston and Sons, 1973.

Anzai, Y., and Simon, H. A. The Theory of Learning by Doing. *Psychological Review,* Vol. 86, No. 2, pp. 124–140, March 1979.

Apte, C. Expert Knowledge Management for Multi-Level Modeling. Report LCSR-TR-41, Computer Science Department, Rutgers University, 1982.

Araya, A. A. Learning by Controlled Transference of Knowledge Between Domains. *Proceedings of IJCAI-83,* Karlsruhe, West Germany, pp. 439–443, 1983.

Baddeley, A. D. *The Psychology of Memory.* New York: Basic Books, 1976.

Bainbridge, L. Asking Questions and Accessing Knowledge. *Future Computer Systems,* Vol. 1, 1986.

Baldwin, J. F. An Automated Fuzzy Knowledge Base. In R. Yager (Ed.), *Fuzzy Systems,* New York: Pergamon Press, 1981.

Baldwin, J. F. Fuzzy Expert Systems. *Proceedings of the International Symposium on Multi-Valued Logic,* Japan, 1983.

Baldwin, J. F., and Guild, N. C. F. FUZLOG: A Computer Program for Fuzzy Reasoning. *Proceedings of the Ninth International Symposium on Multiple-Valued Logic,* Bath, England, 1979.

Balzer, R., Erman, L. D., London, P., and Williams, C. HEARSAY-III: A Domain-Independent Framework for Expert Systems. *Proceedings of the First National Conference of the American Association for Artificial Intelligence,* Palo Alto, CA, 1980.

Bandler, W. Representation and Manipulation of Knowledge in Fuzzy Expert Systems. *Proceedings of a Workshop on Fuzzy Logic and Knowledge-Based Systems,* Queen Mary College, University of London, 1983.

Banerji, R. B. *Artificial Intelligence: A Theoretical Approach.* Amsterdam: North-Holland, 1980.

Barnes, R. M. *Motion and Time Study.* 7th ed., New York: Wiley, 1980.

Barnett, J. A. Computational Methods for a Mathematical Theory of Evidence. *Proceedings of IJCAI-81,* Vancouver, Canada, 1981.

Barr, A. Meta-Knowledge and Cognition. *Proceedings IJCAI-79,* Tokyo, pp. 31–33, 1979.

Barr, A., and Davidson, J. Representation of Knowledge. Stanford Memo HPP-80-3, Computer Science Department, Stanford University, 1980.

Barr, A., and Feigenbaum, E. A. *Handbook of Artificial Intelligence,* Vols. I, II. Los Altos, CA: William Kaufman, 1982.

Barstow, D. R. An Experiment in Knowledge-Based Automatic Programming. *Artificial Intelligence,* Vol. 12, 1979a.

Barstow, D. R. *Knowledge-Based Program Construction.* New York: Elsevier North-Holland, 1979b.

Barstow, D. R. The Roles of Knowledge and Deduction in Algorithm Design. *Machine Intelligence,* Vol. 10, 1982.

Bartlett, F. C. *Remembering: A Study in Experimental and Social Psychology.* London: Cambridge University Press, 1932.

Barwise, J., and Cooper, R. Generalized Quantifiers and Natural Language. *Linguistic Philosophy,* Vol. 4, pp. 159–219, 1981.

Behn, D. R. and Vaupel, J. W. *Quick Analysis for Busy Decision Makers.* New York: Basic Books, 1982.

Bell, A., and Quillian, M. R. Capturing Concepts in a Semantic Net. In E. L. Jacks (Ed.), *Associative Information Techniques.* New York: Elsevier, 1971.

Bellman, R., Kalaba, M., and Zadeh, L. A. Fuzzy Sets. *Information and Control,* 1964.

Belnap, N. D., and Steel, T. B. Jr. *The Logic of Questions and Answers.* New Haven, CT: Yale University Press, 1976.

Bennet, J. S. On the Structure of the Acquisition Process for Rule-Based Systems. *Infotech State of the Art Report,* Series 9, No. 3, 1981.

Bennet, J. S., and Engelmore, R. S. SACON: A Knowledge-Based Consultant for Structural Analysis. *Proceedings of IJCAI-79,* Tokyo, Japan, 1979.

Bennett, J.S., and Hollander, C. DART: An Expert System for Computer Fault Diagnosis. *Proceedings of IJCAI-81,* pp. 843–845, 1981.

Berkeley, D., and Humphreys, P. Structuring Decision Problems and the Bias Heuristic. *Acta Psychologica, 50,* pp. 201–252, 1982.

Besnard, P., Quiniou, R., and Quinton, P. A Theorem-Prover for a Decidable Subset of Default Logic. *Proceedings of AAAI-83,* Washington, DC, pp. 27–30, 1983.

Billings, C. E. and Reynard, W. D. Human Factors in Aircraft Accidents. *Aviation, Space, and Environmental Medicine,* Vol. 55, pp. 960–965, 1984.

Blum, R. L. Discovery and Representation of Causal Relationships from a Large Time-Oriented Clinical Database: The RX Project. In D.A.B. Lindberg and P. L. Reicherts (Eds.), *Medical Informatics,* Vol. 19, New York: Springer-Verlag, 1982.

Blum. R. L. Computer-Assisted Design of Studies Using Routine Clinical Data: Analyzing the Association of Prednisone and Serum Cholesterol. *Annals of Internal Medicine,* Vol. 104, No. 6, pp. 858–868, June 1986.

Bobrow, D. G. If Prolog Is the Answer, What Is the Question? *Proceedings of the International Conference on Fifth Generation Computer Systems,* pp. 138–145, 1984.

Bobrow, D. G., and Collins, A. *Representation and Understanding.* New York: Academic Press, 1975.

Bobrow, D. G., and Norman, D. A. Some Principles of Memory Schemata. In D. G. Bobrow, and A. M. Collins (Eds.), *Representation and Understanding: Studies in Cognitive Science.* New York: Academic Press, 1975.

Bobrow, D. G., and Raphael, B. New Programming Languages for Artificial Intelligence Research. *Computing Survey,* Vol. 6, No. 3, September 1974.

Bobrow, D. G., and Stefik, M. *The LOOPS Manual.* Palo Alto, CA: Xerox Corporation, 1983.

Bobrow, D. G., and Winograd, T. An Overview of KRL, a Knowledge Representation Language. *Cognitive Science,* Vol. 1, No. 1, 1977.

Bobrow, D. G., and Winograd, T. KRL, Another Perspective. *Cognitive Science,* Vol. 3, No. 1, 1979.

Bond, E. H. *Rule-Based Expert Systems.* Infotech State of the Art Report, Series 9, No. 3, 1981.

Bonissone, P., and Johnson, H. Expert System for Diesel Electric Locomotive Repair. *The FORTH Journal of Research and Application,* 1984.

Bonissone, P. P., and Tong, R. M. Editorial: Reasoning with Uncertainty in Expert Systems. *International Journal of Man-Machine Studies,* Vol. 22, No. 3, pp. 241–250, 1985.

Boose, J. H. Personal Construct Theory and the Transfer of Human Expertise. *Proceedings of AAAI-84,* pp. 27–33, 1984.

Boose, J. H. A Knowledge Acquisition Program for Expert Systems Based on Personal Construct Psychology. *International Journal of Man-Machine Studies,* Vol. 20, No. 1, pp. 21–43, 1985.

Boose, J. *Expertise Transfer for Expert System Design.* New York: Elsevier, 1986.

Borgida, A. On the Definition of Specialization Hierarchies for Procedures. *Proceedings of IJCAI-81,* Vancouver, BC, pp. 254–256, 1981.

Bousfield, W. A. The Occurrence of Clustering and the Recall of Randomly Arranged Associates. *Journal of General Psychology,* Vol. 49, pp. 229–240, 1953.

Bousfield, W. A., Cohen, B. H., and Whitmarsh, G. A. Associative Clustering in the Recall of Words of Different Taxonomic Frequencies of Occurrence. *Psychological Reports,* Vol. 4, pp. 39–44, 1958.

Bower, G. H., Black, J. B., and Turner, T. J. Scripts in Text Comprehension and Memory. *Cognitive Psychology,* Vol. 11, pp. 177–220, 1979.

Bower, G. H., Clark, M. C., Lesgold, A. M., and Winzenz, D. Hierarchical Retrieval Schemes in Recall of Categorized Word Lists. *Journal of Verbal Learning and Verbal Behavior,* Vol. 8, pp. 323–343, 1969.

Bower, G. H., and Hilgard, E. R. *Theories of Learning.* 5th ed., Englewood Cliffs, NJ: Prentice-Hall, 1981.

Brachman, R. J. A Structural Paradigm for Representing Knowledge. BBN Technical Report 3605, Bolt, Beranek and Newman, Inc., Cambridge, MA, 1976.

Brachman, R. J. What's in a Concept: Structural Foundations for Semantic Networks. *International Journal of Man-Machine Studies,* Vol. 9, pp. 127–152, 1977.

Brachman, R. J. On the Epistemological Status of Semantic Networks. In N. V. Findler (Ed.), *Associative Networks: Representation and Use of Knowledge by Computers.* New York: Academic Press, 1979.

Brachman, R. J. *An Introduction to KL-ONE.* BBN Technical Report, Bolt, Beranek and Newman, Inc., Cambridge, MA, 1980.

Brachman, R. J. What IS-A Is and Isn't: An Analysis of Taxonomic Links in Semantic Networks. *IEEE Computer,* Vol. 16, No. 10, pp. 30–36, 1983.

Brachman, R. J. I Lied About the Trees. *The AI Magazine,* Vol. 6, No. 3, 1985.

Brachman, R. J., Amarel, S., Engelman, C., Engelmore, R., Feigenbaum, E., and Wilkins, D. What Are Expert Systems? In F. Hayes-Roth, D. Lenat, and D. A. Waterman (Eds.) *Building Expert Systems,* Reading, MA: Addison-Wesley, 1983.

Brachman, R. J., Fikes, R. E., and Levesque, H. Krypton: A Functional Approach to Knowledge Representation. *Computer,* Vol. 16, No. 10, October 1983.

Brachman, R. J., Gilbert, V. P., and Levesque, H. J. An Essential Hybrid Reasoning System: Knowledge and Symbol Level Accounts of KRYPTON. *Proceedings of IJCAI-85,* Los Angeles, CA, 1985.

Brachman, R. J., and Levesque, H. Competence in Knowledge Representation. *Proceedings of the National Conference on Artificial Intelligence,* Pittsburgh, CA, August 1982.

Brachman, R. J., and Levesque, H. J. The Tractability of Subsumption in Frame-Based Description Languages. *Proceedings of AAAI-84,* Austin, TX, pp. 34–37, 1984.

Brachman, R. J., and Levesque, H. *Readings in Knowledge Representation.* Los Altos, CA: Morgan Kaufmann, 1986.

Brachman, R. J., and Schmolze, J. An Overview of the KL-ONE Knowledge Representation System. *Cognitive Science,* Vol. 9, No. 2, pp. 171–216, 1985.

Brachman, R. J., and Smith, B. C. Special Issue on Knowledge Representation. *SIGART Newsletter,* No. 70, February, 1980.

Brady, M. Expert Problem-Solvers. In D. Michie (Ed.), *Expert Systems in the Microelectronics Age.* Edinburgh: University of Edinburgh Press, 1979.

Braine, M. D. S., Reiser, B. J., Rumain, B. Some Empirical Justification for a Theory of Natural Propositional Logic. In G.H. Bower (Ed.), *The Psychology of Learning and Motivation,* Vol. 18. New York: Academic Press, pp. 313–371, 1984.

Bramer, M. A. A Survey and Critical Review of Expert Systems Research. In D. Michie (Ed.), *Introductory Readings in Expert Systems.* New York: Gordon and Breach Science Publishers, 1982.

Brodie, M. L., Mylopoulos, J., and Schmidt, J. W. *On Conceptual Modelling.* Berlin: Springer-Verlag, 1984.

Brooks, F. P., Jr. *The Mythical Man-Month: Essays on Software Engineering.* Reading, MA: Addison-Wesley, 1975.

Brown, J. S., and Burton, R. R. Multiple Representations of Knowledge for Tutorial Reasoning. In Daniel G. Bobrow and A. Collins (Eds), *Representation and Understanding: Studies in Cognitive Science,* New York: Academic Press, 1975.

Brownston, L., Farrell, R., Kant, E., and Martin, N. *Programming Expert Systems in OPS5.* Reading, MA: Addison-Wesley, 1985.

Bruner, J. S., Goodnow, J. J., and Austin, G. A. *A Study of Thinking.* New York: Wiley, 1956.

Buchanan, B. Meta Level Knowledge: Overview and Applications. *Proceedings of IJCAI-77,* Cambridge, MA, 1977.

Buchanan, B. Partial Bibliography of Work on Expert Systems. Report STAN-CS-82-953, Computer Science Department, Stanford University, 1982.

Buchanan, B., Davis, R., and Shortliffe, E. Production Rules as a Representation for a Knowledge-Based Consultation Program. *Artificial Intelligence,* Vol. 8, No. 1, 1977.

Buchanan, B. G., and Duda, R. O. Principles of rule-based expert systems. *Advances in Computers,* Vol. 22, pp. 163–216, 1983.

Buchanan, B., and Feigenbaum, E. A. DENDRAL and Meta-DENDRAL: Their Application Dimensions. *Artificial Intelligence,* Vol. 11, 1978.

Buchanan, B.,and Shortliffe, E. *Rule-Based Expert Systems: The MYCIN Experiments.* Reading, MA: Addison-Wesley, 1984.

Bundy, A. *Artificial Intelligence: An Introductory Course.* New York: North-Holland, 1978.

Bundy, A., Byrd, L., and Mellish, C. S. Special-Purpose, but Domain-Independent, Inference Mechanisms. In L. Steels and J. A. Campbell (Eds.), *Progress in Artificial Intelligence,* London: Ellis Horwood Ltd., pp. 93–111, 1985.

Bylander, T., Mittal, S., and Chandrasekaran, B. CSRL: A Language for Expert Systems for Diagnosis. *Proceedings of IJCAI-83,* Karlsruhe, West Germany, pp. 218–221, 1983.

Carbonell, J. G. AI in CAI: An Artificial Intelligence Approach to Computer-Aided Instruction. *IEEE Transactions on Man-Machine Systems,* Vol. 11, No. 4, pp. 190–202, 1970.

Carbonell, J. G. Learning by Analogy: Formulating and Generalizing Plans from Past Experience. In R. S. Michalski, J. G. Carbonell, and T. M. Mitchell (Eds.), *Machine Learning: An Artificial Intelligence Approach.* Palo Alto, CA: Tioga, 1983.

Carroll, J. M. and McKendree, J. Interface Design Issues for Advice-giving Expert Systems. *Communications of the ACM,* Vol. 30, pp. 14–31, 1987.

Carbonell, J. G., Michalski, R. S., and Mitchell, T. M. Machine Learning: A Historical and Methodological Analysis. *AI Magazine,* Vol. 4, No. 3, 1983.

Cercone, N. J., and Goebel, R. G. Knowledge Representation and Data Bases. *Proceedings of the Fourth National Conference of the Canadian Society for Computational Studies of Intelligence,* University of Saskatchewan, Saskatoon, Saskatchewan, May 17–19, 1982.

Cercone, N. J., and Goebel, R. G. Data Bases and Knowledge Representation for Literary and Linguistic Studies. *Computers in the Humanities,* 1983.

Chamberlin, D. D., Astrahan, M. M., Eswaran, K. P., Griffiths, P. P., Lorie, R. A., Mehl, J. W., Reisner, P., and Wade, B. W. SEQUEL 2: A Unified Approach to Data Definition, Manipulation, and Control. *IBM Journal of Research and Development,* Vol. 20, No. 6, pp. 560–575, 1976.

Chandrasekaran, B. An Approach to Medical Diagnosis Based on Conceptual Structures. *Proceedings of IJCAI-79,* Tokyo, Japan, 1979.

Chandrasekaran, B. Expert Systems: Matching Techniques to Tools. In W. Reitman (Ed.), *Artificial Intelligence Applications for Business,* Norwood, NJ: Ablex Publishing Company, 1984.

Chandrasekaran, B., and Mittal, S. Deep Versus Compiled Knowledge Approaches to Diagnostic Problem-Solving. *Proceedings of the Second National Artificial Intelligence Conference,* Pittsburgh, PA, pp. 349–354, 1982.

Chandrasekaran, B., and Mittal, S. Conceptual Representation of Medical Knowledge for Diagnosis by Computer: MDX and Related Systems. *Advances in Computers,* Vol. 22, pp. 217–293, 1983.

Chang, C. C., and Keisler, H. J. *Model Theory.* Amsterdam: North-Holland, 1973.

Chang, C.-L., and Lee, R. C.-T. *Symbolic Logic and Mechanical Theorem Proving.* New York: Academic Press, 1971.

Charniak, E. A Framed PAINTING: The Representation of a Common Sense Knowledge Fragment. *Cognitive Science,* Vol. 1, No. 4, pp. 355–394, 1977.

Charniak, E. On the Use of Framed Knowledge in Language Comprehension. *Artificial Intelligence,* Vol. 11, No. 3, pp. 225–265, 1978.

Charniak, E. A. Common Representation for Problem-Solving and Language-Comprehension Information. *Artificial Intelligence,* Vol. 16, No. 3, pp. 225–255, 1981.

Charniak, E. The Bayesian Basis of Common Sense Medical Diagnosis. *Proceedings of AAAI-83,* Washington DC, pp. 70–73, 1983.

Charniak, E., and McDermott, D. V. *Introduction to Artificial Intelligence.* Reading, MA: Addison-Wesley, 1985.

Charniak, E., Riesbeck, C. K., and McDermott, D. V. *Artificial Intelligence Programming.* Hillsdale, NJ: Erlbaum, 1979.

Chen, S. On intelligent CAD systems for VLSI Design. *Proceedings IEEE International Conference on Computer Design: VLSI in Computers,* pp. 405–407, 1983.

Cheng, P. W., and Holyoak, K. J. Pragmatic Reasoning Schemas. *Cognitive Psychology,* Vol. 17, pp. 391–416, 1985.

Cheng, P. W. Restructuring Versus Automaticity: Alternative Accounts of Skill Acquisition. *Psychological Review,* Vol. 92, pp. 414–423, 1985.

Chester, D. L., Lamb, D. E., and Dhurjati, P. An Expert System Approach to On-Line Alarm Analysis in Power and Process Plants. *Proceedings Computers in Engineering, ASME,* pp. 345–351, 1984.

Chi, M. T. H., Feltovich, P. J., and Glaser, R. Categorization and Representation of Physics Problems by Experts and Novices. *Cognitive Science,* Vol. 5, No. 2, pp. 121–51, April–June, 1981.

Chi, M. T. H., Glaser. R., and Rees, E. Expertise in Problem Solving. In R. J. Sternberg (Ed.), *Advances in the Psychology of Human Intelligence,* Vol. I. Hillsdale, NJ: Erlbaum, 1982.

Chignell, M. H., and Higgins, T. J. Intelligent Warning Systems for Instrument Landings. *International Journal of Industrial Ergonomics,* 1987.

Chignell, M. H., and Patty, B. W. Unidimensional Scaling with Efficient Ranking Methods. *Psychological Bulletin,* Vol. 101, pp. 304–311, 1987.

Chin, D. N. Knowledge Structures in UC, The UNIX Consultant. *Proceedings of the 21st Annual Meeting of the Association for Computational Linguistics,* Boston, MA, 1983a.

Chin, D. N. A Case Study of Knowledge Representation in UC. *Proceedings of IJCAI-83,* August 8–12, Karlsruhe, Germany, 1983b.

Chisholm, I. H., and Sleeman, D. H. An Aide for Theory Formation. In D. Michie (Ed.), *Expert Systems in the Microelectronic Age.* Edinburgh: University of Edinburgh, Scotland, 1979.

Clancey, W. J. Tutoring Rules for Guiding a Case Method Dialogue. *International Journal of Man-Machine Studies,* Vol. 11, 1979.

Clancey, W. J. The Epistemology of a Rule-Based Expert System—A Framework for Explanation. *Artificial Intelligence,* Vol. 20, pp. 215–251,1983.

Clancey, W. J. The Use of MYCIN's Rules for Tutoring. In B. Buchanan and E. Shortliffe (Eds.), *Rule Based Expert Systems,* Reading, MA: Addison-Wesley, 1984.

Clancey, W. J., and Shortliffe, E. *Readings in Medical Artificial Intelligence, The First Decade.* Reading, MA: Addison-Wesley, 1984.

Clark, K. L. Negation as Failure. In H. Gallaire and J. Minker (Eds.), *Logic and Data Bases.* New York: Plenum Press, pp. 293–322, 1978.

Clark, K. L., and Tarnlund, S. A. Logic Programming. *APIC Studies in Data Processing,* Vol. 16, London: Academic Press, 1982.

Clocksin, W., and Mellish, C. *Programming in PROLOG,* 3rd ed. New York: Springer-Verlag, 1987.

Codd, E. F. A Relational Model for Large Shared Data Banks. *Communications of the ACM,* Vol 13, No. 6, pp. 377–387, 1970.

Codd, E. F. Extending the Database Relational Model to Capture More Meaning. *ACM Transactions on Database Systems,* Vol. 4, pp. 397–434, 1979.

Cognitive Science, Vol. 9, No. 1, Issue Devoted to "Connectionism," 1985.

Cohen, B., and Murphy, G. L. Models of Concepts. *Cognitive Science,* Vol. 8, No. 1, pp. 27–58, January–March, 1984.

Cohen, P. R., and Feigenbaum, E. A. *Handbook of Artificial Intelligence,* Vol. III. Los Altos, CA: Morgan Kaufmann, 1982.

Cohn, L. J. Bayesianism and Baconianism in the Evaluation of Medical Diagnoses. *British Journal of Philosophical Science,* Vol. 31, pp. 45–62, 1980.

Collins A. *Changing Order: Replication and Induction in Scientific Practice.* London: Sage Publications, 1985.

Collins, A. M., and Loftus, E. F. A Spreading-Activation Theory of Semantic Processing. *Psychological Review,* Vol. 82, No. 6, pp. 407–428, 1975.

Collins, A., Warnock, E., Aiello, N., and Miller, M. Reasoning From Incomplete Knowledge. In D. Bobrow and A. Collins (Eds.), *Representation and Understanding.* New York: Academic Press, 1975.

Cottrell, G. Re: Inheritance Hierarchies with Exceptions. *Proceedings of the Non-Monotonic Reasoning Workshop,* New Paltz, NY, pp. 33–56, 1984.

Cuadrado, J. L. and Cuadrado, C. Y. AI in Computer Vision. *Byte,* Vol. 11, No. 1, pp. 237–258, 1986.

Dahl, V. Logic Programming as a Representation of Knowledge. *IEEE Computer,* Vol. 16, No. 10, pp. 106–113, 1983.

Date, C. J. *An Introduction to Database Systems,* Vol. I. 4th ed., Reading, MA: Addison-Wesley, 1986.

Davis, R. Applications of Meta-Level Knowledge to the Construction, Maintenance and Use of Large Knowledge Bases. Report STAN-AIM-283, Artificial Intelligence Lab, Stanford University, 1976.

Davis, R. Knowledge Acquisition in Rule-Based Systems. In D.A. Waterman and F. Hayes-Roth (Eds.), *Pattern-Directed Inference Systems.* New York: Academic Press, 1978.

Davis, R. Interactive Transfer of Expertise: Acquisition of New Inference Rules. *Artificial Intelligence,* Vol. 12, pp. 121–157, 1979.

Davis, R. Meta-rules: Reasoning about Control. *Artificial Intelligence,* Vol. 15, pp. 179–222, 1980a.

Davis, R. Content Reference: Reasoning about Rules. *Artificial Intelligence,* Vol. 15, no. 2, 1980b.

Davis, R. Expert Systems: Where Are We? and Where Do We Go From Here? *AI Magazine,* Vol. 3, No. 2, 1982.

Davis, R. TEIRESIAS: Experiments in Communicating with a Natural Language Knowledge-Based System. In M. J. Simes and M. J. Coombs (Eds.), *Designing for Human-Computer Communication,* New York: Academic Press, 1983.

Davis, R., Buchanan, B., and Shortliffe, E. Production Rules as a Representation for a Knowledge-Based Consultation System. *Artificial Intelligence,* Vol. 8, No. 1, 1977.

Davis, R. and King, J. An Overview of Production Systems. In W. Elcock and D. Mitchie (Eds.), *Machine Intelligence,* Vol. 8, New York: Wiley, 1977.

Davis, R. and Lenat, D. B. *Knowledge-Based Systems in Artificial Intelligence.* New York: McGraw-Hill, 1982.

Davis, R., and Shrobe, H. Representing Structure and Behavior of Digital Hardware. *IEEE Computer,* Vol. 16, No. 10, pp. 75–82, 1983.

de Groot, A. D. *Thought and Choice in Chess.* The Hague: Mouton, 1965.

de Groot, A. D. Perception and Memory Versus Thought. In B. Kleinmuntz (Ed.), *Problem Solving.* New York: Wiley, 1966.

de Kleer, J. An Assumption-Based TMS. *Artificial Intelligence,* Vol. 28, 1986a.

de Kleer, J. Problem Solving with the ATMS. *Artificial Intelligence,* Vol. 28, 1986b.

de Kleer, J., Doyle, J., Steele, G. L., and Sussman, G. J. AMORD, Explicit Control of Reasoning. *Sigart Newsletter,* No. 64, 1977.

de Kleer, J. and Sussman, G. J. Propagation of Constraints Applied to Circuit Synthesis. Technical Memo 485, Artificial Intelligence Laboratory, MIT, 1978.

Deliyanni, A. and Kowalski, R. A. Logic and Semantic Networks. *Communications of the ACM,* Vol. 22, No. 3, pp. 184–192, 1979.

Dietterich, T. G., London, B., Clarkson, K., and Dromsey, G. Learning and Inductive Inference. Report STAN-CS-82-913, Computer Science Department, Stanford University, 1982.

Dietterich, T. and Michalski, R. S. Inductive Learning of Structural Descriptions. *Artificial Intelligence,* Vol. 1, No. 3, 1981.

Dietterich, T. G. and Michalski, R. S. A Comparative Review of Selected Methods for Learning from Examples. In R. S. Michalski, J. G. Carbonell, and T. M. Mitchell (Eds.), *Machine Learning: An Artificial Intelligence Approach.* Palo Alto, CA: Tioga, 1983.

Douglass, R. and Hegner, S. An Expert Consultant for the UNIX System. *Proceedings of the Fourth National Conference of the Canadian Society for the Computational Studies of Intelligence,* University of Saskatchewan, Saskatoon, Saskatchewan, 1982.

Doyle, J. A Truth Maintenance System. *Artificial Intelligence,* Vol. 12, No. 3, pp. 231–72, November 1979.

Doyle, J. A Glimpse of Truth-Maintenance. In P. H. Winston and R. H. Brown (Eds.),

Artificial Intelligence: An MIT Perspective. Cambridge, MA: The MIT Press, pp. 119–135, 1982.

Doyle, J. A Society of Mind: Multiple Perspectives, Reasoned Assumptions, and Virtual Copies. *Proceedings of IJCAI-83,* Karlsruhe, West Germany, pp. 309–314, 1983a.

Doyle, J. Admissible State Semantics for Representational Systems. *IEEE Computer,* Vol. 16, No. 10, pp. 119–123, 1983b.

Doyle, J. Methodological Simplicity in Expert System Construction: The Case of Judgements and Reasoned Assumptions. *AI Magazine,* Vol. 4, No. 2, 1983c.

Drastal, G. A. and Kulikowski, C. A. Knowledge-Based Acquisition of Rules for Medical Diagnosis. Report CBM-TM-97, Computer Science Department, Rutgers University, 1982.

Dubois, D. and Prade, H. Criteria Aggregation and Ranking of Alternatives in the Framework of Fuzzy Set Theory. *TIMS/Studies Management Science,* Vol. 20, pp. 209–240, 1984.

Duda, R. O. and Gaschnig, J. G. Knowledge-Based Expert Systems Come of Age. *Byte,* Vol. 6, No. 9, pp. 238–281, September 1981.

Duda, R. O., Gaschnig, J., and Hart, P. E. Model Design in the Prospector System for Mineral Exploration. In D. Michie, (Ed.), *Expert Systems in the Microelectronic Age.* University of Edinburgh, Scotland, 1979.

Duda, R. O., Hart, P. E., Konolige, K. G., and Reboh, R. *A Computer-Based Consultant for Mineral Exploration.* Menlo Park, CA: Stanford Research Institute, 1979.

Duda, R. O., Hart, P., and Nilsson, N. Subjective Bayesian Methods for Rule-Based Inference Systems. *Proceedings of the 1976 National Computer Conference,* Vol. 45, 1976.

Duda, R. O., Hart, P. E., Nilsson, N. J., Barre, P., Gachnig, J. G., and Reboh, R. *Development of the Prospector Consultation System for Mineral Exploration.* Menlo Park, CA: Stanford Research Institute, 1978.

Duda, R. O., Hart, P. E., Nilsson, N. J., and Reboh, R. *Development of a Computer-Based Consultant for Mineral Exploration.* Menlo Park, CA: Stanford Research Institute, 1977.

Duda, R. O., Hart, N. P. E., Nilsson, J., and Sutherland, G. L. Semantic Network Representations in Rule-Based Inference Systems. In D. A. Waterman and F. Hayes-Roth (Eds.), *Pattern-Directed Inference Systems.* New York: Academic Press, 1978.

Duda, R. O., Nilsson, N. J., and Raphael, B. State of Technology in Artificial Intelligence. In Peter Wegner (Ed.), *Research Directions in Software Technology,* Cambridge, MA: MIT Press, 1979.

Duda, R. O., and Shortliffe, E. H. Expert Systems. *Science,* Vol. 220, pp. 261–268, 1983.

Dyer, M. G. *In-depth understanding.* Cambridge, MA: The MIT Press, 1983.

Edmonds, E. A. Adaptive Man-Computer Interfaces. In M. J. Coombs and J. L. Alty (Eds.), *Computing Skills and the User Interface.* London: Academic Press, pp. 389–426, 1981.

Einhorn, H. J. and Hogarth, R. M. Behavioral Decision Theory: Processes of Judgment and Choice. *Annual Review of Psychology,* Vol.32, pp. 53–88, 1981.

Elcock, E. W. How Complete Are Knowledge-Representation Systems? *IEEE Computer,* Vol. 16, No. 10, pp. 114–118, 1983.

Ericcson, A. K and Simon, H. A. Verbal Reports as Data. *Psychological Review,* Vol. 87, pp. 215–252, 1980.

Ericcson, A. K. and Simon, H. A. *Protocol Analysis: Verbal Reports as Data.* Cambridge, MA: MIT Press, 1984.

Erman, L., Hayes-Roth, F., Lesser, V., and Reddy, D. The Hearsay-II Speech Understanding System. *ACM Computing Surveys,* Vol. 12, No. 3, 1980.

Erman, L. D. and Lesser, V. R. System Engineering Techniques for Artificial Intelligence Systems. In A. Hanson and E. Riseman (Eds.), *Computer Vision Systems,* New York: Academic Press, 1978.

Erman, L. D., London, P. E., and Fickas, S. F. The Design and An Example Use of HEARSAY-III. *Proceedings of IJCAI-81,* Vancouver, BC, pp. 409–415, 1981.

Ernst, G. W. and Newell, A. *GPS: A Case Study in Generality and Problem-Solving.* New York: Academic Press, 1969.

Etherington, D., Mercer, R. E., and Reiter, R. On the Adequacy of Predicate Circumscription for Closed-World Reasoning. *Proceedings of the Non-Monotonic Reasoning Workshop.* New Paltz, NY, pp. 70–81, 1984.

Etherington, D. M., and Reiter, R. On Inheritance Hierarchies With Exceptions. *Proceedings of AAAI-83,* Washington, DC, pp. 104–108, 1983.

Fagan, L. M. VM: Representing Time-Dependent Relations in a Clinical Setting. Ph.D. Dissertation, Computer Science Department, Stanford University, 1980.

Fagan, L. M., Kunz, J. C., Feigenbaum, E. A., and Osborn, J. J. Representation of Dynamic Clinical Knowledge: Measurement Interpretation in the Intensive Care Unit. *Proceedings of IJCAI-79,* Tokyo, pp. 260–262, 1979.

Fahlman, S. NETL: *A System for Representing and Using Real-World Knowledge.* Cambridge, MA: MIT Press, 1979.

Fahlman, S. E., Touretzky, D. S., and van Roggen, W. Cancellation in a Parallel Semantic Network. *Proceedings of IJCAI-81,* Vancouver, BC, pp. 257–263, 1981.

Fain, J., Hayes-Roth, F., Sowizral, H., and Waterman, D. Programming in ROSIE: An Introduction by Means of Examples. RAND Report N-1646-ARPA, The RAND Corporation, Santa Monica, February 1982.

Feigenbaum, E. The Art of Artificial Intelligence. *Proceedings of the Fifth International Joint Conference on Artificial Intelligence,* MIT, Cambridge, MA, August, 1977.

Feigenbaum, E. Knowledge Engineering: The Applied Side of Artificial Intelligence. Memo HPP-80-21, Artificial Intelligence Lab, Stanford University, 1980.

Feigenbaum, E. Expert Systems in the 1980s. *Infotech State of the Art Report,* Series 9, No. 3, 1982.

Feigenbaum, E., and Cohen, P. *The Handbook of Artificial Intelligence,* Vol. III, Los Altos, CA: William Kaufman, 1984.

Feigenbaum, E., and McCorduck, P. *The Fifth Generation.* Reading, MA: Addison-Wesley, 1983.

Feldman, J. A. and Ballard, D. H. Connectionist Models and Their Properties. *Cognitive Science,* Vol. 6, pp. 205–254, 1982.

Fikes, R., and Hendrix, G. A Network-Based Knowledge Representation and its Natural Deduction System. *Proceedings of IJCAI-77,* Cambridge, MA, pp. 235–246, 1977.

Fikes, R. E. and Nilsson, N. J. STRIPS: A New Approach to the Application of Theorem Proving to Problem Solving. *Artificial Intelligence,* Vol. 2, pp. 189–208, 1971.

Findler, N. V. *Associative Networks—Representations and Use of Knowledge by Computers.* New York: Academic Press, 1979.

Findler, N. V. An Expert Subsystem Based on Generalized Production Rules. Report TR-82-003, Computer Science Department, Arizona State University, 1982.

Finin, T. and Silverman, D. Interactive Classification: A Technique for Building and Maintaining Knowledge Bases. *Proceedings of the IEEE Workshop on Principles of Knowledge-Based Systems,* Denver, CO, pp. 107–114, 1984.

Forgy, C. L. *The OPS5 User Manual.* Technical Report, CMU-CS-79-132, Computer Science Department, Carnegie-Mellon University, 1981.

Forgy, C. L. and McDermott, J. OPS, a domain-independent production system language. *Proceedings of the Fifth IJCAI,* Cambridge, MA, pp. 933–939, 1977.

Forsyth, R. *Expert Systems: Principles and Case Studies.* London: Chapman & Hall, 1984.

Fox, M. S. On Inheritance in Knowledge Representation. *Proceedings of IJCAI-79,* Tokyo, pp. 282–284, 1979.

Freeling, A. N. S. Fuzzy Sets and Decision Analysis. *IEEE Transactions on Systems, Man and Cybernetics,* Vol. SMC–10, No. 7, 1978.

Friedland, P. E. Acquisition of Procedural Knowledge from Domain Experts. *Proceedings of the Seventh IJCAI,* Vancouver, BC, pp. 856–861, 1981.

Friedman, L. Extended Plausible Inference. *Proceedings of the Seventh International Joint Conference on Artificial Intelligence,* Vancouver, BC, 1981.

Funt, B. V. Analogical Modes of Reasoning and Process Modelling. *IEEE Computer.* Vol. 16, No. 10, pp. 99–105, 1983.

Gaines, B. R. and Shaw, M. L. G. New Directions in the Analysis and Interactive Elicitation of Personal Construct Systems. *International Journal of Man-Machine Studies,* Vol. 13, pp. 81–116, 1980.

Gallaire, H. Artificial Intelligence and Industry. *Proceedings of the European Conference on Artificial Intelligence,* 1982.

Gallaire, H., and Minker J. *Logic and Databases.* New York: Plenum Press, 1978.

Gardner, H. *The Mind's New Science.* New York: Basic Books, 1986.

Garvey, T. D., Lowrance, J. D., and Fischler, M. A. An Inference Technique for Integrating Knowledge from Separate Sources. *Proceedings of IJCAI-81,* Vancouver, BC, 1981.

Gaschnig, J. Prospector: An Expert System for Mineral Exploration. *Infotech State of the Art Report,* Series 9, No. 3, 1982.

Gaschnig, J. G., Reiter, J., and Reboh, R. *Development of a Knowledge-Based Expert System for Water Resource Problems.* Menlo Park, CA: Stanford Research Institute, 1981a.

Gaschnig, J. G., Reiter, J., and Reboh, R. *Development and Application of a*

Knowledge-Based Expert System for Uranium Resource Evaluation. Menlo Park, CA: Stanford Research Institute, 1981b.

Genesereth, M. R. The Role of Plans in Automated Consultation. *Proceedings of IJCAI-79,* Tokyo, 1979.

Genesereth, M. R. and Nilsson, N. J. *Logical Foundations of Intelligence.* Los Altos, CA: Morgan Kaufmann, 1987.

Genter, D., and Stevens, A. L. *Mental Models.* Hillsdale, NJ: Erlbaum, 1983.

Georgeff, M. P. A Framework for Control in Production Systems. *Proceedings of IJCAI-79,* Tokyo, 1979.

Georgeff, M. P. Procedural Control in Production Systems. *Artificial Intelligence,* Vol. 18, No. 2, pp. 175–21, 1982.

Gevarter, W. B. *An Overview of Expert Systems.* Report NBSIR 82-2505, NASA, 1982.

Gevarter, W. B. *An Overview of Computer Based Natural Language Processing.* Report NBS-83-2687, NASA, 1983a.

Gervarter, W. B. *Expert Systems: Limited but Powerful.* IEEE Spectrum, Vol. 20, No. 8, 1983b.

Giles, R. Semantics for Fuzzy Reasoning. *International Journal of Man-Machine Studies,* Vol. 17, No. 4, pp. 401–415, 1982.

Ginsberg, M. L. Non-Monotonic Reasoning Using Dempster's Rule. *Proceedings of AAAI-84,* Austin, TX, pp. 126–129, 1984.

Glass, A. L. and Holyoak, K. J. *Cognition.* 2nd ed., New York: Random House, 1986.

Goguen, J. A. The logic of inexact concepts. *Synthese,* Vol. 19, pp. 325–373, 1969.

Goguen, J. A. and Parsaye, K. Algebraic Denotational Semantics Using Parameterized Abstract Modules. *Lecture Notes in Computer Science,* Vol. 107, 1981.

Goldberg, A. *Smalltalk–80: The Interactive Programming Environment.* Reading, MA: Addison-Wesley, 1983.

Goldberg, A., and Robson, D. *Smalltalk-80: The Language and its Implementation.* Reading, MA: Addison-Wesley, 1983.

Goldstein, I. P. and Grimson, E. Annotated Production Systems: A Model of Skill Acquisition. *Proceedings of IJCAI-77,* Cambridge, MA, pp. 311–316, 1977.

Goldstein, I. P. and Papert, S. Artificial Intelligence, Language and the Study of Knowledge. *Cognitive Science,* Vol. 1, No. 1, 1977.

Goldstein, I. P. and Roberts, B. Using Frames in Scheduling. In *Artificial Intelligence: An MIT Perspective.* In P. H. Winston and R. H. Brown (Eds.), Cambridge, MA: The MIT Press, pp. 255–284, 1979.

Gordon, J. and Shortliffe, E. A Method for Managing Evidential Reasoning in a Hierarchical Hypothesis Space. *Proceedings of AAAI-84,* Austin, TX, 1984.

Goyal, S. K., Prerau, D. S., Lemmon, A. V., Gunderson, A. S., and Geinke, R. E. COMPASS: An Expert System for Telephone Cable Maintenance. *Proceedings of the IEEE Expert Systems in Government Conference,* Washington, D.C. October 1985.

Greiner, R. and Lenat, D. A Representation Language Language *Proceedings of the First Annual National Conference on Artificial Intelligence,* Palo Alto, CA, 1980.

Grosof, B. Default Reasoning as Circumscription. *Proceedings of the Non-Monotonic Reasoning Workshop,* New Paltz, NY, pp. 115-124, 1984.

Guilford, J. P. *Psychometric Methods.* New York: McGraw-Hill, 1954.

Haas, N. and Hendrix, G. G. An Approach to Acquiring and Employing Knowledge. *Proceedings of the First National Conference of the American Association for Artificial Intelligence,* Palo Alto, CA, 1980.

Haas, N. and Hendrix, G. G. Learning by Being Told: Acquiring Knowledge for Information Management. In R. Michalski, J. Carbonell, and T. Mitchell (Eds.), *Machine Learning.* Palo Alto, CA: Tioga Publishing, 1983.

Hahn, W. The Contributions of Artificial Intelligence to the Human Factors of Application Software. In G. Goos and J. Hartmans (Eds.), *Enduser Systems and their Human Factors.* New York: Springer Verlag, 1983.

Hajek, P. Combining Functions for Certainty Degrees in Consulting Systems. Technical Report, Mathematical Institute, Prague, 1984.

Hamill, B. W. Psychological Issues in the Design of Expert Systems. *Proceedings of the Human Factors Society,* Seattle, WA, pp. 73-77, 1984.

Hendrix, G. G., Sacerdoti, E., Sagalowicz, D., and Slocum, J. Developing a Natural Language Interface to Complex Data. *ACM Transactions on Database Systems.* Vol. 3, pp. 105-147, 1978.

Harmon, P. and King, D. *Expert Systems.* New York: Wiley, 1985.

Hart, P. E. Directions for AI in the Eighties. *SIGART Newsletter,* Vol. 79, January 1982.

Hartigan, J. *Clustering Algorithms.* New York: Wiley, 1975.

Hawkins, D. An Analysis of Expert Thinking. *Journal of Cybernetics,* 1983.

Hayes, J. E., Michie, D. *Intelligent Systems—The Unprecedented Opportunity.* New York: Wiley, 1983.

Hayes, P. J. The Frame Problem and Related Problems in Artificial Intelligence. In A. Elithorn and D. Jones (Eds.), *Artificial and Human Thinking,* New York: Jossey-Bass, 1973.

Hayes, P. J. In Defense of Logic. *Proceedings of IJCAI-77,* MIT, Cambridge, MA, 1977a.

Hayes, P. J. On Semantic Nets, Frames and Associations. *Proceedings of IJCAI-77,* Cambridge, MA, pp. 99-107, 1977b.

Hayes, P. J. The Logic of Frames. In D. Metzing (Ed.), *Frame Conceptions and Text Understanding,* Berlin: de Gruyter, 1979a.

Hayes, P. J. The Naive Physics Manifesto. In D. Michie (Ed.), *Expert Systems in the Micro-Electronic Age.* Edinburgh: Edinburgh University Press, pp. 242-270, 1979b.

Hayes-Roth, B. BB1: An Architecture for Black Board Systems that Control, Explain, and Learn About Their Own Behavior. Technical Report HPP-84-16, Stanford University, Standford, CA, 1984.

Hayes-Roth, B. A Blackboard Architecture for Control. *Artificial Intelligence.* Vol. 26, pp. 251-321, 1985.

Hayes-Roth, F. The Role of Partial and Best Matches in Knowledge Systems. In D. A. Waterman and F. Hayes-Roth (Eds), *Pattern-Directed Inference Systems.* New York: Academic Press, 1978.

Hayes-Roth, F. AI, The New Wave—A Technical Report for R&D Management. Technical Report AIAA-81-0827, RAND Corporation, Santa Monica, 1981.

Hayes-Roth, F., Gorlin, D., Rosenschein, S., Sowizral, H., and Waterman, D. Rationale and Motivation for ROSIE. RAND Report N-1648-ARPA, The RAND Corporation, Santa Monica, November 1981a.

Hayes-Roth, F., Gorlin, D., Rosenschein, S., Sowizral, H., and Waterman, D. The ROSIE Reference Manual. RAND Report N-1647-ARPA, The RAND Corporation, Santa Monica, December 1981b.

Hayes-Roth, F., Klahr, P., Burge, J., and Mostow, D. J. Machine Methods for Acquiring, Learning and Applying Knowledge. Technical Report R-6241, RAND Corporation, Santa Monica, 1978.

Hayes-Roth, F., Klahr, P., and Mostow, D. J. Knowledge Acquisition, Knowledge Programming and Knowledge Refinement. Technical Report R-2540-NSF, RAND Corporation, Santa Monica, 1980.

Hayes-Roth, F., Waterman, D. A., and Lenat, D. B. *Principles of Pattern-Directed Inference Systems.* New York: Academic Press, 1978.

Hayes-Roth, F., Waterman, D., and Lenat, D. *Building Expert Systems.* Reading, MA: Addison-Wesley, 1983.

Hendrix, G. G. Encoding Knowledge in Partitioned Networks. In N. V. Findler (Ed.), *Associative Networks,* New York: Academic Press, 1979.

Hewitt, C. PLANNER, A Language for Proving Theorems in Robots. *Proceedings of IJCAI-71,* London, 1971.

Hewitt, C. Viewing Control Structures as Patterns of Passing Messages. *Artificial Intelligence,* Vol. 8, pp. 323–364, 1977.

Higgins, T. T., and Chignell, M. H. Cognitive Processes During Instrument Landing. *Proceedings of the Human Factors Society,* New York, 1987.

Hinton, G. E. and Anderson, J. A. *Parallel Models of Associative Memory.* Hillsdale, NJ: Erlbaum, 1981.

Hogarth, R. M. Beyond discrete biases: Functional and dysfunctional aspects of judgmental heuristics. *Psychological Bulletin,* Vol. 90, pp. 197–217, 1981.

Hogger, C. J. Derivation of Logic Programs. *Journal of the ACM,* Vol. 28, pp. 372–392, 1981.

Hogger, C. J. Introduction to Logic Programming. *APIC Studies in Data Processing,* Vol. 21, London: Academic Press, 1984.

Hollan, J. D., Hutchins, E. L., and Weitzman, L. STEAMER: An Interactive Inspectable Simulation-Based Training System. *AI Magazine,* Vol. 5, No. 2, pp. 15–27, 1984.

Holland, J. H., Holyoak, K. J., Nisbett, R. E., and Thagard, P. R. *Induction: Processes of Inference, Learning, and Discovery.* Cambridge, MA: MIT Press, 1986.

Hopfield, J. J. Neural Networks and Physical Systems with Emergent Collective Computational Abilities. *Proceedings of the National Academy of Sciences,* USA, pp. 2554–2558, 1982.

Howe, J. A. M. Learning Through Model-Building. In D. Michie (Ed.), *Expert Systems in the Microelectronic Age.* Edinburgh: University of Edinburgh Press, 1979.

Huff, K. and Lesser, V. Knowledge-Based Command Understanding: An Example for the Software Development Environment. Report COINS-82-06, Department of Computer Science, University of Massachusetts at Amherst, June 1982.

Hurst, R. and Hurst, L. *Pilot Error.* New York: Jason Aronson, 1982.

Ishizuka, M. Inference Methods Based on Extended Dempster and Shafer Theory for Problems with Uncertainty/Fuzziness. *New Generation Computing,* Vol. 2, New York: Springer Verlag, 1983.

Ishizuka, M. and Yao, T. P. Inexact Inference for Rule-Based Damage Assessment of Existing Structures. *Proceedings of IJCAI-81,* Vancouver, BC, 1981.

Israel, D. J. The Role of Logic in Knowledge Representation. *IEEE Computer,* Vol. 16, No. 10, pp. 37–42, 1983.

Israel, D. J. and Brachman, R. J. Some Remarks on the Semantics of Representation Languages. In M. L. Brodie, J. Mylopoulos, and J. W. Schmidt (Eds.), *On Conceptual Modelling: Perspectives from Artificial Intelligence, Databases, and Programming Languages.* New York: Spring-Verlag, pp. 119–142, 1984.

Jain, R. Fuzzyism and real world problems. In P. P. Wang and S.K. Chang (Eds.), *Fuzzy Sets.* New York: Plenum Press, 1985.

Jeffrey, R. *Formal Logic: Its Scope and Limits.* 2nd ed., New York: McGraw Hill, 1981.

Johnson, P. E. What Kind of Expert Should a System Be? *The Journal of Medicine and Philosophy,* Vol. 8, pp. 77–97, 1983.

Johnson-Laird, P. N. *Mental Models.* Cambridge, MA: Harvard University Press, 1983.

Johnson-Laird, P. N. and Wason, P. C. *Thinking.* Cambridge, Cambridge University Press, 1978.

Kagel, A. S. The Unshuffle Algorithm. *Computer Language,* Vol. 3, No. 11, pp. 61–66, 1986.

Kahn, G., and McDermott, J. The MUD System. *Proceedings of the First IEEE Conference on Artificial Intelligence Applications,* Denver CO, 1984.

Kahn, G., Nowlan, S., and McDermott, J. MORE: An Intelligent Knowledge Acquisition Tool. *Proceedings of IJCAI-85,* Los Angeles, CA, pp. 581–584, 1985.

Kahneman, D., Slovic, P., and Tversky, A. *Judgment Under Uncertainty: Heuristics and Biases.* New York: Cambridge University Press, 1982.

Kahneman, D. and Tversky, A. Subjective Probability: A Judgement of Representativeness. *Cognitive Psychology,* Vol. 3, pp. 430–454, 1972.

Kahnemen, D. and Tversky, A. On the Psychology of Prediction. *Psychological Review,* Vol. 80, pp. 237–251, 1973.

Kaufman, A. *Introduction to the Theory of Fuzzy Sets.* New York: Academic Press, 1975.

Keller, M. R. A Survey of Research in Strategy Acquisition. Report DCS-TR-115, Computer Science Department, Rutgers University, 1982.

Kellog, C. Intelligent Assistants for Knowledge and Information Resources Management. *Proceedings of IJCAI-83,* Karlsruhe, Germany, 1983.

Kelly, G. A. *The Psychology of Personal Constructs.* New York: Norton, 1955.

Kidd, A. Human Factors Problems in the Design and Use of Expert Systems. In A.

Monk (Ed.), *Fundamentals of Human-Computer Interaction.* London, Academic Press, pp. 237–247, 1985.

Kieras, D. E. and Bovair, S. The Acquisition of Procedures from Text: A Production-System Analysis of Transfer of Training. *Journal of Memory and Languages,* Vol. 25, pp. 507–524, 1986.

Kieras, D. E. and Polson, P. G. An Approach to the Formal Analysis of User Complexity. *International Journal of Man-Machine Studies,* Vol. 22, pp. 365–394, 1985.

Kin, R. and McLeod, D. Semantic Database Models. Report TR-101, Computer Science Department, University of Southern California, September 1981.

King, J. J. Modelling Concepts for Reasoning About Access to Knowledge. *Proceedings of the NBS-ACM Workshop on Data Abstraction, Databases and Conceptual Modelling,* Pingree Park, CO, June 23–26, 1980.

Kintsch, W. *The Representation of Meaning in Memory.* Hillsdale, NJ: Erlbaum, 1974.

Kolodner, J. L. Maintaining Organization in a Dynamic Long Term Memory. *Cognitive Science,* Vol. 7. No. 4, pp. 243–80, 1983.

Kolodner, J. L. *Retrieval and Organizational Strategies in Conceptual Memory: A Computer Model.* Hillsdale, NJ: Erlbaum, 1984.

Konolige, K. *A Deduction Model of Belief.* Ph.D. Thesis, Department of Computer Science, Stanford University, 1984.

Korf, R. E. Toward a Model of Representation Changes. *Artificial Intelligence,* Vol. 14, No. 1, pp. 41–78, 1980.

Korf, R. E. Micro-Operators: A Weak Method of Learning. *Artificial Intelligence,* Vol. 26, No. 1, pp. 35–78, 1985.

Korth, H. F., and Silberschatz, A. *Database System Concepts.* New York: McGraw-Hill, 1986.

Kowalski, A. *Logic for Problem Solving.* New York: Elsevier North Holland, 1979.

Kowalski, A. Logic as a Database Language. Technical Report, Department of Computing, Imperial College, London, 1981.

Krueger, M. W. *Artificial Reality.* Reading, MA: Addison-Wesley, 1983.

Kruskal, J. B. and Wish, M. *Multidimensional Scaling.* London: Sage Publications, 1978.

Kuipers, B. and Kassirer, J. P. How to Discover a Knowledge Representation for Causal Reasoning by Studying an Expert Physician. *Proceedings of IJCAI-83,* Karlsruhe, FRG, pp. 49–56, 1983.

Kulikowski, C. A. Artificial Intelligence Methods and Systems for Medical Consultation. *IEEE Journal on Pattern Analysis and Machine Intelligence,* Vol. 2, No. 5, 1980.

Kulikowski, C. A. Treatment Selection and Explanation in Expert Medical Consultation: Application to a Model of Ocular Herpes Simplex. Report CBM-TR-132, Computer Science Department, Rutgers University, 1982.

Kulikowski, C. A. Knowledge Acquisition and Learning in EXPERT. In R. Michalski, J. Carbonell, and T. Mitchell (Eds.), *Proceedings of Machine Learning Workshop,* University of Illinois at Urbana-Champaign, 1983.

Kulikowski, S. A. and Weiss, S. M. *A Practical Guide to Designing Expert Systems.* New Jersey: Rowman and Allanheld, 1984.

Lachman, R., Lachman, J. L., and Butterfield, E. C. *Cognitive Psychology and Information Processing: An Introduction.* Hillsdale, NJ: Erlbaum, 1979.

Lafue, G. M. E. Basic Decisions About Linking an Expert System with a DBMS. *IEEE Database Engineering,* Vol. 6, No. 4, December 1983.

Lafue, G. M. E. and Mitchell, T. M. *Data Base Management Systems and Expert Systems for CAD.* Report LCSR-TR-028, Computer Science Department, Rutgers University, 1982.

Lafue, G. M. E. and Mitchell, T. *Database Management Systems and Expert Systems for CAD/CAM System Frameworks.* In K. Bo (Ed.), North-Holland, 1983.

Laird, J. Universal Subgoaling. In J. Laird, P. Rosenbloom, and A. Newell, *Universal Subgoaling and Chunking: The Automatic Generation and Learning of Hierarchies.* Boston, MA: Kluwer Academic, 1986.

Langley, P. Representational Issues in Learning Systems. *Computer,* Vol. 16, No. 10, October 1983.

Lenat, D. B. BEINGS: Knowledge as Interacting Experts. *Proceedings of IJCAI-75,* Tbilisi, U.S.S.R., 1975.

Lenat, D. The Nature of Heuristics. Artificial Intelligence, Vol. 19, pp. 189–249, 1982.

Lenat, D., Borning, A., McDonald, D., Taylor, C., and Weyer, S. *Knoesphere: Building Expert Systems with Encyclopedic Knowledge,* Technical Report, Department of Computer Science, Stanford University, 1983.

Lenat, D. B. and Brown, J. S. Why AM and Eurisko Appear to Work. *Artificial Intelligence,* Vol. 23, pp. 269–94, August 1984.

Lehnert, W. and Wilks, Y. A Critical Perspective on KRL. *Cognitive Science,* Vol. 3, pp. 1–28, 1979.

Lesser, V. R. and Erman, L. D. A Retrospective View of the HEARSAY-II Architecture. *Proceedings of IJCAI-77,* Cambridge, MA, 1977.

Levesque, H. J. Incompleteness in Knowledge Bases. In M. Brodie and S. Zilles (Eds.), *Proceedings of the ACM Workshop on Data Abstraction, Databases and Conceptual Modelling.* Pingree Park, CO, 1980.

Levesque, H. J. *A Formal Treatment of Incomplete Knowledge Bases.* Fairchild Technical Report No. 614, Palo Alto, CA: Fairchild Labs, 1982.

Levesque, H. J. The Logic of Incomplete Knowledge Bases. In M. L. Brodie, J. Mylopoulos, and J. W. Schmidt (Eds.), *Conceptual Modelling: Perspectives from Artificial Intelligence, Databases, and Programming Languages,* New York, Springer-Verlag, pp. 165–186, 1983.

Levesque, H. J. Foundations of a Functional Approach to Knowledge Representation. *Artificial Intelligence,* Vol. 23, pp. 155–202, 1984a.

Levesque, H. J. A Logic of Implicit and Explicit Belief. *Proceedings of AAAI-84,* Austin, TX, pp. 198–202, 1984b.

Levesque, H. J, and Mylopoulos, J. A Procedural Semantics for Semantic Networks. In N. V. Findler (Ed.), *Associative Networks: Representation and Use of Knowledge by Computer.* New York: Academic Press, pp. 93–122, 1979.

Lindley, D. V. Scoring Rules and the Inevitability of Probability. *International Statistical Review,* Vol. 50, pp. 1–26, 1982.

Lindsay, P. H. and Norman, D. A. *Human Information Processing: An Introduction to Psychology.* New York: Academic Press, 1977.

Lindsay, R. K., Buchanan, B., Feigenbaum, E. A. and Lederberg, J. *Applications of Artificial Intelligence to Chemistry: The DENDRAL Project.* New York: McGraw-Hill, 1980.

Lloyd, J. W. *Foundations of Logic Programming.* Berlin: Springer-Verlag, 1984.

Lloyd, J. W. and Topor, R. W. Making Prolog More Expressive. *Journal of Logic Programming,* Vol. 1, pp. 225–240, 1984.

Loftus, E. F. *Eyewitness Testimony.* Cambridge, MA: Harvard University Press, 1979.

Loveland, D. *Automated Theorem Proving.* Amsterdam: North Holland, 1978.

Mackworth, A. K. Consistency in Networks of Relations. *Artificial Intelligence,* Vol. 8, 1977.

Maida, A. S. and Shapiro, S. C. Intensional Concepts in Propositional Semantic Networks. *Cognitive Science,* Vol. 6, pp. 291–330, 1982.

Mamdani, E. H. and Gaines, B. R. *Fuzzy Reasoning and its Applications.* New York: Academic Press, 1981.

Marcus, S., McDermott, J. and Wang, T. Knowledge Acquisition for Constructive Systems. *Proceedings of IJCAI-85,* Los Angeles, CA, pp. 637–639, 1985.

Mark, W. Rule-Based Inference in Large Knowledge Bases. *Proceedings of the First Annual National Conference on Artificial Intelligence,* Palo Alto, CA, 1980.

Mark, W. Representation and Inference in the Consul System. *Proceedings of IJCAI-81,* Vancouver, BC, August 1981.

Marriott, F. H. C. *The Interpretation of Multiple Observations.* New York: Academic Press, 1974.

Martin, W. A. Descriptions and the Specialization of Concepts. In P. H. Winston and R. H. Brown (Eds.), *Artificial Intelligence: An MIT Perspective,* Vol. 1, Cambridge, MA: The MIT Press, pp. 377–419, 1979.

Martins, J. P. and Shapiro S. C. Reasoning in Multiple Belief Spaces. *Proceedings of IJCAI-83,* Karlsruhe, West Germany, pp. 370–373, 1983.

McAllester, D. A. *The Use of Equality in Deduction and Knowledge Representation.* Technical Memo 520, Artificial Intelligence Laboratory, MIT, 1980.

McCarthy, J. Epistemological Problems of Artificial Intelligence. *Proceedings of IJCAI-77,* Cambridge, MA, 1977.

McCarthy, J. Circumscription—A Form of Non-Monotonic Reasoning. *Artificial Intelligence,* Vol. 13, No. 1, 1980.

McClelland, J. L. and Rumelhart, D. E. An Interactive Activation Model of Context Effects in Letter Perception: Part I, An Account of Basic Findings. *Psychological Review,* Vol. 88, pp. 275–407, 1981.

McCorduck, P. *Machines Who Think, A Personal Inquiry into the History and Prospects of Artificial Intelligence.* San Francisco, CA: W. H. Freeman, 1979.

McCulloch, W. and Pitts, W. A Logical Calculus of the Ideas Immanent in Nervous System Activity. *Bulletin of Mathematical Biophysics,* Vol. 5, pp. 115–133, 1943.

McDermott, D. A Temporal Logic for Reasoning about Processes and Plans. *Cognitive Science,* Vol. 6, pp. 101–155, 1982.

McDermott, D. Generalizing Problem Reduction: A Logical Analysis. *Proceedings of IJCAI-83,* Karlsruhe, West Germany, pp. 302–308, 1983.

McDermott, D. and Davis, E. Planning Routes Through Uncertain Territory. *Artificial Intelligence,* Vol. 22, pp. 107–157, 1984.

McDermott, D. and Doyle, J. Nonmonotonic Logic I. *Artificial Intelligence,* Vol. 13, No. 1, November, 1980.

McDermott, J. R1: A Rule-Based Configurer of Computer Systems. *Artificial Intelligence,* Vol. 1, No. 1, 1979.

McDermott, J. R1's Formative Years. *AI Magazine,* Vol. 2, No. 2, 1982.

McDermott, J. The Knowledge Engineering Process. *IEEE Database Engineering,* Vol. 6, No. 4, December 1983a.

McDermott, J. Building Expert Systems. *Proceedings of the New York University Symposium on Artificial Intelligence Applications for Business,* New York University, 1983b.

McDermott, J. and Forgy, C. Production System Conflict Resolution Strategies. In D. A. Waterman and F. Hayes-Roth (Eds.), *Pattern-Directed Inference Systems.* New York: Academic Press, 1978.

McDermott, J., Newell, A., and Moore, J. The Efficiency of Certain Production System Implementations. In D. A. Waterman and F. Hayes-Roth (Eds.), *Pattern-Directed Inference Systems.* New York: Academic Press, 1978.

McDermott, J., and Steele, B. Extending Knowledge-Based Systems to Deal with Ad Hoc Constraints. *Proceedings of IJCAI-79,* Tokyo, 1979.

McSkimmin, J. R. and Minker, J. A Predicate Calculus Based Semantic Network for Deductive Searching. In N. V. Findler (Ed.), *Associative Networks: Representation and Use of Knowledge by Computers.* New York: Academic Press, pp. 205–238, 1979.

Medin, D. L. and Smith, E. E. Concepts and Concept Formation. *Annual Review of Psychology,* Vol. 35, pp. 113–138, 1984.

Mervis, C. B. and Rosch, E. Categorization of Natural Objects. *Annual Review of Psychology,* Vol. 32, pp. 89–115, 1981.

Michalski, R. S. A Theory and Methodology of Inductive Learning. *Artificial Intelligence,* Vol. 20, No. 3, 1983.

Michalski, R. S., Carbonell, J. and Mitchell, T. *Machine Learning: An Artificial Intelligence Approach.* Tioga Publishing Company, 1983.

Michalski, R. S. and Chilausky, R. L. Knowledge Acquisition by Encoding Expert Rules Versus Computer Induction from Examples: A Case Study Involving Soybean Pathology. *International Journal of Man-Machine Studies,* Vol. 12, pp. 63–87, 1980.

Michalski, R. S. and Stepp, R. Learning from Observation: Conceptual Clustering. In R. S. Michalski, J.G. Carbonell, and T.M. Mitchell (Eds.), *Machine Learning: Artificial Intelligence Approach.* Palo Alto, CA: Tioga, 1983.

Michie, D. *Expert Systems in the Microelectronic Age.* Edinburgh: University of Edinburgh Press, 1979.

Michie, D. Expert Systems. *Computer Journal,* Vol. 23, No. 4, 1980.

Michie, D. *Knowledge-Based Systems.* Infotech State of the Art Report, Series 9, No. 1, 1981.

Michie, D. High-Road and Low-Road Programs. *AI Magazine,* Vol. 3, No. 1, pp. 21–22, 1982a.

Michie, D. The State of the Art in Machine Learning. In D. Michie (Ed.), *Introductory Readings in Expert Systems,* New York: Gordon and Breach, 1982b.

Michie, D. *Introductory Readings in Expert Systems.* New York: Gordon and Breach, 1982c.

Michie, D. Inductive Rule Generation in the Context of the Fifth Generation. In R. Michalski, J. Carbonell and T. Mitchell (Eds.), *Proceedings of Machine Learning Workshop,* University of Illinois at Urbana-Champaign, 1983.

Miller, G. A. The Magical Number Seven, Plus or Minus Two: Some Limits on our Capacity for Processing. *Psychological Review,* Vol. 63, pp. 81–97, 1956.

Minoura, T. and Parsaye, K. Version Based Concurrency Control of a Database System. *Proceedings of the 1984 ACM/IEEE Conference on Data Engineering,* Los Angeles, May 1984.

Minsky, M. *Semantic Information Processing.* Cambridge, MA: The MIT Press, 1968.

Minsky, M. A Framework for Representing Knowledge. In P. Winston (Ed.), *The Psychology of Computer Vision.* New York: McGraw-Hill, 1975.

Minsky, M. Frame-System Theory. In P. N. Johnson-Laird and P. C. Watson (Eds.), *Thinking: Readings in Cognitive Science,* Cambridge: Cambridge University Press, 1977.

Minsky, M. K-Lines: A Theory of Memory. *Cognitive Science,* Vol. 4, No. 2, 1980.

Minsky, M., and Papert, S. *Perceptrons.* Cambridge, MA: The MIT Press, 1969.

Moates, D. R. and Schumacher, G. M. *An Introduction to Cognitive Psychology.* San Francisco, CA: Wadsworth, 1980.

Moore, R. C. Reasoning About Knowledge and Action. *Proceedings of IJCAI-77,* Cambridge, MA, 1977.

Moore, R. C. The Role of Logic in Knowledge Representation and Common Sense Reasoning. *Proceedings of the Second National Conference on Artificial Intelligence,* Pittsburgh, PA, August 1982.

Mylopoulos, J. An Overview of Knowledge Representation. In M. Brodie and S. Zilles (Eds.), *Proceedings of the ACM Workshop on Data Abstraction, Databases and Conceptual Modelling,* Pingree Park, CO, 1980.

Naga, M. and Tsujii, J. S-NET: A Foundation for Knowledge. *Proceedings of IJCAI-79,* Tokyo, 1979.

Nau, D. S. Expert Computer Systems. *Computer,* Vol. 16, pp. 63–85, February 1983.

Nau, D. S., Reggia, J. A., and Wang, P. Knowledge-Based Problem Solving Without Production Rules. *Proceedings of the IEEE 1983 Trends and Applications Conference,* May 1983.

Negoita, C. V. *Expert Systems and Fuzzy Systems.* Benjamin and Cummings, 1985.

Nelson, K. Some Evidence for the Cognitive Primacy of Categorization and Its Functional Basis. *Merrill-Palmer Quarterly of Behavior and Development,* Vol. 19, pp. 21–39, 1973.

Nelson, K. Concept, Word and Sentence: Interrelations in Acquisition and Development. *Psychological Review,* Vol. 81, pp. 267–285, 1974.

Newell, A. Remarks on the Relationship Between Artificial Intelligence and Cognitive Psychology. In R. Banerji and M.D. Mesarovie (Eds.), *Theoretical Approaches to Nonnumerical Problem Solving.* New York: Springer-Verlag, pp. 363–400, 1970.

Newell, A. Production Systems: Models of Control Structures. In W. Chase (Ed.), *Visual Information Processing,* New York: Academic Press, 1973.

Newell, A. On the Analysis of Human Problem Solving Protocols. In P. N. Johnson-Laird and P. C. Wason (Eds.), *Thinking: Readings in Cognitive Science.* Cambridge, MA: Cambridge University Press, 1977.

Newell, A. The Knowledge Level. *Artificial Intelligence,* Vol. 18, pp. 87–127, 1982.

Newell, A. and Simon, H. *Human Problem Solving.* Englewood Cliffs, NJ: Prentice-Hall, 1972.

Newell, A., Simon, H. A., and Shaw, J. C. Empirical Explorations with the Logic Theory Machine: A Case Study in Heuristics. In E. A. Feigenbaum and J. Feldman (Eds.), *Computers and Thought.* New York: McGraw-Hill, 1963.

Nguyen, T. A., Perkins, W. A., Laffey, T. J., and Pecora D. Knowledge Base Verification. *AI Magazine,* Vol. 8, No. 2, Summer 1987.

Nii, H. P. An Introduction to Knowledge Engineering, Blackboard, and AGE. Report HPP-80-29, Stanford, CA, 1980.

Nii, P. and Aiello, M. AGE (Attempt to Generalize): A Knowledge-Based Program for Building Knowledge-Based Programs. *Proceedings of IJCAI-79,* Tokyo, 1979.

Nilsson, N. J. *Problem-Solving Methods in Artificial Intelligence,* New York: McGraw-Hill, 1971.

Nilsson, N. J. *Principles of Artificial Intelligence.* Palo Alto, CA: Tioga, 1980.

Nilsson, M. A Logical Model of Knowledge. *Proceedings of IJCAI-83,* Karlsruhe, West Germany, pp. 374–376, 1983a.

Nilsson, N. J. Artificial Intelligence Prepares for 2001 *The AI Magazine,* Winter 1983, pp. 7–14, 1983b.

Nisbett, R. E. and Wilson, T. D. Telling More Than We Can Know: Verbal Reports on Mental Processes. *Psychological Review,* Vol. 84, pp. 231–259, 1977.

Norman, A.C. and Fitch, J. P. Implementing LISP in a High-Level Language. *Software Practice and Experience,* Vol. 7, No. 6, 1977.

Norman, D. A. *Perspectives on Cognitive Science.* Hillsdale, NJ: Erlbaum, 1981.

Norman, D. A., and Rumelhart, D. E. *Explorations in Cognition.* San Francisco, CA: Freeman, 1975.

O'Shea, T. Rule-Based Computer Tutors. In D. Michie (Ed.), *Expert Systems in the Microelectronic Age.* Edinburgh: University of Edinburgh Press, 1979.

O'Shea, T., and Eisenstadt, M. *Artificial Intelligence: Tools, Techniques, and Applications.* New York: Harper & Row, 1984.

Osherson, D. N. and Smith, E. E. On the Adequacy of Prototype Theory as a Theory of Concepts. *Cognition,* Vol. 9, pp. 35–38, 1981.

Osherson, D. N. and Smith, E. E. Gradeness and Conceptual Combination. *Cognition,* Vol. 12, pp. 299–318, 1982.

Palmer, S. E. Fundamental Aspects of Cognitive Representation. In E. H. Rosch and B. B. Lloyd (Eds.), *Cognition and Categorization.* Potomac, MD: Erlbaum Press, 1977.

Papert, S. *Mindstorms.* New York: Basic Books, 1980.

Parker, D. S. and Parsaye, K. Embedded Multivalued Dependencies and Transitive Dependencies, *Proceedings of the 1980 ACM SIGMOD Conference,* Los Angeles, CA, 1980.

Parsaye, K. Higher Order Abstract Data Types, *Ph.D. Dissertation, Computer Science Department, UCLA,* December 1981.

Parsaye, K. Database Management, Knowledge Base Management and Expert System Development in Prolog. *Proceedings of the ACM SIGMOD Database Week Conference,* San Jose, CA, 1983a.

Parsaye, K. Prolog, A Programming Language with a Built-in Relational Database, *ComputerWorld,* October, 1983b.

Parsaye, K. Logic Programming and Relational Databases, *IEEE Transactions on Database Engineering,* December, 1983c.

Parsaye, K. The Next 700 Expert System Languages. *Proceedings of the IEEE COMPCON Conference,* San Francisco, 1985a.

Parsaye, K. A Perspective on Expert Systems. *Communications of Unix /usr/group,* 1985b.

Parsaye, K. An Evolutionary Path to Expert Systems. *Proceedings of the IEEE Expert Systems in Government Conference.* Washington D.C., 1985c.

Parsaye, K. Knowledge Compilation: Expert Systems on Personal Computers, *Proceedings of the 21st Annual Meeting of the Association for the Advancement of Medical Instrumentation,* Chicago, April 1986.

Parsaye, K., and Lin, K. Y. An Expert System Structure for Automatic Fault Tree Generation for Emergency Feedwater Systems for Nuclear Power Plants. *Proceedings of the Second IEEE WESTEX Conference,* Anaheim, CA, June 1987.

Parsaye, K., and Murphree, S. Using Auto-Intelligence for Knowledge and Expertise Transfer Between Humans. *Proceedings of the Third Annual Artificial Intelligence Conference,* Long Beach, CA, April 1987a.

Parsaye, K., and Murphree, S. Automating the Knowledge Acquisition Process. *Technical Report 6-22-87, IntelligenceWare, Inc.,* Los Angeles, CA, 1987b.

Parsaye, K. and Sampaio, A. B. C. The Formal Specification and Testing of Hardware Building Blocks, *Proceedings of the 1982 ACM Computer Science Conference,* Rolla, MO, March 1981.

Patel-Schneider, P. F., Brachman, R. J., and Levesque, H. J. ARGON: Knowledge Representation Meets Information Retrieval. *Proceedings of the First Conference on AI Applications,* Denver, CO, 1984.

Patil, R. S., Szolovits, P., and Schwartz, W. B. Causal Understanding of Patient Illness in Medical Diagnosis. *Proceedings of IJCAI-81,* Vancouver, BC, pp. 893–899, 1981.

Pentland, A. P., and Fischler, M. A. A More Rational View of Logic or, up Against the Wall, Logic Imperialists. *The AI Magazine,* Winter, pp. 15–18, 1983.

Peterson, C. and Beach, L. R. Man as an Intuitive Statistician. *Psychological Bulletin,* Vol. 68, pp. 29–46, 1967.

Peterson, M., and Waterman, D. A. Rule-Based Models for Legal Expertise. *Proceedings of the First Annual National Conference on Artificial Intelligence,* Palo Alto, CA, 1980.

Pitz, G. F. and Sachs, N. J. Judgment and Decision: Theory and Application. *Annual Review of Psychology,* Vol. 35, 1984.

Politakis, P., Kulikowsk, C. A. and Weiss, S. Designing Consistent Knowledge Bases for Expert Consultation Systems. Technical Report DCS-TR-100, Computer Science Department, Rutgers University, 1979.

Pople, H. E., Myers, J. D., and Miller, R. A. DIALOG INTERNIST: A Model of Diagnostic Logic for Internal Medicine. *Proceedings of IJCAI-75,* pp. 849–855, 1975.

Puff, C. R. *Handbook of Research Methods in Human Memory and Cognition.* New York: Academic Press, 1982.

Quillian, M. R. Semantic Memory. In M. Minsky (Ed.), *Semantic Information Processing.* Cambridge, MA: MIT Press, pp. 227–270, 1968.

Quine, W. V. O. *Elementary Logic.* rev. ed., Cambridge, MA: Harvard University Press, 1980.

Quine, W. V. O. *Methods of Logic.* 4th ed., Cambridge, MA: Harvard University Press, 1982.

Quinlan, J. R. Discovering Rules by Induction from Large Collections of Examples. In D. Michie (Ed.), *Expert Systems in the Microelectronic Age,* Edinburgh: University of Edinburgh Press, 1979a.

Quinlan, J. R. Induction over Large Databases. Memo HPP-79-14, Computer Science Department, Stanford University, 1979b.

Quinlan, J. R. Fundamentals of the Knowledge Engineering Problem. Infotech State of the Art Report, Series 9, No. 3, 1982a.

Quinlan, J. R. Semi-Autonomous Acquisition of Pattern-Based Knowledge. In D. Michie (Ed.), *Introductory Readings in Expert Systems.* Gordon and Breach: New York, 1982b.

Quinlan, J. R. INFERNO: A Cautious Approach to Uncertain Inference. *The Computer Journal,* Vol. 26, No. 3, August 1983.

Quinlan, J. R. The Effect of Noise on Concept Learning. In R. S. Michalski, J. G. Carbonell, and T. M. Mitchell (Eds.), *Machine Learning: An Artificial Intelligence Approach.* Vol. II, Los Altos, CA: Morgan Kaufmann, 1986.

Raphael, B. *The Thinking Computer: Mind Inside Matter.* San Francisco, CA: Freeman, 1976.

Reboh, R. Using a Matcher to Make an Expert System Consultation Program Behave Intelligently. *Proceedings of the First National Conference of the American Association for Artificial Intelligence,* Palo Alto, CA, 1980.

Reggia, J. *Knowledge-Based Decision Support Systems.* Ph.D. Dissertation, University of Maryland, 1981.

Reggia, J. A., Nau D. S. and Wang, P. Diagnostic Expert Systems Based on a Set Covering Model. *International Journal of Man-Machine Studies,* 1983.

Reiter, J. E. A Review of the Prospector Project. *IEEE Database Engineering,* Vol. 6, No. 4, December 1983.

Reiter, R. A Logic for Default Reasoning. *Artificial Intelligence,* Vol. 13, October 1980.

Reitman, W. *Artificial Intelligence Applications for Business.* Norwood, NJ: Ablex, 1984.

Rendell, L. A. Toward a Unified Approach for Conceptual Knowledge Acquisition. *AI Magazine,* Vol. 4, No. 4, pp. 19–27, Winter 1983.

Rich, C. Knowledge Representation Languages and Predicate Calculus: How to Have Your Cake and Eat It Too. *Proceedings of AAAI-82,* Pittsburgh, PA, pp. 193–196, 1980.

Rich, E. Users Are Individuals: Individualizing User Models. *International Journal of Man-Machine Studies,* Vol. 18, pp. 199–214, 1983a.

Rich, E. *Artificial Intelligence.* New York: McGraw-Hill, 1983b.

Richie, G. D. and Hanna, F. K. AM: A Case Study in AI Methodology. *Artificial Intelligence,* Vol. 23, pp. 249–68, 1984.

Rieger, C. An Organization of Knowledge for Problem Solving and Language Comprehension. *Artificial Intelligence,* Vol. 7, pp. 89–127, 1976.

Rips, L. J. Cognitive Processes in Propositional Reasoning. *Psychological Review,* Vol. 90, pp. 38–71, 1983.

Rips, L. J., Shoben, E. J., and Smith, E. E. Semantic Distance and the Verification of Semantic Relations. *Journal of Verbal Learning and Verbal Behavior,* Vol. 12, pp. 1–20, 1973.

Roberts, A. W., and Visconti, J. A. The Rational and Irrational Use of Systemic Microbial Drugs. *American Journal of Hospital Pharmacy,* Vol. 29, pp. 828–834, 1972.

Roberts, R. B., and Goldstein, I. P. The FRL Primer. *MIT AI Lab Memo No. 408.* Massachusetts Institute of Technology, Cambridge, MA, 1977.

Robinson, J. A. A Machine-Oriented Logic Based on the Resolution Principle. *Journal of the ACM,* Vol. 12, pp. 23–41, 1965.

Rosch, E. Natural Categories. *Cognitive Psychology,* Vol. 4, pp. 328–350, 1973.

Rosch, E. Cognitive Representations of Semantic Categories. *Journal of Experimental Psychology: General,* Vol. 104, pp. 192–233, 1975.

Rosch, E. Principles of Categorization. In E. Rosch and B. B. Lloyd (Eds.), *Cognition and Categorization.* Hillsdale, NJ: Erlbaum, 1978.

Rosch, E. and Mervis, C. B. Family Resemblances: Studies in the Internal Structure of Categories. *Cognitive Psychology,* Vol. 7, No. 4, pp. 573–605, 1975.

Rosenblatt, F. *Principles of Neurodynamics.* New York: Spartan, 1962.

Rosenbloom, P. S. and Newell, A. The Chunking of Goal Hierarchies. In R. S. Michalski, J. G. Carbonell, and T. M. Mitchell (Eds.), *Machine Learning: An Artificial Intelligence Approach,* Vol. II. Los Altos, CA: Morgan Kaufmann, 1986.

Rosenschein, S. J. Plan Synthesis: A Logical Perspective. *Proceedings of IJCAI-81,* Vancouver, BC, pp. 331–337, 1981.

Rumelhart, D. E. Schemata: The Building Blocks of Cognition. In R. Spiro, B. Bruce, and W. Brewer (Eds.), *Theoretical Issues in Reading Comprehension.* Hillsdale, NJ: Erlbaum, 1980.

Rumelhart, D. E., McClelland, J. L. and The PDP Research Group. *Parallel Distrib-*

uted Processing: Explorations in the Microstructure of Cognition, Vol. 1. Cambridge, MA: The MIT Press, 1986.

Rychener, M. D. Approaches to Knowledge Acquisition: The Instructable Production System Project. Technical Report, Computer Science Department, Carnegie Mellon University, 1981.

Rylko, H. M. *Artificial Intelligence: Bibliographic Summaries of the Select Literature.* Lawrence, KS: The Report Store (in 2 vols), 1984, 1985.

Sacerdoti, E. D. *A Structure for Plans and Behavior.* New York: American Elsevier, 1977.

Sammut, C. Concept Learning by Experiment. *Proceedings of IJCAI-81,* Vancouver, BC, 1981.

Sammut, C., Banerji, R. B. Learning Concepts by Asking Questions. In R. S. Michalski, J. G. Carbonell, and T. M. Mitchell (Eds.), *Machine Learning: An Artificial Intelligence Approach,* Vol. II., Los Altos, CA: Morgan Kaufmann, 1986.

Sandewall, E. Representing Natural Language Information in Predicate Calculus. In B. Meltzer and D. Michie (Eds.), *Machine Intelligence 5,* Edinburgh: Edinburgh University Press, 1970.

Sargent, R. G. *Progress in Simulation and Modeling.* New York: Academic Press, pp. 159–169, 1982.

Schank, R. C. Conceptual Dependency: A Theory of Natural Language Understanding. *Cognitive Psychology,* Vol. 3, pp. 552–631, 1972.

Schank, R. C. *Conceptual Information Processing.* Amsterdam: North-Holland, 1975.

Schank, R. C. Representation and Understanding of Text. In H. A. Simon (Ed.), *Models of Thought.* New Haven: Yale University Press, 1979.

Schank, R. C. and Abelson, R. P. *Scripts, Plans, Goals, and Understanding.* Hillsdale, NJ: Erlbaum, 1977.

Schank, R. C. and Childers, P. G. *The Cognitive Computer.* Reading, MA: Addison-Wesley, 1984.

Schank, R. C. and Colby, K. M. *Computer Models of Thought and Language.* San Francisco, CA: Freeman, 1973.

Schank, R. C. and Riesbeck, C. K. *Inside Computer Understanding: Five Programs plus Miniatures.* Hillsdale, NJ: Erlbaum, 1981.

Schmolze, J. G. and Brachman, R. J. Summary of the KL-ONE Language. *Proceedings of the 1981 KL-ONE Workshop, Fairchild Laboratory for Artificial Intelligence Research,* Palo Alto, CA, 1982.

Schubert, L. K. Extending the Expressive Power of Semantic Networks. *Artificial Intelligence,* Vol. 7, pp. 163–198, 1976.

Selfridge, O. G. *Pandemonium: A Paradigm for Learning.* London: Her Majesty's Stationary Office, 1959.

Shafer, G. *A Mathematical Theory of Evidence.* Princeton, NJ: Princeton University Press, 1976.

Shapiro, A. The Role of Inductive Learning in Expert Systems. Research Report, Department of AI, University of Edinburgh, 1983.

Shaw, M. L. G. (Ed.), *Recent Advances in Personal Construct Psychology.* New York: Academic Press, 1981.

Shaw, M. L. G. PLANET: Some Experience in Creating An Integrated System for Repertory Grid Applications On a Microcomputer. *International Journal of Man-Machine Studies,* Vol. 17, pp. 345–360, 1982.

Shaw, M. L. G. and Gaines, B. R. A Computer Aid to Knowledge Engineering. *Proceedings of British Computer Science Conference on Expert Systems,* Cambridge, pp. 263–271, 1983.

Shaw, M. L. G. and Gaines, B. R. Techniques for Knowledge Acquisition and Transfer. *Proceedings of the AAAI Workshop on Knowledge Acquisition for Knowledge-Based Systems,* Banff, Canada, November, 1986.

Shneiderman, B. *Software Psychology: Human Factors in Computer and Information Systems.* Cambridge, MA: Winthrop, 1980.

Shortliffe, E. H. *Computer-Based Medical Consultation: MYCIN.* New York: Elsevier, 1976.

Shortliffe, E. H. Medical Consultation Systems: Designing for Doctors. In M. J. Simes and M. J. Coombs (Eds.), *Designing for Human-Computer Communication,* New York: Academic Press, 1983.

Shortliffe, E. H. and Buchanan, B. G. A Model of Inexact Reasoning in Medicine. *Mathematical Biosciences,* Vol. 23, 1975.

Shortliffe, E. H., Buchanan, B., and Feigenbaum, E. A. Knowledge Engineering for Medical Decision Making: A Review of Computer-Based Decision Aids. *Proceedings of the IEEE,* Vol. 67, No. 9, 1979.

Shortliffe, E. H. and Fagan, L. M. Expert System Research: Modeling the Medical Decision Making Process. Report STAN-CS-82-932, Computer Science Department, Stanford University, 1982.

Shortliffe, E. H., Scott A. C., Bischoff, M. B., Campbell, A. B., van Melle, W., and Jacobs, C. D. An Expert System for Oncology Protocol Management. In Buchanan, B. and Shortliffe, E. H. *Rule-Based Expert Systems: The MYCIN Experiments.* Reading, MA: Addison-Wesley, 1984.

Shrager, J. and Finin, T. An Expert System that Volunteers Advice. *Proceedings of the National Conference on Artificial Intelligence,* Pittsburgh, PA, August 1982.

Siekmann, J. and Wrightson, G. *Automation of Reasoning,* Vols. I & II. Berlin: Springer-Verlag, 1983.

Siklossy, L. *Let's Talk LISP.* Englewood Cliffs, NJ: Prentice-Hall, 1976.

Simon, H. A. Information processing models of cognition. *Annual Review of Psychology,* Vol. 30, pp. 363–396, 1979.

Simon, H. A. *The Sciences of the Artificial.* Cambridge, MA: MIT Press, 1981.

Simon, H. A. and Gilmartin, K. A Simulation of Memory for Chess Positions. *Cognitive Psychology.* Vol. 5, pp. 29–46, 1973.

Sleeman, D. and Brown, J. S. *Intelligent Tutoring Systems.* New York: Academic Press, 1982.

Slovic, P. and Lichtenstein, S. Preference Reversals: A Broader Perspective. *American Economic Review,* Vol. 73, pp. 596–605, 1983.

Smets, P. The Degree of Belief in a Fuzzy Set. *Information Science,* Vol. 25, pp. 1–19, 1981.

Smith, E. E. and Medin, D. L. *Categories and Concepts.* Cambridge, MA: Harvard University Press, 1981.

Smith, E. E. and Oshershon, D. N. Conceptual Combination with Prototype Concepts. *Cognitive Science,* Vol. 8, pp. 337–363, 1984.

Smith, E. E., Shoben, E. J., and Rips, L. J. Structure and Process in Semantic Memory: A Featural Model for Semantic Decisions. *Psychological Review,* Vol. 81, pp. 214–241, 1974.

Smith, P. J., Giffin, W. C., Rockwell, T. H., and Thomas, M. Modeling fault diagnosis as the activation and use of a frame system. *Human Factors,* Vol. 28, pp. 703–716, 1986.

Snedecor, G. W., and Cochran, W. G. *Statistical Methods.* 6th ed., Ames, IA: Iowa State University Press, 1967.

Sowa, J. F. Semantics of Conceptual Graphs. *Proceedings of 17th Annual Meeting of the ACL,* La Jolla, August 1979.

Sowa, J. F. A Conceptual Schema for Knowledge-Based Systems. In M. Brodie and S. Zilles (Eds.), *Proceedings of the ACM Workshop on Data Abstraction, Databases and Conceptual Modelling.* Pingree Park, Colorado, 1980.

Sowa, J. F. Interactive Language Implementation System. *IBM Systems Research Journal,* October 1981.

Sowa, J. F. *Conceptual Structures.* Addison-Wesley, New York, 1983.

Sridharan, N. S. and Schmidt, C. F. Knowledge-Directed Inference in Believer. In D. A. Waterman and F. Hayes-Roth (Eds.), *Pattern-Directed Inference Systems.* New York: Academic Press, 1978.

Stallman, R. M. and Sussman, G. J. Forward Reasoning and Dependency-Directed Backtracking in a System for Computer-Aided Circuit Analysis. *Artificial Intelligence,* Vol. 9, pp. 135–196, 1977.

Stampelos, J. G. and Apostolakis, G. A Methodology for the Analysis of Dynamic Human Actions. *Proceedings of the International Topics Meeting on Probabilistic Safety Methods and Applications,* San Francisco, February, 1985.

Steele, G. L. and Sussman, G. J. Constraints. AI-Memo 502, MIT Artificial Intelligence Lab, Cambridge, MA, November 1978.

Steels, L. Reasoning Modeled as a Society of Communicating Experts. Report MIT-AI TR 542, MIT Artificial Intelligence Lab, 1979.

Stefik, M. An Examination of a Frame-Structured Representation System. *Proceedings of IJCAI-79,* Tokyo, 1979.

Stefik, M. Planning and Meta-Planning. *Artificial Intelligence,* Vol. 16, No. 2, 1981.

Stefik, M., Aikins, J., Balzer, R., Benoit, J., Birnbaum, L., Hayes-Roth, F., and Sacerdoti, E. The Organization of Expert Systems, A Tutorial. *Artificial Intelligence,* Vol. 18, October 1982.

Stefik, M. and Bobrow, D. G. Object-Oriented Programming: Themes and Variations. *AI Magazine,* Vol. 6, No. 4, pp. 40–64, 1986.

Stefik, M, Bobrow, D. G., Mittal, S., and Conway, L. Knowledge Programming in LOOPS: Report on an Experimental Course. *AI Magazine,* Vol. 4, No. 3, pp. 3–13, 1983.

Stefik, M. and de Kleer, J. Prospects for expert systems in CAD. *Computer Design,* Vol. 22, No. 5, pp. 65–76, 1983.

Stonebraker, M., Wang, E., Kreps, P., and Held, G. The Design and Implementation of INGRES. *Journal of ACM Transactions on Database Systems,* Vol. 1, No. 3, pp. 189–222.

Stonebraker, M., Woodfill, A. J., and Anderson, E. Implementation of Rules in Relational Data Base Systems. *IEEE Database Engineering,* Vol. 6, No. 4, December 1983.

Sussman, G. J., and Steele, G. L. CONSTRAINTS: A Language for Expressing Almost-Hierarchical Descriptions. *Artificial Intelligence,* Vol. 14, No. 1, pp. 1–40, 1980.

Suwa, M., Scott, A. C., and Shortliffe, E. H. An Approach to Verifying Completeness and Consistency in a Rule Based Expert System. Report STAN-CS-82-922, Computer Science Department, Stanford University, 1982.

Swartout, W. R. Xplain: A System for Creating and Explaining Expert Consulting Programs. Technical Report, USC-ISI, March 1982.

Swartout, W. R. The GIST Behavior Explainer. Technical Report ISI/RS-83-3, Information Sciences Institute, 1983.

Szolovits, P. *Artificial Intelligence in Medicine.* Cambridge, MA: Westview Press, 1982

Szolovits, P. and Pauker, S. G. Categorical and Probabilistic Reasoning in Medical Diagnosis. *Artificial Intelligence,* Vol. 11, 1978.

Taylor, F. W. *The Principles of Scientific Management.* New York: Harper & Brothers, 1911.

Tesler, L. The Smalltalk Environment. *Byte,* Vol. 6, No. 8, 1981.

Toffler, A. *The Third Wave.* New York: Bantam Books, 1981.

Torsun, I. S. *Expert Systems: State of the Art.* New York: Addison-Wesley, 1983.

Touretzky, D. S. Implicit Ordering of Defaults in Inheritance Systems. *Proceedings of AAAI 84,* Austin, TX, pp. 322–325, 1984a.

Touretzky, D. S. *LISP: A Gentle Introduction to Symbolic Computation.* New York: Harper, 1984b.

Treleaven, P. and Lima, I. Japan's Fifth-Generation Computer Systems. *IEEE Computer,* Vol. 15, No. 8, 1982.

Turner, R. *Logics for Artificial Intelligence.* London: Ellis Horwood, 1984.

Tversky, A. and Kahneman, D. Availability: A Heuristic for Judging Frequency and Probability. *Cognitive Psychology,* Vol. 5, pp. 201–232, 1973a.

Tversky, A. and Kahneman, D. Judgments under Uncertainty: Heuristics and Biases. *Science,* Vol. 185, pp. 1124–1131, 1973b.

Tversky, A. and Kahneman, D. The Framing of Decisions and the Psychology of Choice. *Science,* Vol. 211, pp. 453–458, 1981.

Ullman, J. D. *Principles of Database Systems.* 2nd ed., Rockville, MD: Computer Science Press, 1982.

U. S. Department of the Air Force. *Air Force Manual 51-37: Instrument Flying.* Washington, DC: Department of the Air Force, 1984.

U.S. Department of Transportation. *Instrument Flying Handbook,* AC 61-27C. Oklahoma City, OK: Federal Aviation Administration, Flight Standards National Field Office, 1980.

van Emden, M. H. and Kowalski, R. A. The Semantics of Predicate Logic as a Programming Language. *Journal of ACM*, Vol. 23, pp. 733–742, 1976.

van Melle, W. A Domain-Independent Production Rule System for Consultation Programs. *Proceedings of IJCAI-79*, Tokyo, 1979.

van Melle, W. The Strengths and Weaknesses of EMYCIN. *Proceedings of the Expert Systems Workshop*, San Diego, August 1981a.

van Melle, W. *Systems Aids in Constructing Consultation Programs*. Ann Arbor, MI: UMI Research Press, 1981b.

van Melle, W., Scott, A. C., Bennet, J. S., Pears, M. *The EMYCIN Manual*. Report STAN-CS-81-885, Stanford University Computer Science Dept, 1981.

von Neumann, J. and Morgenstern, O. *Theory of Games and Economic Behavior*. New York: Wiley, 1944.

Wahl, D. An Application of Declarative Modeling to Aircraft Fault Isolation and Diagnosis. In P. A. Luker and H. H. Adelsberger (Eds.), *Intelligent Simulation Environments*. pp. 25–28, 1986.

Walker, M. G. How Feasible Is Automated Discovery? *IEEE Expert*, Vol. 2, No. 1, Spring 1987.

Wallis, J. W. and Shortliffe, E. H. Explanatory Power for Medical Expert Systems. Report STAN-CS-82-923, Computer Science Department, Stanford University, 1982.

Warren, D. Efficient Processing of Interactive Relational Database Queries Expressed in Logic, *Proceedings of the Very Large Databases Conference*, Nice, September 1981.

Waterman, D. A. Exemplary Programming in RITA. In D. A. Waterman and F. Hayes-Roth (Eds.), *Pattern-Directed Inference Systems*. New York: Academic Press, 1978a.

Waterman, D. A. A Rule-Based Approach to Knowledge Acquisition for Man-Machine Interface Programs. *International Journal of Man-Machine Studies*, Vol. 1, 1978b.

Waterman, D. A. User-Oriented Systems to Capture Expertise: A Rule-Based Approach. In D. Michie (Ed.), *Expert Systems in the Microelectronic Age*. Edinburgh: University of Edinburgh Press, 1979.

Waterman, D. An Investigation of Tools for Building Expert Systems. RAND Report R-2818-NSF, The RAND Corporation, Santa Monica, 1983.

Webber, B. L. and Nilsson, N. J. *Readings in Artificial Intelligence*. Palo Alto, CA: Tioga, 1981.

Weiner, J. L. The Nature of Natural Explanations: Theory and Application. Technical Report SDC-SP-4028, System Development Corporation, Santa Monica, 1979.

Weiner, J. L. BLAH: A System Which Explains Its Reasoning. *Artificial Intelligence*, Vol. 15, 1980.

Weiss, S., and Kulikowski, C. EXPERT: A System for Developing Consultation Models *Proceedings of IJCAI-79*, Tokyo, pp. 942–947, 1979.

Weiss, S. M., and Kulikowski, C. A. *A Practical Guide to Designing Expert Systems.* Totowa, NJ: Rowland & Allenheld, 1984.

Weiss, S. M., Kulikowski, C. A., Amarel, S., and Safir, A. A Model-Based Method for Computer-Aided Medical Decision-Making. *Artificial Intelligence,* Vol. 11, No. 1, 1978.

Weiss, S., Kulikowski, C., Apte, C., and Uschold, M. Building Expert Systems for Controlling Complex Programs. Report LCSR-TR-40, Computer Science Department, Rutgers University, 1982.

Weizenbaum, J. ELIZA—A Computer Program for the Study of Natural Language Communication Between Man and Machine. *Communications of the ACM,* Vol. 9, pp. 36–45, 1966.

Westfold, S. J. Very-High-Level Programming of Knowledge Representation Schemes. *Proceedings of AAAI-84,* Austin, TX, pp. 344–349, 1984.

Weyhrauch, R. W. Prologemena to a Theory of Mechanized Formal Reasoning. *Artificial Intelligence,* Vol. 13, pp. 133–170, 1980.

Whaley, C. P. Collecting Paired-Comparison Data With a Sorting Algorithm. *Behavior Research Methods and Instrumentation,* Vol. 11, pp. 147–150, 1979.

Whitehead, A. N., and Russell, B. *Principia Mathematica.* Cambridge: Cambridge University Press, 1910.

Wickelgren, W. A. *Cognitive Psychology.* Englewood Cliffs, NJ: Prentice-Hall, 1979.

Wickens, C. D. *Engineering Psychology and Human Performance.* Columbus, OH: Charles Merrill, 1984.

Wiederhold, G., and Milton, J. Applications of Artificial Intelligence in the Knowledge-Based Management Systems Project. *IEEE Database Engineering,* Vol. 6, No. 4, December 1983.

Wielinga, B. J., and Breuker, J. A. Interpretation of Verbal Data for Knowledge Acquisition. *ICAI '84:* Advances in Artificial Intelligence. Amsterdam: Elsevier Science Publishers, 1984.

Wiener, N. *Cybernetics.* New York: Wiley, 1948.

Wilczynski, D. Knowledge Acquisition in the Consul System. *Proceedings of IJCAI-81,* Vancouver, BC, 1981.

Wilensky, R. Meta-planning: Representing and using knowledge about planning in problem solving and natural language understanding. *Cognitive Science,* Vol. 5, pp. 197–233, 1981.

Wilkins, D. E. Domain-Independent Planning: Representation and Plan Generation. *Artificial Intelligence,* Vol. 22, No. 3, pp. 269–302, 1984.

Wilks, Y. *Expert Systems and Natural Language Analysis.* Infotech State of the Art Report, Series 9, No 3, 1981.

Wilks, Y. and Bien, J. Beliefs, Points of View, and Multiple Environments. *Cognitive Science,* Vol. 7, No. 2, pp. 95–121, 1983.

Winograd, T. *Understanding Natural Language.* New York: Academic Press, 1972.

Winograd, T. Frame Representation and the Declarative/Procedural Controversy In D. G. Bobrow and A. Collins (Eds.), *Representation and Understanding: Studies in Cognitive Science.* New York: Academic Press, 1975.

Winograd, T. *Formalisms for Knowledge.* In P. N. Johnson-Laird and P. C. Wason

(Eds.), *Thinking: Readings in Cognitive Science.* Cambridge, MA: Cambridge University Press, 1977.

Winograd, T. Beyond Programming Languages. *Communications of the ACM,* Vol, 22, No 7, 1979.

Winograd, T. Extended inference Modes in Reasoning by Computer Systems. *Artificial Intelligence,* Vol. 13, pp. 5–26, 1980.

Winograd, T. *Language as a Cognitive Process.* Volume 1: Syntax. Reading, MA: Addison-Wesley, 1983.

Winograd, T. and Flores, F. *Understanding Computers and Cognition.* Norwood, NJ: Ablex, 1985.

Winston, P. H. Learning Structural Descriptions from Examples. In P. H. Winston (Ed.), *The Psychology of Computer Vision,* New York: McGraw-Hill, pp. 157–209, 1975.

Winston, P. H. *Artificial Intelligence.* Reading, MA: Addison-Wesley, 1984.

Winston, P. H. and Brown, R. H. *Artificial Intelligence: An MIT Perspective.* Cambridge, MA: MIT Press, 1979.

Winston, P. H. and Horn, B. K. P. *LISP,* 2nd ed. Reading, MA: Addison-Wesley, 1984.

Winston, P. H. and Prendergast, K. A. *The AI Business: Commercial Uses of Artificial Intelligence.* Cambridge, MA: MIT Press, 1984.

Wong, H. K. T. and Mylopoulos, J. Two Views of Data Semantics: A Survey of Data Models in Artificial Intelligence and Database Management. *INFOR,* Vol. 15, No. 3, October 1977.

Woods, D. D. Cognitive Technologies: The Design of Joint Human-Machine Cognitive Systems. *AI Magazine,* Vol. 6, No. 4, pp. 86–92, 1985.

Woods, W. A. What's in a Link: Foundations for Semantic Networks. In D. G. Bobrow and A. M. Collins (Eds.), *Representation and Understanding: Studies in Cognitive Science.* New York: Academic Press, pp. 35–82, 1975.

Woods, W. A. What's Important About Knowledge Representation? *Computer,* Vol. 16, No. 10, October 1983.

Wos, L., Overbeek, R., Lusk, E., Boyle, J. *Automated Reasoning: Introduction and Applications.* Englewood Cliffs, NJ: Prentice-Hall, 1984.

Wos, L., Pereira, F., Hong, R., Boyer, R., Moore, J., Bledsoe, W., Henschen, L., Buchanan, B., Wrightson, G., and Green, C. An Overview of Automated Reasoning and Related Fields. *Journal of Automated Reasoning,* Vol. 1, No. 1, pp. 5–48, 1985.

Yates, F. A. *The Art of Memory.* Chicago: University of Chicago Press, 1966.

Yuchuan, Y. and Kulikowski, C. A. Multiple Strategies of Reasoning for Expert Systems. Report CBM-TR-131, Computer Science Department, Rutgers University, 1982.

Zadeh, L. A. Fuzzy Sets. *Information and Control,* Vol. 8, 1965.

Zadeh, L. A. Fuzzy Logic and Approximate Reasoning (in Memory of Grigor Moisil). *Synthese,* Vol. 30, pp. 407–428, 1975.

Zadeh, L. A. Fuzzy Sets as A Basis for A Theory of Possibility. *Fuzzy Sets System,* Vol. 1, pp. 3–28, 1978a.

Zadeh, L. A. PRUFA Meaning Representation Language for Natural Languages. *International Journal of Man-Machine Studies,* Vol. 10, pp. 395–460, 1978b.

Zadeh, L. A. A Theory of Approximate Reasoning. In J. E. Hayes, D. Michie, and L. I. Mikulich (Eds.), *Machine Intelligence,* New York: Wiley, 1979.

Zadeh, L. A. A Note on Prototype Theory and Fuzzy Sets. *Cognition,* Vol. 12, pp. 291–297, 1982.

Zadeh, L. A. Commonsense Knowledge Representation Based on Fuzzy Logic. *Computer,* Vol. 16, No. 10, October 1983a.

Zadeh, L. A. A Computational Approach to Fuzzy Quantifiers in Natural Languages. *Computer Mathematics Applications,* Vol. 9, No. 1, pp. 149–184, 1983b.

Zadeh, L. A. The Role of Fuzzy Logic in the Management of Uncertainty in Expert Systems. *Fuzzy Sets and Systems,* Vol. 11, pp. 199–227, 1983c.

Zadeh, L. A. A Simple View of the Dempster–Shafer Theory of Evidence and Its Implications for the Rule of Combinations. Berkeley Cognitive Science Report No. 33, Institute of Cognitive Science, University of California, Berkeley, November, 1985.

Zadeh, L. A, Fu, K. S., Tanaka, K., and Shimura, M. *Fuzzy Sets and Their Applications to Cognitive and Decision Processes.* New York: Academic Press, 1975.

Zloof, M. M. Query-by-Example: The Invocation and Definition of Tables and Forms. *Proceedings of the International Conference on Very Large Data Bases,* September 1975.

Zucker, S. W. Production Systems with Feedback. In D. A. Waterman and F. Hayes-Roth (Eds.), *Pattern-Directed Inference Systems.* New York: Academic Press, 1978.

INDEX